BALI, 50 YEARS OF CHANGES

A Conversation with Jean Couteau

Eric Buvelot

Translated by Diana Darling

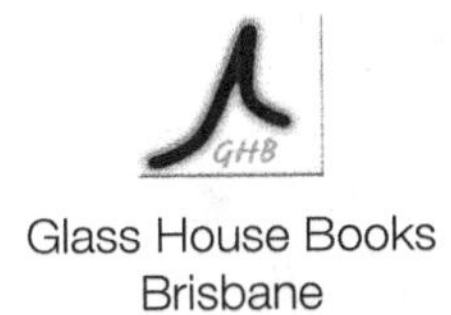

Glass House Books
Brisbane

Glass House Books
an imprint of IP (Interactive Publications Pty Ltd)
Treetop Studio • 9 Kuhler Court
Carindale, Queensland, Australia 4152
sales@ipoz.biz
http://ipoz.biz
First published by IP in 2022
© IP, and Eric Buvelot and Jean Couteau (text), Diana Darling (English translation)
French edition, © 2021, Editions GOPE, 74930, Scientrier, France

Printed in 14 pt Avenir Book on Helvetica Neue 11 pt.

ISBN: 9781922332905 (PB) 9781922332912 (eBook)

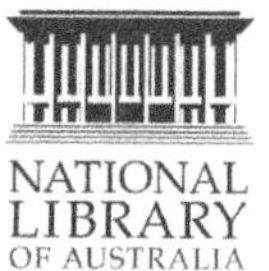

A catalogue record for this
book is available from the
National Library of Australia

Contents

Foreword

"It takes two to speak the truth. One to speak, and another to hear."
– Henry David Thoreau

What happens when two men sit down to discuss the passion, wealth, righteousness and evolution of the people of their adoptive home? Will they reveal insights or yet more clichés of paradise? What can we learn about and glean from the culture being gazed upon? Would we learn more about human cultural adaptation, or more about the lenses used for looking upon changing human worlds?

As a Balinese, I read through these pages with a mix of awe at the breaking of taboos of discussing certain subjects and horror at the highlighting of some practices I grapple with within my own extended family, yet with a tenderness: Here are two men who are attempting to understand the culture of my people, our idiosyncrasies and contradictions. Here are two observers who are holding up a mirror to Bali. Here are two thinkers who have, in their own way, created a portrait of Balinese society: A snapshot of a woman of a certain age at the cusp of yet another great transformation. The woman may not enjoy seeing her wrinkles bared for the world to see, but it is also hard not to accept the token of love in all this attention.

The conversations in this book do not purport to convey an objective truth. From Lao-tzu to Jacques Derrida, to the more recent Charles Eisenstein, the fallacy of objective meaning has been widely recognized. The truths presented in this book are subjective, and usefully so. Balinese myths are full of subjective truths that are contradictory without being any less conciliatory. Only the initiate is encouraged to attempt understanding; novices are enthralled by the story, accepting that different passions and reasons drive each of us on in life. Our stories are told to keep us in wonder of the infinite possibilities of the world while embracing the fire in our own bellies, harnessing them to power our journey to pursue our own truths.

Growing up in Bali, we are told that things just are the way they are. Don't try to explain them! Understanding is for later. When pressed into the role of a guide to foreign guests from an early age, I often felt the magic of creation when I attempted to explain my world to visitors. As I uttered my explanations, it became so! Fifty years of receiving such magic from his hosts and informants, and almost as many years of weaving them into vignettes in Balinese, English and French, have similarly transformed Jean Couteau. Prompted by the questions of Eric Buvelot, Jean makes sense of the stories he has received.

> Eda ngaden awak bisa, depang anake ngadanin, ..."
> (Do not think yourself capable, let others name it, ...)
> – Opening lines in a Balinese folk song

The intensity of the outside world's gaze upon Bali has become familiar. We have come to expect it. Aware of our insularity, we rely on outsiders to tell us what they see: to hold a mirror up for us. Let me reveal an elephant in the room: a tradition-bound Balinese could never have published the observations in this book. Our social taboos against speaking critically of our own are too strong. Jean Couteau has received the encouragement of his Balinese mentors and peers to keep writing precisely because many of these issues need to be aired and brought out into the open. While he draws out a map of his ideas about the Balinese, perhaps he is opening avenues for further discussions among us.

Jean Couteau's long engagement with Balinese society as an observer, curator and commentator is not to be taken lightly. While he does not shy away from revealing the crass humor of the Balinese *warung* typical of Singaraja, his north Bali home, it is pertinent to underline that in recent years he has lived mostly in urban Denpasar, to the south of Bali. While the people of the south tend to be subtle, our northerners are known for being outspoken, like Jean. He is often invited to speak on artistic and cultural topics with both urban and rural-based intellectuals of Bali in public debates as well as private discussions where ideas flow more freely. This book captures Jean's anxieties about the changes presently unfolding in Bali's society as we embrace and navigate a mechanistic material world. Another elephant in the room is that, while being an honored guest, Jean Couteau has never lived under the pressure of the obligations that come with being a member of Balinese societies, be they duties to the customary village (*desa adat*), clan (*kawitan*) or artistic guild (*sekaa*), among other responsibilities that come with membership. Almost all married Balinese face these pressures and more, coloring their everyday decisions.

Organized by the four categories of human pursuits of Catur Purusha *Artha* (*Puruṣārtha* in Sanskrit), this book lays out the many conversations between Jean Couteau and the inquisitive Eric Buvelot within these 'purposes of being human' by starting with the more external action-oriented impulses of passion (*Kama*) and wealth (*Artha*) before observing the more latent inward restraints of virtue (*Dharma*) and enlightenment (*Moksa*). Balinese philosophy sees these four areas as the quadrants of a mandala, where every person is an artist who can focus on the details of a particular quadrant at different stages of their lives, while keeping in balance with the other quadrants in their mind's eye.

In following these conversations and their exploratory tangents, we begin to appreciate the concerns of two speakers observing a culture shifting from myths about their world and themselves towards logic and reason. We may intimate that there is a concern that this shift in worldview is happening without open debate. I agree that many of these discussions need to happen more among the Balinese, and also find these discussions useful in reflecting upon the greater trajectory of human stories. By the pressure-cooker of modernity, in two to three generations Bali is shifting through cultural milestones Europe underwent over two to three millennia. Read this book reflectively. How do you see the world and the way it is changing? What are your roles in these changes?

In the pages of this book, perhaps you are about to encounter what you have learned to perceive as 'the other'. Let me share with you the nuance in two Balinese words used to describe the human 'other' when we encounter them. The first, which Jean and Eric have internalized by now, would be the word *tamu*, which means guest or visitor. The *other* is an honored passerby, walking among us temporarily. Give them a wide berth to stumble upon things of interest. When we speak of the opinions of others, we use the word *anak* or child. Children are listened to in Bali, because in their newness and innocence they make pronouncements that are pure and insightful. Take delight, and allow the delight to open up perceptions for reflection.

– Kadek Krishna Adidharma, Waitarere, 19 October 2020

Translator's Note

When two Frenchmen sit down to talk about serious matters, the language is likely to soar. Listening in on this can be a delight when the language is still French. But when it is translated into English, the sensation of flight may turn to vertigo. In the Anglophone world, simplicity is prized, and the fewer syllables the better. But to transform the very French conversation of this book into plain journalistic English would be an injustice to the character of the two men involved – Eric Buvelot: at once generous and meticulous; and Jean Couteau: jovial, ardent, and inclined to oratory. So the translation process was one of trying to balance the sound of the conversation with the editorial need to turn it into something comfortable for the reader.

But there was more to it than that. As these interviews show, the little island of Bali is an extremely complicated place. Bali 50 years ago was rather like it was a thousand years ago, and it was unlike anywhere else on earth. It was like an heirloom tapestry – whole, beautiful, full of intricate tales and details, incomprehensible and yet coherent. This made it fascinating, and, as this book explains, that fascination has left big thumbprints all over Bali's landscape and its psyche. Where Bali was once inscrutable, it has become almost illegible. Thus, the courage of the authors to explore Balinese reality and the changes it has suffered (or enjoyed) over the past 50 years. And thus, too, the fact that, as the anthropologists put it, everything in Bali is contested.

Resolving contested issues is not easy. Widespread literacy in Bali dates only from the 1970s, as Jean Couteau tells us, about the time he first settled here. Thus, it's hard to find the sort of facts in Bali that you find in industrialized societies, such as statistics, a shared historiography, and so forth. Whatever rules and laws there are – and there are many, all sorts, everywhere – are a work in progress.

One contested area that affected this translation is the spelling of Balinese terms. The Balinese language is written in its own script, which is derived from Javanese and ultimately Sanskrit. This script does not correspond exactly to the Latin alphabet, and there has always been debate among interested people (they are very few) about how Balinese should be spelled in Latin script. Perhaps the closest thing to an official standard may be found in the dictionary *Kamus Bali-Indonesia Tahun 1993*, edited by I Wayan Warna. Although it is neither perfect nor complete, I have used this as my source for the spelling of Balinese words and terms here.

But not without argument! In Bali there is currently a movement of cultural longing for the glamour of Old Java and Old India, as if the light were brighter in those days. One way to express that nostalgia is, surprisingly, in spelling –

specifically, to add an 'h' where none is called for, in order to make Balinese words look more like Javanese or Sanskrit words. For example, a priest-puppeteer in Balinese is a *dalang*, whereas in Javanese he is a *dhalang*. The basic Balinese alphabet, unlike the Javanese, does not have a character for 'dh'. Also, the spelling of the (most common) Balinese name for the Supreme Deity is 'Sang Hyang Widi Wasa.' And yet, Balinese authors of books and blogs passionately write 'Widhi' instead of 'Widi'. In the production of this book, Jean Couteau argued in favor of the most current spelling; I argued in favor of adhering to the Warna dictionary in order to have an objective standard. (He eventually conceded.) But the Warna dictionary is itself contested. Purists, like Michel Picard, often cited in this book, point out that the prefixes of certain Balinese words in the dictionary have been Indonesianized, rather than respecting the orthography of the original script – for example, 'pedanda' instead of 'padanda'. These hybrid spellings have become so common as to be effectively correct. Perhaps the lesson here is that, in Bali, everything is a bit true.

Meanwhile, the translation of 50 *ans de changements* into English means that more Balinese are likely to read it, a wish that Kadek Krishna Adidharma expresses in his Foreword, even as he notes its critical character. The Balinese people have a genius for tact, and it would be painful to inadvertently offend them with the wrong choice of a word. This was a consideration in the course of translating, not only to me but also to Eric and Jean.

One of the pleasures of this project was working with these two thoughtful people. Another was the many readings it required, and the opportunity each time to think about things that normally linger just beyond one's awareness when you live in Bali. Reality, always equivocal, is especially difficult to discern in Bali, because it is further obscured by being part magical and part folie de grandeur. Add to this 50 years of the encroachment of the modern world with all its unexpected disruptions, and the picture requires a very particular observer to make sense of it. Eric Buvelot and Jean Couteau have done that in detail.

– Diana Darling, Ubud, Bali

Glossary of Key Terms

1965-1966: a period when communists and their sympathizers on the left were systematically massacred or imprisoned by the *Orde Baru* (New Order) of General Suharto.

Adat: customary law. The *adat*, hitherto local and oral, has been systematically written down, which has opened it up to the intervention of the state and modernity. It has become a field of contention between national modernity and multiple local resistances.

Agni hotra: ancient Indian fire ritual described in the Vedas. *Agni* = fire, *hotra* = healing. Recently introduced in Bali as part of ongoing re-Indianization.

Anak Agung: title indicating the rank of a person, here the descendant of a king or prince.

Arjuna: one of the five heroic brothers in the epic *Mahabharata*. He is the handsome seducer, and his image is found on certain coins, which were believed to make girls fall into the arms of their pursuers.

Bali Aga: Balinese people who still retain traditions and customs that predate the Hinduism brought by Java.

Balian: traditional Balinese healer and shaman.

Banjar: communal neighborhood organization; a legal unit of the basic village community, in which only married males have the vote.

Barong, Banaspati Raja: mythological Balinese guardian effigy resembling a lion or dragon.

Bemo: a contraction of the words *becak* (pedicab) and *motor* (motorcycle), which first designated a motorized tricycle, then a small public taxi.

Bhagavad Gita: central part of the epic poem Mahabharata and one of the fundamental writings of Hinduism. The text was not known to the Balinese before Independence, but the story of Arjuna's dialogue with Krishna was already known through the *wayang* shadow-puppet theatre.

Bonnet, Johan Rudolf (1895-1978): was a Dutch painter who passed much of his life in Ubud; with Walter Spies he helped in the renewal of Balinese art.

Brahmana: Brahmin; traditional priestly high caste, among whom are the *pedanda* high priests.

Bugis: ethnic group from South Sulawesi

Bule: literally, "albino". A term currently used in Indonesia to designate Caucasians.

Cokorda: title indicating the rank of a person, here a higher member of the aristocracy; literally "feet of the gods," *cokor i dewa*, in Kawi. Also spelled *Tjokorda, Tjokorde*.

Drama Gong: a mix of modern and traditional Balinese theatre accompanied by gamelan.

Gria: residence of *brahmana* families.

Jero tapakan: a man or woman with the power to communicate the will of forces of the invisible world; a trance medium.

Kawi: generic name given to old and middle Javanese, sometimes to middle Balinese as well. After the invasion of Bali by the Javanese in 1343, Kawi became the literary language of the courts. It is still used in theater when princely characters address their ministers and lower officials. Readings of Kawi literature are still part of Balinese ritual. There are also circles of Kawi readers.

Kos: modest rental lodgings.

Lontar: palm-leaf manuscripts; traditional books, sometimes containing magic lore.

Losmen: modest guest house, usually family-run; from the French *logement*.

Majapahit: former kingdom located in eastern Java. Founded in 1292, it reached its peak in the 14th and 15th centuries. Majapahit troops invaded Bali in 1343. Many of the Balinese nobility trace their origins to this Javanese kingdom.

Niskala: the intangible world, corresponding to the unseen forces through which the Balinese people live their lives and which they honor through offerings and rituals. The term *sekala* refers to the seen world.

NTT: Nusa Tenggara Timur, province comprising the eastern Indonesian archipelago.

Nyepi: the Day of Silence, which marks the new year of the Saka lunar calendar in Bali. The only official national Hindu holiday in Indonesia.

Ogoh-ogoh: large bamboo and papier-mâché monsters paraded on the eve of Nyepi, the Day of Silence.

Orde Baru: the New Order, the military regime of Suharto (1965-1998).

Ormas: mafia-style gangs qualified as societal organizations: *ormas*, acronym for *organisasi masyarakat*, "social organization".

Pamangku, mangku: temple priest; different from the high priest, who officiates for a clientele.

Pancasila: the five principles of the Indonesian state philosophy. 1) belief in one God; 2) a just and civilized humanity; 3) the unity of Indonesia; 4) democracy guided by wisdom through deliberation and representation; and 5) social justice for all Indonesian people.

Parisada Hindu Dharma: Indonesian Council of Hindu Affairs. Presently Parisada Hindu Dharma Indonesia (PHDI).

Pecalang: member of a village militia and, by metonymy, the militia itself.

Pedanda: Brahmin high priest.

Pendatang: literally, new arrivals, a popular term designating Indonesian immigrants from other islands.

Puputan: collective suicidal battle of the raja of Denpasar and his court in 1906 in the face of advancing Dutch troops; culturally sanctioned fight to the death; repeated in 1908 in Klungkung and on other occasions in Balinese history

Puri: "palace;" residence of nobility.

Reformasi: name of the period of democratic reform following the fall of Suharto in 1998 and still ongoing at the time of writing (2020).

Reklamasi: a huge reclamation project in Benoa Bay in south Bali, which is strenuously opposed by the local Balinese population.

Sang Hyang Widi Wasa: the absolute divine order; God. *Sang hyang* = divinity; *widi* = law, order; and *wasa* = all powerful. In former times, this name was known only to a few scholars. It was introduced as an object of worship in the 1920s by the first reformers of Balinese religious tradition.

Sasak: ethnic group from Lombok.

Satria: the caste of princes, warriors, and the nobility.

Spies, Walter (1895-1942): a German painter, musician and choreographer who spent a long time in Java and Bali. He is known for having played a role, with Rudolf Bonnet, in the renewal of Balinese art and for helping to make Javanese and Balinese cultures known internationally.

Sudra: also *wong jaba*, or "outsiders," are the lowest caste, comprising some 85-90% of Balinese.

Sulinggih: high priest who has undergone the *dwijati* initiation rites. From *su* = high and *linggih* = seat, meaning 'most exalted'. Most commonly used for non-*brahmana* high priests.

Tri Hita Karana: Balinese concept that defines the "three causes of well-being": harmony among humans, with the natural environment, and with God.

Triwangsa: members of the three upper castes (*brahmana, satria, wesia*).

Vedas: sacred Hindu scripture from early India.

Warung: small, very simple roadside café, shop, and eating place.

Wayang: a theatrical tradition in Java and Bali, chiefly in the form of shadow-puppet theatre.

Introduction

This book is a series of interviews with Jean Couteau, an esteemed collaborator and friend. It is the result of twenty hours of recorded discussion over several months on a subject that has fascinated us both for many years: Bali.

At the beginning of this story was a mutual desire to do a project together based on our long friendship. Jean has been in Bali since the 1970s, and I since the 1990s; between us we have decades of experience living on the island. The 1970s were in fact the beginning of the island's metamorphosis, with the boom in tourism and extraordinary economic development in Indonesia. In the past 50 years, there has been more change in Bali than there has been in the past millennium!

This has hardly gone unnoticed. Many observers have recorded these upheavals in academic studies, publications, and in the press. All recognize that Bali, like Hawaii, Tahiti, or any other "paradise on earth," has undergone a radical transformation under the impetus of development. This is especially clear from an anthropological point of view, where the object of study is generally another society observed over a short period of time. Our approach in this book of interviews is more socio-historical, with this flagrant peculiarity (some would say this flaw): we are part of the sociological object that we analyze. But this is precisely where our strength lies. We, elements of external origin, bring a vision of the inside of this fantasized society to the outside, but also from the inside.

We have chosen the form of a book of interviews for several reasons, chiefly that of spontaneity. Indeed, the changes assaulting Balinese life are happening before our eyes, and we do not always fully understand them. The interview form allows a more journalistic than scientific approach, and has the advantage of allowing us to ask questions without having to give definitive answers; indeed, we wished to avoid an academic mode. A second advantage is that spoken language is more readable. One may open the book to any chapter, or even to any page. Topics are layered and therefore inevitably recur over the course of the dialogue: we have tried to approach them in a different way each time, a concern reflected by the structure of the book, divided into four parts presenting four angles of reflection. Moreover, conversation produces generalizations or excesses. For example, when we say "the Balinese" in the course of the dialogue, it can actually mean different kinds of people, even though it sounds like a generalization. These are the vagaries of talking, which sometimes introduces emotion and subjectivity. I would add that the choice of the interview form is a sort of tribute to Jean and his lifelong work. In a sense, he is also at the center of this book; he is undeniably a part of it, because he is so much a part of Bali, an island both of us still love passionately to this day, for its beauty and the kindness of its people. Balinese and Indonesian intellectuals respect Jean for his closeness to Bali, not to mention the Anglophone sphere, in which he is a leading authority on Bali. The books he has published and the articles he has written on a regular basis are mostly printed in these two languages, Indonesian and English. It is only the French who have not yet discovered him. So, making Jean a secondary subject of this book was also part of my original intention. The interview format fulfills this function perfectly and does justice to his remarkable work on Bali at the same time. Indonesians and English-speakers will instantly understand this choice.

Bali: a paradise marketed in a capitalist world, frozen forever in its exotic clichés, to the extent that the Balinese themselves hesitate to question this role of which they find themselves prisoners. Bali-as-paradise is a fantasy that everyone has an interest in maintaining, for the benefit of structural development, economic growth, and personal enrichment, by Balinese, by other Indonesians who benefit from it, and by the visitors who consume their portion of paradise. This deliberately nurtured collective illusion does not make it easy to see things clearly. "Nothing has changed!" they say, and often Balinese are the first to say so. *Bali, 50 Years of Changes* aims to identify the sociological changes that many refuse to see. As Jean would say, "The more changes modernity produces, the more these changes are denied." Or, people come to terms with it by looking to tradition, to religion, for justifications that assure that this is all in the order of things. Bali is the subject of constant change, to which the population apparently adapts intelligently and opportunistically, but, in the discourse on Bali, everyone acts as if nothing is changing.

In fact, there are a number of discourses on Bali that of the Balinese themselves, that of tourism, that of the Indonesian and Balinese governments, that of politicians, of intellectuals, of the press but all convey the idea that the culture of Bali is capable of absorbing mutations and therefore that it does not change or changes little. And to some extent this is true. Compared to the other "paradises on earth" cited above, Bali has probably resisted the steamroller of capitalism better and has lost less of its own identity. This famous culture, which has so greatly fascinated so many, which has been studied by scholars, adored by artists and intellectuals from all over the world and which was also at the origin of tourism marketing, is this culture the bulwark that protects the Balinese? Probably, yes, with some adjustments, often detrimental elsewhere. But does this Balinese culture have the same power of attraction to visitors today? Without a doubt, no. For us, the object of these discussions was never to exhaustively cover the history and the social or cultural life of the island, but to underline little-known aspects and those developments that many refuse to see. Nevertheless, by Jean's own admission, it may be that, depending on the dialogue, we place ourselves in a very Western analytical tradition, that is to say too dialectical, and perhaps we especially emphasize contradictions and conflicts rather than the harmony so dear to the Balinese. As an interviewer, I fully embrace this journalistic approach that Jean tries to reframe as he responds. If the traditions of harmony can blind, those of argument can imagine conflict where there is none. However, everything changes in Bali, like it or not. With Westernization, with individual rights, with autonomy of the person, with education, tourism, consumption, and 'the Indonesian project', unprecedented mutations are transforming Balinese society and culture year after year.

During these interviews, we try to address all facets of these sociological transformations over the past 50 years, the COVID-19 health crisis unexpectedly marking the final milestone in 2020. I have divided the themes we are discussing into four main parts, according to the principles controlling the four aspects of life in Hinduism: *kama*, *arta*, *darma* and *moksa*.[1] It should be noted that this is more of an editorial device than the reflection of anything relevant to Balinese beliefs. Indeed, some would object to describing the religion of Bali as purely Hindu. And yet, this is indeed one of the most disturbing developments in Bali, and perhaps the most subtle. From a cult of ancestors, tinged with Indian remnants and passed through Java, what is practiced in Bali today is becoming Indianized and internationalized, moving from a village religion to a global religion although, in fact, there are many Hindus in India who do not recognize their religion in Bali either. One more upheaval, which in the end doubles as a paradox.

In Kama, we approach disruptions from the perspective of youth, passion, sex, creativity, life forces. In Arta, we describe changes that are linked to the economy: sectors of activity, prosperity, money, land, investments, and so forth. In Darma, we reflect on how notions related to order, morals, law, good manners, social balance, and social customs are rethought today in relation to modernity. Finally, in Moksa, the idea is to approach more spiritual or philosophical subjects from a theoretical, conceptual, even metaphysical point of view. It is also in the last part of the book that we discuss how development and modernity challenge the Balinese conception of the world and the universe.

This is not the first time that Bali has changed. Before it was a celebrated paradise marketed to tourists for the benefit of Indonesian economic development with all the upheaval induced by modernity, the island and its culture had already been through the revisionist mill of the colonial Dutch. They were the first aided by an international intelligentsia to describe Bali as an "earthly paradise," an idealist and Rousseauist vision of a harmonious society located outside the world and time itself. And yet, before that, Bali was seen in the region as an island of spells and demons, inhabited by dark forces that struck fear in anyone forced to visit it, an island of proud warriors willing to commit mass suicide rather than surrender to the enemy. Also, the island was one of the most important sources in the Indian Ocean of the slave trade. Its name, "Bali," is found in the word *"balian,"*

---

[1] The four Hindu principles/stages of life: First is Kama, desire. Then Arta, the principle of wealth. Third is Darma, notions of what is good and wise. Finally, Moksa, the principle of dissolving into the void of the cosmos (these are given in Balinese spelling).

meaning sorcerer, one who communes with the forces of the invisible world. All this is far from "paradise". It is almost only in Indonesian popular culture that this frightening image of Bali is still remembered, especially in certain films or novels that perpetuate the fear generated by this island of wizards and that for many represented more hell than heaven. But in the modern and official discourse of the Republic of Indonesia, as well as in that of the Balinese themselves, the image of paradise on earth has officially taken over.

In the face of modernity, Bali is a society that affirms that nothing changes when everything has been turned upside down. Is this denial of reality really the way to negotiate all these changes? We are entitled to ask this question. And asking it shows that we have confidence in the Balinese people and their ability to adapt. But at what cost? As Tancrède says in *The Leopard*, the novel by Giuseppe Tomasi di Lampedusa, which takes place in Sicily during the Garibaldian period and which was admirably adapted to the screen by Luchino Visconti: "Shouldn't everything change so that everything becomes again like it was?" After all, postmodernism and deconstruction teach the Balinese to get rid of tutelary figures and "rebuild" themselves in their own way. But it is not for us to lecture. Neither do we fall into blissful admiration. This book of conversations is meant only to discuss realities, from within and almost in real time. It is not a scientific work, but it is indeed a work of in-depth reflection, at the very moment when mutations are occurring and are not yet quite clearly identified. And this sort of investigation has not yet been done, at least not in a comprehensive way, since the idea that "nothing changes in Bali" is so current. We realized that when we wanted to describe the great complexity of contemporary Bali, we would have to clarify a great deal for the written version, hence the abundance of footnotes here. These notes, which can unfortunately slow the pace of reading, are nonetheless necessary to establish the objectivity of a point or to supplement it, in a historical or simply contemporary perspective.

The first time I met Jean was at the end of 1996. I had been living in Bali for less than a year. Surprisingly, at the heart of this encounter is a Japanese vintage motorcycle that I still own a quarter of a century later. Having always been a biker, I had some difficulties riding a moped every day when I arrived in Bali. So I was looking for a more satisfying machine that would also please my interest in fine mechanics. One day, by chance, I found a Suzuki GT380 for sale. A three-cylinder, two-stroke, 1970s machine that I had liked as a teenager and that I had never had the chance to own. I bought it from a guy in Denpasar called Andre. This was a 1975 model, complete, in good condition. On the day of the transaction, Andre and I were chatting about this and that, as one does in Indonesia. When he asked me what my occupation was, I replied that I was a writer. Immediately he wanted to take me to the nearby home of another French writer. In Indonesia, it is sometimes difficult to refuse an invitation, even impromptu after all, I was there to buy a motorcycle, not to meet a compatriot but before I knew it, there I was on Andre's heels heading to Jean's house.

We found him preparing a collection of his daily column in the *Bali Post*, which was published as a book much later under the title *Bali 2day Modernity*. He told me about his Indonesian mentor, Usadi Wiryatnaya, as well as his illustrator, Wayan Sadha, with whom he worked from 1989 to 1990 at the magazine *Archipelago*, then at the *Bali Post* from 1990 to 1994, collaborating for the "English Corner" page of this local daily. This was a page he edited under at least twenty assumed names and which was eventually discontinued for printing an article "Mecca's ancestors in Balinese belief," a sensitive subject in this religious nation of Indonesia. So, I returned home with a new motorcycle and a photocopied collection of his columns, with instructions to tell him what I thought soon.

After these first friendly exchanges around his work, we lost sight of each other. Jean and his family lived in Australia for a few years, and I did not return to journalistic activities until many years later as editor of *La Gazette de Bali*. In this context I wrote a portrait of Jean in 2005, painting him as an "adventurer of arts and letters," to make him better known to the French of Indonesia. As contributor to other Indonesian newspapers such as *Gatra*, *Tempo* and, above all, *Kompas*, as well as the Bahasa Indonesia translator for Jean-Paul Sartre and Michel Foucault, Jean was, paradoxically, already better known to Indonesians than to French people at the time. And I am not talking here about the French in France, who unfortunately do not know him well enough. Subsequently, I often interviewed him on subjects linked to Bali, or more simply asked him to write for the newspaper when current events needed his illumination.

Finally, there is something more about Jean that might help you better understand the value of his work in general and the meaning of this work in particular. He is a man of his time, that is, of his youth in the 1960s and '70s, with its ideals of fraternity and its thirst for discovery of others. These values seem to have dried up today in our world of withdrawal into oneself, something that afflicts even the Balinese, which worries Jean about the future of Bali.

Thus, Jean. He has fundamentally remained faithful to the humanist values of his time, which have guided him throughout his life in his work and which also govern the approach of this book. Although he is a scholar with an advanced academic degree and a lifetime of living in Bali, Jean has always engaged with ordinary Balinese as equals. Indeed, they are the primary source of his knowledge of Bali. Jean loves nothing more than sitting in a *warung*, drinking coffee and chatting with local villagers. This is how he has accumulated pages and pages of anecdotes and stories about everyday Balinese culture. This is also how he was able to probe deeply into the local psyche and hear the anxieties and misunderstandings that have sprouted from the rapid changes affecting the island. The anthropologist who arrives and leaves, and whose vision is narrowed by the focus of investigation, will never discover what Jean has patiently discovered about the Balinese soul by simply chatting in Balinese with people over a glass of coffee.

As I wrote in an article in the *Jakarta Post,* on the occasion of the publication of his book *Myth, Magic and Mystery in Bali*, anyone who thinks that Bali has no more secrets to reveal should read one of Jean's books.

Indeed Pak Kadek, as he is called by the Balinese, has never ceased to scrutinize Bali, tirelessly going to meet all sorts of people princes, artists, laborers getting lost in remote villages to discover a farmer and his daily life close up. Few foreign observers of Balinese culture have made such a broad and deep foray into Bali. Of the many books on Bali published in the West describing its people and culture, while often fascinating and well documented, almost none have the force of intimacy that Jean's works have. This is perhaps because, as he says, "In meeting people different from me, I have always looked for how we are alike." In his accounts of Balinese culture and daily life, there are details unknown to the public and even to "specialists". In short, Jean Couteau is a uniquely sensitive and knowledgeable observer, ideally equipped for deciphering the upheavals operating in Bali, of which he has been a privileged witness for half a century.

– Eric Buvelot

Yogyakarta, 11 Mei 1980

kami yang segelintir
aku yang sedikit
ucapan yang sedikit
terdesak, terdesak, terdesak
sebelah baratnya ada segelintir
sebelah timurnya ada separo
terjepit senyum
terjepit tangis
tetapi, kami bersemi
lahir di atas batu

There are just a few of us
I am insignificant
My words are few
Overwhelmed, overwhelmed, overwhelmed we are
To the west there are quite a few
To the east half of them
Squeezing our smile.
Squeezing our tears.
But we shall grow new shoots,
Born upon our rock.

– Made Wianta [Yogyakarta, 11 May 1980]

PART ONE

KAMA

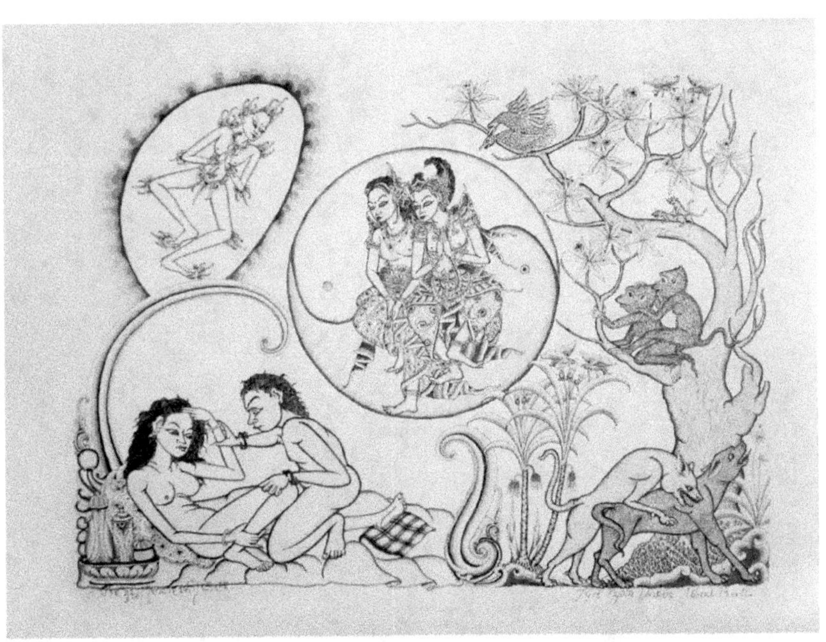

Conception by I Gusti Nyoman Darta. 42 x 60cm, paper.

1. Love, Courtship, Romantic Relationships, Marriage, Status of Women

In this discussion, we look at the question of romantic relationships among the Balinese. In the deep local tradition, it seems that Balinese love is mostly about male-orchestrated sex. Women have little say in the matter. Divine forces also come into play, because sexuality here is also a matter of descent, in that one is allowing the ancestors to "come down," to reincarnate. It is the men who are in charge. We examine the conditions and circumstances of traditional love relations, in regard to virginity, marriage between castes,[2] customary kidnappings, interreligious unions, rape, and polygamy. Modernity has changed traditional behaviors, which are now mutating, becoming more in line with Western customs and gender norms. Some modern Balinese deny these evolutions, or deny the persistence of traits considered too archaic. Then we look at new amorous practices among the Balinese: courtship, cohabitation, adultery, divorce, and how they have evolved in the 21st century. We review the commercialization of exotic Balinese weddings for tourists, up to the recent gay mock-wedding. Finally, Jean recounts recent developments in regard to female emancipation.

ERIC BUVELOT. **Did the notion of love exist in the past?**

JEAN COUTEAU. In the deep tradition of Bali, love reverberates in cosmic relationships. In Balinese pictorial depictions of love scenes, we often see gods alongside humans, for example Sang Hyang Ratih[3] with Sang Hyang Kamajaya.[4] So it is divine power that activates humans. The appearance of the feeling of love is the intervention of Sang Hyang Deleng,[5] the god of the gaze. But he's still a god.

It's love at first sight.

Yes, acting in love with forces from the heavens, prior to the present incarnation. Falling in love is said to be *jatuh karma*: obeying our karma / karma ripens. When we incarnate, we leave the *tegal penangsaran*,[6] or Balinese purgatory, to return to the world of humans, but often we also have to pay a debt, in this case in love, incurred during the previous incarnation or even during the stay in purgatory.

Is it really that far from the Western concept of love?

---

[2] *Caste*: we use the word generically to describe a closed titled group, which has nothing to do with India other than its nomenclature. This subject is discussed in Chapter 6.

[3] *Sang Hyang Ratih*: goddess of the moon.

[4] *Sang Hyang Kamajaya*: god of love.

[5] *Sang Hyang Deleng*: the god of amorous glances.

[6] *Tegal penangsaran*: literally, the field of sadness, sorrow.

It's completely different. The Western concept of love is here, but it only arrived with modernity, particularly through films, starting in the 1950s with open-air screenings.

But, in the West, in the idea of love, isn't there also a mythical, even mystical, dimension that escapes the human will?

In the West, love is more personal. It's an individual choice. Here in Bali, everything is determined by karma, by previous incarnations, by the intangible world of *niskala*.

What about women?

This is another aspect. Traditionally, women had no voice. Choice in love was exclusively with the male.

So, can we say that love or the idea of love was a purely sexual matter?

Yes, as a priority, because women are "taken". The key word is "take," *ngambil* in polite language, *ngejuk* in the rough version. Something very direct. In some situations, it was almost impossible for women to refuse a sexual demand. This has changed with education, modernity, and the associated feminist discourse, but it is still the case in some groups.

But then, the woman is completely reified, merely an object ...

Yes, absolutely. True, in some classical writings, the woman is described as waiting for the man of her life, and such. But above all, she is the object of contests. She has no right to speak.

So, has all this changed considerably over the past 50 years?

Yes, especially because of two new developments: education and mobility. The meeting place of young people until recently was during performances of *Drama Gong*,[7] *Wayang Kulit*[8] or *Topeng*[9] during temple festivals. Fifty years ago, the population of Denpasar was only about 150,000, whereas now it's nearly a million.[10] Society was still mostly rural. Young people didn't go to party in Kuta, where there were only a few hundred hippies and who were very much frowned upon. Most Balinese, with the exception of a tiny Dutch- or Japanese-trained elite, remained in their villages. Boys and girls met at the frequent theatrical performances, held at night, that accompanied religious ceremonies, most often on an improvised stage (*kalangan*) lit by an acetylene lamp. These events were

----

[7] *Drama Gong*: a mix of classical and modern Balinese theatre accompanied by gamelan.
[8] *Wayang Kulit*: shadow-puppet theatre, traditional in Java and Bali.
[9] *Topeng*: a form of masked dance-theatre.
[10] The population of Denpasar was 897,300 inhabitants in 2017. This does not include unlisted migrants from other islands, nor other elements of the urban area, which spreads into Sukawati, Kuta, Nusa Dua, and Tabanan.

very crowded. Typically, in the first row were the children, sitting cross-legged on the ground. Behind them were the girls, standing; and pressed behind the girls were the boys, themselves pressed from behind by the enthusiastic crowd. It was there that flirting took place, a spectacle within the spectacle, with sweet words, promises, and furtive pinching.

Yes, it still exists!

Village festivals are no longer as popular as they once were. The young Casanovas go to the city, or to Kuta, and they prefer modern music to gamelan.

Do these village festivals still remain the main place, the means, of meetings for young people?

Yes and no, because although the religious ceremonies are still carried out as actively as ever, boys and girls from good families are all urbanized. And that changes everything. A new hierarchy appears: graduates vs. non-graduates, which transforms the mechanisms of flirting.

But for some villagers, this still goes on ...

Yes, but with the migration of young people to the towns to look for work, everything changes. Formerly, a boy would meet a girl at a performance and ask her if he could visit her at her parents' house. If she liked the boy, when he showed up at her house, she would greet him with a smile and sit down with him for a chat. Otherwise, she would offer him a coffee and do her best to quickly disappear. On the parents' side, if the boy did not meet their expectations, they would keep him company until he got bored and left. On the other hand, if he came from an affiliated clan group, they gave him some freedom. With time, and some patience, the young man considered a candidate would approach his sweetheart. Many things could happen. It must be said that virginity is not necessarily required at the time of marriage, except in Brahmanic and some princely families. Anyway, in these situations the boy is actually stuck.

What do you mean?

He's obliged to marry the girl. Incidents of *blatuk memedi* (dropping a girl after making love to her)[11] do exist, but is considered improper behavior, especially when the young man has been accepted by the parents at home. This is especially so since young people of the village who see a boy coming out of a girl's house late at night are sure to call out to him and ask him where he's been and where he is going. Indeed one of the implicit functions of the youth group *(muda mudi)*[12] is to

---

[11] *Blatuk memedi:* this is play of vulgar words: *blatuk memedi, suud me… tuk mengedi,* playing on the sounds "tuk" and "di". *Blatuk memedi* = a frightening demon.
[12] *Muda mudi:* village association of all unmarried young people.

oversee each other. It should be noted that this was before motorbikes. Everyone walked everywhere. So there was already a kind of sexual freedom, but in a very controlled framework. There followed a formal request, the *mapadik*, followed by the actual wedding, with all the ceremonies customary to the place and clan.

What is marriage by kidnapping?

When parental permission is lacking, the girl can in fact, with the help of her suitor, set up her own *ngerorod* (kidnapping). As soon as the fleeing couple declare the so-called "kidnapping" to officials at their place of refuge, they come under their protection. Few parents dare to oppose it. In time, there is reconciliation. The romantic aspect of this sort of wedding often leads observers of Balinese society to read it as a sign of women's freedom. It's debatable! For one thing, occasionally parents do force young lovers to break up. This is one of the main causes of suicides, as the lovers, inspired by old Balinese stories, are sometimes convinced that in this way they will reincarnate together.

No other possibilities, then?

In other cases, there is the *plegandang*, now banned, but which, for this reason, has changed its name; it is called *ngejuk* (to take), already mentioned earlier. Twenty years ago, this was still a fairly common type of marriage: a boy sexually forces a girl. If he marries her, there is no fault. And if she cries, a visit to the balian will eventually calm her down.[13] If you ask Balinese if this practice is still common, educated people answer "no," out of identity pride, but if you dig a little, you discover of stories of this type. The notion of consent still has some way to go.

So this still exists?

It is no longer frequent, and people deny its existence in official speeches and with foreigners. And anyway, women in general accept their fate. This type of behavior reflects a certain tradition of violent but acceptable masculinity. It comes down to the fact that women, once again, have few rights, at least in the deep tradition.

Is this seen as prestigious for a man?

Yes, to capture a woman shows a certain virility! People laugh a lot about the grandfather who kidnaps a grandmother in the marketplace. But anyone who considers himself "modern" would deny this. It doesn't fit the image of the paradisiacal Bali instilled in all Balinese from childhood.

---

[13] The refusal, accompanied by disorder (tears, screams) is sometimes interpreted as coming from the *niskala* (invisible world) and treated as such: the role of the *balian* is then to expel the magical forces which have seized the young woman. The *balian* healer and shaman—plays a considerable role in the life of the Balinese. He is the intercessor of the intangible forces of the *niskala* and, for this purpose, is consulted about many things. His role is in some ways more important than that of the high priest (*sulinggih*), except to the latter's disciples. The high priest, through his holy water, takes care of the cosmic balances; the *balian* manages the crises of everyday life.

So, there is a parallel evolution towards modernity and a continuation of old practices by those who do not adapt well to this modernity...

Yes, necessarily. Of course.

What opposition separates these two parallel elements? Rich and poor? Graduates and non-graduates? Rural and urbanized?

I think the main opposition is between village and town. The opposition between cultivated and uncultivated people exists, but it seems less relevant to me because we also find this myth of aggressive virility in educated and modern circles.

So, what does the notion of love correspond to in Balinese culture?

Let's say that first is the desire for a child, which opens up the possibility for ancestors to reincarnate. Couples still often request it in a temple, usually a family or clan temple. This is *nakti*. In the domestic temple, in fact, one doesn't address the great Hindu gods for this purpose, but the ancestors, because it is they who will come back to "ask for rice" (*ngidih baas*), that is, to incarnate. This reincarnation sets in motion both cosmic material forces, called the *panca maha buta*,[14] and the soul of a deified ancestor *(betara)* in the process of reincarnation, who descends by the paths of love.

So, cosmic forces are at work ...

Yes, that's why in paintings when you see people making love, the cosmic forces and the gods are present. It's the same mechanics. Human beings are basically reflections of the cosmos, a meeting of spirit and matter. Triggered by Sang Hyang Deleng, love provokes the meeting of the two *kama*,[15] the red *kama* and the white *kama*, which symbolize the sperm and the ovum. Through this sexual act, the soul descends and inserts itself into the fetus, which is called *Sang Hyang Jabang Bayi*, that is, the baby, a little god! When the child is born, it is indeed common to call it *dewa*, or god because it is an ancestor who descends. Everything that will allow the ancestor to reincarnate is therefore at the heart of the urge of love. These kinds of beliefs are, however, starting to be somewhat less central today, as this aspect of Balinese religion is gradually giving way to a more formal Hinduism. This shakes up a lot of things.

Here, too, I imagine that in the villages, people are closer to these traditions than in the towns.

Yes, the important thing is that the ancestor returns. This has always been the case. In everyday life, for example, offerings are made to the ancestors, because they are expected to come back among the members of their family. By the way, I've noticed that when Balinese speak about their own ancestors, some use the first person singular. "I was there ..." they say.

---

[14] *Panca maha buta*: the five fundamental elements that constitute the world and its contents.
[15] *Kama*: desire, above all sexual, in Hinduism.

The presence of the ancestor is therefore felt even in the inner self of individuals ...

Yes, and people are always trying to find out how souls circulate. So, shortly after birth, they visit a *balian* to find out which ancestral soul has incarnated, and shortly after death they seek to know, again through a *balian*, where the soul is located, what it might want on its ritual journey to the realm of deified ancestors above the mountains. The worst is when some deficiency, particularly in regard to ritual, makes an *atma kesasar*, a wandering soul.

Very interesting, but let's return to the theme of love, if you don't mind.

Love, in the sense you're talking about has developed through mobility. This mobility was originally the privilege of the elites, who looked for their mate beyond the boundaries of their village. Everything changed with the advent of motorbikes in the 1970s and '80s. They increased the mobility of ordinary villagers. People from Ubud started going to the beach, for example, which took flirting to a whole new level.

What do you mean? How has this new mobility changed love habits?

If a boy likes a girl, he can then take her away, out of sight of the community. Besides motorcycles, another factor was schooling, which became widespread during the same period. Until the 1970s, most girls had only a primary school education at best. And the boys weren't much better off.

Let's go back to mobility, that paragon of modernity.

Mobility has indeed changed everything. At the turn of the '70s and '80s, when I started to express myself better in Indonesian, then in Balinese, there were many stories in the press of boys who took their girlfriends on motorcycle tours. At the time, there was a lot of talk about the bad influence of the West on young people's behavior. But there has always been voyeurism here, even watching lovemaking, on the beach or elsewhere, without the help of the West.

So, a revolution of morals caused by motorbikes?

Yes, and also through school, because the girls were there together with the boys. Not to mention another phenomenon of the 1970s: the start of the garment industry boom with the establishment of production workshops in Denpasar and Kuta, which employed thousands of young girls. This took them away from their village and gave them some autonomy, while also contributing to urbanization.

That allowed meetings outside the village, right?

Yes, of course. It was the start of a new way of relating to sexuality. Especially when boys picked up girls after work. It created meeting opportunities that did not exist before. Not to mention the money earned through work.

And I imagine that this mobility contributed greatly to the awareness of the people of Bali as a whole. Whereas, before, it was village identity that was primary ...

Yes, changes in their relationship to space modified people's perception. Urbanization, education, and mobility have altered Balinese identity, including romantic relationships, which were transformed. There is also something that should perhaps not be overlooked: in those days, boys used to go to brothels outside their village, often in groups, and were quite open about it. I remember coming across a local English teacher on a motorbike at a stoplight, and, by way of standard greeting, I asked him, "Where are you going?" "To the brothel in Kedonganan!" he replied, and took off in a burst of laughter.

Young people still go to brothels. And I would say that Balinese men are very fond of Javanese women, who provide the main contingent of these brothels. The Javanese woman is seen as the ideal mistress ...

Yes, the Javanese woman often arrives in Bali in poverty. She's an outsider and has no impact other than sexual on Balinese reality. She does not represent any danger, except to the wives, of course, and does not generate any significant social disturbance. This is part of deep-seated prejudices. But Western women are also seen as women with easy morals.

Yes, a Western mistress is more disruptive to the social balance ...

Because the power of money also changes things. The Balinese man expects material benefits from a relationship with a Westerner. This is the story of local gigolos.

While the Javanese woman doesn't bother anyone, the Western woman turns everything upside down ... But let's come back to the young Balinese woman. Is she expected to remain a virgin before marriage?

It depends on her caste. For some high caste families, yes. Otherwise, what matters is not that they are virgins but that they do not have multiple adventures. And in principle, the boy who deflowers a girl is more or less obliged to marry her. I collected stories in Ubud about girls who were considered less than nothing because they had had a few adventures. But these kinds of stories are usually hushed up. In the end, the boy is always right, as long as he respects the caste distance. He decides whether or not to marry the girl he deflowered.

So, the man is lord and master?

I'm reminded of a story that happened at our home in Denpasar in 2000. We had a *pembantu*[16] who came from East Bali. We had been away for two days, and several weeks after our return, she told me that the next-door neighbor had come during that absence and forced the door open despite her refusal to open, then raped her.

---

[16] *Pembantu*: household helper.

The master of the house is responsible for the physical integrity of the helper who lives in his house.

Yes, absolutely. So, I took the matter in hand and, passing word to his brother, I asked the neighbor to come to my house to talk about the problem. That evening, in front of my house, there were thirty young men, plus the rapist's father. The girl came out and was insulted, called a whore. She screamed that she had been raped and pointed to the guy. The tension mounted. It could very easily have turned bad. Fortunately, the neighborhood leader arrived and calmed things down. After this heated confrontation, she told me she would quit: she said I risked being ostracized from the village and having stones and rubble thrown on my roof every day. There it is: in a case like this, the youths gang up against the victim, who is considered an intruder. She came from somewhere else, so she had no network protecting her, and besides, she wasn't pretty, which is a disadvantage in traditional society.

How are girls protected? By limiting their freedom of movement? Even today, girls are rarely alone in the villages.

There's the illusion that girls have relative freedom of movement in Bali because, unlike Muslim women, they are not veiled. But no. In the villages, outside their immediate environment, they used to go about most often in groups.

A girl alone, left to her own devices, is she easy prey?

Yes, in a way, and without wanting to dramatize, taking the opportunity is seen as quite normal in the context of Balinese masculinity, especially in the villages. They say that a woman alone is like fish already in the frying pan, *cara be di pengorengan*. The distribution of power between genders is clear. Descent and inheritance are in the male line. The Balinese speak of the male as belonging to a higher cosmic principle, the *purusa*, which also means phallus. Nominally, on the strictly Hindu level, this principle has its female counterpart, *pradana*. The *pradana* symbolizes the material, while the *purusa* evokes the spiritual, at least according to the local version of the lingam / yoni of classical Shaivism. This dualism, under many names and variants, has become part of local traditions. In some villages, until a few years ago, a man who wanted to find a wife would lie on the ground on his stomach and beg Pertiwi, the earth goddess. The woman seeking a spouse did the opposite; she would lie on her back and speak to Akasa, the sky god. What matters is to harness the cosmic forces. But forget cosmic balance: If the man is "above" the woman, it is not only because the sky is above the earth!

Is symbolism so present to remind everyone of their role?

In the villages, sexual symbolism is indeed omnipresent, most often as a sign of fertility. For example, in the village of Kayu Putih in Buleleng, one of the local deities is Betara Celak Kontong, the penis god, represented by a huge phallus. But this is not gratuitous pornography. It corresponds to the desire for incarnation we were talking about earlier. By pouring water on the phallus, one obtains a kind of holy water which is then used during a prayer asking an ancestor to please incarnate.

These sexual symbols can be found in religious space, in temples.[17]

Or in nature, at least initially. On the road to Garuda Wisnu Kencana Park, halfway up the slope, there is a temple which is the perfect illustration of this. It started forty years ago with a few large roots intertwined in such a way as to resemble vaginal lips and a pubis. All it took was for a woman, longing for a child, to place an offering there in the hope of obtaining offspring. When she got pregnant, other women followed suit. With the same result. Later, trances and good souls helping, the place was endowed first with a perimeter, then with secondary altars for other "visiting" deities. And one day it was decided that the place was a full-fledged temple and needed an officiant (*pamangku*). The forces of the *niskala*, the invisible world, are typically at work in the service of fertility.

Do such things still occur today?

Now it's a bit more complicated. People are better educated and often skeptical: they are trying to rationalize their religion. They are perfectly aware that things do not make sense, at least for those who are modern. What's more, this rationalization is a veritable modernization project of the Indonesian Department of Religious Affairs.

Can you give an example?

Today, in school, children are told that when they make an offering to a spirit residing in a small altar in the middle of the forest, it is to a *manifestasi* of *Sang Hyang Widi Wasa*.[18] Thus, polytheism, the fundamental animism of the indigenous religion, is camouflaged under the abstract garb of modern Hinduism and its theory of the balance of cosmic forces, Indian version whereas in the local tradition, one is dealing with the forces of nature.

Right. But can we come back to marriage and mobility?

In the past, marriages normally took place within the same clan groups or between groups of similar status. Today, that is less the case. More and more people are letting their daughters marry men from a lower caste unthinkable before independence in the mid-20th century. In former times, this had terrible consequences and parents did everything they could to prevent such a union.

---

[17] Balinese temples: it is very difficult to describe the complexity of the temple system. There are family temples, community temples, temples of village founders, of clan, of irrigation systems, of professions, of mountains, of the sea, of the cardinal points, and more. There are also multiple altars or shrines (*palinggih*) in the temples, addressed to the invisible lords of the place. Temples enclose the Balinese in a web of intersecting social networks that produce the bulk of the Balinese mentality.

[18] *Sang Hyang Widi Wasa*: the absolute divine order; God. *Sang hyang* = divinity; *widi* = law, order; and *wasa* = all powerful. In former times, this name was known only to a few scholars. It was introduced as an object of worship in the 1920s by the first reformers of Balinese religious tradition.

But inter-caste marriages were taken into account in particular, with those who had the title "Jero" after marrying someone from a higher caste ...

Yes, but it only existed for women marrying a man of a higher caste. It did not exist for men marrying a higher caste woman. An *Ibu Jero* is a lower-caste woman who marries a man of a higher caste, like a *satria*.[19] It's a title, but it also announces her origins. If a girl from the *brahmana* (Brahmin) caste, the highest caste, marries a man from another caste, not only does she lose her membership in the community of ancestors in her group, but her father has to change his language when he speaks to her and use Low Balinese only. She has become an alien and can barely return to her family of origin.

Today, however, transgressions occur more and more often.

Yes, people even joke about it. But in the old days it was difficult. This is why there were many *brahmana* women who remained celibate and became *dayu tukang*, that is, makers of offerings. Moreover, the prosperity of *brahmana* houses often rests of them, because these offerings are more or less directly marketed. And a Balinese who uses such services for his own ceremonies can only pay generously, because his image in the clan is at stake. These are the women who run this Brahmin trade.

What if a Brahmin woman marries a foreigner?

It's probably easier. But the status issue is still there, that's where the shoe pinches. People will speak to her in English and avoid Balinese, because she has become a foreigner in the full sense of the word. At worst, when her father meets her, he will speak to her in Low Balinese and may even refuse to eat with her. These Brahmin women have a bit of the reputation of girls brought up by Benedictines in Europe, that is, either overly serious or easy women! Their situation is simply impossible, even if caste prohibitions are less marked than in the past. In the old days, before the independence of Indonesia, a Brahmin or even a *satria* girl would not marry a man of a lower caste without risk. This could go as far as the physical elimination of the unfortunate suitor.[20]

And today?

There is a double attitude among the *brahmana*. Some extoll openness, a legacy of their tradition as scholars. It's no coincidence that there were many communists among the Brahmins, before 1965–1966.[21] Others, probably less numerous, adopt the opposite posture, reinforcing *brahmana* attitudes, in particular by adopting

---

[19] *Satria*: the caste of princes, warriors, and the nobility.

[20] Here Jean Couteau remembers a Brahmin friend indicating her aunt to him with these words: "You see this woman, my aunt. Well, before Independence, she had a *satria* lover who hid in the ceiling. They caught him and killed him."

[21] 1965-1966: a period when communists and their sympathizers on the left were systematically massacred or imprisoned by the *Orde Baru* (New Order) of General Suharto.

behaviors and dietary habits imported from India, thus becoming ideological vegetarians!

If we could come back to marriage …

The basic unit of Balinese citizenship is the couple it is the hearth, as in ancient France: the home. So you have to get married. The Balinese do not understand that someone can wish not to get married.

It reminds me of a question: is cohabitation possible today?

Yes, it may happen now that a boy and a girl live together without being married when they reside in the city. It's important to remember that what is required of a man is not so much to be faithful as to be responsible. This means that if there is a child, he will have to recognize it and take care of it. This is what generates polygamy. Luckily everything can be fixed fairly easily, for the traditional Balinese wedding is the *biakala*: in its simplest form, a few offerings on the ground addressed to the lower cosmic forces; that's enough to legalize a union from a customary point of view. Nowadays, of course, there is an obligation to register the marriage at the village administration level and with the Department of Religious Affairs. But basically it can be dealt with very simply unofficially. And this has many advantages.

Like what?

As soon as a marriage is formalized and registered, the union of the two families generates obligations. If the marriage fails, it creates tension. The woman will not divorce, because it can be extremely painful for her to return to her home environment, under the control of her father. Besides, the patrilineal system in Bali means that her children belong to her husband, and if she leaves him, she must leave her children behind. Most women prefer to endure the humiliation of staying with a husband who has taken another wife, more or less legally.

Is polygamy legal in Bali?

In the deep historical tradition, it has never been an issue. Some kings had hundreds of wives and concubines. Under Indonesian law, polygamy is not allowed unless the first wife gives her consent, which is a concession to Muslim parties, whose leaders are sometimes polygamous. In any case, this is the law of 1974. It seems that some villages in Bali prohibit it. I am thinking in particular of the village of Penglipuran, in Bangli. In practice, however, polygamy is present almost everywhere and well documented.[22]

Do women accept this situation?

Necessity rules. In Bali, when a woman marries a man, she also marries his clan,

---

[22] Polygamy in Indonesia: a contemporary documentary film on this subject is *Bitter Honey* (2014) by Robert Lemelson.

that is, his ancestors. She changes her ancestral affiliation. She passes from the ancestral gods of her father to those of her husband, and takes on the related ritual tasks. This sometimes cuts women off from their previous modern networks, and it also complicates divorce cases. Any woman who divorces must perform a double ceremony: that of divorce, and also one that allows her to return to her family of origin. She "becomes a girl again" (*mulih daha*), it is said. And this is generally frowned upon! So, what happens? Well, the scorned wife prefers to stay with her husband and therefore implicitly authorizes him to take a new wife. Thus quite a few men indulge in polygamy in Bali: they may have several more or less camouflaged families who are often not officially registered. However, on a customary level, this has the force of law. Children are not born without a father; they remain affiliated with the family of the progenitor.

But does it happen today that it is the woman who files for the divorce?

Yes, it's becoming more frequent, because despite what I have just said, women have more autonomy now. It is a phenomenon of modernity, linked to education and urbanization. But in traditional circles, the wife whose husband is unfaithful is often considered to be wrong anyway. "The wife must be aware of who she is,"[23] they say, or worse: "If a woman can't satisfy her husband's needs, it's normal that he should go elsewhere."[24] These are remarks by women, I'm told.

What is the predominant reason in these requests for divorce?

The husband's infidelity, in general, which is much more common than the other way around, and which transmutes into polygamy. Filing for divorce is a sign of modernity and autonomy.

How is polygamy perceived?

In modern discourse, this is frowned upon, but in the sociological reality of ordinary people, it is perfectly acceptable, as long as it is not formalized as such. It happens when you live separated for a while, or when you marry again and just "forget" to divorce. It must be said that in pre-colonial times, the lord of Ubud, for example, had some 130 wives and concubines. The women employed in his service at the palace, the *penyeroan*, were considered to be automatically available sexually. This is why the famous painter and sculptor Gusti Nyoman Lempad was furious at one of the former princes of Ubud, after he placed one of his daughters in the palace.[25] Remember that traditionally the notion of sexual choice did not exist for women. It was normal that the woman might not want a man, but it was also normal that the man could force her. This was part of reality. Modern educated Balinese tend to deny all of these phenomena, in the name of an identity purified of all dross. They refuse to see social reality. But when

---

[23] *Anak yen dadi anak luh, pang tatas ke dewek.*

[24] *Kenken nyi ngayahin anak muani nyi-ne, apa ia sing bisa ngwarung kapah-kapah.*

[25] Tjokorde Gede Sukawati, the prince of Ubud at the beginning of the 20th century, had several wives and over a hundred concubines.

you talk to the women here, they tell you what's really going on.

Is polygamy very common?

No, it is rather rare. And most often linked to social status.

So, the poor are not polygamous? As in Islam, you have to be able to support several wives and children.

Yes, that's it. And we could even say that the Balinese *biakala* ceremony, addressed to the lower forces when taking a new wife, corresponds to the *nikah siri* ceremony of Muslims. Everyone believes that the marriage is legal, but it is not, at least not according to national law. It takes place outside the legal village framework.

There's a type of marriage not established in the civil registry that allows sex tourists from the Middle East to come and marry and divorce a prostitute in the space of a few days, as happens in Bogor [26] for example …

With a difference, though: in Bali, the *biakala* wedding doesn't cost a lot …

In Bogor it became a particularly profitable business for some imams! Materially, how is it for the new bride in Bali? Does she benefit from any particular material comfort? Independence from older wives?

The wives live separately. Usually, it is the "strongmen" in the village who take other wives. Otherwise, among Balinese who have polygamous tendencies without having this local boss profile, there are those who find themselves a Western woman, which is sometimes problematic. More than once, a Western woman who married one of those famous beach boys from Bali discovered later that the man of her life already had a wife and children in the village. Some accept it, more or less willingly. As long as the women have money, they have respect.

In this case, it's a question of hidden polygamy.

Yes. In the 1930s, an Ubud prince found himself an elegant French wife in the 16th arrondissement of Paris. She imagined herself becoming queen of Bali, but she was not the first or only wife. But she had become a princess, so she easily resigned herself.

As ever in Bali, nothing is ever made very clear.

[Laughs] These days there is still a tendency to moralize behavior. Firstly, because one doesn't want to be criticized by the Islamic community …

Yes, but polygamy is also Muslim.

---

[26] Bogor: City in Western Java located at the foot of Mount Salak, south of Jakarta, formerly known as a Dutch vacation resort, now a weekend destination for Jakartans.

The Balinese joke about it, but they do not declare their polygamy like some Muslims do. That said, there are also more and more Muslims who refuse polygamy, women in particular, including those who wear the headscarf.

I have the feeling, on the contrary, that polygamy has regained some strength in recent years among Indonesian Muslims ...

Sometimes it's hard to tell; there's movement and counter-movement. This is the duality of interpretations of the text. There is literality and contextual reading those who take the text literally want jihad, polygamy; others only read the "good" sura.

Let's come back to cohabitation: I see Balinese couples more and more often who aren't married. It's Western-style, that is, they try it out before considering an official union.

Yes, this is relatively new and can only operate outside the home communities, in the towns. It's part of the new behavior, it's modern; because traditionally it's unclean. And it's considered a negative Western influence. They might also resort to an informal marriage. It can also be a matter of being secretly agnostics, increasingly common in Bali. At least they are agnostics outside their village.

So, cohabitation or informal marriage is quite common today?

Yes, quite common.

Can we now turn to the issue of interfaith marriage?

Usually when a Balinese man marries a Muslim woman, the man goes through the motions of becoming Muslim. For the Balinese, having two religions, in practice if not formally,[27] is not a problem, because religions, they often say, are all the same. They are like rivers, which all descend from the mountain and all flow into the sea.

But, in Indonesia, doesn't the woman take her husband's religion?

Yes, the Balinese woman will become Muslim, and will most likely adopt the headscarf, as the pressure will be strong in this direction from her new co-religionists. We are witnessing a certain hardening of identities: re-Islamization against re-Indianization.

Is there a tradition relating to these marriages? Because there has always been a strong Muslim community established in Bali ...

There is a notable evolution in this matter. Previously, the exchanges of women between these two communities were almost equal. Now it is more and more in the direction of Balinese towards Islam.

---

[27] One's religion appears on the national identity card. It is compulsory to have a religion in Indonesia.

Why?

Because Muslims no longer give their women as wives, even though this practice still persists in some Balino-Muslim villages where Muslims have settled for centuries. But the observance of religious rules in Muslim communities is increasingly strict. And the Balinese, too, are hardening their attitudes.

The belief in reincarnation must also create problems in conversion to another religion.

Of course. The main issue the Balinese faces is that, after death, he will reincarnate. This saturates Balinese reality. Take the case of a Balinese who changes his religion by marrying a Muslim woman in Java. He never returns to Bali and disappears without giving any news. But one day, in his home village, one of his nieces has an accident. She comes out of it … and then, a few weeks later, a sudden illness seizes her. She is taken to the *balian* (shaman) who, after offerings are made and mantras uttered, is suddenly possessed and cries out: "I'm hot, I'm hot, free me!" It is the uncle who became a Muslim who, having died, is now in Balinese Hell and demands attention through the balian's intercession. His lost soul (*atma kesasar*) demands the Balinese rites of death: cremation, sending the soul to the mountain heights, etc. Otherwise, his soul will continue to prey on the living. It's an impossible conundrum. The old man is buried in the direction of Mecca, but his soul is at a loss what to do: on the one hand, buried in the city cemetery, it awaits the promised heavenly nymphs of Islam; on the other, tortured, it asks to be freed from its endless wandering.

That certainly complicates things. What can we say about the Balinese wedding for foreigners?

I made fun of this about twenty years ago in one of my daily *Bali Post* columns. Balinese weddings for tourists were very much frowned upon then, but now it's grown into a booming business. Without the "Hindu" aspect, however. Most of the brides and grooms are Christians, with pastors officiating and pseudo-offerings, although there are also people who get dressed up in Balinese temple clothes, or even convert as a sort of New Age indulgence. We find that in Nusa Dua. It doesn't shock anyone anymore.

Except when it comes to gay marriage, as has happened several times in recent years. This caused an uproar, in the newspapers and within religious and political bodies. We can mention here the former governor Made Mangku Pastika[28] vilifying this mercantile drift of religion …

These are phenomena of hypermodernity, and are part of the commodification of Balinese culture. Again, what's most important in the marriage ceremony are the offerings to the lower forces different from the pageantry that is sold to tourists today. It remains to be seen whether in these touristic marriages the officiant recites meaningless pseudo-mantras. It's all rather sad, because it arouses all kinds of fantasies that should be a thing of the past.

---

[28] Made Mangku Pastika: governor of Bali in the periods 2008-2013 and 2013-2018.

You've spoken of the status of women, emphasizing the burdens of tradition. But what about the history of feminism and, more generally, the evolution of the status of women over the long term?

There are several competing phenomena here. First, the normative and legal intervention of the Dutch, who banned *masatia*, or widow-sacrifice, during large royal cremations, and then *pelegandang*, or marriage by kidnapping. Of course, there was also a feminist movement. This was largely the product of education and more generally of enthusiasm for *kemajuan* (progress) in the years preceding the Japanese occupation.

So, we can say that the notion of emancipation is part of a long-term evolution toward modernity?

Yes, the feminists from Dutch colonial times were almost exclusively young girls from the lower nobility or the local chiefdom. They were a tiny minority, due to the very low female literacy rate.[29] In fact, it was only in the 1920s that the first school for girls was opened. This relative backwardness did not prevent them from being radical, though. Equal rights, rejection of polygamy, criticism of the caste system it did not take long for the discourse of those Balinese women to tap into the political radicalism of the day. They paid dearly for it.

What do you mean?

Those who most vehemently advocated attacks on tradition, caste, and feudalism were the radical socialists, therefore nationalists, and communists. Their discourse became politicized as early as the 1930s, with the founding of the association of Balinese women, Poetri Bali Sadar. After the Japanese occupation (1942-1945) and the war of independence from 1946 to the end of 1949, feminist figures took a religious turn, like Ibu Gedong Oka, who became one of the founders of Parisada Hindu Dharma[30] and an advocate for the Indianization of Balinese Hinduism. Others retreated to more "feminine" functions in health or education, such as Gusti Ayu Rapeg. Others, among the most radical, became members of Gerwani (the association of women activists that became affiliated with the Indonesian Communist Party) before disappearing in 1965-66, often physically, during the anti-communist repression.

What was the position of the military regime vis-à-vis female emancipation?

It blocked any radicalization of feminism, if not always in the discourse, at least in its concrete effects educational, religious, health. It did not ban polygamy, as I said before. In fact, it did not really touch tradition, because it was among the supporters of tradition or rather of traditions, because there are many traditions in Indonesia that it found its main political support.

---

[29] Literacy in Bali: according to the 1920 census, only 0.25% of women over fifteen could read and write, compared to 6.78% of men, see the book *Wanita Bali Tempo Doeloe: Perspektif Masa Kini*, p. 17, by I Nyoman Darma Putra, Pustaka Larasan, 2007.
[30] Parisada Hindu Dharma: Indonesian Council of Hindu Affairs.

Yes, but as far as I know, it was the New Order military regime that set up many women's development programs. How do you explain that?

There is indeed a paradox. The Sukarno regime, before the New Order, adopted the women's emancipation rhetoric, but it did not have the means to implement it. The military regime set in motion economic development. It therefore soon had the means. But it took care to limit the sociological consequences of the economic changes it engineered.

In what way?

The New Order implemented many programs that led to lifting the peasantry out of poverty. Some were addressed to women, especially those aimed at improving family welfare[31] and organizing birth control. Co-education of girls and boys also became widespread, with increased schooling of girls. Apart from these targeted actions on the ground, the regime also created conditions for the real emancipation of women through their widespread access to salaried work.

You praise the military regime!

No, I'm talking about realities. But there was a downside. The regime did not want full emancipation of women. It hated the idea that a woman could have control over her body. What it envisaged was only for the wife to be a junior partner of her husband in the couple. Here we find the old Javanese background of the New Order. For Javanese, the woman is the *konco wingking* of her husband (the partner who follows).

So, what can we conclude?

That there was real progress for many Balinese women, who live, not in a bilinear system, as in Java, with equal rights of inheritance, but in a totally patrilineal system. In Bali, there is no ambiguity. It's the *purusa*, and therefore the penis, that always wins the day.

Does the current period, known as *Reformasi*,[32] represent progress for women?

No, I would say it is often the opposite. As in the Sukarno era after Independence, the discourse is of progress. But besides the feminist discourse, there is also the identity discourse, which is more dominant. In Java, Islam is trying to bring women into line. Sharia law is advancing, with effects not only on the manner of dress, but also on inheritance.[33]

---

[31] This is the *Pemberdayaan Kesejahteraan Keluarga* (PKK) program, which means "strengthening family prosperity". It still exists today in every village in Indonesia as an association of the married women of the community.

[32] *Reformasi*: name of the period of democratic reform following the fall of Suharto (1998) and still ongoing at the time of writing (2020).

[33] Inheritance in Java: one hears of families who are replacing the traditional Javanese egalitarian system with the Sharia system two parts for a son to one for a daughter.

Could one say that it's better in Bali?

Not really. Of course, now there are all kinds of local feminist associations, Bali Sruti, LBH Apik, and others. There are also female creators: artists, writers, designers. Moreover, if you come across activists of Balinese identity among them, women you will hear that there are Balinese priestesses, the famous *tapini*. If you persist, you will be told that there were heroic queens during the colonial conquest. But, when a friend of mine, a Brahmin woman and a future senator, published an article[34] twenty-five years ago in which she said that women should be entitled to their own ancestral temple, what was the reaction of religious authorities? Silence. The condition of Balinese women is changing, but the patriarchal heart of Balinese society, subordinate to *purusa*, is not about to change.

I imagine we will have the opportunity to talk about it again.

Yes, because that is what keeps the island from becoming a paradise for women.

---

[34] See Ida Ayu Agung Mas, in *Bali di Persimpangan Jalan*, Usadi Wiryatnaya dan Jean Couteau, (ed.) Denpasar: Nusa Data Indobudaya Editions, 1995.

2. Sex, Gender, Sexuality, Sexual Practice

This chapter is about sexuality in Bali as it is conceived and practiced. While sexual pleasure was exclusively for men, the notion of sexual pleasure was for princes. Traditionally, woman's genitals are considered impure and thus so is sexuality. It is therefore necessary to symbolically purify it through rituals, the first being that of marriage. But how did couples first meet? Was premarital sex possible? What happened if an unmarried girl got pregnant? What about abortion? Illegitimate children? We explain that the Balinese woman was treated as an object, that she had no romantic choice. What has happened since the global values of human rights were introduced to Bali? What sort of feminism for these modern Balinese? But, also, why the craving for pornography? What is its relation to homosexuality? To transgender people? To pedophilia? Today there are many cultural misunderstandings due to the pervasiveness of Western values, such as interracial sexuality, almost unknown 50 years ago yet very common today. Bali has become a land of sexual freedom for Indonesians themselves. Is it therefore at the forefront of personal emancipation, of Indonesian sexual liberation? Or are we simply witnessing the ravages of capitalism on a traditional society? We ask ourselves: is liberation really achievable? Or even desired by the Balinese themselves?

ERIC BUVELOT. **How has sexuality evolved in Bali?**

JEAN COUTEAU. The sex of a woman is a considered a wound; it is impure because of blood, which is considered ritually unclean. Thus, menstruation prevents women from going to the temple or participating in ceremonies. Balinese men talk freely about the vagina; they'll say that they like it tight, and claim that Western women's sex is *goloh*, meaning a little loose, or *benyek*, soft. This sort of talk reveals all kinds of fantasies. But the key concept here is impurity, with the fact that sexuality, the notion of desire, is —

Exclusively masculine?

Yes, it is patriarchy enshrined in traditional literature. With emphasis on *kama*. The *kama,* which refers to the stage of life when the human being devotes himself to love and reproduction, is one of the four elements of the philosophical construction of life. There is *kama*, then *arta*, then *darma* and finally *moksa*, which are combined in this order of priority according to the phases of life[35] and the age of a person. That is to say, there is a stage, the *grhasta*, the time of forming a family, when one's life is devoted to *kama*.

Why this need to classify?

Because the main function of sexuality, from a Balinese point of view again, we go back to the authentic Balinese tradition is to allow the arrival of a *sentana*, of a male heir, who will take care of future ancestors, especially their cremation. It is said that without *sentana* to take care of them in the afterlife, souls will hang upside down from a bamboo for centuries, in a kind of limbo in the world of the dead.[36] It is therefore very important to have a male heir.[37]

So, traditionally, sex is only for the procreation and reincarnation of an ancestor?

Basically, yes.

Isn't sex for pleasure in the tradition?

Yes, kings, princes had access to all the women they wanted. There is a famous image in a temple[38] of an old man masturbating. There are also the herbs that constrict the vagina for male pleasure, of course. But the important thing here is to bring the ancestor into this world.

Do people do anything else besides copulate to bring this about?

Targeted prayers are made to the ancestors in various temples at the family level, in the *sanggah* or family house temple,[39] and at the level of the kinship group, in the clan temple. They ask for the intercession of the ancestor. We find this in the story of Sutasoma,[40] but also in my biography of Tjokorde Agung Sukawati. His parents went to Pura Gunung Lebah to request that the ancestral gods come down from the mountain in their unborn offspring. It's very serious.

---

[35] *Kama, arta, darma, moksa*: these are the *catur asrama*, the four principles of life. This, along with *karma*, is one of the few truly Hindu notions constantly conveyed by Balinese shadow theatre. Before the *grhasta*, there is the period of *brahmacari*, apprenticeship / celibacy, and then the *wanaprasta*, period of retreat "in the forest," to end in wisdom or *bhiksuka*. However, there is no tradition of a true forest or mountain retreat. The retreat translates only into access to the priesthood when old age approaches, or through visits to temples known for their holy waters.

[36] This is the story of *Jaratkaru*, taken from *Adiparwa*, an ancient text in Old Javanese.

[37] Heir: when there is no heir, one can adopt a boy (*nyentana*) or adopt the husband of a girl in the clan, but in practical terms this poses all kinds of problems in regard to the inheritance.

[38] Eroticism in temples: necessarily in an "impure" part of the temple, in reliefs symbolizing the lower world.

[39] Family house temple: a simple shrine or small temple in the family courtyard, depending on the means and rank of the family; in houses of the nobility, it is called a *mrajan*.

[40] *Kakawin Sutasoma* is a 14th-century poem in Old Javanese which depicts the life of Lord Sutasoma, who became a Buddha. It is also the text behind the Indonesian national motto: *Bhinneka Tunggal Ika* or Unity in Diversity.

Is this concern as intense in all castes? Or do the lower castes have a less divine approach to sexuality?

Yes, certainly, I think that the ancestral presence and the theories about *kama* are also less significant when one moves away from the traditional centers of power occupied by high castes, in which the cosmic theories of Hindu-Javanese origin circulate. In the villages, pragmatism reigned. In some of them, twenty-five years ago, there was a sort of curfew. Boys were allowed to visit girls at their homes, but they were not to come home after nine or ten o'clock at night, except with the implicit permission of the parents which means that the boy is going to be included in the family. The girl may lose her virginity on this occasion, but the boy will have to marry her. To have a *bebinjat*, a bastard, is unthinkable, impossible, because then the child would have no ancestral temple of origin, of reference. Because of this, sexuality is traditionally very controlled, in order to cleanse it.

"Cleanse," you say?!

Yes, you have to cleanse, or purify, if you prefer. Sexuality sets in motion the lower forces, the *kala*, which must be neutralized. This is why the central marriage rite, the one that religiously formalizes it, is called *biakala*, which literally means "to pay the *kala*". The ritual consists of simple offerings to the *kala*, placed on the ground. Actually, the union must be announced to the *trisaksi*, the three witnesses from the three levels of the world that of the gods and ancestors, of humans, and of demons. In addition to the *biakala*, one must also introduce the bride to the gods of the family temple network and the local community. There are complex rituals for all this. A marriage is also an alliance between families, and this is why they are most often between families of the same status.

So, ceremonies purify everything, including abortion?

Abortion cannot be tolerated in the Balinese world. Why? Because it means that the incarnating soul cannot come to term. If we disturb a reincarnation, it is as if we had an accident: there is disorder at the level of the invisible world (*niskala*). The incarnate soul is left wandering, which is very serious. People therefore see the *balian*,[41] who will solve the problem with a ritual. Aborted fetuses are buried in a specific part of the cemetery, the *setra bebajangan*, to await subsequent cremation.

In Bali, however, there are angel-makers!

Yes, clandestine abortion does exist. It is sometimes practiced by masseuses, even certain doctors.

Where do boys pick up girls, traditionally?

During temple festivals, at the time of dance performances, as I said earlier.

---

[41] *Balian*: shaman.

But there is another important place the river, when bathing or washing clothes. There are all kinds of stories about this. Men in general are upstream and women downstream. I think of the story of Lod-lod Peng, a monster that terrorizes Balinese women because of his disproportionately long penis that moves like a snake in water. It emerges from the river where the women bathe. These are stories of sexual terror. In other stories, women find themselves pregnant because there are too many eels in the streams where they bathe.

What about sexual vulgarity, pornography?

References to sexuality are constant and are not necessarily seen as vulgar. Little boys are called *kocong* (erection) and little girls, *tjebeng* or *weg* (slit), for example. And this, after being called *dewa / dewi* (god / goddess) at their birth. Sexuality is associated with fertility, especially in Selat where there is a tradition of giant puppets miming sex.

Is there a popular pornography, the dirty joke in the Western sense?

Yes, between the symbol and the joke, sex is everywhere. So, making love is said to be *ganti oli* (change the oil). Having an erection is *pasang dongkrak* (put on the kickstand). Note that these two examples of popular language borrow from the world of motorbikes and therefore from modernity. Another mechanical figure is: *Ampere sing menjalan* (the spark plug is dead) which describes male impotence.

Does this colorful language also exist within the high castes?

Yes, there is a similar kind of behavior and language. It's a bit like with bourgeois families in Europe. When vulgarity arises, it is over-emphasized. The woman of rank is respected, but not the common girl, to whom the man of quality must have access. In any case, what is certain is that formerly Balinese women did not even think about whether they had the choice to practice their sexuality, nor to refuse the sexuality of the man.

What do you mean by "have the choice"?

Even if she inwardly says "no," she cannot persist in her refusal. She will have to surrender. If she is truly won over, she'll surrender easily. If she goes astray, she will say that she succumbed because her lover practiced magic: he had an Arjuna coin[42] or an overly large ring; she's not responsible for having been seduced. It was the forces of the *niskala*, of the invisible world, that compelled her to surrender. I also remember the story of a modern Balinese novel:[43] a girl is kidnapped; she balks, refuses; the boy employs a *balian*. If she keeps crying and screaming, it's a sign that she's possessed. Then she is controlled, she's broken, and finally she gives in.

---

[42] Arjuna, one of the five brothers in the epic *Mahabharata*. He is the handsome seducer, and his image is found on certain coins, which were believed to make girls fall into the arms of their pursuers.

[43] *Tresna Ajur Lebur Setonden Kembang,* by Djelantik Santha, no date, Denpasar.

Does this still happen today?

Probably... Because in the end, the girl usually accepts her fate. She internalizes the violence to which she is subjected, she accepts it, because the whole of society is against her. Recourse to a *balian* often happens in marriages that are coerced by families, when boys kidnap girls with the consent of the parents on both sides.

These phenomena are no doubt more marginal today?

If you ask Balinese today, many say that *pelegandang*, forced elopement, no longer exists because it was banned in the days of the colonial Dutch. But abduction remains associated with a certain conception of virility, and is therefore accepted, in a certain way, by the girl. The important thing in a kidnapping is that the boy performs a purification ceremony quickly, summoning the *balian*. This is usually done with the agreement of a part of his entourage. I heard of a case in Karangasem where a girl was abducted and she found herself cornered in a room. The family was there, and they let it happen. The boy wanted to formalize the kidnapping in front of his family members, but the girl managed to escape. The next day, the boy met her at her home to remind her that she had to marry him, because he had managed to take her. She refused. For her it was rape, and the marriage ultimately did not take place.

These practices again indicate a strong association of virility with sexual violence.

This exists in many societies in eastern Indonesia, as it once existed in our countryside in the West. The important thing here is to dominate the woman, to dominate her sexually, and then, with the weight of religious practice, rites, people who expect her to submit. The notion of choice for women did not exist until a few decades ago, and this helplessness was perfectly internalized.

So, was happiness an unknown notion for Balinese women in the past? Unless they fell in love with their kidnapper ...

I think they had to be really lucky to end up with a husband they liked. In former times, when women were employed in princely houses as *penyeroan*,[44] the prince had the right to use the girl as he chose. If for example a family had the fortune to be given a few rice fields by an *Anak Agung*[45] or a *Cokorda*,[46] what could be more normal than for the prince to ask the pretty girls of the family to work for them? It was impossible for the parents to refuse. And when the prince presented himself to claim his due, impossible to reject him. All social pressures are at work in a case like this. The woman surrenders.

---

[44] *Penyeroan*: in the service of the prince.

[45] *Anak Agung*: title indicating the rank of a person, here the descendant of a king or prince.

[46] *Cokorda*: title indicating the rank of a person, here a higher member of the aristocracy; literally "feet of the gods," *cokor i dewa*, in Kawi. Also spelled *Tjokorda, Tjokorde*.

Once again, we see the Balinese woman treated as object.

And, beyond that, at the local level, women are not even full citizens of the *banjar*.[47] It reminds me of the situation of L. R. R., a well-known local feminist, scholar, and activist, who fights for equal status between men and women. But in her banjar, there is not much she can do, she said, except in the name of her husband.

Isn't tradition changing?

Yes, indeed, first through education, and then also with modernization itself. When I first arrived in Bali in the 1970s, there were few or no motorbikes. Boys and girls met at public dance performances at temple festivals. The advent of motorcycles in the 1980s increased the possibilities for meetings and visits. The young man could finally take his girlfriend to the coast, wait with her for the sunset and the moment when his vocabulary would suddenly change: "I really want you ..."

It's straightforward, to say the least!

Yes, but not always; it can be suggested. There are also veiled ways of denying the attention of a suitor. The impatient motorcyclist may find that his passenger wants to delay things, saying for example: "The weather is cloudy today, perhaps it will be nicer tomorrow ..." It obviously depends on the social and cultural level of the players in this motorcycle flirtation.

Either way, is it masculinity that is active and valued?

Yes. The model here is the theatre, with a coded combination between, on the one hand, extreme refinement and mastery of emotions, and, on the other, great vulgarity and total loss of control. The characters speak to each other in High Balinese with extreme politeness, and all of a sudden, everything goes wild! Violence and vulgarity. This is a general pattern of behavior in Indonesia, but it is very marked in the Javano-Balinese world.

So, how did behavior finally start to change?

Well, there was the expansion of space beyond the village brought by motorbikes, the new autonomy given to women, the model of the Westernized bourgeoisie of Jakarta brought by television ...

And then also behaviors brought by tourists? Through the cinema? Even porn cinema ...

Formerly in Ubud, just across from the *puri*,[48] there was a cinema. And that's where the young people would come to meet discreetly. It was the start of liberation, of sexual freedom. They could kiss and fondle each other in the dark. From one

---

[47] *Banjar*: communal neighborhood organization; a unit of the basic village community, in which only married males have the vote.
[48] *Puri*: "palace;" residence of nobility.

session to the next, before sitting down, you had to check the condition of the seats!

I mentioned porn because from the 1990s it became easy to get hold of it, for example by discreetly buying forbidden VCDs in the market.

Yes, it's true. It was also common at the time for women of high society to get together to watch porn movies. But the main difference in behavior depended on the location. The south of the island, Kuta, was a world apart. It was often there that "things" happened. Until recently, this area of the island was not considered representative of Bali by the Balinese themselves.

Were there any sexual practices that were taboo or unknown in former times that are no longer so, due to recent developments in society?

What I do know is that the Balinese woman was sexually very passive. I also know that the Balinese were often surprised by Westerners' sexual demands. There were often misunderstandings, especially with regard to homosexuality, based on a difference in bodily behavior. When the Westerner shakes hands, he creates a physical bond, but he also keeps the other at bay. It is the same when he puts his hand on the other's shoulder. For the Balinese, the body language is different. Youths may touch one another, sleep together, without any sexual ambiguity.

Yes, that does not imply that you are homosexual. In fact, two men are often seen walking together, holding hands or shoulders. This is where intercultural misunderstanding lies ...

Yes, the relation to the body is very different. People often keep each other company without having to talk to one another. For them, to communicate is to be together, without necessarily having to exchange words. But this is changing: Balinese bodily behavior is changing with modernity.

Yes, but let's come back to sexual practices and their evolution.

Julius Jacobs[49] in the 19th century was the first observer to write about the sexuality of the Balinese. Whether it was more the fantasy of a colonial official than a depiction of Balinese realities, I don't know. But, and here we are getting into homosexuality, he writes about *mecenceng juwuk*, where women rub their genitals together in the scissor position. Yet, I believe there are sexual behaviors in Bali that were not traditionally classified as deviant, but that are now. By this I mean that queries about sex from the West have helped to classify certain ordinary practices as homosexual, when they were not previously. The intrusion of the West has altered classification systems, has brought about a questioning about sexual behavior and identity.

---

[49] Julius Jacobs (1842-1895) was a Dutch physician who visited Bali in 1881 and published a work entitled *Some time among the Balinese: A travel description with notes on Hygiene, Land and Ethnology of the islands of Bali and Lombok*, in which he described pedophile behavior among the Balinese.

And what can we say about the pornographic drawings of Gusti Nyoman Lempad?

Many artists have made and still make pornographic works I am thinking in particular of some artists from Batuan purely to fulfill Western commissions, although some scenes are based on tradition. Otherwise, the Balinese have representations that we could classify as pornographic but which, for them, are symbolic.

Like the fertility symbols in temples, for example?

Yes, of course ... But this is still a Western classification.

Since Balinese women are traditionally so passive, it would be interesting to know what Balinese men see in Western women?

An instrument of political emancipation. To sleep with a white woman is to challenge the historical domination of white males over the native woman. Sex creates a kind of equality. In colonial times, white women slept only with princes;[50] then it was artists; now it's taxi drivers. The barriers are disappearing.

Isn't it prestigious to have a Western wife?

Yes, if one can enroll her in the Balinese system. A Balinese married to a Western woman will Balinize her through religion that is, she will convert to Hinduism and adopt Balinese religious customs which the admiring Westerner, critical of her original identity, enthusiastically accepts.[51] The happy husband is not going to put his kids in an international school: after all, he took the white woman, which is no small feat. Unless, of course, he is already modern himself, or has lived outside of Bali. Because, as I pointed out, everything is changing. We can no longer see everything through the prism of tradition. More and more Balinese are becoming cosmopolitan and escaping the norms. Individualized sexual behavior can no longer be considered marginal. We see this not only in the tourist ghettos of southern Bali, but also in other urban spaces, and even in Ubud.

But is there a Western-style over-sexualization?

I don't think so. It must be said that the Balinese who are into Western-style disorders drugs, drink, frantic promiscuity remain a tiny minority.

Let us return to the relationship with the body. What about the mouth here? One doesn't do anything with it, is that right?

No, it's the nose that counts. To kiss, *madiman*, means "to sniff". The kiss on the

---

[50] The most famous colonial romance in Bali is that of K'tut Tantri, pseudonym of Muriel Stuart Walker, author of the book *Revolt in Paradise* (1960).

[51] Balinization of Westerners: the reverse can certainly take place as well, with a Western man taking on the Balinese religious culture. Generally, it's the woman, except if the Westerner is so-called "New Age," in which case his or her Balinization may be of a new form, a kind of Hinduism fabricated in California.

mouth[52] came from outside. It must be said that as long as people chewed betel, it was hardly appetizing.

If a woman's sex is a wound that never heals, I imagine the man did not put his mouth to it.

Certainly not. There exist *lontar*[53] that discuss sex, but they mainly address issues related to erection, reproduction, and the prayers that must be made before taking action.[54] It gets more into cosmology than eroticism that is, the replication of the human couple and the cosmic couple, *buana alit / buana agung*.

Could we come back to homosexuality?

The big misunderstanding with gay Western men who come to Bali is that, seeing the very intimate physical behavior between male Balinese, they believe they are accessible. I remember one of my Balinese friends telling me how surprised he was when a Western visitor suddenly revealed his homosexuality to him. The reason is simple: ambiguity often pervaded the relations between Balinese and Westerners. In Ubud, a few decades ago, some gay Western men would arrive with lots of gifts. Having received a watch or a nice shirt, the father of, let's say Made, would then allow his fifteen-year-old son, often quite naively, to accompany, let's say Mr. Smith, in his discovery of north Bali. One can imagine the kinds of surprises and dramatic situations the boy could be suddenly faced with.

You're describing the encounter with the Western world. But, before, in traditional society, did homosexuality have a place?

Meeting people who had effeminate behaviors like *waria*, transvestites was frequent and was not a problem. Some female dances were performed only by males, and vice versa. There were no behavioral barriers such as those imported by the West and Islam. In the end, the behaviors are more complex than the categorizations that the West imposes on them.

I read in Adrian Vickers[55] that certain princes had *waria* in their courts.

Yes, before colonial times. They also had whites and dwarves. Princes were supposed to be surrounded by people from all over, in order to symbolize their control over the world.

And is there female homosexuality?

It depends on the meaning you give to words. The practice of *mecenceng juwuk*, mentioned earlier, women caressing each other sexually, was considered normal, and not as any deviation.

---

[52] *Omed-omedan*, the annual ritual culminating in kissing on the mouth, performed by young people in the Sesetan district of Denpasar, is relatively recent in origin, around a hundred years old.

[53] *Lontar*: palm-leaf manuscripts; traditional books.

[54] That said, there is an entire pharmacopeia for treating female genitals.

[55] Adrian Vickers is Professor of Southeast Asian Studies at the University of Sydney and a specialist on Bali and Indonesia.

Is sexual liberation happening in Bali?

Without a doubt, and for all kinds of behavior. Whatever the Balinese say, there is an emergence of global standards, many of which are competing: Western standards, bourgeois neo-puritans, Islamists, etc. School and, increasingly, social media play a key role in this. Let us say, though, that having a mistress in an open manner remains inappropriate, at least for the new local bourgeoisie. As soon as you act outside the norms, you generate impurity. Then you must hold a ritual ceremony to restore the balance. For example, in the case of a couple who have divorced and are starting to have sex again, they have to do a ceremony. There is no question of lying or hiding, because everyone will know anyway. And this will generate even more impurity!

You always have to put things back in order.

Yes, there is this normative need and constant necessity to preserve cosmic balance.

If there is no liberation of the human being, there can be no sexual liberation.

I don't think it can be thought of that way in Balinese society especially since there are prejudices about the West. It's high time that the West realized this: the Westernization that modernity brings is traumatic for people from other cultures. Besides disrupting economic mechanisms and social structures, Westernization disturbs different ways of thinking and behavior.

The great upheaval of values?

Yes, it started with what we said earlier: the relationship to space changes with mobility. The Balinese have moved from being villagers to becoming educated and urban, and there everything changes, first of all sexual and intellectual behavior. Traditionally, the Balinese sought wives in or near their village except those who had a larger geopolitical mindset, that is, mainly aristocrats, who would take wives in other spaces in order to consolidate their system of alliances. All of this is changing.

If the sexual liberation of Balinese women remains imperfect, is that of other Indonesians who come to Bali more successful?

I see where you are going with this. Yes, there is a national trend to come to Bali to seek freedom, especially among homosexuals and transgenders from Islamized backgrounds. Some people also come to look for a white partner.

In the imagination of Indonesians, Bali is undoubtedly a land of freedom. Especially since the moral rigor, which weighs more and more due to the Islamization of Indonesian society, leaves less and less choice ...

Yes, you are right, Bali is considered *maksiat* for some Muslims, a place of sin.[56] On the other hand, some people from Jakarta, Java, Sumatra or elsewhere come to Bali for moral slumming. Or to be free. It is fascinating for some to witness Western perdition as spectator-voyeurs.

It doesn't seem that the Balinese assume this position of Bali as a land of freedom for their Indonesian fellow citizens. It seems more that they are positioning themselves in a bid for virtue.

Yes, it's very interesting. The other day, I was talking about something with a Balinese artist friend. All the vulgarity found in the south of the island the nightclubs, prostitution, alcohol, drugs, bar fights, delinquency no Balinese artist has ever portrayed this in any work. The artists remain locked into their over-idealization of Bali as "paradise" and so on. The only one whose works speak of Kuta's vulgarity, cosmopolitanism, is Ashley Bickerton.[57] The Balinese do not accept that their island is presented as sullied even if they themselves say so.

What is the fundamental difference in Bali between a man and a woman, sexually?

The man is the only actor. Basically, the woman has few rights. Of course, in this area, as in others, we are witnessing a feminist reinterpretation of tradition. They say that *rwa bhineda* an old Balinese principle of the complementarity of opposites, such as earth and sky, man and woman should be applied so that women are granted a status equivalent to that of men. They insist that is the deepest and hence the genuine tradition. No less interesting is that others, confusing their wish and reality, deny that there is patriarchal domination. In practice, however, despite a demand for change, the system of descent and control of family temples remains based on the primacy of *purusa*.

What can we say about interracial sex?

As I said before, when it comes to Western women, there is a certain kind of disdain or contempt. This is well described by Nyoman Darma Putra, who sees the relationship with Western women as a favorite theme of short stories written in the 1980s.[58] Also, when it comes to interracial sex, there's something very real: a lot of Western men come to Bali with sexual fantasies. If you fly a lot, ask your male neighbors on the journey about the purpose of their trip. You'd be surprised.

There are also many Japanese women who come to Bali with a wish for sex, or even to find a husband.

---

[56] According to Jean Couteau's wife, who teaches at a university in Bali, her Javanese students are not at all proud to be studying in Bali. They are even hesitant to say that they are graduates of this university because, seen from outside, they are suspected of having spent their time in the nightclubs of Kuta.

[57] Ashley Bickerton is an Anglo-American contemporary artist based in Bali since 1993.

[58] *A Literary Mirror: Balinese Reflections on Modernity and Identity in the Twentieth Century* by Nyoman Darma Putra, Brill Publishers, 2011.

Yes, that's right. There are also pedophiles hunting in the villages of north Bali. Predatory behavior mixed with sexual exoticism!

How are these foreigners in search of sex perceived by the Balinese?

People say only good things about Japanese women, because they marry their Balinese. For men, it's more complicated. When I lived in Blanjong, not far from the brothel district in Sanur, I remember that buses full of Japanese men would come there. At that time, there were relatively few Westerners frequenting these Sanur prostitutes. The pick-up scene with Western tourists takes place on the beaches of Kuta, where the famous Kuta Cowboys operate. And there are young women from Jakarta or other big cities who come to Bali to look for a foreign husband, *bule*,[59] or whatever. Books have been written about this kind of Indonesian adventuress!

Why this phenomenon?

Well, simply because Westerners don't require their lovers to be virgins! But I would say that with Balinese women this sort of adventurism is not so usual. They have never been inclined to look for foreign husbands, except very recently, which goes hand in hand with schooling and urbanization, in short, the autonomy of women. The perception of mixed unions has nevertheless evolved in Indonesian society at large. In some circles, this is no longer stigmatized. But ambiguities and misunderstandings, economic and otherwise, remain, as well as sexual fantasies.

Yes, what can we say about this? If both sides are fueled by fantasy, these ambiguities can lead to misunderstanding.

It is true that when a Balinese woman, or an Indonesian woman in general, hooks up with a Westerner, it can have very harsh social consequences for her. And Westerners aren't aware of this!

Is she considered a "whore," to put it vulgar terms?

Yes. Which also means that she can end up becoming a "*bule* woman," and switch from one to the next before she finds someone who suits her!

But this union with a foreigner also allows a kind of turnabout of fate. Is that the fantasy? It probably creates social jealousy ...

Yes, absolutely. There are two scenarios then: the woman, taken by the Westerner, disappears from the Balinese ritual world. Or and this is becoming more frequent the Western man, victim of exoticism, is Balinized by inclusion in the clan, and Hinduized, with all the social, religious and above all economic expectations that this implies.

---

[59] *Bule*: literally, "albino". A term currently used in Indonesia to designate Caucasians.

Speaking of fantasies, the Japanese woman is highly desired in the Balinese but also Indonesian imaginations. In the local psyche, she combines the servility of the Asian woman and the looser morals of the West.

Yes, that's it, absolutely. There are a lot of mixed Japanese-Balinese couples.

It is interesting that while porn cinema is banned in Indonesia, the Japanese porn actress Miyabi[60] is considered Indonesians' favorite foreign film actress!

Fantasy about interracial sexuality is rampant. It began with the West: the desire for the exotic woman is an effect of the colonial conquest. In former times, high-caste Balinese women would have nothing to do with foreigners. They had no contact with the Dutch.

Today, that's no longer the case ...

Of course, and this is another evolution in modern Bali. And yet we should note that in interracial couples there is often little communication. People have trouble conversing, they don't communicate well. They wonder what the other is talking about! The relationship is often based on clichés, more than any real exchange.

Shouldn't we simply trust people to progress in this communication? For example, through love or sensuality?

Of course... Even if the cultural variable is a factor, personality indeed also plays a determining role. Some couples get along very well.

---

[60] *Miyabi*: known internationally by her real name, Maria Ozawa.

3. Desire, Creativity, Youth, Culture, Lifestyles

Here Jean Couteau and I try to review the changes that have taken place in the expression of desire, the arts, and creativity. First of all, we look at art what it was, what it is becoming. It appears that Balinese art today is all about identity. This is more a matter of asserting yourself as a Balinese than developing your culture. Jean explains that the Balinese have gone from symbol to "truth," from the informal to the rationalized. In Balinese dance, a wind of sexual freedom seems to blow with the controversial *Joged Bumbung,* but was sexual desire traditionally expressed in art? Bali is today a national scene for contemporary art. Is this an affirmation of modernity, or of Balinese-ness within that modernity? Are we witnessing the end of Balinese cultural memory? Tourism is also an identity, explains Jean. But with changes in language and in the way of thinking, the arts become poorer. Is dance that has become an icon of itself still culture? Modern literature is dynamic and a sign of Bali's integration into Indonesia. Lifestyles, vibrant cultures, music, and youth movements is Bali now on the international map of places that matter? Does Bali have a say in the world? We try to shed some light.

Eric Buvelot. **How was desire expressed in traditional Balinese theatre?**

Jean Couteau. Traditional Balinese theatre is extremely codified. In the typical situation of a palace scene, the women are either absent or, when they enter the scene, they are idealized figures who are not allowed to express the slightest desire. Everything seems to be under control until, suddenly, there is an explosion ...

What do you mean?

At first in the timbre, the words, the gestures everything is controlled, extremely refined, and then suddenly it becomes violent, within the very heart of the story but also at the level of gestures and language. Another sign of this rupture is the appearance of the clowns. Their speech and gestures are often sexual or, sometimes there are vulgar women, because women who display sexual behavior are vulgar by definition. They are commoners.

Vulgar in the sense of "common" then?

In both senses of the word "vulgar". In the *Drama Gong*[61] a guy will say to a girl, *"Saya butuh cintamu"* and she might reply, *"Saya cinta butuhmu."*[62] We find this all the time: the code and its opposite. Also interesting is that when a woman

---

[61] *Drama Gong:* a mix of modern and traditional Balinese theatre accompanied by gamelan.
[62] A play of words on *butuh,* which means "need" in Indonesian and "testicles" in Balinese. The boy says, "I need your love," and the girl says, "I love your balls."

becomes old and ceases to be desirable, she is regarded as a witch. In traditional Balinese stories, we often find anecdotes of heroes who flirt with gorgeous girls, who quickly turn out to be *raksasi*, that is, monsters. For women, therefore, it is a mutation from beauty to monstrosity. This expresses both the rejection of female aging and the rejection of female autonomy. Thus, the woman is either completely idealized (like an object) and nubile, or if she asserts autonomy, she's wicked. We therefore understand that, with traditional Balinese men, there is no notion of sentimental expectation toward the woman. She's there. He takes her, then throws her away. In theatre and in reality, women are always waiting. Gender inequality permeates the entire Balinese cultural system.

As in the West, with *Snow White* or the *Iliad* and the *Odyssey* ...

Yes, but without the modern questioning. Although in the *Panji*[63] stories there is the appearance of sexual ambiguity. The hero sometimes disguises himself as a woman to gain access to his beloved – a recurring theme in the tradition.

Does this theatre, steeped in Hindu myths, also tell the story of common people? Or is it a mix?

This theatre is not really steeped in Hindu myths. These myths are a shell at best, because the theatre features characters from Indian epics. Although the general frame is that of Indian mythology, at each performance, especially in the *wayang*,[64] the episodes are reinvented and refer to situations that are always local. For example, if Arjuna must face a monster to obtain a magic weapon, the scenario, or *pakem*, remains purely native. The Balinese dress their theatre with an Indian nomenclature, but the content is local.

So, it's an appropriation.

Yes. Let's take the case of Arjuna in *Arjuna Wiwaha*.[65] When the gods see Arjuna meditating on the slopes of Mount Indrakila, they decide to test his ability to resist temptation. They want to know if he will be able to vanquish Niwatakwaca, a monster that threatens the abode of the gods. Seven divine nymphs, each of which symbolizes one of the cardinal temptations, are dispatched to the mountain where the hero is immersed in meditation. This story has nothing to do with India. It's a local addition to the Indian epic Mahabharata. The point is to present a model of behavior: the hero must meditate, but without forgetting his social responsibility to kill "monsters".

Are there only heroes?

There are also the common people, who appear in the sequences of the clowns.

---

[63] *Panji*: the stories of *Panji* are a collection of stories from Java dating from the classical period (between the 13th and 15th centuries).
[64] *Wayang*: a theatrical tradition in Java and Bali, chiefly in the form of shadow-puppet theatre.
[65] *Arjuna Wiwaha* or the "Wedding of Arjuna" is a long poem in Old Javanese (Kawi) written in the 11th century during the reign of the king Airlangga.

In a typical representation of *wayang*, the heroes speak to each other in Kawi,[66] translated into High Balinese by the clowns, who represent the common people. Then the clowns remain alone together and the language changes to Low Balinese. Thus, we go from the idealized level of heroes to the aristocratic level, then to everyday life.

What are these clowns doing? What are they saying?

They behave in a vulgar way to be funny, but their role is very important. Behind this comic vulgarity, they remind the Balinese of their obligations toward the village, the temples, the ancestors. They also recall the social norm: stratification, language, and the like. It's a real educational system, traditionally the main means of disseminating the norms and values of society. This is fundamental. It is why the Balinese people of old, even though often illiterate, could be so sophisticated with regard to symbols. But now it's changing. With modernity, the Balinese have moved from a theatrical form of spreading the values of an agrarian society to education through schools with the rational norms of a modern society. Imagine the shock! To which you have to add the current shock of modern media and the absolutism of opinion they engender. In short, if the theatre is flexible, the school is text, it's rigid. This is therefore a very big cultural change: the Balinese are going from the informal to the rational and from the symbolic to fixed truth. The flexibility of ancient beliefs is replaced by the stiffness of the reference to texts of Indian origin. Do the Balinese complain about this transformation? No. They idealize it, which has consequences. In the past, people could joke about beliefs, about weird gods like the Betara Celak Kontong,[67] which we talked about earlier. Rowdy jokes are still possible today, but one no longer makes jokes about Vishnu or Krishna,[68] nor about contemporary Hindu religion.

Is current cultural modernity entirely focused on religious identity?

No, this is a long-term development that began a hundred years ago, in the early stages of modernity when some Balinese began to question the notion of historical change and transformation in the world.[69] Then colonization brought the notion of progress, which for these Balinese was a hectic mix: criticism of

---

[66] *Kawi*: Old Javanese.

[67] Betara Celak Kontong: the phallus god, a local divinity.

[68] There used to be a septic-tank-emptying company that advertised itself on its trucks with the name "Kuras WC Krisna" (Krisna Toilet Cleaning). Impossible today; it is now blasphemous.

[69] Toward the turn of the 20th century, a text appeared in Balinese: *Tutur Kehananing Gumi Prancis* (Commentaries on the situation of the Land of France). See the article by Helen Creese, "Curious Modernities: Early Twentieth-Century Balinese Textual Explorations," *The Journal of Asian Studies,* Vol. 66, No. 3, August 2007, pp. 723-758.

the caste system,[70] a desire for revolution and national independence,[71] and efforts to define their religion as Hindu.[72] But these were still internal debates among the educated elites, which were tiny.[73] It is only very recently that, through education, modernity has deeply affected all sectors of society. This is happening at the same time as there is a new fixation on identity, and although limited to narrow circles the appearance of all the themes of our globalized hypermodernity (human rights, women's rights,[74] other sexualities, and so forth).

Today, if there is a need for identity affirmation in Bali, isn't this because identity is called into question due to the presence of many foreign identities in its terrain? Previously, identity didn't have to be substantiated. It went without saying ...

Absolutely. In former times, Balinese culture was essentially the only culture on the island. Of course, Indonesianization had already started when the colonial Dutch established schools that taught in the Malay language. But the core culture of the island, some 90%, remained Balinese. The Balinese did not have to define nor to display their identity, as it was not confronted with other identities, as we see today.

And what are these new identities?

First, of course, there's the national culture, with its system of symbols, its norms, the idea of the nation, the economy, and so forth. But there are also ethno-demographic changes. Today in some urban areas, between 30% and 40% of the population is of non-Balinese origin. And these changes are taking place at the same time that the local "Hindu" religion is in the process of being structured through contact with modernity, redefining itself by mimetic adoption of Indian elements and by theological distancing in regard to other religions, in particular Islam. If all of this is not handled well, it could have dramatic political consequences. Recent developments are not all encouraging.

---

[70] From the 1920s, with the first educated elites. See *Kebalian – La construction dialogique de l'identité balinaise,* by Michel Picard, Association Archipel, 2017.

[71] Revolution: The Balinese participated in the struggle for national emancipation from the 1930s. Many monuments celebrate their resistance to the return of the Dutch between 1946 and the end of 1949, after the Japanese occupation (1942-1945). From simply "national" at the beginning, the notion of revolution then split between nationalist and communist branches, until the anti-communist repression of 1965-1966. See Geoffrey Robinson (1995).

[72] Hinduism: It was especially after Independence that educated Balinese elites began to systematically structure their religion. In 1947, Ida Ketut Jelantik published *Aji Sangkya,* a modern Shivaite Balinese vision of Hindu cosmogony. On the evolution of religious identity, see Michel Picard (2017).

[73] Less than 10% of the population could read and write before World War Two; 25% at the advent of the military regime of the New Order in 1965. This same regime generalized literacy between 1966 and 1980. Currently, the majority of children are in school until the end of high school.

[74] Women's rights: Cok Sawitri, for example, published *Sitayana* (2019), a version of the *Ramayana* revised and modified by a woman's vision.

What do you mean?

The 2018 elections delivered two senators, out of four for Bali, who for the first time introduced messages based on identity, with the election of both a hard-right-leaning Hindu Arya Wedakarna, close to Modi's BJP in India and a Javanese presenting himself in the name of Islam, Haji Bambang Santoso, moderate certainly, but nevertheless a confirmed Muslim. Religion has thus entered the local political discourse. According to Wedakarna and his supporters, it is not they who are not nationalists (that is, faithful to the national idea), since they respect Pancasila and its principle of equal treatment of religions; it is fundamentalist Muslims, who want to replace Pancasila with Sharia law.

Okay. Back to the notion of desire in Balinese artistic expression. What can we say about dance? I have the impression that there is an expression of great sensuality here.

We must keep in mind that in Bali, there are, roughly speaking, two levels of culture. There's the culture of upper castes, that of the Brahmin *gria* and princely houses (*puri*), and on the other hand, popular culture. The upper level is an Indianized hybrid dating from the Majapahit[75] invasion in 1343, the other has remained more indigenous. So, there is a culture of control and another of, shall we say, permissiveness and many graduated variations in between. In dance, we find expressions of an idealized sexuality, as in the Tamulilingan,[76] where we see the male and female dancers approach each other, almost touching noses.

Yes, here they kiss with the nose!

Yes, the nose first. There is always this duality between extreme control and extreme leniency. The female stereotypes are, on the one hand, hyper-feminine with their domination internalized and idealized by the women of the *puri*; and on the other hand, vulgar with sexual laxity in other sectors of the population. Of course, this duality is not specific to Bali, it is found in many societies, but here it is especially obvious. Among the common people, when women are flirtatious and show it in dance in the Joged it's vulgar, which everyone finds hilarious.

It seems to me that in traditional Balinese dances, women, although sensual, are always constrained by their sarong. It reveals their shapes but also hides their skin, their attractions. The movements occur mainly with the upper body, arms, hands, head, eyes. The lower body seems to be imprisoned by the sheath of the sarong. With the emergence of the

---

[75] Majapahit: an East Javanese kingdom founded in 1292, at its height in the 14th and 15th centuries. The aristocracy of Bali trace their origins to Majapahit.

[76] *Oleg Tamulilingan* or Dance of the Bumblebees is an elegant and very sensual choreography created by the famous dancer Mario (real name Ketut Marya) inspired by the mating dance of two bumblebees.

Joged Bumbung,[77] the dancer has now released her lower body, shows her legs, spreads them, to seduce a chosen partner in the audience, like a stripper would.

There is indeed a reversal of behavior. There is a demand for vulgarity ...

Yes, and this dance is very popular in the villages and at the same time denounced by the authorities, who condemn it out of moral outrage.

I think this is part of the dualism of stereotypes we were just talking about. As for the *Joged Bumbung*, it has existed in its current form since the 1930s, but corresponds to a much older tradition.

From a caste perspective, it's a dance for the common people. Are there higher, more noble forms of expression that also express desire and sensuality?

Yes indeed, the princesses in the theatre and the Legong[78] dancers are like odes to femininity. But it's the opposite that's popular. In certain dance-dramas, there are scenes of voyeurism. We find that in particular in the *Arjuna Wiwaha* story, mentioned earlier.

That is to say?

Arjuna and his wife are spied on having sex! This means that voyeurism has a long history in Bali. Of course, as always with this kind of thing, many people deny it.

What can we say about the Legong, this dance which features very young girls of ten, twelve years old, very made-up?

It's idealized femininity. These are the types of women that were presented to palaces, for the princes and kings of the old days. Made available to them.

But they are not women; they are twelve years old!

That was the reality.

In Bali, how does one express desire in art? Did it go as far as explicit representations of sexuality?

In the Balinese painting of the 1930s, we see kidnappings, and even quite pornographic things. But most of these explicit images have a symbolic function: the torments of hell in particular.

---

[77] *Joged Bumbung:* traditional Balinese dance performed during the wedding season, just after the harvest, and which has taken a very erotic turn in recent years, to the point of alarming the authorities.

[78] *Legong* is thought to express the epitome of femininity in Bali. Girls begin learning this dance as young as five, and perform it until adolescence.

Are there ancient objects, bas-reliefs, sculptures, paintings, with sexual connotations?

Outside of symbolism, no. However, let us not forget that in the tradition, the woman is not an autonomous subject. I am thinking here of those *sayembara*[79] of literature, those contests for which the reward is a princess. That explains everything. Although there is also the model of mad love, for example the story of the guy who is so in love with his wife that when she dies, he throws himself into her cremation fire.[80] He wants to find her in the realm of dead souls, in order to reincarnate at the same time with her.

How are these stories featured? Is art mainly illustrative?

Yes. Traditional art consists above all in a pictorial representation of scenes from the theatre, and in particular the *wayang*. It had a function: to ensure the maintenance of the collective memory in a pictorial way, most often by way of great epics such as the *Mahabharata*, the *Ramayana* or the *Panji* tales. The iconography itself is derived from *wayang*, the shadow theatre. A good example is found in what's called the Kamasan style of painting. In the 1930s, these representations mutated, although they always used a similar system, that is, a narration whose illustrative aspect is dominant, and inscribed on a space that is totally filled.

What triggered the modernization of art in the 1930s?

The arrival of Westerners, new techniques, and also a questioning of traditional representation. Remember that in the past, in Balinese theatre, music, and dance, everything was extremely codified with recurring motifs, at once visual, gestural, and in sound.[81] The case of painting deserves attention. From the 1920s and '30s, with the general introduction of paper through newly opened primary schools in some villages, the organization of space and the representation of the body began to change. This was the highlight of the so-called traditional painting,[82] particularly in Ubud where a small group of foreign artists had settled, chiefly

---

[79] *Sayembara*: an ancient practice in which a girl of marriageable age is married to a suitor, sometime following a contest or some feat.

[80] "Angling Dharma": a Javanese epic poem whose story is frequently performed in Drama Gong theatre.

[81] Discussed in *Steps to an Ecology of Mind* by Gregory Bateson, University of Chicago Press, 1972.

[82] The term "traditional painting" is to be understood here in a particular sense. This is not pre-colonial painting, which was largely derived from *wayang* iconography, but a similar aesthetic type of painting, with repeating icons, using new materials (India ink wash, paper support, then canvas), new representational techniques (better anatomy, better organization of space) and dealing, in addition to mythological subjects, with scenes from everyday life.

Walter Spies[83] and Rudolf Bonnet.[84] With this contact, a new style emerged, combining classical aesthetics with a more structured organization of space and a more realistic representation of the person, but without the analytical aspects of Western figuration.

Was it modern painting?

Some observers have used the word. It depends where you draw the line between tradition and modernity. But in my opinion, no, because the aesthetic remained traditional. Modern Balinese painting proper came later. It was a qualitative leap. It came from the city, therefore from modernity, and it did not develop until the first artists returned from studying art in Java in the 1960s. It was at first a figurative kind of painting, most often post-expressionist with exotic themes similar to that found in paintings made in Bali by Westerners. But soon enough, as many non-Balinese Indonesian artists moved to Bali, the outlook of the Balinese began to change, and painting with it. Instead of presenting Bali in a way that featured an exoticism aimed at tourists, they began to look at Bali for its own sake. In the 1970s, Nyoman Gunarsa introduced the techniques of action painting to translate the movement of dance. Then came Made Wianta[85] who, after a period of surrealist black and white, introduced an abstraction that was structurally very Balinese.

Why are Balinese artists attracted to abstraction?

Bali adapted very well to abstraction, or perhaps pseudo-abstraction, because abstraction allowed artists to express the prevailing symbols of their intellectual space of the time, that is, Hinduism. The process is clear: while Balinese intellectuals were structuring their beliefs into modern Hinduism, artists were putting Hindu concepts into abstract form. The play of opposites, the trinity, the cosmic wheel: these cosmological schemes of Hindu thought appeared in art at the same time that the *Parisada Hindu Dharma* (Council of Hinduism) was instilling them in society, that is, since its foundation in 1959. Thus, during the 1970s and '80s, there emerged the few Balinese artists who made a name for themselves in Indonesian abstract and contemporary art.[86] Actually, there is only one artist from the Balinese technical and iconographic tradition who creates a purely Balinese modernity, and that is Ketut Budiana. He deals with the cosmic dynamic as such, thus a modern, philosophical theme, but with a typically Balinese iconography. The result is quite extraordinary phantasmagorical art.

---

[83] Walter Spies (1895-1942) was a German painter, musician, and choreographer who spent a long time in Java and Bali; he contributed, with Rudolf Bonnet, to making the Javanese and Balinese cultures known internationally.

[84] Johan Rudolf Bonnet (1895-1978) was a Dutch painter who spent much of his life promoting Balinese painting, mainly that of Ubud and the surrounding area.

[85] Made Wianta (1949-2020) is one of the major contemporary artists of Indonesia.

[86] We can mention here Nyoman Erawan and Wayan Sika.

What does all this reveal?

It's an affirmation of modernity, but also of the Balinity, the Balinese-ness, within that modernity. Now, we are witnessing a new twist: a questioning of the modern world, but with reference to the global world. It's a reverberation of the fact that Bali, sold globally as "paradise," now feels it must play a role in the global conscience. The theme of ecology arose early on. In the 1990s, the painter Made Wianta used a car in one of his installations. For the new millennium, he organized a performance with the word "peace" written on a cloth two kilometers long in all the languages of the world.

What role did non-Balinese Indonesian painters play in the development of Balinese painting?

The first Indonesian artists were trained in Java through contact with Dutch artists mainly at the beginning of the 20th century. They diverged from the Dutch when emerging nationalism in the 1930s led them to abandon exoticism and adopt a more social form of expressionism. Just after Independence, in 1950, these Indonesian artists, like Westerners, "discovered" Bali. They had open studios in Denpasar and Sanur and thus trained the first Balinese artists to take an analytical, that is, non-traditional approach. At that time there was no art school in Bali. It was only later, starting in the 1960s, that Balinese went to study at art schools in Java.

Did non-Balinese Indonesians make the same kind of art as foreigners?

Unlike foreigners, who highlighted the exotic, Indonesians from the outset accentuated their common Indonesian identity. Two great Indonesian artists have made part of their career in Bali: Affandi and Srihadi Sudarsono. Affandi painted violent expressionism directly from the tube; Srihadi paints visual meditations dealing with the insignificance of human beings in the cosmos. Nothing to do with Western painting nor with modern Balinese painting, which at first was imbued with exoticism, then very quickly with veiled Hindu religiosity.

Are there any contemporary Balinese artists today working outside of Balinese identity?

Made Wianta is almost the only Balinese artist to have explored this trail. He refuses to be labelled narrowly as Balinese, and positions himself as an Indonesian artist. The others tend to express their Balinity in modernity. Ecology is a favorite theme. I think of artists like Made Bayak addressing the issue of *Reklamasi*.[87] Yes, Bali is always the primary theme.

So, there are no contemporary Balinese artists without Balinity?

There are a few isolated cases mostly artists trained and living outside Bali. The

---

[87] *Reklamasi*: a huge reclamation project in Benoa Bay in south Bali, which is strenuously opposed by the local Balinese population.

best known is indisputably Nyoman Masriadi, who was the first Indonesian artist to deal with new modernity, that of modern media, and related modern vulgarity. For example, his works represented cell phones, to better mock the use people made of them. But that was 15 years ago. His antithesis is Putu Wirantawan, who paints visibly cosmological themes without directly referring to Balinese iconography. But his meticulously pictorial style reveals an unmistakably Balinese touch. Sutawijaya expresses the encounter between Bali and the West by making his body a metaphor for the world. So, there is no explicit denial of Balineseness; to the contrary, we find it now in a new universalized form. Mangu Putra, who subjects Balinity to Indonesian nationalism, is also interesting. Wayan Karja goes from a representation of Balinese cosmic dynamism, the *pangider-ider*, to the representation of the universal cosmic void. Speaking of Balinity, the most natural is that of Djirna, who calls the invisible *niskala* world of Bali to life in bizarre installations beyond classification. Well worth mentioning are Suklu and his highly personal drawings and Kun Adnyna's promising inroads in history and space. On the whole, even artists who deal with ecology, like Made Bayak, or those who reject the commodification of the land, remain focused primarily on their Balinese identity.

And women?

With women painters, there is a rupture. They speak for themselves and not about religion or Bali as a theme of identity or ecology. They don't particularly do much technical or conceptual research. They just talk about their bodies as an object of desire for others and of traumatic obsession for themselves. Two extraordinary artists stand out very clearly: Murni [88] and Satya Cipta.[89] Both use a linear language, Murni rather *art brut* or outsider art, Satya Cipta more sophisticated and more classically refined but no less expressive. Through them and a few others, women are shaking up Balinese art.

Is the ArtBali cultural center that opened in 2018 in Nusa Dua, with the idea of doing annual exhibitions, a response to the opening of the MACAN Museum in Jakarta?

Yes, but ArtBali is a concept set up for national Indonesian purposes. The language is contemporary, with increasingly hybrid local components. It's a rather artificial structure set up by the Bekraf.[90] Ultimately, it's about presenting the Indonesianness of modern Bali.

When you think of contemporary art in Indonesia, today Jakarta is on the map, thanks to the MACAN museum. But, otherwise, we think mainly of Yogyakarta and Bali. Are you telling me, though, that this

---

[88] Murni: I Gusti Ayu Kadek Murni (1966-2006).
[89] Satya Cipta: born in 1998.
[90] Bekraf: Badan Ekonomi Kreatif (Indonesian Creative Economy Agency), a non-ministerial Indonesian government institution charged with defining government policy in the creative industries.

ArtBali center is a government initiative and that it has no authenticity?

Yes, that's it. If anything genuinely new appears in Bali, it will be elsewhere, in Canggu, for example, in the most international part of Bali, and anyway outside all areas associated with genuine Bali. The problem is that there is not yet any real spontaneous hybridization taking place. When it comes to culture and creativity, the touristic south of Bali remains marginal for most Balinese themselves. This is the place of desire, the place of Evil, the place of foreigners. This is where people from Jakarta go. They might be on an adulterous escapade, but they still want to be able to eat Padang,[91] that is, halal. The south embodies it all, Indonesia's Sodom and Gomorrah, but also halal and Islam!

Have we been witnessing, over the past decades, the end of Balinese cultural memory?

Yes! Or at least its total transformation. And I think it's the most important transformation that has taken place on the island in seven hundred years, since the invasion of Majapahit in 1343 a transformation based on economic and ecological changes. There is an ongoing mutation of the language, from Balinese to Indonesian,[92] then towards English. There is a change in the way of thinking, which was symbolic, narrative and relative, and which is becoming abstract, national and even international, with the need for the internal logic inherent in this new way of thinking. This results in the establishment of standard forms, hesitantly at first, then gradually structuring themselves, and hardening in almost every area.

Text is taken to be a fixed truth …

Yes, that of Balinese modernity. Traditionally, everything was relative, fluid, nothing was standardized, except the rites, of course, and on a very local scale. People weren't yet self-conscious, everything happened spontaneously without the need for consistency. All this is changing. It's also linked to the presence of the "other" in the cultural realm, but also in reality.

Dance is mainly what made Bali's artistic reputation. Has it changed a lot?

Since the glory days of the 1920s and '30s, when images of little Balinese dancing girls spread around the world, yes, everything has changed. Until then, dance was performed exclusively for religious festivals and rituals. There were dances to welcome the deities during their visits, like the Pendet, when the gods seized one or more dancers who went into a sudden trance in front of the ancestral shrines. There were dances that replayed the history of clans especially Topeng mask dances or that replayed scenes from classic epics like the adventures of

---

[91] Padang: a region of Sumatra renowned for its cuisine and its many restaurants throughout Indonesia.

[92] Even seminars on the Balinese language are in Indonesian.

Panji. Sacredness varied, but was present everywhere. The trance dances often took place in the higher, innermost courtyard of the temple; the more secular dances though none were really secular took place in the outer part, where there was often a large open pavilion.

So, dance wasn't a spectacle?

It was first a rite. Anyway, with the exception of the trance taking place in the inner courtyard, most dance performances were watched sitting on the ground, just a few meters away from the dancers. Coming out from behind a makeshift curtain, the dancers were suddenly among us, no barriers, hands reaching upwards, legs drilling into the ground. Everything was in the eyes and the hands. It wasn't the choreography that mattered; there was no conscious choreography, more a stylized convention of movement. What mattered was the magical presence, the Balinese *taksu*. Before dancing, the dancer prayed at a special *taksu* shrine and did not dance until he had summoned ancestral memory into himself.

This type of dance still exists!

Yes, of course, just like sudden trance, if only because some ritual dances are expressly for trance, as the very sign of the presence of the gods. But they remain more intimate and hidden, except perhaps in rural mountain villages. Or when they become part of folklore, as in Kesiman or Denpasar. But then, how can you judge if a trance is real or feigned among a hundred cameras in search of the unique document? But these phenomena have decreased with education, because there is a decrease in the role of magic. It used to be that for a child born in the week called *Wayang*, a *wayang* play with the story "Sapuh Leger" would be held, to keep the child from harm. Few people believe that now, so this type of performance is less common. And yet! In times of crisis, all it takes is for a temple priest or inspired *tapakan* (medium) to say in trance that a certain god asks to be awakened and the god will be roused with the support of trance and dance. Once awakened, the god will be part of the ceremonial dancing for years, during each temple anniversary.

Education and urbanization create a lot of change, don't they?

It goes back and forth a bit. Change is first of all disorder. And disorder calls for the voice of the gods, for trance. Sanur, in the heart of the tourist area, has long been known for its extraordinary trances. Not to mention the temple of Petitenget, in another area dense with tourism, and its possessed dancers who stab their eyes with a *keris* while shouting: "*Tiang ngayah, tiang ngayah!*" (I serve, I serve my divine master!) So, the evolution is complex. But, generally speaking, education raises the level of rationality. The *tapakan*, who go into trance naturally, are dying one by one, and with them the dances of possession fade away. You don't see college professors suddenly going into trance. Everyone would laugh.

If the ritual dances decrease, are there fewer dances in total?

Perhaps. Dance was gradually, and intellectually, desacralized to become the spectacle and product it is today. Look at what the Europeans did in the 1930s, Walter Spies, in particular. They wanted dance performances, but not too long, not too much repetition, and it had to start on time. They asked for cuts and a reduction in the role of the accompanying storyteller, which has disappeared in many cases. Dance thus became a spectacle, presented before an audience of privileged guests, first in Belaluan, then in the *puri* of Ubud and elsewhere, or at the Bali Hotel in Denpasar. Seeing this, some Balinese got involved in the creation of new styles of music and dance, often based on pre-existing sounds and gestures. Then Walter Spies gave it a go, assisted by the famous Wayan Limbak. We know the result: the Kecak which then incorporated elements of the Ramayana. But this was just the beginning. Since foreigners wanted shows with chairs and armchairs, before long the Balinese made theatres, with chairs and armchairs. And they ended up sitting there themselves. This became widespread from the 1980s, when the old wooden pavilions were replaced everywhere by big concrete structures, to the despair of Made Wijaya.

Yes, Made Wijaya[93] denounced this destruction of architecture without being able to do anything about it.

Even beyond beauty becoming ugliness, everything has changed. No more *kalangan*, the open performance ground around which musicians, dancers and spectators crowded in communion.[94] Dance was no longer judged by the detail of the hand and eye, but by the choreography, created on demand. After Independence, all that remained was to perfect the development: create a conservatory, KOKAR, in 1960; teach dance by analysis rather than by mimicry; be inspired by last year's gestures to create new works; feminize dance to please the spectator; then put on big shows. So, now we have the past, present, and future of Balinese dance: ritual dances in decline; *kreasi baru* (new creations) for the general Balinese public; and a product sold in hotels to satisfy the craving for authenticity of the naive West and the image-seeking Indonesian state. To complete the picture, add festivals, aimed at waking up the memory of the past.

Is nothing being done to ensure the survival of ancient forms of dance?

In some villages, like Peliatan, Batuan and Sukawati, traditional dances are so linked to religious life that transmission takes place naturally. But Bali has also intellectuals who are aware of the need of a strong cultural polity, such as Made Bandem, a major figure in Balinese dance and culture. When he was rector of the Denpasar Art Institute, he not only helped produce *kreasi baru* and extraordinary choreographed productions for entertainment, but, borrowing

---

[93] Made Wijaya (1953-2016): Australian landscape designer based in Bali and renowned chronicler of Balinese culture. Author of *Architecture of Bali* (Archipelago Press, 2002) and other works.
[94] For reflections on this kind of theatre and its influence on modern theatre, see *Le théâtre et son double*, Antonin Artaud, 1938, Gallimard.

from old terminology, he popularized a system for classifying dances,[95] to isolate and preserve those which have a ritual function. The object of this classification was to prevent desecration. There are some other notable efforts of preservation, in particular, the establishment of a historical documentation center under the leadership of Bandem's son Marlowe. But, as far as I know, there has been no systematic documentation made of living and threatened performing arts, of the last surviving genuinely traditional dancers and artists, those whose memory was shaped before academies and television transformed everything.

Aren't you exaggerating?

Yes, of course, because alongside this transformation, there is also the opposite, resilience. In Batuan and a couple of other villages, the Gambuh dance still survives. During temple festivals, when one literally welcomes the ancestors for a few days, the Gambuh is performed, accompanied by melodies played on giant bamboo flutes, telling of palace love stories and conflicts from 500 years ago, in the Kawi language used at the time by the nobility, of Javanese origin. Thus the palace, and its "foreign" rulers, are still the model. All Balinese dances are said to originate in the Gambuh. People like Made Bandem above are well aware that it must be preserved. And it is indeed resilient.

But even if the sacred character is being lost, isn't the survival of a secular art form better than nothing?

This is what we must say. But we see the result, and the problem: today's international culture is a maelstrom that sweeps away everything in its path. What endures is only what is iconic. An identifiable product. Is dance that is only an icon of itself still really culture? Is memory only an identifiable product? I doubt it.

What kind of conditions does this create for new generations? For the young?

Traditionally, culture was communicated in the village through shadow theatre performances and dance-dramas that told the stories of ancestors, princes, and local figures. Forty years ago, all the young people of the village attended these performances. It was the only available entertainment. Now, young people go to towns, they go to the cinema, to nightclubs, or, for the more intellectual, they do modern theatre. And when there are temple festivals in the village, it's not uncommon today to see rock bands. It's no longer just traditional dance-drama. In the 1980s, Bali's memory evolved in just ten years from that of the shadow-puppet theatre to that of television.

I imagine that today it's mainly the internet and social networks where the Balinese position their identity.

Yes, they view themselves and construct their identity based ever less on the

---

[95] This terminology comprises: the *wali*, ritual dances required for religious ceremonies; *bebali* dances to accompany the rite; and *balih–balihan* for entertainment.

reality of traditional memory, which fades with the death of each old master, and ever more on the image of their island as it is produced locally and internationally by modern media. This is where the magnitude of current changes is measured. From a communication that took place only at the village level bathing at the river, at temples, during dance performances the Balinese gradually passed to exchanges with the Indonesian nation, then with the whole world. And all this happened in just a few decades, with the advent of school, then motorbikes, the *bemo*[96] and now the internet. The relation to space has changed and all the points of reference have been jostled! It makes your head spin.

Why wouldn't these modern means of communication be used for a strengthening of cultural memory?

Let's say that what is left of traditional cultural memory is of course highlighted. But the volume of this memory of Balinese knowledge by Balinese themselves is greatly diminishing.

So, younger generations are losing this memory?

They lose its positive content. What remains of it is transferred from the peasant population to urban artists, specialists and intellectuals. It locks itself in the conservatories. And living symbols become standardized norms, then identity, that is, a means to define oneself in relation to others. The shift is obvious. But it's not just the cultural aspects that change. The economy is no longer agrarian. In a more macro way, people talk about the eternal rice fields while the economic importance of rice fields shrinks every year. It's as if people can't confront reality. The Balinese do not want to adapt their symbolism to their new modernity, so what's left to them? They focus on identity, which they overemphasize. With all these ongoing changes, this end of the old Balinese cultural memory, can the Balinese find an alternative, create another memory, at once genuinely open and Balinese?

Maybe that will allow the Balinese to reinvent themselves!

That's what we must hope. If possible, without losing, if not the social structure, at least the extraordinary and typically Balinese way of being together.

Faced with this steamroller of development, wouldn't Bali have extra assets compared to other societies in the Indonesian archipelago?

The Balinese have an organized cultural memory, a writing system, and a literature, certainly more Indianized, even Hindu, than the religious rituals. So, we can ask the question: how could the Balinese intellectuals of the 1970s,

---

[96] *Bemo*: a contraction of the words *becak* (pedicab) and *motor* (motorcycle), which first designated a motorized tricycle, then a small public taxi.

survivors of 1965-66,[97] indulge in the reform of their culture to cope with tourism, in the same way that, 20 years earlier, they indulged in the restructuring of their religion, in order to deal with the threat of Islam and Christianity, the religions of the book? Maybe they were wrong; maybe they made the mistake of wanting to standardize things on the pretext of saving what they could. That said, they are certainly more in command of their destiny and the expression of their identity than, say, the people of Sumba or Papua.

Is tourism actually the main factor of change?

Yes, but tourism is also at the origin of a very special type of identity. The real issue with today's tourism is that the paradise of Bali is no longer just "created," as Adrian Vickers put it,[98] referring to Dutch colonial politics, but it is also deliberately fabricated. We see this in tourist performances, in Buddhist statuary for hotel décor, or in trekking tours on elephants, and even camels, which were never endemic in Bali. A completely artificial exoticism has been fabricated. I think of those Hollywood-inspired shows at the Bali Safari & Marine Park where there's a mix of Balinese music and dance with a love story between a Balinese prince and a Chinese lady, all for the marketing of Bali to Chinese and Western tourists. Although the story based on history, this is Disney! The narrative mode is completely transformed. It's the modern West with Balinese music and costumes added to remind the audience that they're in Bali. This is what's on offer to tourists these days: local aesthetic devoured by the Americanized West, with chinoiserie decoration to signal that it's about China, too. And all this was created by Balinese. Hello the future!

So, what about cinema? On TV, they show Bollywood films or Indian TV series, some of which are adaptations of great Indian epics ... What do the Balinese think?

This presents them with a different kind of storytelling about Hinduism than their own. It's part of the relearning of Hinduism that's going on. The Balinese adore these shows.

Despite the West's infatuation with Bali, international cinema has shown little interest in it. But Indonesian cinema has always seen what the "paradise created" has conscientiously erased: the demonic face of Bali. For Indonesian cinema, Bali is the island of *balians* and sorcerers, not a paradise, but a hell ...

Yes, after all, other Indonesians know Bali better than Westerners. Or perhaps

---

[97] There is obviously a political aspect. One of the most political intellectuals, I Made Kembar Kerepun, was regent of Gianyar from 1965 to 1969. He then played a considerable role in the discussions on tourism and, later in the reform of the status of the priesthood, towards a more democratic priesthood. See below. See also *The Dark Side of Paradise: Political Violence in Bali*, Geoffrey Robinson, Cornell UP, 1995.

[98] Adrian Vickers (1953-) is a professor in the Department of Southeast Asian Studies at the University of Sydney, and a specialist on Bali and Indonesia. He is renowned for his book *Bali: A Paradise Created* (Penguin Books Australia, 1989).

this Balinese paradise is perceived differently, simply because the Balinese woman has never been, until very recently, accessible to foreigners.[99]

Yes, but there was a very real fascination with bare-breasted Balinese women, which can be traced in old photos, films, and documentaries. This fascination should have resulted in more films, and yet there are few anyway, not at the level of erotic tension that Bali has incited in the Western psyche …

Yes. To which must be added that one does not find in Bali the Buddhism that is so fantasized by the West.[100] And the West has long refused to fully accept Balinese aesthetics and iconography the occupation of space, the repetition of forms, monsters …

Yes, the rational West could not accept the Balinese universe and reinvented it in its own way …

Kamila Andini, the daughter of the Javanese director Garin Nugroho, made a film in 2017 entitled *Sekala, Niskala*, on the visible and invisible Balinese worlds. Once again, an Indonesian film that, interesting as it is, confirms Bali for what it is in the Indonesian imagination. The forces of the *niskala* invisible world are constructed as always being negative.

What about literature in Bali?

Modern literature is one of the signs that Bali is successfully incorporated into Indonesian multicultural space. Poetry in particular has a big place, not least thanks to Umbu Landu Paranggi, a Sumbanese who for 35 years edited two pages of the daily newspaper *Bali Post* devoted to literature. He toured villages, attended meetings, identified talents, organized competitions, and published their works once a week. It shows that the national culture is extremely lively in Bali. The poet Warih Wisatsana continues this role with the Bentara Budaya cultural center, created by the national newspaper *Kompas*.[101]

What about the more traditional aspects of local literature?

The past has long been resilient in Balinese mentalities. Until recently, there were scholars who wrote in Kawi, Old Javanese. For example, the *Kakawin Gajah*

---

[99] Except when the foreigner exalts the mythical image of Bali, such as the painter Le Mayeur and his wife Ni Pollok in the 1930s to 1950s or, more recently, the painter Antonio Blanco and his wife Ni Ronji.

[100] The Buddhist component of the culture, derived from the Siwa-Boda Javanese tradition, plays a very minor role in daily religion. Buddhist texts, however, are at the core of the mantras uttered by the Boda priests, whose holy waters are necessary for the completion of some ceremonies. It is tourism, through decoration, that gives Buddhism a visibility it does not have in the original culture.

[101] *Kompas*: the main national Indonesian daily newspaper.

Mada,[102] a long classical poem on the Javanese conquest, was written by one of the uncles of the present prince of Ubud. There was the great 20th-century priest-poet, Ida Pedanda Made Sidemen. In Denpasar, there is a bookstore where they sell mostly books of *geguritan*[103] in modern Balinese. But most new Balinese literature is published in Indonesian.

What is the dominant genre?

There is a lot of poetry written in Bali. In Indonesian. Novels are mostly written by women. Long constrained by tradition, women explode in literature. They highlight their problems as women, like Oka Rusmini about marriage and the atmosphere of violence that surrounds women's lives. There is also Cok Sawitri, very focused on Balinese identity and fanatically ethnocentric. She offers a feminist reinterpretation of classic themes such as the *Calon Arang* [104] and the *Ramayana*. Among men, we should mention Gde Aryantha Soethama, who writes articles and short stories dealing with the impact of the West, and of Western women in particular. Abu Bakar, a non-religious Muslim, talks about the difficulty of representing himself outside religious frameworks. In Balinese, Djelantik Santha talks about the kidnapping of women.

Are all these authors making their mark on the Indonesian scene?

Yes, of course. Apart from the last one, all those I have just mentioned are known nationally, which shows that Bali is fundamentally Indonesian. The unitary dream works. Educated Balinese think of the Indonesian national space as their primary space with the right to settle anywhere, to have temples everywhere, and to think of Indonesian space as potentially Hindu. And yet, the process is not yet complete. There is a paradox here: Senator Wedakarna defends the religion of Bali on behalf of a marginal Indonesian nationalist party (PNI Marhaenisme). Behind a display of nationalism, he risks stimulating separatist desires. He creates the conditions for possible conflict, not with regard to Indonesian nationalism proper, but to religious and identity crystallization.

In that case, Pancasila[105] is hijacked ...

Yes, instead of being guidelines for the establishment of a humanist modernity, it becomes a venue of religious rivalry, where each religious group must assert itself to the detriment of others.

---

[102] *Kakawin Gajah Mada*: a work of poetry recounting the life of Gajah Mada (d. 1364), a military chief and vizier of the Majapahit kingdom.

[103] *Geguritan*: a style of popular poetry that is read aloud in small groups.

[104] *Calon Arang*: an account believed to date from the Javanese kingdom of Majapahit. It tells the story of Calon Arang, a widow and witch from the village of Girah. Popular theme for religious dance-drama.

[105] *Pancasila*: the five principles of the Indonesian state philosophy. 1) belief in one God; 2) a just and civilized humanity; 3) the unity of Indonesia; 4) democracy guided by wisdom through deliberation and representation; and 5) social justice for all Indonesian people.

Let's talk about music. Balinese gamelan has taken on modern accents in recent years by mixing with other genres of music, *kolaborasi*, as they say here, according to the good old recipe of world music of the 1980s.

Music is where there has been the most change. When I first came to Bali in the 1970s, there were a couple of radios on Kuta beach playing Western music, but everywhere else in the *banjar*, there was only Balinese music. It has changed a lot. Now there's no Balinese music in the bars and restaurants on the south coast. That said, Balinese music endures and even is exported, to Europe, to France, to the United States.[106]

Yes, well, this is mostly through conservatories. But what about the modern evolution of Balinese music?

I think of the 1930s and the creation of a new type of gamelan, the *gong kebyar*. Since then, there have been no dramatic changes except the recent work of Gede Yudhana, who makes contemporary Balinese music. There is also the work of the singer Ayu Laksmi, or even Dewa Bujana, or the virtuoso guitarist Balawan.

On a more popular level, we won't talk about the insipid Bali pop and its silly lyrics, but it is interesting to mention the countless reggae groups that have firmly established themselves on the local scene since the 1990s or even the punk group Superman Is Dead, very engaged in the fight against *Reklamasi*.

Yes, this is the modernity brought by the youth. In the 1970s, the educated urban society was tiny but, just emerging from the heavy constraints of the Sukarno years,[107] it was very much Western-oriented, especially the young people. In fact, from the outset, this urban society was more Indonesian than narrowly Balinese. Its members were often Indonesians of Chinese or Punjabi descent, each of which lived in their own area of Denpasar. They were also the first to set up businesses on the beaches. Thus, it was "Indians" actually Indonesian Punjabis who set up the famous Goa 2001 bar in Seminyak.[108] It was also the epoch of Pak Kadek, who started 6×6 [109] and today is one of the richest men in Bali. All those youth were open to the outside world, but marginal in regard to their original space. There were also young people from good Balinese families, from Brahmin or princely families, who had studied in Yogyakarta or Bandung, and who were

---

[106] We must mention here the role of the Institut Seni Indonesia (Indonesian Art Institute), where Jean Couteau taught for a long time, and the role of Made Bandem and his wife Swasti Bandem, who are largely responsible for the modernization and internationalization of Balinese dance and music.

[107] Sukarno, the founding president of Indonesia (1945-1966), prohibited modern Western music.

[108] It should be noted that while the men of these communities, when they were not in Java or abroad, went to the beach to rub shoulders with the hippies, while the women were confined to tending the shop. Moreover, if the beach was a place of mixing, the town was a place of segregation of groups.

[109] 6×6: pronounced "Double Six," a famous open-air night spot on the beach, now gone.

eager to build a modernity mixing traditional elitism and modern appetites. Now this modernity is everywhere.

There's something more to say about these phenomena of modernity developing in Bali. Before, they were always out of step with global fashions that is, late. Today, that's no longer the case. When we see the hipsters and other digital nomads of Canggu, we understand that this is where it's happening and nowhere else.

Yes, that's clear. Bali used to be an imitator of fashions from elsewhere, now it's a trendsetter! Kuta has become a hotspot for fashion, especially beach fashion, with its now well-known Bali Fashion Week. The same with jewelry and design. That said, we must add that, except for the hotel industry, this international Bali in the south of the island is largely controlled by foreigners. Thus, there is a rift between the internationalized Bali of the south and the rest of society, frozen in the cult of tradition. Is this a holdover from the politics of the past? Perhaps. Let's not forget that 20 or 30 years ago, the West represented decadence, debauchery. Officials of the *Orde Baru*[110] wanted its money, but not its culture. Now this culture is part of everyday life either directly through tourism or indirectly through education and the media.

What will today's new tourists change?

Are you thinking of the tourists from China? From India? It's obvious that if they come in large numbers for a long time, they will make their mark on Balinese society.

Finally, what can we say about the craze of beauty pageants in Bali?

Some members of the new bourgeoisie, national as well as Balinese, seek social recognition in terms of other criteria than tradition caste status in particular. There is the criterion of money, but also of beauty. Some Balinese women are eager for these contests that deal them a new hand.

---

[110] *Orde Baru*: the New Order, the military regime of Suharto (1965-1998).

4. Delinquency, Crime, Violence, Marginalization

What about violence and crime? Did they exist in Bali? To what extent in modern Bali? Jean Couteau recounts that in earlier times, there was no room for difference, for marginality, even if it existed. Today, as in the past, problems of this type are often managed by the community, although without a concept of law. Social control takes precedence over everything, upstream of the law. Since the arrival of democracy, this control has passed from the hands of the military to community organizations, sometimes nothing more than organized gangs. We note that this period also marked the increase in discrimination against non-Balinese. Did brothels exist in former times? Did the men get drunk? Did people use drugs? Pedophilia, which exists locally, is now used to stigmatize the supposed decline of the West in sex tourism cases where it is all about vocabulary, we explain. As for sex tourism between consenting adults, the role of gigolos has been prominent for a long time, but is fiercely denied officially. Has the nightlife world, which has developed with tourism, brought its share of additional problems? We explain that foreign mafias have recently established themselves in Bali. Are the Balinese prepared to face all these external assaults? Jean and I recall that it was the dirty money of Suharto's New Order that was laundered in Bali. Finally, we talk about gambling and the convoluted legality of cockfights.

ERIC BUVELOT. **What's it like to be marginal in Bali?**

JEAN COUTEAU. In traditional Balinese society, there was basically no marginalization. People were integrated into the village and there was no room for difference. Even the *balian* were part of the system. Everyone was expected to behave in a "normal" and prescribed manner. There was very little personal autonomy. That said, because being aberrant was a social rarity, when it did appear it was dramatic. In the time of the kingdoms, Balinese who behaved very badly often for sexual reasons, for example by having a relationship with one of the king's wives well, they tied a stone to their neck and drowned them. In other cases, they were exiled to Nusa Penida or Nusa Dua. Or in a more distant past, they were sold as slaves, in Batavia, or later, at the end of the 18th century, in the Île de France or on the Île Bourbon (today Mauritius and Reunion).

Why such harsh measures?

First of all because there were no prisons. Imagine a young prince sleeping with the king's first wife: if his relationship was discovered, he had no choice, he had to flee. Fortunately for him, there was still space in Bali. The young prince, accompanied by a dozen of his followers, would take refuge in the mountains and, in no time, they were clearing the forest! If you read the *babad*, the chronicles of the kingdoms, you'll see that many villages, and even principalities, were created in this way. The alternative was death or slavery.

Marginality also applies to people with mental disabilities.

Yes, they are tied up, literally, or caged in backyards still today. If Michel Foucault had come to Bali, he could have rewritten his *Madness and Civilization: A History of Insanity in the Age of Reason*. In some cases, the mentally ill are integrated into the system. They have the status of *melik*, visited by the gods, and become *balian* or *jero tapakan*.[111] They are called upon, for example, to select officiants such as *pamangku*.[112]

So, no marginality because it is impossible?

It used to be impossible. Now it has become possible, for sociological reasons among others. Bali's population is no longer homogeneous. A hundred years ago, Muslims were few in number, little more than 1% of the population. They were integrated into the rites and held specific functions most often as mercenaries, merchants, butchers, or medics. In short, they were part of the system.

And today?

Today, they are indeed on the margins, albeit much more numerous. In addition to the native Balinese Muslims, there are now *pen-datang*,[113] who constitute 15-20% of the population of the island. They are most often urban; some are not registered. They are less well integrated than the earlier communities because they live apart and do not speak Balinese. While the former feel and want to be Balinese, the latter display their difference. But we must also mention a marginality that appeared very suddenly between 1965 and 1966 the political marginality of the communists. In a way, the Indonesian political leaders did with the communists what Balinese kings did with the marginalized. They forced them into exile, in this case on Buru Island, or simply killed them.

Forced labor or the mass grave!

This must be seen in a socio-historical perspective: here, there has never been room, ideologically, for a complete questioning of reality, after the Western manner. Modern marginality arose first of all because of socio-economic changes in particular around conflicts linked to the control of land, and then, nowadays, because of ethno-demographic changes. In 1960, when the government of Sukarno wanted, in the name of a European idea of social justice, to carry out land reform and thus reduce the power of so-called feudalism, it shook the whole

---

[111] *Jero tapakan*: a man or woman with the power to communicate the will of forces of the invisible world; a trance medium.

[112] *Pamangku*: temple priest; different from the high priest, who officiates for a clientele.

[113] *Pendatang*: literally, new arrivals, a popular term designating Indonesian immigrants from other islands.

system, at a terrible cost. First, there were massacres following the fall of Sukarno, then the communists were ostracized for decades. But it is paradoxically now, 60 years later, that we see the most perverse effects: this reform has resulted in the appearance of modern land titles, that enable the transformation of collectively owned land into private land, and then the sale of that land to outsiders. A very traumatic transformation.[114]

Which led to the dispossession of the land of the Balinese.

Yes, it is no longer the Balinese who control the land, at least in the coastal regions. They have sold it to non-Balinese, or leased it out to foreigners on so-called freeholds. We are seeing the emergence of a new phenomenon of marginality: landless Balinese, those who have sold everything. It's tragic. They are still affiliated with their temples, but they no longer have a place of residence; they have dispossessed themselves. There are still very few cases like this, but the fact that it does exist is worrying. Do not dream of a bright future.

Can you say more about the events of 1965-1966?

Access to land was traditionally conditioned by belonging to a clan, being in a village, or by fealty to a Brahmin or noble family or local potentates. This defined part of land rights, networks of ritual obligations and, inevitably, political choices, which were not those of the individual but of the group. The national land reform of 1960 shook up the system of social obligations, then made it rigid. Traditionally, when the master or the strongman of the place told his men to go to war, to kill, well, they killed.[115] This is what happened, in its own new way, in 1965-66 during the massacres of communists in Bali.

No way to get out of it?

No; some Balinese killed because their own survival that was at stake if they refused. There was a novel political aspect to these massacres, but it was marginal. To me, it had more to do with nascent modernity, linked to the conflicts of Independence and the expulsion of the colonizer. After all, it was Westernized intellectuals who introduced these notions of control over history, of transformation of society, of revolution. They didn't know what they were playing with.

Yes, of course. But we also often hear of problems of jealousy, rivalry, which would have taken these purges to particularly bloody levels here.

---

[114] Land ownership: we must understand the shock that this change in the status of land caused. In the Balinese tradition, the ownership of the land was separate from that of the trees growing on this land. Jean Couteau remembers having seen Balinese people continue to make offerings to the coconut palms at Club Med Bali and climb the trees to harvest the nuts. When the land was leased for the resort, the Balinese owners ceded their rights to the land, but not to the trees they had planted.

[115] The reality is indisputably complex. See Geoffrey Robinson (1995).

Yes, obviously, even though jealousy was not expressed as such; it sometimes hid behind suspicions of black magic. But if people like Frantz Fanon,[116] Jean-Paul Sartre and other advocates of the end of oppression had been able to see the layers of horror they brought about, and in the name of what cause that death came, perhaps they would have drawn other conclusions.

Were Chinese-Indonesians particularly targeted?

No. The Chinese were not victims as such in Bali. It must be said that they have a better image here than in the rest of Indonesia. In Bali, they were never the intermediaries of the Dutch, except some, in the north especially, during the short colonial period in Bali. And then the Dutch occupied the island when the colonial policy was milder, after 1900. The Chinese were therefore not in charge of collecting taxes on the markets, the roads, the rivers, and so forth, as in other parts of Indonesia. Moreover, the first Chinese who settled in Bali did so with the agreement of the local princes. So, they were never as marginalized as in other parts of Indonesia.

So, they were well integrated?

Yes, there are Chinese in Bali who are no longer seen as Chinese. Compared to the Balinese notion of the other, there is a certain inclusiveness when that other is Chinese. There are Balinese temples with an altar for Chinese ancestors, for example. There really have been traditional ways of absorbing ethnic marginality in Bali.

I've noticed that Chinese-Balinese people often master the Balinese language.

Yes! And often they are addressed by people in High Balinese. Also, the Chinese woman, with her white skin, represents an ideal as in the Barong Landung effigies, the story of the black-skinned king Jaya Pangus and his white Chinese wife. Still, the Chinese, being foreigners, could not settle in Bali without the permission of the prince.

So, the Chinese, marginalized elsewhere, were not so in Bali; is that true today?

They are starting to become marginalized, because, like many Muslims, most Chinese in Bali now are from Java; they are not Chinese-Balinese. Not only are they buying land all over Bali, but they come and settle here as Christians, with their habit of ethno-religious separation, inherited from Java's history.

And the other foreigners? The whites?

Whites have always been marginal here. Colonials aside, they came last, in the

---

[116] Frantz Fanon (1925-1961) is a French essayist from Martinique and one of the founders of Third World thought.

1970s. They did not come to fit in, but to enjoy the "Bali paradise" on the cheap, while taking advantage of the weak state presence, despite Suharto's dictatorial regime. They could pretty much do whatever they wanted. There was no control over their behavior, neither social nor legal. This is probably why the hippies were infatuated with Bali. However, the press often castigated the decadence of the West that they embodied, and thus they were real outsiders. Not content with the real paradise of Bali, they indulged themselves, joint after joint, in the languor of artificial paradises. That said, for many Balinese of the time, the foreigner was not only decadence, but also the notion of progress and that of contradiction, including politics. Indonesian artists and writers understood this well, and came to Bali to rub shoulders with the deviance and freedom made possible by the presence of foreigners.

Were there Balinese who were perceived as outsiders in Bali?

Yes, the beggars, who were originally absent in the south. But in the 1970s and '80s, there were women who started coming south with their children from poor villages in the arid northeast of Bali. First, these women bartered onions from the mountains for a small basket of rice. With the arrival of tourism, they shifted to places where there were foreigners, where there was money.

Are they the same ones we see begging at traffic lights today and that are regularly rounded up by the social services?

Yes, from being merchants, they became beggars with children, then some became traffickers of children. Originally, the women had no idea what was going on between their offspring and these generous foreigners. So, they let things happen. Yet it was sexual violence in the extreme, since it was psychologically integrated as normal. There was no possibility of defense. And this phenomenon went on for decades in Bali, the children being provided with false papers, including passports if needed. Moreover, the mobilization against pedophilia has appeared only recently, with a little anti-*bule* refrain thrown in, not without objective reason.

What else has introduced marginality to Bali?

First, there is a new white marginality of national communities, French, Italian, Australian, etc. The new whites no longer have a reason to integrate. They watch their TV on Android, their national news on cellphone; and Indonesians speak English much better than they did twenty or thirty years ago. After years in Bali, many whites speak at best only a "colonial" kind of Indonesian, good for giving orders. There are also the gay communities; but they have, in addition to some clubs in Jakarta, their Indonesian spaces of tolerance, which they find for the most part in Kuta. Finally, there are the small Javanese merchants who started coming in the 1980s. They tried to settle in Sanur, Kuta, even Ubud. Back then we often heard officials from those municipalities say they had to get rid of them. And in practice, many have indeed been deported.

In Ubud, this is hardly surprising, because it claims a powerful Balinese identity. Mosques are prohibited there, for example ...

Not officially, but in fact. There are mosques everywhere, including in Kuta, but some traditional villages (*desa adat*) have been able to evict their *pendatang*. This was done in concert with the emergence of a new phenomenon in the 1980s, the creation of village militias. Note that, in the tradition, as soon as the security of the village is threatened, the *kulkul bulus*[117] is struck and all the men of the village have to come out with knives and clubs. Beware of thieves, real or imaginary.

These phenomena of street justice also occur in the suburbs of large cities in Indonesia, where the social and ethnic fabric has become a veritable patchwork of migrants from all over the Archipelago ...

Yes, but there are specific contingencies in Bali. I remember a Balinese friend telling me, twenty years ago, that he was "obliged" by his *banjar* to participate in an attack on a neighboring *banjar*. He disagreed. He had friends in this other *banjar* with whom he played music in the same *gamelan* group. But if one refuses these obligations, there are sanctions.

What are the sanctions?

Ostracism. If the fault is a serious one, one risks a penalty on the dead! People will not come to help at the next cremation in the family, or they will not want to carry the body. In the event the conflict with the village worsens, most often at the level of a clan, the graveyard can be closed to the offender(s), unless he is a strongman, in which case he can cause a split in the *banjar*. This tends to keep the population in good order, to avoid marginality.[118]

This helps to avoid certain conflicts ...

Yes, but it is a mistake to imagine Bali as a place of full social harmony. Without mentioning the massacres of 1965-1966 and their contemporary political legacy, there is a lot of conflict in the villages, dozens of cases each year.[119] Much of this conflict concerns land, which has now become a scarce and expensive commodity, and whose control is subject to all kinds of manipulation.

These days people talk about administrative sanctions, fines ...

---

[117] *Kulkul*: a traditional tool of communication, a drum of bamboo or hollow wood that allows villagers to broadcast messages according to the manner in which it is struck. *Kulkul bulus* is a very fast rhythm that signals an emergency.

[118] There are now several cremation centers in Bali. This allows people to circumvent customary rules and thus weakens the punitive force of ostracism from the village.

[119] This is according to Wayan Windia, professor emeritus of Balinese customary law. In a series of articles devoted to conditions in the villages and published in the magazine *Sarad*, he said on p. 10 of the issue of 20 April 2010, "Between 1999 and 2005, there were no less than 112 cases of conflict in traditional Balinese villages (*desa pakraman*), of which 50.9% concerned a conflict between the village and one of its members, or a group of its members, and 49.1% concerned a conflict between the village and one or more external parties, individual or collective."

Yes, of course. For ordinary infringements or absences, the fines are minimal. It is above all a matter of recalling social control. But someone who's been expelled from the village and asks to become a member again can be asked to pay tens of millions of rupiah. You might ask, why ask for reinstatement in a village which expelled you? It's simple: because Balinese life is organized around ancestral temples, and the ancestors are lavish in "signs". It is they who most often ask for reinstatement a *balian* (shaman) helping or not.

Does the community get involved?

Yes, within the framework of the village, there's no question of infringing the collective decision of the village, unless it is a group, usually a clan, which rebels. Then there will be a split. But the community can also get involved in a positive way. I remember 35 years ago, the son of one of the houses where I lived stole some money from me and I found out. I could prove it and told the family about it. How was he punished? The kid was put under surveillance. So, it was resolved through peer review. All of this is handled by family friends and the *banjar*, through the intercession of powerful people, of respected figures.

Where does this spirit of communal resolution come from?

There is the strictly Balinese aspect, of course. But there is also the meeting of the Balinese tradition and the participation of the masses in politics, which dates from the Japanese period. When the Japanese occupied Bali in 1942, they were at first welcome. They set up youth movements (*gerakan pemuda*), which in 1945 became the spearhead of the struggle for independence, before splitting into multiple movements and political parties with related perverse effects. In the 1950s there were *Logis*[120] bandits, who were in fact disgruntled former fighters. If you add to that the Third World ideology of Bandung, the conflicts between intellectuals linked to the land reform of 1960, and the anti-communist repression of 1965-1966, you end up with the creation of village militias in the pay of the army, in addition to the *koramil* (military posts), responsible for security at the *kecamatan* (district) level. It is this repressive system that gave their first form to mass, mafia-like, organizations like Laskar Bali and Baladika that emerged after the fall of the military regime in 1998.

The *koramil* still exist.

They no longer have the same repressive powers. In the 1970s, an Indonesian who wanted to move or sleep in another village had to carry a permit and report to the local authorities. There was no freedom of movement except for the few Western tourists in Bali, but that's another story. Indonesians who had passports at that time were a tiny minority only for the country's elite! It was another world. Misery. When I went to Singapore to renew my visa, my Balinese friends would ask me to bring them a watch. Some were still dressed in rags. It's hard to imagine

---

[120] Logis: the former Logis combatants, once demobilized, were disappointed and spiraled out of control.

that today. There was not a tenth of the paved roads we see now.

Can you describe that time for us?

To get to Ubud, you had to take the bus to where the giant baby statue is today in Sakah, between Batuan and Mas. After 4pm, there was no more transportation, you had to walk. There were only three buses a day to Ubud. As you passed the iron bridge at Sukawati, the driver would stop to make offerings. Until the 1980s, on the main road through Sukawati, the *dalang*, the masters of shadow theatre, could still give performances by the roadside. At night there were no passing cars. No traffic! As the sun was setting, many Balinese could be seen sitting on the asphalt road: the temperature was ideal for warming up their buttocks.

Back to social control and its relation to marginality …

Yes, what's happened since *Reformasi* is the establishment of local autonomy, at island and regency level, but also at village level. The *desa pakraman*[121] was given greater autonomy. The *pecalang*[122] appeared, and the term *"krama tamiu"* (village guests) was created to designate Javanese residents of the village, but also all outsiders. It was also around this time, notably after the Islamist bomb attacks, that a provisional identity card (KIPEM) was made compulsory for all *pendatang*.

Yes! It was also at the same time that we witnessed social disorder in Bali, especially in Kuta where prostitution and drug trafficking had flourished in the street since the 1990s, in public view and in proportions that are difficult to imagine today.

Yes, the power formerly vested in the military through the *koramil* and other paramilitary militias soon fell to the *pecalang* in the *Reformasi* era. They first cleaned up the area, even on the beaches where the army had previously authorized the opening of bars. Then the local repressive power gradually passed from the village *pecalang* into the hands of mafia-style "mass organizations,"[123] which also claimed to represent order and protect Bali, like Laskar Bali, Baladika, and others. And beach bars have returned, as have schemes with politicians and affiliations with political parties, now democratic.

Finally, it should be noted that the *pecalang* are chosen by the *banjar*. They are generally strong, rather young guys from the village who cannot refuse this obligation which will last for several years.

Yes. They reappeared at village level during the rise of conflicts between political parties, in particular between the PDI-P of Megawati,[124] which has historically been favored by the Balinese, and Golkar, which was powerful during the *Orde*

---

[121] *Desa pakraman*: traditional village.

[122] *Pecalang*: member of a village militia and, by metonymy, the militia itself.

[123] Mass organizations: often referred to as *ormas*, for *organisasi masyarakat* (social organizations).

[124] Megawati Soekarnoputri, a daughter of Sukarno, Indonesia's first president, and herself president from 2001 to 2004.

Baru of Suharto. The PDI had been held on a tight leash during the thirty-two years of military rule and had scores to settle with Golkar. In 1998, this resulted in a few dozen deaths in the Buleleng region, and many *pecalang* became agents of political parties.

This reshuffling of cards also worked for the sale of land.

Indeed, the smartest *pecalang*, with or without Laskar caps, have become land agents, thus taking a role previously granted to local Suharto favorites. This former mafia affiliated with the Suharto military regime had mastered the art of expelling populations, in order to carry out increasingly gargantuan projects. Today, it is no longer so simple, as we see with the *Reklamasi* case.

It was also from the time of the establishment of the *pecalang* that we saw signs at the entrance to villages saying: *"pemulung dilarang masuk"* (access prohibited to scavengers).

Yes, the first open discrimination dates from this period, when some villages prohibited the rental of *kos*[125] to Javanese or the sale of land to non-Balinese Indonesians. In other cases, they imposed a very high floor on rentals, to dissuade *pendatang* from residing in the village. However, it should be added that this discrimination was ad hoc.

Today the government of Indonesia has banned these regional self-government laws. Measures of this type, sometimes taken at a very local level, are therefore obsolete.

Yes, the KIPEM[126] has disappeared. One of President Jokowi's first-term projects was to ban all laws that conflicted with national law. It is more difficult for him, however, to cancel similar measures outside Bali, in particular those areas which make the wearing of the Islamic headscarf compulsory.

I would like to know: did alcohol, bars, brothels exist before the arrival of tourism?

Yes, they've always existed. In some places along the main roads, there were *warung*[127] run by pretty girls. They provided for the needs of men with a bit of cash, on the roadsides, hidden away by thick trees. Those found on the Denpasar-Singaraja road for the stops of high officials on the move were famous. Gentlemen's pee stops. With modernity the name has changed. We now call them *kafe cewek*.[128]

Yes, but today's *kafe cewek* are more aimed at truck drivers, if I may say so.

---

[125] *Kos*: modest rental lodgings.
[126] KIPEM: a provisional identity card for outsider residents of the district.
[127] *Warung*: small, very simple roadside café, shop, and eating place.
[128] *Kafe cewek*: roadside café that is also a place of prostitution. *Cewek* means "girl".

Yes, they've always been here. It was once common for young men to go to brothels in groups. They openly admitted it. Now, of course, there are still ejaculatory stops on the Java road for truck drivers and their sixteen-year-old assistants. But, for the penniless, the places of pleasure have changed. There was Lumintang, there is now Padang Galak. There are massage parlors and karaoke bars. Even for the poor, Bali has gone upmarket.

You are telling me that Bali has become Bangkok. It is still far from that!

In Kuta, I don't know, but, in my opinion, prostitution is a marginal phenomenon. Bali is not Bangkok. Above all, do not confuse *warung cewek* with ordinary *warung*. These have always existed in the villages for farmers returning from the fields. They had their heyday in the 1980s. What to do with a pretty daughter after she has been through elementary school? Send her to work in the garment industry in Denpasar or Kuta? No, if possible, it was better to build a hut next to the family compound, put in a few benches, add bamboo walls and, with toothpaste and little packets of shampoo on sale, and wait for the motorbikes of the young men of the village and elsewhere to stop by.

Did men formerly get drunk? Today, it is not uncommon to see young people in the villages clustered on a *bale bengong*[129] with bottles of alcohol and listening to rock.

This surprised me during my first years in Bali. On New Year's Eve, for example, I didn't dare go out because after midnight the young men were all dead drunk! While the Balinese New Year's Eve, *Nyepi*, is marked by displays of symbolic excess, with the processions of *ogoh-ogoh*,[130] the Gregorian new year is marked by real excesses. It should be added that drunkenness is associated with a deterioration in group behavior.

What are you thinking of?

I am thinking here of the lynchings of soup vendors (*tukang bakso*) who were accused at one time of deliberately poisoning the food they sold. Or worse, of the lynching at the end of 1999 of four snake charmers in Denpasar on their way home from the last show of the millennium and whose legal consequences are unknown. In times of tension like twenty years ago, all it took was a sharp response to a question from local youth sitting high in a bamboo *bale bengong*. Easy then to denounce passing *pendatang* as thieves. The rumors didn't wait for hoaxes to produce racism and violence. Today, it is rarer, and it not so much Javanese who are the victims, but rather new arrivals from the eastern part of the Archipelago.

---

[129] *Bale bengong*: small raised-platform structure of wood or bamboo with a roof, for relaxing and meeting.
[130] *Ogoh-ogoh*: monsters of bamboo and papier mâché that are paraded on the eve of Nyepi, the day of silence.

Yes, especially since migrants from NTT[131] often work in the security professions, which must create jealousy, especially among the Laskar Bali ...

Yes, people from NTT are the latest migration wave. They face the Laskar Bali, most of whom work for different political parties. This accentuates the rivalries. That said, such drifts are becoming rarer. No doubt because we are in a period of economic expansion, but also because the public discourse, such as reflected in the press and on television, no longer condones this type of behavior.

Getting back to prostitution, it's always been around, hasn't it?

There was already some in the past, in Tuban, Lumintang, Blanjong. The army was behind the first settlements, such as Blanjong, Sanur, established by naval officers as early as the 1950s and '60s. Now there is the mega-complex of Padang Galak which is reputed to be Bali's biggest prostitution district.

What are the social impacts of this?

They have always been part of the landscape. They are assimilated, especially since many pimps are Balinese. They pick up the girls in East Java, where many women divorce very young. Married at fourteen, they divorce at fifteen. The parents did their duty: they married them off as virgins. In any case, once divorced, these women have to eat. Fortunately, there is the Balinese Eldorado just across the strait. Love made possible. In the West, we label all these phenomena. We isolate them, make them into problems. This makes it possible to act, medically in particular. Here, people deny the reality of brothels.

Or rather it is disguised with a false name. We call prostitution a *penyakit masyarakat,* a societal disease, and the brothel is a *lokalisasi,* a localization, an administrative term from the Suharto era during which these places were legal and even monitored from a health point of view ...

Yes, *penyakit masyarakat* is a euphemism that weakens its impact. Indonesians adore euphemism. It's like racism: it's not named, not intellectually structured, but it's there nonetheless. Today, denying this reality of brothels complicates health treatment.

Were these epiphenomena introduced by international tourism, or by national tourism?

Very good question because, Bali being a non-Muslim place, it is often considered by the people of Java and elsewhere as depraved. This is not exactly a coincidence, since after all there are many Westerners here practicing an elastic sexual morality. In the eyes of many, this makes it a place without morals, and therefore not without attractions. Besides, if Westerners came to Bali since the 1930s to see

---

[131] NTT: Nusa Tenggara Timur, province comprising the islands of eastern Indonesia.

bare-breasted Balinese women, Jakartans came as early as the 1980s to see bare-breasted Western women on the beaches. The fashion is somewhat past, however.

Is sex tourism here grafted onto a reality that already existed?

Yes, but it has undeniably given it a new dimension. Javanese prostitutes arrived in large numbers in the 1980s, "accompanying" construction workers hired in Java to build hotels during the boom. Bus and truck drivers on the Bali–Java route[132] were also regular clients of prostitutes. I remember a photographer friend who used to prepare packs of happy photos for them for their families back in Java, so they wouldn't worry. Photos or not, hello HIV/AIDS. Today, the official figure is over 6,000 sex workers, but the reality is undoubtedly much more.

The new dimension of local prostitution linked to tourism is above all the extraordinary flowering of independent prostitutes who work in bars and nightclubs for foreign customers. And these don't appear in the statistics.

All the more so since these occasional prostitutes, who often do not admit to being so, are also candidates for marriage with a "rich" foreigner in search of exoticism. They have been disappointed in love, perhaps illicit or violent. They are single, divorced, or unmarried mothers; in short, all the marginalized women who do not find what they are looking for in their home environment. Some work in hospitality professions, because they have a better level of English. This is a cliché, I admit, but it remains nonetheless a very real sociological phenomenon and rather recent, since the end of the 1990s.

It must be said that if the establishment of local laws since *Reformasi* allowed Bali to tackle the excesses linked to prostitution, the same phenomenon was exerted on drug trafficking. In the 1990s, besides the prostitutes who had invaded the sidewalks of Kuta, there were also dealers who offered their products in full view of everyone ... It's hard to imagine that today!

I know that, in the 1970s, when I first stayed here, smoking a joint was considered normal in Kuta. You could be drinking coffee at a café on the beach, and your companion at the table would be quietly rolling his joint. At the time, it was not considered a societal disease. I remember that Jean-François Bizot, who had just taken over *Actuel* magazine, asked me to write an article on the subject, particularly on the use of magic mushrooms. But this did not correspond to any reality in Balinese culture and I refused to do it. Thinking of that topic, at the heart of this market of artificial paradises were local youths, often more or less marginalized because of their ethnic origin Chinese, Punjabi.

Some of these pioneers were at the origin of the tourist boom in Kuta ...

Yes, they invested, they felt the wind coming their way in contact with these early

---

[132] Bali and Java are connected by a ferry service.

hippies and surfers. But until the 1980s, tourism was not yet a major phenomenon, as it has become.

Otherwise, magic mushrooms made the reputation of Kuta, with many points of sale. The ban is only very recent. But can we come back to pedophilia?

Pedophilia is an old story ...

I would like to note on this subject that the pedophilia cases that involve foreigners and which come out from time to time in the media are always a pretext for anti-foreigner diatribes.

Yes, it is a reality, there are some local figures, whom we will not name here, who stir up anti-foreign sentiment. Pedophilia is a golden pretext for them, because, that said, there is no smoke without fire: when it is not foreigners, it is in contact with foreigners that the phenomenon is revealed, as in a famous ashram of eastern Bali. Because foreigners bring their neuroses and sexual pathologies to Bali with them.

Interestingly, the word "pedophilia" has only recently entered the Indonesian vocabulary and remains steeped in the mystery of its Greek roots. It is used to stigmatize an evil which is said to be uniquely Western; and it will be avoided in a case involving only locals. There are people use the Indonesian word *cabulan*, which doesn't mean much.

It's even normal here.

Yes, the word *cabulan* is a vague term that designates inappropriate, dirty, shameful touching, in short, that which offends morals. It is a portmanteau that helps to hide the reality of the facts and which includes both a wandering hand and a rape!

We come back again to the power of words, which creates a new reality, this time pedophilia linked to tourists. Would there be, then, a traditional pedophilia? It's not named as such, but it does exist, of course. In fact, it went without saying for the princes to provide themselves with very young girls. There was no age barrier at the time. And what about boys who touch each other when they sleep together in the *bale bengong*, for example. What they do is not named, nor categorized as sexual, but to foreigners looking for sex, one can imagine the effect and the problems posed ...

Are the problems associated with modernity resulting in an increase in the number of suicides in Bali?

I couldn't say. Traditionally, suicide was mainly linked to matters of love. It was the notion of *jatuh karma* that came into play, the notion of having found your ideal partner in life. It is as if lovers were predestined, from a meeting they had in the "abode of dead souls," to meet such and such a person in this life here. And if the parents did not agree about the union for reasons of social status, it could end up in a suicide.

Are the new causes of suicide linked to current issues? Stress, poverty, debt?

It's difficult to say, because the Balinese are not used to expressing these problems in socio-economic terms. Look for example at the phenomenon of schoolgirls having sudden collective fits of hysteria; this is always explained by the presence of spirits. One of them would have behaved badly vis-à-vis the village *duwe*,[133] etc. When a girl goes into trance at school, no one questions whether she is having personal problems. People say she is possessed, they wonder what ritual fault was committed. When a young person drowns in a river, it's not because he has stumbled and fallen into the water, it's because he has been taken by a spirit of the river.

So, death does not take on the same heaviness as in Western culture .

Certainly not. Especially since whoever leaves will come back. It gives a certain lightness. Traditional Balinese say that reincarnation is not the *samsara*[134] of Hinduism, but simply a return to the paradise of Bali.

Let's move on to the phenomenon of gigolos, the famous Kuta cowboys, these local playboy surfers, very often non-Balinese, who are at the heart of a sex tourism specialty well known here, especially among female Japanese and Australian tourists. A Singaporean film director[135] turned it into a documentary that in the process sparked the anger of local authorities to the point that they tried to stop him by issuing a notice through Interpol ...

It must be said that the Balinese have an extraordinary quality: they have an unparalleled sense of service and are renowned for this in the tourism and hospitality industry around the world. There are thousands of them on Mediterranean or Caribbean cruises. They also excel at a more personal type of service. When some women, be they young or faded, see the muscles of a handsome boy with bronze skin, they cave in. It's love, pure or cynical. Unfortunately, the moment comes when the mother of the beautiful boy falls ill, or it's the upcoming cremation of his grandfather. The foreign woman has to pay. It's classic. But these boys are so kind that these women are amazed, and conquered. They are not used to such kindness. Many will return the following year to find their *Wayan*. Some will marry, some forever, others for the moment, alone or shared with his wife.

Officially, this phenomenon is fiercely denied, as if it was detrimental to the honor and dignity of the local male; it's astonishing!

---

[133] *Duwe*: the master spirit of a place.

[134] *Samsara*: the cycle of successive lives and their conditioning related to karma.

[135] *Cowboys in Paradise* by Amit Virmani (2009). Jean Couteau was one of the informants for the filming of this documentary.

I've personally known a number of these gigolos ... But here, in principle, people don't talk about these social phenomena; they know that they exist, and they tolerate them as long as they remain vague and nameless. By naming them, one adopts the posture of telling people what to do, so common among foreigners. In Indonesia, the emphasis is not on dysfunction, but on harmony. Even if this is ultimately a myth, it also generates its reality! Just as in France, cultural skepticism also generates its reality of grumbling and disorder.

Let's move now from sexuality to violence. Has the West brought its violence to Bali through tourism?

You'd have to know the statistics on the subject, and compare the current situation with that before the arrival of tourism. These numbers probably don't exist. As far as I know, this country is not a violent society, except when everything suddenly changes, resuming the pattern of classical theatre. While apparent crime is relatively low, perhaps less than in Europe, latent, structural violence, especially against women, seems obvious to me.

The nightlife has undoubtedly brought its share of violence?

Going out at night in Bali or even anywhere in Indonesia is a rather reassuring experience. That said, let us remember here that Kuta is not Bali in the eyes of the Balinese, it is an unclean place. Kuta is anyway unclean from a Muslim perspective, even though it is one of the few places on the island where you can eat perfectly halal and not find roast pork on display in public. This double network of impurity makes the possibility of crime and violence obvious. Ultimately, people think, it is the foreigner who is responsible for this imbalance. This is part of the latent, ill-structured, but real prejudices.

It is also surprising to see how little Bali was prepared for the arrival of foreign mafias, the Russian mafia, for example, but more particularly that of Australian biker gangs, which are very established here and launder considerable sums in the nightlife industry and real estate. These activities create crime with the settling of scores, murders ...

There is indeed a criminality of foreign origin, with its drug dealers, killers, and crooks. Unfortunately, I don't know much about this subject![136] Also note that recent legal changes regarding access to land, and leases in particular, until then closed to foreigners, have allowed the arrival of a rather unsavory sort of mafia, which has no reason to envy the local mafia. You can't name names here, but some are rich and famous local figures today.

I fear that Bali is not sufficiently prepared to defend itself against all these assaults.

There is now an office of Interpol in Bali.

---

[136] See airport literature for more information.

This wasn't the case in the 1990s, and Bali had become a haven for many gangsters on the run from all over the world; they could stay here tranquilly.

To return to the subject of dirty money laundering, it's Suharto's New Order that is behind many land investments in Bali. A veritable mafia was anchored here, based on power networks, and it was this official mafia that sowed the first seeds of what makes Bali attractive to foreign mafias today. I remember a time whenever I entered a hotel, there at the reception was a portrait of the owner, with his title or position a judge from Jakarta, for instance, or a colonel in the army effectively saying: "I am someone important, I have connections, move on," to possible *ormas* racketeers.[137]

So, Bali has always been a money-laundering machine. How do the Balinese react to this?

Today there are legal instruments: there is Interpol, as we said, and there is also the KPK,[138] but as for mafia networks, nobody talks about it.

Are cockfights legal?

Normally, this is prohibited beyond the three rounds required to perform certain ceremonies, because ritual events of any importance must be witnessed by the denizens of the three levels of the world: the gods (*dewa*); the forces of lower world (*buta*); and the humans (*manusa*). And at the beginning of each ceremony, there is a blood offering for the *buta*, usually the blood of a rooster. But for the biggest ceremonies, as in Besakih, it is the blood of a buffalo that will be spilled.

Yes, some cows are sacrificed by being thrown into the sea[139] or into the crater of a volcano. But a sacrifice is not a combat …

Yes, but it is the same religious offering of blood; whether you cut the rooster's throat or it bleeds in a fight, it's the same. Of course, people try to increase the number of cockfights because it's a gambling opportunity. And it continues today, even though there are fewer cockfights than in the past. Until the 1980s, I remember that there were cockfights almost every day in the neighborhood of Pemedilan in Denpasar. Around this time, Balinese began to sell their land and they had more money. There were many who bet the proceeds of their sale in cockfighting. Entire families were ruined. Made Mangku Pastika, when he was appointed chief of police for the island, was the first to try to stop this delusional practice, and to succeed to a certain extent.

---

[137] *Ormas*: mafia-style gangs qualified as societal organizations: *ormas*, acronym for *organisasi masyarakat*, "social organization".

[138] KPK: Komisi Pemberantasan Korupsi, the national anti-corruption agency.

[139] There have been occasional cases of bestiality, with the abused cow declared guilty of desire and therefore impure. So, she is sacrificed to the sea. Jean Couteau thinks that feminists should take up this issue.

Has cockfighting always been linked to betting?

Yes, always. You see it in the *geguritan*[140] stories, some of which date back several hundred years. But some people even bet on cricket fights.

Or when they play dominoes, it's for money, too …

Chinese-Indonesians are very active in cockfighting in Bali. Another reason that gambling at cockfights has persisted despite the bans is that the villages need money to fund their ceremonies. They collect a tax on these fights. It is more or less tolerated: the police close their eyes and accept a little envelope. Nevertheless, there is significantly less cockfighting today. That said, there are also cockfights that are completely illegal, that is, with no connection to any ceremony. These are organized by local *preman*,[141] often the strong arms of local politicians. Some bookies have even had political careers here. A lot of money flows in these bets. All the men of the village are present. There are *lontar* that explain how to choose a cock for combat.

I've heard of billions of rupiah being staked.

Yes, without a doubt particularly when Chinese-Indonesians participate. Note that there are never any women in the arenas where cockfighting takes place. Apart from those who sell food or drinks.

Today, in the 21st century, in an Indonesia where gambling is strictly prohibited, there is nevertheless a lot of online gambling, poker and the like, often in the hands of Chinese-Indonesians. Would cockfighting be gradually replaced by these online games?

It's difficult to say … especially since it is almost impossible to obtain information about these illegal practices. People have always gambled a lot in Bali. At any temple festival, you will find people gambling, if only with dice or dominoes!

---

[140] *Geguritan*: style of popular poetry recited in small groups.
[141] *Preman*: thugs, henchmen; from the English "free man".

PART TWO

ARTA

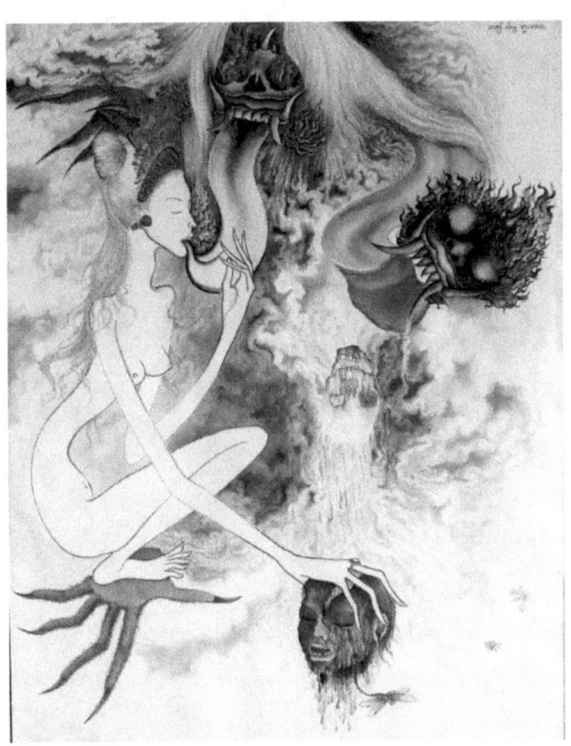

Somya of Mount Agung by Satya Cipta, 2019,
57x76cm, gold, Chinese ink, vermilion on arches.

5. Economic Development, Prosperity, Structural Upheaval, Caste

Economic development has brought about many physical changes affecting the appearance of Bali, including what Jean Couteau calls a "loss of control over beauty". Urbanization and the changes it imposes are also transforming the social fabric in urban areas with the arrival of more and more people from outside Bali. Originally, tourism was the driving force behind these transformations, but today many sectors of economic activity that are not directly related to it are thriving in turn. Until the eruption of the COVID-19 pandemic, the economy was roaring and carried everything in its path. In times of contraction, tensions can arise between communities, and lynchings have occurred against Javanese or, today, new arrivals from the eastern islands. Jean explains to us that a local proletariat has also emerged since a migrant proletariat entered into competition with the most disadvantaged Balinese. Originally, tourism was designed in high places for big power investors. This allowed the emergence in Bali of a rather well-accepted outsider bourgeoisie, the newly rich, whose descendants still prosper today. A class of nouveau riche Balinese has also emerged at the same time, usually linked to these big investors, often in a subordinate role. In the internal Balinese universe, these upheavals have allowed calls to rise for a revision of the caste system; and some of these reformers draw inspiration from the Hindu tradition they find in the *Vedas* to justify a desire for the readjustment or re-examination of the condition of women not always in the way you would expect! In contemporary democratic Bali, we try to identify the profile of candidates for the elections. A petty bourgeoisie has managed to appropriate many good economic ideas brought by the West since the 1970s. The role of education, which spread in the 1980s, is essential in this rapid development, which has also claimed many collateral victims. In short, while capitalism has produced wealth, it has also produced destruction, as Jean notes. And today, religion and identity are an obsession.

ERIC BUVELOT. What are the main upheavals to which Bali has been subjected?

JEAN COUTEAU. There has been a transition from an agrarian society to a service society, with related changes. Today, half of the Balinese population lives in towns. The first impact of this urbanization is on the landscape. When I arrived in Bali, social life was organized around the village; there were no buildings along the roads. Between Denpasar and Nusa Dua, it was the countryside. The same between Denpasar and Ubud, where apart from the villages of Celuk and Sukawati there was nothing, everything was green. Bali went from occupying space around traditional villages, structured from upstream to downstream around the three village temples[142] with the houses all oriented in the same direction, and built on the same model to an occupation of space along the roads and on the entire south coast of the island, in a sort of huge urban conglomerate of shapeless architecture.

How do you feel about it?

When one knew Bali in another era, it's a great disappointment. It's above all a loss of control over beauty, this densification of the habitat to the detriment of the rice fields of old, which were a humanized nature. Nowadays, it is almost impossible to find genuine traditional houses in Bali, as they can still be seen in tourist guides, with the family temple and the inner courtyard intact.

Why?

Because in the traditional houses of 50 years ago, the brothers and their families are now crowded in there all together. In the past, when land was still available, the father gave a piece of non-irrigated land to each of his sons, who build a new house compound which was the duplicate of their paternal compound, and followed the *kosala-kosali* pattern of classic Balinese habitat. Today, that's over.

What are the consequences of this compression of urban housing?

The first concerns religion. There is a distance from the origins. When people live in the city, they no longer address their ancestors directly, through their traditional family temple, the *sanggah / mrajan*; they now often have a multipurpose shrine in their home through which they remotely address (*nyawang*) the gods of their village. The densification also has aesthetic consequences, such as the construction of the *sanggah* on a rooftop. In short, there are changes not only in the realm of religion, but of space.

So, there are many aspects of change that we are not aware of today?

Yes, there is the demographic aspect, that of the occupation of space, and also that of work. In the 1970s, most occupations were linked to the agrarian world. Since then, the tertiary sector has developed, offering services oriented towards tourism, supported by a discourse on culture and identity, and an iconic that is, self-referencing and highly recognizable handicraft production to better drive the point home. Through all this, the self-image of the Balinese was automatically transformed.

What else?

With the new occupations, dress has changed: men have gone from sarong well ventilated and easily transformable into a loincloth tight around the waist to pants, and from bare feet to rubber sandals, then to shoes. In terms of socialization,

---

[142] Temple of the territory upstream (*pura desa*), of the ancestral navel (*pura puseh*) and of the dead (*pura dalem*).

it went from the village *warung*,[143] run by the beauty of the moment under her mother's eye, to the noodle and dumpling shop, run by the first Javanese migrants. Then to Kentucky Fried Chicken and other McDonald's-style restaurants (except in Ubud, of course). Meanwhile in Petitenget, Payangan, and the Bukit, hotels and villas were being built for the rich on vacation. As the Balinese opened up to democracy, they discovered social distance, and of course, social class.

Was the change so complete?

Of course, with a demographic aspect of which no one can measure the consequences: the rise in strength of minorities. Bali's population is around 15-20% Muslim today. This has a huge economic impact: the Javanese provide cheap labor, particularly in construction, which keeps costs relatively low. They also work in many small trades, constituting a real under-proletariat, very mobile, often without fixed habitat or, on the contrary, grouped in a *kampung Jawa*.

Not only in town but also in the countryside. Don't we see them as agricultural workers?

Absolutely, especially in the rice-growing areas of Badung and Gianyar. In their daily life, they remain external to Balinese life, although they settle in certain spaces that they Javanize, such as the *pasar malam*.[144] Other Javanese remain seasonal. They live in makeshift shelters near their construction sites, and return regularly to Java where their wife and children await them. These flows play a very important role in the Balinese economy.

What are the local effects?

Some could become harmful, because, alongside the growth of this non-Balinese urban proletariat, we are witnessing the urbanization of the poorest Balinese. It is indeed the poor Balinese who are urbanizing today. Those who moved to the city thirty or forty years ago were the rich – the Brahmins, the high caste people who could buy land when it was still affordable. Now the price of land is out of reach for all the new poor. So, there is an unprecedented cohabitation in towns between an imported proletariat and a Balinese proletariat.

All these young Balinese who live in often insalubrious *kos*?

Yes, and who find themselves in competition with the Javanese proletariat, which is generally better equipped in the labor market. You can imagine what can happen in the event of a slip.

Why the Javanese?

We often hear that the Balinese have no work ethic. That's wrong. Traditionally,

---

[143] *Warung*: small, very simple roadside café, shop, and eating place.
[144] *Pasar malam*: night markets.

men got up very early to go to the fields. Back home, around 9 o'clock, they were sculpting or painting. But they cannot compete with the Javanese. Because the newcomers are ready to accept any working conditions, at any cost while the Balinese are at home, with their pride, their village references and their land. Less proletarianized, Balinese labor is more expensive.

Are there no other competitors besides the Javanese?

Yes, there are *pendatang* from NTT, who come from the eastern Indonesian archipelago. First there were people from Flores, about fifteen years ago. Now the Sumbanese …

Bali offers them possibilities for a better life, as their islands are isolated in the far east. Bali is the first dynamic economic hub they find on their way into exile.

Especially since, paradoxically, life is often more expensive in distant islands, because of transportation costs. This is a handicap that President Jokowi is trying to erase by developing the infrastructure.

Let's come back to the competition between local and outsider proletariats. Has the number of poor exploded in Bali?

No. According to the *Bali Post*, the poor are only 7% of the population! That was before the COVID-19 pandemic stopped tourism, however. But it depends on where you draw the line of poverty. Even if money circulates mainly in cities, there are, thanks to religion, mechanisms for redistribution to the countryside. When a Balinese who has become a city dweller is far from his village, he can no longer participate in compulsory community work for ceremonies. So, he engages someone to replace him, a cousin for example, who will represent him during this collective work. And he pays him in one way or another. There are rebalancing mechanisms through the religious community.

Can you give another example of these mechanisms?

Take the example of a civil servant of some rank who at age fifty-five returns to the village for his retirement. There, by virtue of his acquired social position in the city, he becomes a local leader, for example *bendesa*,[145] *kelihan*,[146] or, at least, a man of influence. Concerned about the prestige of his village and his own, one day he will ask, during the monthly *paruman*[147] that the village "wake up" some deity that has been "asleep" for too long. There are "signs," he says. The villagers agree. This sets in motion the routine for producing ritual: consultation with the high priest; definition of the size of the *gebogan*[148] offerings, the type of costume for processions of young women, etc. There are costs, which are often

---

[145] *Bendesa*: village leader responsible for customary matters.
[146] *Kelihan*: (or *klian*) group manager; literally "elder," from *kelih*.
[147] *Paruman*: general village assembly.
148 *Gebogan*: a type of temple offering that women carry on their heads in procession.

considerable. But from an economic point of view, this serves as a local stimulus, especially as urbanized villagers whose ancestral temple remains in the village, will, of course, be involved. In the end, there is something for everyone except for the truly poor, who dare not have an opinion.

Religion is therefore an economic sector in Bali, it is difficult to deny this evidence.

Yes, I would estimate the expenses of a typical family at 20% of their income for offerings, ceremonies, and all that has to do with religion. These activities were formerly very little monetized, because the immediate environment furnished supplies, in *janur*,[149] in bamboo, fruits, and so forth. But they now constitute a true parallel microeconomics. However, this economy has little to do with the modern urban economy, which is no longer controlled by the Balinese.

What do you mean?

The much-vaunted notion of "cultural tourism" has indeed generated its opposite. Why? The 1970s were the heyday of the New Order of Suharto, let's not forget. The Balinese elites, scalded by the anti-communist massacres of 1965-1966 for which they were partly responsible, were wary of any social dynamism: Bali had to remain politically and therefore sociologically and culturally untouched, for their greater benefit. For that to happen, it was necessary to isolate the tourists. Also, an isolated tourist enclave corresponded more to the expectations of foreigners keen on virgin paradises. Tourism was therefore welcome, but without its decadence. In short, it was necessary to ensure that tourists were clustered away from the population, went by bus or private car to visit villages designated as tourist destinations, and had as little contact as possible with the Balinese. Hence the idea of parking them in hotels in Nusa Dua, which at the time was still far away from everything. Nice idea, advocated by the World Bank, except for this: who has benefited from financing for the development of tourism? Accomplices of the regime and very rich non-Balinese, while the local petty bourgeoisie had to be content with whatever they got. However, it was this Balinese petty bourgeoisie who was best able to preserve the Balinese cultural aspect of tourism.

Yes, but Nusa Dua was a failure in that it did not ultimately prevent tourism from developing everywhere, without the slightest control ...

Yes, because in terms of financial volume, this has consolidated the supremacy of capital of non-Balinese origin over local capital, from the outset minimizing the role of the Balinese in this economy linked to tourism. This naturally had an impact on the culture with the selective iconization of some aspects of Balinese-ness at the expense of others. Thus, the image of Bali escaped the control of the Balinese. The more enlightened elites who had advocated "cultural tourism" are now tearing their hair in frustration.

---

[149] *Janur*: palm-leaf used by housewives for making offerings.

What other phenomena has this engendered?

The emergence of a semi-resident non-Balinese bourgeoisie, I would say.

Yes, but a local bourgeoisie has also been formed thanks to tourism.

Except that the outsider is stronger. Jakartans who come here regularly are more powerful, especially in the south, which explains the reactive ethnocentric behavior of the Balinese. Social stratification is becoming ethnic at the island level. Members of the upper castes, even princes, are certainly less powerful than these new rich from outside. But, luckily, they are not in competition: they work together; they are each other's agents. The outsiders are active in national networks, the Balinese in local networks. And besides, the newcomers, Chinese-Indonesian and others, don't care about the whole symbolic apparatus on which the power of the Balinese elites rests. For them, no huge cremations, no Balinese mansions that are the equivalent of the old *puri*. It is different for the newly rich Balinese.

Does that create tensions?

I would say that it goes rather well, because the new and old elites complement each other. Among the Balinese, they often have ritual networks in common. They find themselves side by side in certain large ceremonies, where they vie with each other in courtesy. That said, high priests, princes, and Brahmins are always given a well-defined place, apart and higher up than the common people, except the most notable among them, who are treated as peers. As for foreigners and other Indonesians, except close friends, they are not supposed to be present. Inevitably, in this mishmash of the caste system and the class system, the second is gradually replacing the first, even if the substrate of the caste system endures, at least in terms of language and gesture, by co-opting the newly rich and powerful. The secret of this astonishing harmony undoubtedly lies in the interweaving of social, economic, and religious networks: everyone knows each other.

Can we say that as long as these newly rich people contribute their share to community and religious life, they de facto have their place?

Yes, but it's very complex. Thus, in certain temples, in particular the temples of the territory, the *pura penataran*, the shrine of the ancestors of the prince of the place rubs shoulders with those of the most powerful clans, located a little lower. Groups are therefore more than associated they are linked by ritual, while remaining hierarchical. Their members meet at temple festivals, major cremations, and weddings. Which doesn't mean there aren't tensions; they are just veiled.

What do you mean?

Nobody forcefully demands equality anymore, as they did when Indonesia was newly independent, but some Balinese nonetheless say, most often as an aside, or in the press, that the classic Balinese caste system does not conform to the system defined in the **Vedas**,[150] which are Indian. Indeed, according to these Balinese modernists, it is the professional position one actually occupies that defines one's a caste, called *varna*, and not, as in Bali, *wangsa*, the status inherited by descent. This is therefore an opportunity for some thinking heads of modern Balinese Hinduism to openly question the power and privileges of the traditional three upper castes, the *triwangsa*.[151] Supporters of the upper castes who feel threatened by these upheavals tend to quietly harden their position of caste. Some Brahmins turn in on themselves.[152] Members of other groups reread their family history to announce that they are descendants of kings, and therefore *satria*. The system is shaken. But it still keeps its coherence. I hope we will talk about it again.[153]

Does the nation of Indonesia have a say in these upheavals?

Of course. In general, nationalists are critical of the caste system. We find this positioning since the beginning of the 20th century.[154] At the time, it was mainly a consequence of the introduction of Western values, demands for equality and democracy. Since then, sociological changes resulting from economic change have taken over: there are people from lower castes – and women who, through education, come to occupy important positions who are upsetting certain traditional behaviors. The egalitarian pressure of the West also continues to be felt, in a new form: it is now the pressure of feminism and human rights conveyed by NGOs, the press, and some international organizations. It is no longer the notion of progress as such that is promoted, as in the days of Sukarno, who was a strong critic of feudalism.

Does it work?

Yes, because there is now a kind of reversal. It is in tradition the reread, revised, and corrected tradition that people now seek equality of status, even feminism. It is no longer in revolution.

How? By reinterpreting ancient texts?

Yes, according to the same procedures which make it possible to deny the superiority of the high castes, people reread the **Vedas** to reform the status of women. They draw on Hindu concepts of polarity between man and woman *lingga / yoni,* or *pradana / purusa* in Balinese to affirm the equality of the sexes.

---

[150] *Vedas*: sacred Hindu scripture from early India.
[151] *Triwangsa*: see *Kasta dalam Hindu: Kesalafahaman Berabad–abad (Caste in Hinduism: Centuries of Misunderstanding*) by Ketut Wiana and Raka Santri (1993).
[152] For example, IBM Dharma Palguna, in *Shastra Wangsa,* Sadampaty Aksara (2018) has recently published a corpus of traditional texts that shows that *triwangsa* privileges have long been disputed, well before colonization.
[153] See Chapter 10.
[154] On caste, see *Kebalian – La construction dialogique de l'identité balinaise, Association Archipel* (2017) by Michel Picard, pp. 40-41.

This allows them to reject the Western concept of feminism while affirming that equality between men and women exists in the **Vedas**, and that women are therefore equal to men. In other words, progress was already there in religion if you interpret it correctly; the West didn't invent anything.

What can we say about women?

Their situation is complex. Because, while they do have a greater role in the modern economy, and therefore there has been real progress, there has also been, in certain areas, a deterioration of their economic condition. For example, in the past, among villagers who had little land, women grouped together in associations of harvesters (*seka manyi*), through which they obtained a percentage of the harvested crop. This disappeared after the introduction of the scythe and the arrival of Javanese farm workers forty years ago.[155] These women therefore found themselves marginalized, even if their associations have endured.

Is that why we see them today in the grueling construction and earthworks labor?

Yes, it's a workforce that is still sometimes hired through the remainder of these associations. There was therefore a kind of proletarianization of the already poor women of the villages that accelerates their urbanization. But do they have a choice? If they stay in the village, they can survive only by *munuh*, gleaning. Women's autonomy sometimes comes at a high price.

There is one image that greatly shocks Westerners here, and that is to see a truck driver smoking his cigarette in the shade while women are loading or unloading the truck in the hot sun.

These are the women I just mentioned. Remember that in the days of agricultural Bali, men would get up at 4 a.m. to go to the fields until 9 or 10 a.m. They were also responsible for watching over the village and the temples at night. But I understand that this proletarianization of women shocks today.

Have we witnessed in the last 50 years an impoverishment of the great princely families?

Yes, it's undeniable. To maintain their prestige and pay for cremations and other rites, they often have to sell their land. They try to cling to power through politics and bureaucracy, where the old networks still operate. On the other hand, some Brahmins have become rich. A lot of *Dayu*[156] have become excellent businesswomen, especially in the business of offerings.

What about the petty bourgeoisie? We know that the prosperity of a

---

[155] The change in the status of land with access to full ownership, following the agrarian reform of 1960, gave peasants a freedom in the use of land that they did not have under previous tenure regimes.

[156] *Dayu*: female *brahmana*, from the title "Ida Ayu" (she is beautiful).

community can be measured by the size of its middle class. But here in Bali, as we have seen in recent years, especially with the housing boom and road traffic, there has been an extraordinary enrichment of people often from modest backgrounds.

Yes, there is no question, although many of them are in fact employees of non-Balinese companies and investors.

The standard of living has nevertheless improved considerably!

Yes, that made the caste system obsolete in the urban south of the island. In the old days, status was given forever. A person died as he was born, prince or beggar. There was little escape. The arrival of Westerners, and money, has changed the situation; it has allowed social ascent. Among the new fortunes established in Bali over the past 50 years, we find those who first benefitted from passing Westerners, sometimes in rather borderline conditions. Also, those who created all kinds of businesses with the hippies and other early adventurers. Traffickers and gigolos of all stripes; sellers of wooden penises from Sebatu; collectors of the hair of beautiful Balinese women for the wigs of old Parisians; polyglot former seminarians; not to mention the really honest intermediaries ... All these people literally launched development and generated a new local elite, of economic origin, not an inherited position in society.

Isn't the role of education even more essential to this recent boom?

Yes, but in a second stage, especially from the 1980s, when skills development became necessary. In the 1960s, probably more than 70% of the population was still illiterate or almost. Now everyone has or is aiming for a high school diploma or higher. But there are ideological constraints in education. The fall of Sukarno in 1965 and the rise to power of the military certainly boosted the economy. But ideologically, in education as well as in culture, anything controversial was erased. I am thinking of Marxism, of course, and the related idea of social justice as a concrete practice.

Yes! Here there is traditionally no culture of contradiction, and the military regime has not helped matters.

At the university, only the partisans of functionalism or their imitators remained post-1965. It's no coincidence that Udayana University has created a department of cultural studies. In these so-called "cultural" studies, economic determinants, i.e., the approach to raw social reality, have long been deliberately downplayed as if everything happened at the level of discourse, of culture. We can see the result at the national political level, where one speaks neither of conflict of interests, nor of the establishment of collective negotiations. No one talks about morality, Good versus Evil. And one brings out postmodernism whenever it is useful to criticize the universalism of the West. The critical analytical approach that was common in the days of Independence was badly damaged by the military regime. The cost might be high in the future, because it is religion that is the carrier of political discontent.

The difference, the opposition of points of view, disappeared with the massacres of the communists and all that represented the left in the 1960s. Today there is a single political discourse. You have to be a patriot, religious, and participate in the development of the nation.

Yes! But I think the root causes are more than just political. In Bali, as in Indonesia in general, it is virtually impossible to criticize power: the *Cokorda*, the *Professor Doktor*, the elderly sage, the Westerner, the *kyai*[157] or cleric, in short, all those who hold any power. Why? Because it's rude to contradict! It's not the content of speech that matters, it's the speaker's status. How to get out of this conundrum? How to create intellectual instruments, concepts, which can give a grip on reality?

Obviously; but let's refocus on Bali and its economic development.

Yes, let's talk a bit about economic diversification. All kinds of services have arisen from tourism. For example, in Klungkung or Baturiti, there used to be rice fields in the hills. Many have disappeared to be converted into market gardens growing produce for the hotel industry when it's not fields of flowers to decorate villas and hotels. There are even vineyards now! Think also of the development of crafts to meet the massive demand from Western buyers, such as in Tegallalang, or of the digital nomads of which Canggu seems to have become the new Eldorado. Not to mention the rice fields destroyed to build villas. Thus, land use has been massively modified to adapt to the needs of tourism.

In recent years, people have also felt the urge to put Bali on the map of medical tourism, at least since the term of Made Mangku Pastika, the previous governor of Bali.

Bali is still a long way off in terms of capacity and skills, especially as national law prohibits foreign doctors from practicing in Indonesia. But the idea persists. And it might be a good one.

Does the new personal autonomy acquired with modernity benefit everyone?

We see it for women.[158] And young people. But this personal autonomy is not so broad, nor so easy to carry! Because it is full of contradictions. Besides being limited, it is constantly ideologically denied or criticized because of its origins: the intrusive West is behind it, described as capitalist and colonial, individualistic and permissive. And indeed it shakes up society. All in all, the Balinese usually have only a constrained autonomy, more effective in business than in thought and behavior. They escape the village to embrace the market and the orientation of being "Hindu" or Balinese. Not to become themselves.

---

[157] *Kyai*: Muslim sage.
[158] Women are very prominent in the professions of health and education. Thus, Prof. A.A. Raka Sudewi was rector of Bali's main university, Udayana, from 2017 to 2021.

What does this imply?

People become pragmatic; they want to succeed. And to achieve success, they crash whatever circles of power there may be. The old obsession with status is still there. Hence the fashion for ostentatious signs, such as adding a string of diplomas to your name that's as long as your arm "Prof.," "Dr.," "drs.," "MM," as many as you can. And mad consumption. I think of all those poor people who put themselves into debt for months or years just to show off with the latest iPhone.

This is an outward sign of wealth; it allows you to show off.

The smartphone even indirectly modifies sexuality!

What do you mean?!

Well, yes, the smartphone makes erotic images easily accessible and above all increases the possibilities of meetings, thanks to messaging. This frees young people from the grip of the village, which is loosening. There are also ideological effects, not yet really measured, and ongoing political consequences. In short, it's not easy to understand and manage all these changes. A task for sociologists.

Indeed. How has this new personal autonomy affected the relationship with the land?

Apart from the fact that land has become a generalized market good, little is known. No serious study has yet been done on the subject: its actual use, the nature of the contracts that determine its use, the origin of those who control it: nothing is known. In short, the sociologists at Udayana University, who are so interested in Foucault [159] and Baudrillard, [160] should also pay attention to the situation of land rights and use.

And in terms of religion, what does personal autonomy involve?

As with consumption, there's the possibility of making choices. There is now a proliferation of sects in Bali, like Sai Baba which comes from India and has its own hospital here. Some Balinese abandon the cult of ancestors for new cults. What matters is prayer, *bhakti*, addressed to the divine and directed upwards. People are becoming less concerned with the ancestors, who are closer, who come down to visit and are welcomed with dances and offerings. Some modernist priests recommend these evolutions. Religion is thus becoming abstract, based less and less on belief in the direct perception of the forces of the *niskala* [161] and the related rites, which are often criticized, and more and more on the cosmic speculations of Indian Hinduism or on an indefinite expectation of the divine.

---

[159] Michel Foucault (1926-1984), French philosopher known for his critiques of social institutions and for his work on the history of sexuality.
[160] Jean Baudrillard (1929-2007), French philosopher and theoretician of contemporary society.
[161] *Niskala*: the invisible world.

Aren't these sects the modern adaptation of an ancient phenomenon, which flourishes on an expectation of the divine and is already well anchored in the culture of Indonesia in general?

Yes, but it's different today, especially in the structuring. They are modern sects. The aim of these sects is to make people independent of their origin, cut off from their ritual roots in the village. Traditionally, this relationship with the magical, the divine, did not affect the cohesion of local communities. Now many Balinese are building an identity that is more pan-Balinese and pan-Hindu than local.

Isn't there a certain snobbery in this new esotericism?

Yes, indeed.

The big consumerism boom happened in Bali in the 2000s. Today, there is an unparalleled choice of consumer goods, greater than all Indonesia except Jakarta, especially when it comes to the number of shopping malls. What does this tell you?

Regarding investments, these giant shopping centers are often built by outsiders, and a few years ago I would have said the same about the customers who frequent them. But two new malls have just opened in Denpasar. It has an impact. Keep in mind that among Balinese, if a son asks his father to buy him a motorbike, he can't refuse: parents have a debt towards their male descendants, because it is the sons who will take care of their cremation. This stimulates consumption.

These days, it's no longer a motorbike they ask for, it's a car!

You'd have to look at the figures, but I think today there must be one car for every eight or ten inhabitants.[162] And Bali's urban space, for the most part an interlacing of small alleys, is not at all suitable for cars.

On the island, what impact has this shuffling of the cards for 50 years had on politics?

One of the problems in the history of Indonesia, and also that of Bali, is that after the eradication of communism in 1965-66, all discourse on the redistribution of wealth has completely disappeared. But inequality and poverty persist nonetheless. Now the main discourse is about ethno-religious identity, affirmed or refused, and this occurs throughout the Archipelago. It is the only political speech one hears nowadays: some fear national disintegration, others wish to Islamize the country as if Indonesia as a nation were still an ongoing project.

Shouldn't we link this to the fact that after thirty-two years of Suharto's

---

[162] There are 3.2 million vehicles registered in Bali (20% cars and 80% motorbikes) for a population of 4,225,000 people. This figure does not include vehicles circulating in Bali that were registered elsewhere (source *Radar Bali*, 2018).

reign, when political speech finally freed itself on the occasion of *Reformasi* and the implementation of democracy, the place was immediately taken by those concerned with identity and religion, who had been muzzled before?

Yes, the first discourse to assert itself was that of identity.

Local identities, radical Islam, these voices immediately took to the political arena.

In Bali, too, and it continues to this day. It should be added that in politics, only members of the educated bourgeoisie make a truly individual choice when they vote. For the most part, the choices are collective. Decision-makers from kinship groups, *banjar* and other communities approach candidates saying, if we vote for you, what do we get in return, how much money to restore our temple? There follows a game of pressure and consensus that few Balinese can resist.

Good, but let's talk about the profile of these candidates today. Who are they? New rich, or members of the upper castes?

Representatives of the upper castes have diminished since the establishment of elections at all levels of constituencies. In the time of the *Orde Baru*, the Brahmins were over-represented, but they were nominated, not elected. They made sure to get the top jobs in local government. But it's over. Wayan Koster, the current governor of the island, and his predecessor Made Mangku Pastika, are of low caste.

What can we say about politicians and *ormas,* these mafia gangs in Bali?

These links already existed at the time of Suharto, but they have taken on an important dimension since *Reformasi* and especially since the Islamist attacks. Their success corresponds to the return of local identity in political discourse. This is what they symbolize. Some are ethnocentric, others are nationalists. Today, they have penetrated local politics to such an extent that it's almost impossible to eradicate them. Not even the Chief of Police in Bali can do much against them.

Are the developments we've been talking about affecting the image of Bali?

Bali is a completely capitalist universe today. It is a fundamental evolution, which will undoubtedly have profound political consequences in the long term, but ideologically, everyone acts as if nothing has changed. People constantly reaffirm, in all speeches, all discussions, the eternal immutability of the foundations of Balinese culture, its agrarian origin, the principles of *Tri Hita Karana*[163] underlying it, etc. There is a refusal to accept the realities.

---

[163] *Tri Hita Karana*: Balinese concept that defines the "three causes of well-being" harmony among humans, with the natural environment, and with God.

It's cultural in Indonesia to deny reality, especially when the reality is inconvenient. And it's Western to name what is wrong, then people deny it. It's a principle of blindness.

It's a performative mentality here, modeled by mantras, as if what is announced actually corresponds to reality. In Indonesia, there is a real difficulty in objectifying, in taking distance from the construction, a social object, a psychological object.

We often hear that the Balinese are tight-fisted. What does that mean?

In Bali there is always a demand for exchange; everything is calculated extremely closely, especially in a village environment. When a Balinese participates in a village or clan ceremony, he is obliged to provide his share of all kinds of things, which will be strictly counted.

At the same time, international surveys regularly place Indonesians among the most generous people in the world. This is a funny paradox!

The Balinese who gives has an expectation. Mauss has written on the subject, on the notion of the gift. I always refuse Balinese gifts, except those from close friends. At the same time, for this reason one is always very well received, there is a real sense of exchange.

Has this new wealth changed mentalities in relation to money?

But everything has changed in Bali! The problem is why? It's useless to say, as too many Balinese do, that nothing has changed. One soon arrives at the notion of "essence," of the "folk soul," a worn-out idea that some Western countries, like Germany, have experienced with terrible consequences.

The Balinese soul seems to me very strong and ready to face the challenges of tomorrow. Perhaps even stronger than those of other peoples of the world, and in any case stronger than those of other peoples of Indonesia. The Balinese are very involved in the discourse on themselves, which is their strength, in my opinion.

You have a more positive outlook on this subject than I do! You are right in the sense that there is not, or not yet, a real rupture in society. Even if the ideology produced in Bali is a little illusory, it works, it has the merit of maintaining certain fundamental balances. Villages are weakening, ties to village and religion are loosening, economic differences are creating tensions, but it still holds! There are resistance mechanisms! Me, I have a kind of fundamental pessimism that I base on history in general: capitalism produces wealth but also destruction. This is perhaps what remains French in me, a cultural affirmation of contradictions, while Indonesians emphasize harmony.

In today's disoriented world, plagued by capitalism, wouldn't Bali be the bearer of values that could benefit everyone?

There is the fact of the ethnic "other," of the religious "other," whose otherness has never been accentuated in the tradition. But, at the same time, we see this otherness developing everywhere, in all social mechanisms particularly with the rise of an increasingly exclusive confessional discourse, and not only among Muslims, among the Balinese as well. Will the Balinese avoid the trap of literal interpretation of the sacred texts? This will be the ultimate test! Indonesia is the bearer of a local humanism, but will it be able to digest the rhetoric of otherness emphasized in a considerable part of contemporary education systems? It's possible; it all depends on how it is handled. Many Balinese are aware of these issues. Which is why they would like greater provincial autonomy by obtaining the status of *daerah istimewa*.[164] It would protect Bali from interference from the central power in the event of a too strong Islamization of Indonesia.

Indonesia is doing better than many other multicultural countries. I remember that Jacques Attali predicted the disintegration of the Archipelago after the fall of Suharto, on the model of Yugoslavia. This still has not happened more than twenty years later.

That's the problem with these futurologist experts: they draw conclusions from what's going on in the West. Here, there is really a resilience in Bali, in Indonesia. It must be encouraged. The big question is, will capitalism be more brutal here than elsewhere? So far, it holds. Why? Because the Balinese village is resisting. Even if land, work, and culture have become commodities, even if young people go to the city, the village remains, thanks to its temples, the central place of Balinese identity.

To conclude this discussion, are there any very rich Balinese? We know that local fortunes have been made quickly, say, for twenty, twenty-five years.

There are, of course, in the hotel industry, in Sanur and Kuta. Some indisputable Balinese fortunes: Gusti Ngurah Anom, Wayan Kari, the Wiranatha brothers but they are small compared to the fortunes of non-Balinese. Some of today's nouveau riche started their fortunes as intermediaries with Jakartans or Chinese-Indonesians. Typical result of the corruption of the *Orde Baru* of Suharto. The money was placed in Bali, in land and hotels.

---

[164] *Daerah istimewa*: "special region," a status sought by Wayan Koster, the governor of Bali at this writing (2020).

6. Increase in Wealth, Investments, Speculation, Luxury

Is Bali a place of global luxury? Jean Couteau and I ask ourselves the question, trying to trace what has made the island a glamorous place since the elitist tourism of the 1930s. After all, Western artists who developed a passion for the island during this time were often sponsored by Balinese royal courts. As for the tourists who marveled at the beauty of the island and its inhabitants, they mostly belonged to an Anglo-Saxon elite who arrived in the wake of Charlie Chaplin. Jean reminds us that in Bali, the appearance of sexual freedom played a part in this image of luxury. And yet, reality is more complex; and now not much is left of this vaunted luxury, as mass tourism seems to have supplanted elite tourism. After all, apart from the Nusa Dua resort, designed in the 1970s, there has been no genuine tourism development planning since then. Are there really all sorts of tourism in Bali now? We no longer know, really, although many Balinese like to believe that their culture is the only reason why tourists visit their island. Jean affirms that the rich and famous continue to come. But they are invisible. Yes, there certainly remains a chic niche and, between Fashion Week and wine production, Bali still tries to maintain its image as a mythical island, even in the face of mass tourism from emerging countries.

ERIC BUVELOT. Does it make sense to speak historically of luxury in Bali? Wasn't that for kings or princes? In a tightly collective society like Bali's, there wouldn't be much hedonism.[165]

JEAN COUTEAU. Clifford Geertz[166] has written a lot on this subject. Expressing one's Balinese-ness was doing a potlatch[167] on a royal scale! Kings did not so much fight militarily as they confronted one another with the grandeur of their courts and the magnificence of their ceremonies. Competition took the form of contests, rituals, and phantasmagorical architectural works, and it still goes on in a way. The *Cokorda* of Ubud admitted to me recently that with all the money flowing about, temple festivals are more lavish now than they ever were in his father's day.

What was the influence of the Dutch?

---

[165] Or rather, hedonism is strongly criticized, but in a philosophical context, as in the story of the ravenous Cupak or the older story of Gagak Aking and Bubuksah.

[166] Clifford Geertz (1926-2006), celebrated American anthropologist of Weberian tradition and known, among other things, for his work on Java and Bali. He wrote, among others, *Negara: The Theatre State in Nineteenth Century Bali*, Princeton University Press (1980).

[167] Potlatch: a more or less formal ceremony, based on the gift, in certain ethnic groups of America, the Pacific, and India.

They initially turned ceremonial prestige to their advantage. They also destroyed court life, gradually emptying *puri* of their vital forces, the young princes, and thus leaving dances and theatre in the custody of the villages. On the other hand, their maritime routes allowed foreign tourists to discover Bali. After the *puputan*,[168] the Dutch created a road network, making the island a unified economic area. It should be noted that before their arrival, the Balinese kingdoms were separated by steep river gorges, natural borders difficult to cross usually over bamboo bridges. It was with the construction of these roads that the first tourists were able to actually visit Bali. They arrived by sea via Singaraja, then the capital and port of entry, and finally alighted in Denpasar, at the Bali Hotel.

These first wealthy tourists date back to the 1930s?

A little earlier, if we include Dutch officials as tourists. They are the ones who discovered the sites that became tourist destinations. They are also the first to have thought that tourism should preserve the authenticity of Bali.

So, it was in the 1930s that the image of Bali as a luxury destination was born?

Yes, the first visitors were mostly rich people, and probably a few adventurers, generally people from very wealthy backgrounds or pretending to be, a little decadent, and cosmopolitan. They were people who liked to be among their peers. For Balinese aristocrats, receiving prestigious foreigners raised their status in the eyes of the populace. Walter Spies, Rudolf Bonnet were sponsored by princes. Their Balinese mentors valued the reputation of their guests as distinguished people in the foreign community. They vied with one another over them: how proud a prince was to have an important foreigner in what was left of his court! Especially if one of them, in this case Walter Spies, could also play a Balinese tune in the palace courtyard on a piano prepared for the occasion.

In the 1930s, Bali represented the dream of a heavenly elsewhere, a fairly common cliché, repeated in American films of the time. Have American tourists played a truly important role in shaping the image of Bali as a luxury destination?

I would say certain Americans… It should be added that certain Western elites of the time rejected what was happening in the West: the rise of nationalism, of fascism, of Nazism, of communism, which foreshadowed the catastrophe to come. Indeed, cosmopolitans before the First World War were returning to the forefront of the artistic and cultural scene for example, the modernists of the Bauhaus under the Weimar Republic in Germany, or the painters of the School of Paris in France.

---

[168] *Puputan*: fight to the death of the kings of Denpasar in 1906, and of the king of Klungkung in 1908, in the face of superior Dutch troops; culturally sanctioned suicidal fight to the death.

Yes, it is interesting to note that Walter Spies, before coming to Bali, had been the lover of Friedrich Wilhelm Murnau, one of the most iconic filmmakers of German Expressionism.

Yes, capitalism was wreaking havoc through the ultra-nationalism of the 1920s and '30s. To escape it, some ended up in Bali. And there was also the Victorian aspect of this period, with its repressed sexuality. In the United States, the Hays code ensured the strict morality of the films that came out of Hollywood.

And here in Bali, the women were walking half-naked in the road!

Yes, in Western eyes anyway. Balinese people gave the appearance of unbridled sexual freedom, while in the West it was the era of Freudianism and surrealism: sexuality was slowly rising to the surface.

This epoch would produce the glamorous image of Bali through numerous photographs and documentaries which showed a civilization both sophisticated and savage, the perfect symbol of sexual exoticism.

Yes, that was when the myth of Bali was born.

Then it will go away for decades, with the struggle for independence, the troubled and chaotic years of the Sukarno period, the purges of the sixties. Bali will go off the radar of the West and fall back into oblivion.

Yes and no, the Dutch actually returned to Bali after the Japanese surrender in early 1946 to look for "terrorists" hidden in the mountains.[169] *National Geographic* devoted an article to Bali from that time. No, I would say foreigners tried to recreate Bali, but it wasn't really about the glamor of the Thirties. Rather, it was a return to the "natural order of things". Although after the recognition of Independence by Holland (late 1949), it was Sukarno who embodied for a time the notion of luxury and glamor in Bali ...

Yes, he came with great pomp to Bali with his ministers.

He had the Tampaksiring palace built there, as his second home, and arrived by helicopter! Bali was his garden. Nationalist as he was, he espoused all the Western clichés about Bali! For him, women with perfect breasts were part of Bali's importance. He bought paintings in which all the Balinese women were bare-breasted even though the country's republicans were against it; indeed, they obtained a decree that compelled women to cover themselves. Contradiction!

He had that quality of an international jet-setter that showed itself with stars like Elvis Presley or Marilyn Monroe ...

Yes, he played the international star!

---

[169] This was the resistance movement led by Ngurah Rai, defeated in a *puputan* on 20 November 1946.

Whereas later, during the *Orde Baru*, it was Suharto's son Tommy who played the star with his playboy looks, his investments in Bali, his escapades in the casinos and then, ultimately, his takeover of Lamborghini in the 1990s.

Yes, let's say the *Orde Baru* tried to awaken the glamor side of Bali. About tourism and investment, I have my own theory. The elites of the 1970s, led by Ida Bagus Mantra[170] and survivors of the traumas of the 1960s, wanted to develop Bali while keeping it unchanged, "so that Bali remains Bali". It was of course also a way of keeping their traditional power intact while claiming the opposite. This demand for authenticity also corresponded to the myth of Bali as paradise inherited from the 1930s, maintained by foreigners, especially by the French, who still want Bali to remain Bali today.

Yes, it's this famous demand for authenticity that French tourists still insist on today. "Authentic" is a sacred word! As if the other peoples of this earth did not also have the right to development, to modernity! I have always found it very annoying.

Yes, always this demand for authenticity! At the same time, in those days there were already Balinese apprentice capitalists, middle-class people who were setting up businesses for tourists, opening homestays and *losmen*.[171] I'm thinking here of Nyoman S. Pendit,[172] who, unlike Ida Bagus Mantra, wanted to develop a community-based tourism, especially in Kuta. But the *Orde Baru* listened only to Ida Bagus Mantra and the French experts from SCETO.[173] However, to build a luxury tourist enclave such as Nusa Dua, a lot of capital was needed. So, who were given financing facilities?

Those close to Suharto, the ruler of the day!

Voilà! That is, in the name of preserving Balinese identity and space, they did the exact opposite. These are the indirect effects of a certain tourism policy. Bali would be much better today if financial facilities had been granted instead to the Balinese, in favor of boutique hotels rather than big hotels.[174]

---

[170] Ida Bagus Mantra (1928-1995) was governor of Bali from 1978 to 1988. A Santinikatan-educated intellectual, he was also one of the main supporters of the tourism policy of the post-1965 military regime, albeit in an idealistic way.

[171] *Losmen*: modest guest house.

[172] Nyoman S. Pendit (1927-2014) was, like Ida Bagus Mantra, a Santinikatan-educated intellectual. A prolific author of book on Balinese history and tourism, he once wrote (translation): When it becomes too much to bear, even ants will resist being trampled, as the outbreaks of the *puputan* battles (lit. fight to the finish...demonstrate. In *Membangun Bali*, Pustaka *Bali Post*, 2001: 42.

[173] SCETO : Société Centrale pour l'Équipement Touristique Outre-Mer. This company carried out a study on the Nusa Dua project financed by the United Nations Development Program under the direction of the World Bank.

[174] Boutique hotel: This was the solution advocated a little later by Ida Bagus Adnyana Manuaba, who had campaigned for this in the *Bali Post*. He indirectly ran for the governorship of 1988, but was Ida Bagus Oka who was appointed, who opened the doors freely to capital from Jakarta.

Weren't you a lecturer at Club Med Nusa Dua in the 1980s?

Three times a week, I gave lectures on Balinese society. They gave me a room for the night. It was a trendy place, the best Club Med in the world. One met ministers there, international personalities; that's where I met Régis Debray,[175] for example! The Sultan of Brunei, then considered the richest man in the world, had invested in the Nusa Dua Beach Hotel in the grounds of Nusa Dua. I don't know if he is still the owner. But Bali still had an image of luxury in the 1980s. So, it's no coincidence that the Suharto family literally took it over.[176] You had to see the effects of speculation on Nusa Dua! The Balinese who had sold their land were not always sure what to do with their money, as the banks were unreliable and sometimes shut down brutally, ruining their customers. Nusa Dua had turned into a land of plenty for the people who had land there, when they weren't swindled, which often happened to the original owners.

There must have been some local fortunes made at this time?

Yes, with the first guides, the first beach boys, sometimes doubtful types, some very good guys, too…

So, finally, has it always been relevant to associate Bali with luxury since the 1930s?

Yes, I think it's always been so.

Today, it is not quite clear what Bali's image is. In the 2000s, there was a lot of talk in Balinese newspapers about where tourism should go, with luxury tourism or mass tourism as the alternatives. I would say they took both turns at the same time, one to the detriment of the other, of course.

I think luxury is very localized today. It is found only in certain hotels and certain villas. And one never sees the very rich people who come to these places.

A question now arises: how can one sell an image of luxury if this luxury is invisible, precisely because of the mass tourism which makes everything ugly? You could say that apart from Nusa Dua, which remains the only truly planned tourism project, there has never been a coherent tourism development plan in Bali, which has led to the chaos one sees today.

Yes, there was never any control of land use, of land speculation, of the movement of populations. The only urban project to date that required the development of a cadastre is the administrative and residential district of Renon, in Denpasar. Another quality of this project was to respect the spirit of Balinese architecture

---

[175] Régis Debray is a French writer, philosopher and senior official, who was engaged alongside Che Guevara in the 1960s.

[176] See *Bali, Jakarta's Colony: Social and Ecological Impact of Jakarta-based Conglomerates in Bali's Tourism Industry* by George Aditjondro, Murdoch University (1995).

while modernizing it. It was a Balinese attempt at control.

How did Bali go from the distribution of land by sponsorship of the powerful to a market system completely based on supply and demand?

This happened simply because of the shift from customary rights to property rights, recognized at the national level a process that is still underway in the Indonesian archipelago. The roots of this transformation can be found in the *Agrarian Law of 1960*, which aimed to avoid the creation of large land holdings in the style of South American haciendas, but this had the indirect effect of favoring the privatization of land throughout the territory.

And its commodification!

And no one really knows what happened to the land, because, as mentioned before, there has never been a precise investigation into its evolution. No one has any idea what's going on there! But this is what allowed all the investment in Bali, and this is how the great Balinese fortunes have been built up today, by becoming intermediaries for Jakarta's investors, especially in the 1980s and '90s. All the local smart guys moved to the coasts. It started with the local Chinese, formerly residents of Singaraja or the mountainous plantation areas. They were the first to settle in Kuta, along with a few Indians. This is normal, because they were already established in older tourist circuits. The Chinese of Jakarta followed, and this is not counting the judges, colonels, officials of the tax service and others recycling in Bali the dirty money of the *Orde Baru*.

Has this phenomenon of land speculation grown to the point where it is totally out of control today?

There are no more forced sales of land like in the heyday of the *Orde Baru*. I also think that the land market in Bali is on the decline. It should be noted, however, that it is still more expensive to buy land in Bali than in many European countries.

Since the 2000s, there has been a boom in real estate agencies. Before, this was almost unknown here ...

It was simply forbidden. Since then, the legislation has changed and authorizes their establishment, including large international agencies.

The first Ray White agency was opened in 2004, but the very first agencies were created at the end of the 1990s.

I know that Indonesian law in this area has been relaxed, allowing a kind of renewable lease for foreign residents, to whom formal full ownership is nevertheless still prohibited.

This phenomenon has not been favorable to the image of luxury in Bali, paving the way for an increasingly intense fragmentation of land to build minimalist villas with swimming pools the size of a bathtub and boxed in by gray walls with no view.

Yes, luxury in Bali is not what it used to be, especially since it does not come with any interest in Balinese culture. In the past, people used to come to Bali for Bali. There were real exchanges between foreigners and Balinese. It was exotic, of course, but there was a willingness to discover differences; it went hand in hand with a certain cultural veneer. Foreigners were interested in dance, in painting. Now it's over.[177]

I remember Tommy Suharto had big luxury projects for Bali, his Intercontinental hotel in Jimbaran, of course, then the ambitious New Kuta project in Pecatu, for which entire populations had been evicted, and a marina project never finished, to cite only those. Today, we see more and more luxury cars driving here, and every year there's Fashion Week...

Yes, there are also national and international celebrities who come here regularly. But I don't know if Bali is still so popular with Westerners. But I believe that objectively, here, as everywhere in the world, there is a diminishing of very beautiful spaces.

It is true that Bali's image of luxury is also linked to its beauty!

Yes, although for me the beauty of Bali is crumbling a little more every year. But for people coming here for the first time, it still works ... Personally, I find the island has been made ugly. In the past, beauty was everywhere. Now you have to look for it, in the recesses of the countryside if the swings[178] and quad vehicles have left them intact!

Yes, but despite this ugliness, the myth persists!

It's undisputable. Bali has become such an icon! And then, there is the Balinese smile!

Yes, the Balinese smile is a luxury in this grim world.

I think that Westerners who come here and believe themselves empowered to provide advice to everyone would have a lot to learn in this area.

Is Bali, Indonesia-wide, like the French Riviera?

Yes, there is no equivalent elsewhere in the Archipelago. It is also where Chinese-Indonesians can go out of their hotel into the street without fear: one does not take them for Chinese, one takes them for ordinary people. The Chinese have always been better integrated in Bali than elsewhere.

It is also true that some foreigners have succeeded in creating luxury brands associated with Bali ...

---

[177] A sign of this phenomenon: the new generation of foreign painters no longer paint thematically Balinese, but abstract or contemporary art.

[178] Swing: a recent and very popular tourist attraction featuring swings over a scenic view.

Yes, for example John Hardy in jewelry or Paul Ropp in fashion. Some big deals have been done in Bali.

Bali was indeed the starting point for some large fortunes of foreign origin.

There was the creation of a certain bourgeoisie of foreign entrepreneurs who started with nothing at the end of the 1970s.

It created a lot of jobs. For example, the French clothing brand Animale, which employed a lot of people in the 1990s.

In the clothing industry, the majority of employees were women. Many companies contracted out work in villages, allowing certain populations to generate income without having to go to town. We must also mention the role of handicrafts, with impact that was not only economic, but also sociological and cultural. In Badung and Gianyar, entire villages are working on the production of handicrafts linked to tourism. This has manifest positive effects. It fixes populations in their villages of origin and therefore allows cultural activities such as music and dance to continue. The phenomenon of migration to the city is thus reduced compared to other regions.

It should be noted that there has never been any investment from multinationals in Bali, with the exception of hotel chains, probably because everything is on a small scale here ...

I know that some Indonesians have thought of creating a kind of Silicon Valley in Bali, supposed to attract talent spontaneously. But it didn't work. Bali remains economically focused on tourism. The clothing industry has gone to China, like many crafts. On the other hand, goldsmithing remains an important sector, which it already was traditionally. Design is also a strong point.

Yes, there's the late Linda Garland, who designed and decorated, with the talent of local artisans, the luxury properties of stars like Mick Jagger and David Bowie in the Caribbean.

This is another aspect of the Balinese economy. There are indeed decorators and architects who sell Bali internationally. Made Wijaya[179] is undoubtedly at the origin of this fashion. It's a buoyant economic sector. There are four or five architects in this niche, Popo Danes being certainly the best-known Balinese architect to work internationally. Here we have yet another glamorous dimension of Bali.

The Garuda Wisnu Kencana Cultural Park with its recently inaugurated giant statue of Vishnu, is this glamorous?

Yes, I think so. The designer of the statue, Nyoman Nuarta, is a friend by the

---

[179] Made Wijaya (1953-2016), né Michael White, an Australian landscape designer and cultural observer based in Bali.

way. I support him because he offers a modernist conception of Balinese-ness. His view is that you can do things that are Balinese, that look like Balinese, but that are modern. In this context, the planned statue had to remain faithful to the traditional iconic system, while taking on a dimension other than that known in village Bali. The original idea was not from Nyoman Nuarta, but from a somewhat special minister of the *Orde Baru*, Joop Ave.[180] Naturally, some criticize the statue, some for its size, others for its reference to classical statuary iconography.

And we are also in a dimension of prestige that the Balinese appreciate to the highest degree. A perfectly glamorous enhancement of a certain Balinese-ness, an ideal statue to appear on the cover of a beautiful glossy magazine.

Yes, but this statue is also national, because it must serve as an icon for Indonesia. In fact, according to Nuarta, it operates on two levels. It links Bali to Indonesia and Indonesia to Bali. This is the fundamental purpose of this statue, and I have supported this project in public for the same reasons. It will also help channel mass tourism. Chinese tourists will stay one more day to visit it! This is the first thing that holidaymakers on an organized tour want go and see. On the symbolic level, there is a little anecdote to add: in the Balinese compass rose, Vishnu, the god of water, must occupy the position north. Brahma, which represents fire, must be in the south. But it turns out that this statue was erected in the south of the island. So, what did the Balinese formalists do? They put a small statue of Brahma even further south, thus respecting the order of things.

What are this park and this statue the symbol of?

I would say they represent an intervention from the outside by their enormity, very different from what the Balinese are accustomed to. Nyoman Nuarta is himself a Balinese from outside, from Bandung; very nationalist. He arrived in Bali with a different truth than that promoted by many Balinese personalities. This project made people cringe, but was truly visionary: it integrates local symbolism with national symbolism!

What other major prestigious project deserves to be mentioned?

The airport! And the second airport, if it ever gets built.

Regarding luxury, we must also note the introduction of Balinese wines, vineyards ...

Yes, another element that positions Bali in the world of luxury. It is the only place in Indonesia, the country with the largest Muslim population in the world, where wine is produced. It is said to have been introduced by a former papal guard in the 1960s. Since it was then a sacramental wine, we can paraphrase Henri IV and say that Bali is well worth a mass!

---

[180] Joop Ave (1934-2014) was Minister of Tourism, Posts and Telecommunications between 1993 and 1998.

7. Middle Class, Education, Qualifications, Standard of Living

This interview is about understanding the development of the economy and what changes this has brought about. Literacy, the arrival of doctors from Java, electrification, improved hygiene, the start of tourism on a larger scale and also its transformation have all sparked the emergence of a middle class. Culturally, the Balinese have started to restructure their customs. Jean Couteau explains that they went from myths and symbols to standardization of religion and a concern with identity. Some villages are proud of their enrichment from tourism. Since wealth attracts wealth, there has been a frantic circulation of capital with the commodification of land, and it is still unabated today. In these latest developments, Jean believes that mass tourism but also sports tourism have displaced cultural tourism. From a sociological point of view, class has overtaken caste; modernity has allowed people of low extraction to acquire status. Although there has been progress, the big losers in these developments are women. Why? Descent and inheritance are still in the male line. Despite unprecedented advances in the economy, not everyone is happy: in fact, the role of capital is more important than that of work. So how do you acquire capital? We also look at Bali's new social stratification. What about the evolution of relations between castes? What about external or even foreign contributions to social stratification? Jean believes that in Bali, there is no cosmopolitanism in the positive sense of the term and that the middle class does not produce its own criticism.

Eric Buvelot. **When did the first signs of the consumer society appear in Bali?**

Jean Couteau. I would say around the mid-1970s with the appearance of soaps and toothpastes in *warung* in Denpasar and Ubud. The toothpaste was a Chinese brand called Maxam that still exists. But the first significant cash flows were from tourism. For example, the young people of Penestanan, near Ubud, would sell their paintings in Kuta, stamped "Young Artists" and destined for Italy or France, the big markets of the time. It was during this period that Ubud's first fortunes were made. And this money from tourists immediately turned into land purchases. Purpa, Agung Rai, Neka, so many people today linked to Balinese art began to make their fortune with this boom that came with the sudden opening of Indonesia.

You were talking about soaps and toothpaste just now, is that also when hygiene improved?

There was indeed a considerable improvement in hygiene at that time, also due to the policy of the *Orde Baru*. The government distributed Turkish toilets in the villages. Before that, people would defecate in the *teba*, behind the family enclosures, where pigs and dogs cleaned up the remains. No one used soap, and people brushed their teeth with a twig of *kayu putih*.[181] The children hung out in the dirt; the houses were built not of concrete but of pounded earth. The most modest houses were often made of bamboo and dried mud. Or bricks for better-off families. Everything was made with local materials and local techniques. There was still a constant physical contact with nature. This had other implications, especially in art, as well as ease with the body and beauty. But, in terms of hygiene, it had dramatic consequences, especially on infant mortality. So, it was a time that saw the advent of money and consumption, but also, luckily, the *puskesmas*[182] and the first physicians in numbers, in the late 1970s and early 1980s.

How did this affect everyday life?

The main upheaval took place in the relationship to nature. Until the 1970s, it was still old Bali. Everyday objects were made from natural elements found around the village bamboo, wood, *janur*[183] and so forth. Packaging was banana leaves. No one used cement or cinder blocks: sun-dried brick or dried mud, thatch, and volcanic stone were enough for any structure. Vehicles were very rare. Denpasar was just a large village where a few *bemo* circulated. In this still-agrarian space and society, the Balinese moved with an easy, very natural grace of the body, wrapped in a sarong or sometimes, for men, with a *kencut*, a cloth tied around the waist. Everyone lived at ground level, crouching or sitting cross-legged. As for aristocratic culture, the imagery was still that of shadow theatre and dance, and therefore a language of symbolism, not of school and TV. All that has changed. People now sit on chairs. The female breast is absolutely hidden behind a bra and *kebaya*.[184] The sarong has almost disappeared for men. In short, dress has become standard for everyone, a sign of the body being taken in hand by the supra-village world and the modern sphere. These changes towards modern consumption came with the increasing circulation of money since the 1970s. In Kuta, the hippies began to enrich the Chinese and Indian families of Denpasar, in the process attracting misfits from Jakarta and other rebels who came to Bali to mingle with Westerners.

In this still-peasant world, spitting, burping and even farting did not pose any problem of decorum?

There was an extraordinary bodily ease. Starting with the children, who played freely outdoors. They experienced nature directly. Eating was like shitting: one stood aside, in a corner. This can still be seen today in some villages. People used to bathe *en masse* in the river. A favorite pastime of women was de-lousing each other's hair; sometime they pissed standing up.

---

[181] *Kayu putih*: tree of the Myrtaceae family; eucalyptus in English.

[182] *Puskesmas*: government-sponsored health clinic.

[183] *Janur*: palm leaf.

[184] *Kebaya*: traditional tight-fitting jacket from the Majapahit epoch worn by women as a blouse in Indonesia, Brunei, Malaysia, and Malays of Singapore.

Good, but back to burps and farts ...

It's not all gone; if you go to a *warung* frequented by truckers or drivers this is often where Balinese cuisine is the best you can still hear the sound of chewing. No control of mouth sounds, burping... On the contrary! All is very natural. In the past, I have known villages where, during ceremonies, people literally threw themselves on banquets. The remains of princely meals were still thrown to the common people, all the more greedy as these leftovers had a sacred value. They were part of the princely power.

Did these princes have better codes of decorum?

Since colonization, they had adopted Dutch manners. The prince of Ubud had a telephone and a car from the beginning of the 20th century. They had to have more refined manners, like in shadow theatre. But, in early childhood, they were as natural as the common people.

In short, are spitting, burps and farts on the verge of extinction?

Now? The burp, absolutely not. Spitting, yes. The fart, I have nothing to say about it. What changed the situation was the arrival of the table, the bed, running water, the bathroom ... and tourists.

I go to the countryside a lot, and I can tell you that many Balinese people are still bathing in rivers and canals ...

Like the peasants whose rooms were heated by cows in the Vendée region of my veterinarian father ... Still, many people here behave differently now. The relationship to the body has undeniably changed, so much so that some can't even imagine that women used to go around bare-breasted. As for the beauty of the bodies, having piped water in the house, riding motorbikes, and eating Kentucky Fried Chicken have had their effects on the once superb bust and waist of women. A seamstress friend of mine told me that clothes have gone up two sizes in the past ten years.

Some men and women still bathe naked in the river, in full view of everyone, and grandmothers still walk bare-chested at all hours of the day in the villages, even in the city.

Yes, it's true. Change takes time. This resilience of tradition makes it hard to generalize and that's true of all the topics we are discussing here.

Are they starting to eat together as a family, at home?

Yes, more and more. In the past, they ate squatting here and there, often alone, tending to a simple need. Except of course at ceremonial times such as weddings and tooth-filings, when prestige and the assertion of status take over. But everything is changing, especially with the help of TV commercials and Jakarta soap operas.

Back then, was Ubud on the tourism map as it is today?

There were two or three *losmen*. I remember Puri Ubud, another called Mutiara, and Tjokorda Joni renting out guest rooms. I remember post-1968ers who lived in bamboo huts on the other side of Campuhan, after the old iron bridge. The road was unpaved. It was a whole other physical space.

Describe for us the health conditions of those years in the 1970s ...

Life expectancy was very low. When a woman was asked how many children she had, she would count on her fingers, quoting their Balinese first names one after the other, and then she might reply: "Seven, but I have only four left." Infant mortality was terrible, it was quite dramatic. People did not know their age. For the most part, there was no civil state at the time they were born to register births. So, people would say: "He was born just before the Japanese arrived" or "I started running after girls at the time of the Agung eruption." These events served as benchmarks to define approximate age.

Literacy has also played a role.

Yes, the 1970s were the great years of emerging literacy. But now, I'm going to say something dreadful: they were also the great years of military rule. That regime first understood that development can only happen through the introduction of skills, money, and investment, all from outside. It worked.

The *Orde Baru* was therefore instrumental in the development of the country in general and Bali in particular, at that time ...

Absolutely! Schools opened everywhere, even in the most remote areas of the island. They were the regime's first social investments, followed by public dispensaries and clinics: the *puskesmas*. At the time, there were still very few doctors; almost all of them were in Denpasar. They were often famous people, some from Java, all men. I remember Professor Murdowo, who wrote books on Balinese culture. Today, there are something like five hundred doctors in Bali! And the local university produces more than 50 new doctors a year. These are tremendous changes.

What about electrification?

When I arrived in the 1970s, there was no electricity yet in Ubud. People used kerosene or pressure lamps. There were only one or two motorcycles. Agung Rai, the owner of the famous Ubud museum-resort ARMA, bought a motorbike in 1971 to sell Ubud paintings to the hippies of Kuta. I remember French people who came every year to buy women's hair for wigs. Others ordered statues with big penises from the sculptors of Sebatu to resell them in the markets of France. It was a time of postcolonial fantasies. I had a typewriter, which was a big deal for the locals. Very difficult to find someone who could repair it!

It's difficult to imagine that all these changes have taken place in just

50 years, when we see the number of schools and universities on the island today and the range of specializations they offer, in particular in the tourism professions.

Yes, although we may wonder about the general quality of Indonesian education, still very poorly ranked in PISA[185] surveys. For Westerners, school produces learning but also questioning. With exceptions, of course, it's not like that here at all. For years, the object of teaching has been to standardize everything: daily life, hygiene, and, of course, religion. It is particularly marked in this area. Religion is still at the stage where many people are looking for explanations. Beliefs, texts, rites and traditions until recently had the status of magical, untouchable truth. But it was not organized as a cohesive whole. Now, truth must be explained, rationalized and thus justified. And this is done with reference to Indian thought and texts as the authoritative source. All religion is thus passed through the rationalist mill, which is the main job of religious universities. The results are now pervading the internet, including Google.

So, the Balinese have passed in a few decades from the peasant village to the modern world ...

Yes. I remember, when I was an advisor and then a lecturer at Club Med, the management of the establishment struggled to hire Balinese GOs,[186] the "friendly organizers" who engaged with the guests. It was very difficult for them to keep Balinese GOs for several seasons and to assign them abroad. After two or three months in Cherating or Mexico, they invariably asked to return to the village to take care of their ancestors. Going abroad for a Balinese villager was almost unthinkable. The GO might suddenly declare: "*Sing nau!* (I can't take it anymore!)" and refuse to do anything until a plane is found for him to return home. Today, the only God who concerns them, Sang Hyang Widi, is much less demanding than the original ancestors of the village. He lets the young people leave.

Balinese hotel staff are in great demand, especially for cruise ships, for example.

Yes, absolutely. Since the 1990s, labor merchants have been coming to Bali in search of human resources for foreign hotels.

The Balinese are said to have this natural faculty, which is highly prized in the hotel industry, to produce service, a quality inherent in themselves, in addition to their professional qualifications, like their smile, one might say. It's hard to imagine that Bali, traditionally known as a land of black magic, evil spells and proud warriors, has now become a provider of kind, model hotel workers. One more fabrication?

---

[185] PISA: Program for International Student Assessment is a regular OECD (Organization for Economic Co-operation and Development) study of 15-year-old high school students in 70 countries.

[186] GO: *Gentils organisateurs*, staff expected not only to work but to entertain the guests at the Club Med.

I don't think so; there is some truth to this. Also, they like to be in groups. The Balinese now travel the world thanks to the tourism professions. In Greece, I met a group of Balinese who worked on a cruise ship. They like to stay together, they often put on shows together. It all evolved rapidly.

There is nonetheless a stark contrast between the image of old Bali and modern Bali! Is there an official discourse on this?

I think, yes, in newspapers, schools, etc. But habits have indisputably changed. In the past, any serious discussion started with a betel exchange. Chewing betel nut was part of good manners.

Why did this habit disappear?

Because it destroys the gums!

Yes, but what caused this change? Was it the *Orde Baru's* health discourse?

That played a role, via village associations, Dharma Wanita,[187] the Pemberdayaan Kesejahteraan Keluarga[188] program. It was the "top-down" development style of the military regime which often worked better than the more democratic "grassroots" system put in place since then. It was also the era of village tourism, which contributed to the hospitable image of the Balinese. In the 1970s, people's houses in the villages of Sukawati, Batuan, and Ubud were indeed open to tourists. One had direct access to the painters, sculptors, and artisans of the place. It was perfect for communication. There was less social distance between tourists and Balinese than now. Near the temples of tourist villages, small souvenir shops offered things made in that village. Today, all that is almost gone. The sale of handicrafts has become a virtual monopoly of souvenir supermarkets like Krisna and a few others.

What is the role of tourism schools in these developments?

Sophistication. The BPLP,[189] ancestor of the STP,[190] was opened in 1978 with an original framework mandated by the World Bank. It was part of the Nusa Dua concept. The training given was considered excellent. Originally, most of the teachers were foreigners. I myself taught the geography of tourism there. I lived in Ubud, but it took only an hour to get to Nusa Dua on my old motorbike, despite the condition of the roads. The bypass did not yet exist; it was built later, after the hotels in Nusa Dua. Suffice it to say that I zipped along!

What impact did this first school of tourism have on the standard of living?

---

[187] Association of officials' wives. Even though it was traditionalist in outlook, it promoted practical improvements in conditions for women.
[188] Grassroots program aiming at improving families' welfare conditions.
[189] BPLP: Balai Pendidikan dan Latihan Pariwisata Bali. Formerly the School of Tourism.
[190] STP: Sekolah Tinggi Pariwisata. Academy of Tourism.

First of all, a transformation of tourism itself, which went from family tourism, around *losmen* or homestays, based on the kindness of Balinese families, to a structured, standardized tourism, no longer based on word of mouth but on marketing mechanisms. Tourists now have very organized, highly structured experiences. This change corresponds to the collapse of local mini-capitalism in the face of the large investments I mentioned earlier. There was also training for tour guides, with professional certification. But as this profession took shape, it moved away from the description of actual Balinese culture, which has become less and less village-based in its character and more and more modern Hindu. Today, guides often give the illusion that Balinese religion is uniquely structured around the cosmic dynamics of the Hindu trinity, as if the animist aspect and ancestor worship were not dominant. The profession as a whole was transformed: it went from improvised and independent guides of the 1970s impoverished intellectuals, Christian seminarians who had broken with their vocation, who spoke a little English but knew their village to tourism marketing and communications professionals who now work online and devour Indian texts.

Isn't it easier that way?

Of course... Instead of talking about the complexity of rituals, calendars, and ancestor worship, it is easier to hide behind the Hindu trinity of Brahma, Vishnu and Shiva!

Is there a hidden intention behind this new construction?

Yes and no. It's also the product of school. After all, these modern guides are among the first in the population to be university trained. As soon as they graduated, or even before then, the most talented among them preferred to become guides rather than lecturers at the university! Which doesn't mean their information is more relevant. But there, I exaggerate. There are some great guides. And some former guides are among the island's wealthiest people.

And today there is specialization by language and culture of the visiting tourist.

Yes, certainly. That's yet another level of sophistication. Another consequence of this tourism was the development of handicrafts. In the region of Gianyar, there arose, starting with the guides, a local petty bourgeoisie of skilled craftsmen. All their children go to university.

Fifty years is two generations; in such a short time, social progress seems extraordinary!

The leap is extraordinary. But it comes with a regression.

People often talk about the negative impact of tourism on societies. In the case of Bali, couldn't we say that the Balinese know better than others how to preserve themselves?

Yes… It is important that you say that. What I regret is that too many Balinese have taken refuge in the standardization and creation of an imaginary Bali that comes with tourism. In fact, the world of customary life is diminishing, along with that of agriculture, and inevitably, of local culture. But in popular discourse, every good Balinese continues to assert that Balinese culture is defined around the customs of its agrarian culture, its *adat*.[191]

Isn't it better to keep a shrunken culture than no culture at all?

You are more optimistic than I am! The Balinese have gone from experiencing a magical kind of reality to seeking explanations and a fixation on identity, within just a few decades. In the West, glorification of past cultural identity is not part of everyday discourse. People talk more about the future. The past is managed in museum form, but one is only interested in the future. Whereas here, people talk about a past fixed on a mythical identity moment, which is a sign of a society under attack in its foundations and not aware of it.

Back to the middle class … There is a provision now that recommends that hotels employ local people when they establish themselves somewhere. This is often a source of tension, as the people available on site might not have the required skills.

Yes! It works in some places, usually when owners are aware of local constraints. They are usually Balinese, or enlightened Chinese-Indonesians, as at Padma in Ubud. But when relations with local villagers are poorly managed, one sees the consequences sooner or later. Let's say that this hotel or villa uses a road that had been built by *swadaya*[192] ten years ago on private land. If the investor doesn't want to give a contribution to the village or hire local young people, they might close the road to him. If the owners of a villa behave badly, they might build a pigsty next door! It's classic protest. Villagers know how to unite when necessary.

There has nevertheless been significant economic development at the village level in recent years.

Yes, and that translates into larger ceremonies.[193] This also creates tensions. Because from the moment the decision is made to have a big ceremony let's say a big *odalan*,[194] after consultation with a high priest everyone must pay their quota, usually each couple or "kitchen".[195] While this allows some to assert their prestige, others find themselves impoverished. This prestige asserts itself in relation to other villages, or other castes, and is also reflected in political life.

---

[191] *Adat*: customary law. The *adat*, or *awig-awig*, hitherto oral, has been systematically written down, which has opened it up to the intervention of the state and modernity. It has become a field of contention between national modernity and multiple local resistances.

[192] *Swadaya*: obligatory communal labor.

[193] Seen particularly in the villages of Karangasem, one of the poorest regions of Bali.

[194] *Odalan*: cyclically held temple festival.

[195] Home, hearth in the old sense.

It's true, some villages show off and display an indisputable opulence: beautiful houses, beautiful cars …

This is often the case with people who have become successful elsewhere; when they return to the village, they flaunt their wealth, and their power as well. But there are other phenomena, such as the development of a certain type of agriculture, catering to hotels for example. This promotes the economic development of certain regions, growing flowers, vegetables … The land is adaptable to the needs of tourism.

Land that almost everywhere, especially on the coasts, has passed into foreign hands.

Much was sold to people in Jakarta or Surabaya and then rented out to Westerners. But many Balinese who sold on the coast are reinvesting in the interior. There is therefore a frantic circulation of capital through the commodification of land; this has negative social impacts, which are extremely difficult to control due to the lack of information on land use.

When we see all this land speculation, can we conclude that cultural tourism is over?

Of course, it is over; now we are witnessing the advent of eco-tourism, which is not cultural at all. People come here to trek, and it spreads tourists all over the inland, where they never went before. It also attracts quads, 4x4s and motorcycles on tours that are not at all green. There is also the new trend of swings[196] on Instagram, set up in the most beautiful landscapes of the island, including in protected areas, in Pejeng, for example. Dreadful!

Since the governor started banning plastic bags in Denpasar, I've noticed that in the countryside, there is a beginning of ecological awareness. Even on local roads between the rice fields, one starts to see trash bins!

It's the dissemination of ecological instruction through traditional local collective mechanisms, the *banjar*, and so forth. This can be effective at the village level.

Yes, but for plastic and garbage, the message took more than twenty years to get through! And I'm not sure we're really there yet …

For birth control, the village approach was very effective. The process is slower for the environment, although it is undoubtedly underway. Because, in fact, the development of tourism has broadened the scope of activities of the *sudra*,[197] the ordinary people, many of whom have become as wealthy as their co-villagers of the high castes. This shakes up the traditional social structure, generating a mixture of the stratification of castes into classes, which varies from place to place.

---

[196] Swings: giant swings installed at the edge of scenic valleys.

[197] *Sudra*, also *wong jaba*, or "outsiders," are the lowest caste, comprising some 85 or 90% of Balinese.

For example?

In Kuta, or in Denpasar, where there are a lot of Javanese, foreigners, and other outsiders, the caste system is barely operative, except in the Brahmin *gria* and the local *puri*. But in villages, caste stratification is more resilient. There is always the *Cokorda*, the *Anak Agung*, and when there are ceremonies, it is they who receive the others, it is they who are seated higher. In some cases, the caste system maintains itself only in the matter of language levels, even though class has overturned caste in order of precedence. These are transitional phenomena.

Can you give an illustration?

I imagine a Brahmin who works as a waiter in a restaurant in Sanur. Here comes a young *sudra* who "made it" in Kuta as a guide, for example. He arrives in a beautiful car and settles down for lunch with a tourist. Suddenly he find himself face-to-face with the son of his village *surya*.[198] This Brahmin, to whom he should normally defer in the village, will serve him or wash his plates. He should speak to this Brahmin waiter in High Balinese, but he will most probably address him in Indonesian. In a less ambiguous situation, people will choose to speak in Middle Balinese. It all depends on where and when. During a ceremony, the traditional language customs will take over.[199] On the other hand, I remember meeting with a group of Balinese in Switzerland, and there, abroad, all divisions disappeared; everyone spoke in Low Balinese. Everyone laughed and nobody cared. Low Balinese is the language of friends. High Balinese, which accentuates differences in rank, creates stiffness.[200] There is a wide range of situations and solutions.

Out of the shackles, propriety disappears?

Yes! Except that some new rich of low origin dream of belonging to nobility in order to better fit into the classical value system. Some will even see a *balian* who will invent for them in all sincerity, sometimes with the help of trance, a prestigious heredity although this will have to be accepted in the networks of corresponding noble clan temples, which is not easy! Wedakarna, one of the four current senators, declared himself to be a descendant of the kings of Majapahit. Of course, some don't care, while others take it very seriously! Because, while some Brahmins appear to be getting more caste-conscious, refusing to eat with common people, others, as well as many *sudra* are now rereading the caste system according to the standard established in the **Vedas**, outside of history, and therefore reject the stratification inherited from tradition. According to them, one belongs to a caste according to the profession that one actually practices, not because of one's

---

[198] *Surya* (sun): name given to the high Brahmin priests by their ritual clientele (*sisia*).

[199] Jean Couteau reports the case of a villa where the employees collectively protested the hiring of an *Anak Agung*. Why? Because they would have had to speak to him in High Balinese, which would have changed and stiffened their mode of communication.

[200] Jean Couteau personally avoids speaking Balinese with people he doesn't know well. They may get upset if he uses too low a level of Balinese. If they speak to him in High Balinese, the communication will remain formal.

birth. This is a democratic and "revolutionary" reinterpretation of sacred texts, not Balinese, but Indian which complicates things that are already complicated, especially with regard to the priesthood. To become a high priest in Bali, one has to undergo a complex initiation in which one becomes "twice born" (*dwijati*). Now one finds high priests who were born as simple *sudra* or other caste but who, by successive initiations, became *dwijati*. This is the case of *empu, begawan, rsi, dukuh*, and others, all high priests, but none of whom are Brahmin by birth.

Didn't that exist in the past? Weren't there mechanisms that allowed for these changes of status to the priesthood?

There were priests unrelated to the Brahmanic system, but they operated in their own geographic and clan spaces, far from the interference of princely powers. For this reason, it was out of the question to grant them the respect and power due to *brahmana*.[201] Now, all high priests have the status of *sulinggih*,[202] and all *sulinggih* can participate in the greatest rites, in particular those of the temple complex at Besakih. They generally operate within the framework of their clan group, with their own *sisia* and their own liturgical vocabulary, more Sanskrit than Kawi (Old Javanese), but they also prepare holy waters of all kinds which complete the rites. Modernity has made it possible for non-Brahmin high priests to claim de facto equality.[203] You can see here that the fight for equality is not just in secular politics. It goes through a recasting of the religious.[204]

Have women benefited from this fight for equality?

Yes, in part. Some could already become high priestesses through their husbands. They are now becoming politicians, as the wife of, daughter of ... The fact that political posts governor, regents, regional and national deputies, senators are the result of democratic elections opens more and more doors for them, which was not the case before the *Reformasi* era, when these positions were filled by appointment or a committee of electors. Developments are nevertheless complex. Socio-economic changes are certainly giving ever more space to women in

---

[201] The high priests were of three types, corresponding to different traditions: 1) *pedanda Siwa*, corresponding to a Shivaite tradition; 2) *pedanda Buda*, to a Buddhist tradition; 3) *rsi Bujangga*, to a Vishnuite tradition, each with its particular ritual and mantric corpus, as well as its clientele of *sisia*. The high priests *pedanda Siwa* and *pedanda Buda* are Brahmins from suitable clan groups. The *Bujangga rsi* claim Brahmin status, but it is generally not granted to them. *Pedanda Buda*, *pedanda Siwa* and *rsi Bujangga* constitute the *Tri Sadhaka*.

[202] *Sulinggih*: high priest who has undergone the *dwijati* initiation rites. From *su* = high and *linggih* = seat, meaning 'most exalted'.

[203] To better understand the complexity of the subject, see *Kebalian – La construction dialogique de l'identité balinaise*, by Michel Picard, Association Archipel (2017), in particular Chapters VI and VIII.

[204] Jean Couteau specifies that it is not always easy, because there are intangible incidences (*niska-la*). The new *sulinggih* sometimes expand their clientele seekers of holy water to the detriment of the Brahmin clientele. But if, having left the traditional attachment of your family to a particular Brahmin high priest, you fall ill, they may tell you: "It is the vengeance of the ancestors ..." Imagine the psychic disorders that may follow!

the state sector or the private sector. They gain autonomy and power, and may eventually come into power. But the paradox is that, even with these advances in the world of work and modern life, nothing can be taken for granted, because tradition continues to dictate a large part of daily life in Bali.

Why?

Well, because descent, inheritance, and therefore the control of ancestral temples, is always through the male line, the *purusa*. It's as difficult to question as the word of God in the Quran. Ultimately, sociological changes and ideological conflicts are inextricably mixed. This creates tensions, but can also ease them. I would say that, for the time being anyway, the typical Balinese woman ultimately goes with her Balinese identity rather than feminism: many Balinese women say that the situation of women in Bali is excellent. This is a denial of reality! It is better, but not good. There is a similar phenomenon among Indonesian Muslim women: in Indonesia, everyone has heard that Aisha, the young wife of the prophet, was a feminist before her time she could ride a camel.

Let's come back to the mix between castes and classes, this time in the important posts and functions of society in Bali.

High-caste people are represented in all sectors of society. In general, they are found more in the middle and upper administration. It is not a coincidence. There was a series of Brahmin governors: under the military regime, Brahmins inevitably entered the circles of power. Yet, since *Reformasi*, governors are directly elected by the population and there have been two *sudra* elected governors, one after another, Made Mangku Pastika, then Wayan Koster. But nepotism also plays a role. In the education sector, there are regional institutions where positions have long been awarded largely on the basis of family and clan ties. This distorts the selection mechanisms, and the quality of teaching not to mention the deleterious effects it has in the long term.

Let's talk a bit about medicine. I would like to know if middle-class Balinese still go to the *balian* or if they have gotten used to the doctor, this relative newcomer ...

It's interesting. I would say people go to the doctor, but that's not all. They also go to the *balian*, who often gives care which he gives a modern-sounding name: *alternatip* (alternative medicine). For the same reason, people no longer speak of *desti teranjana*, one speaks of *mejik* (magic). They endow the old medicine of healers with modern garb. So, there's a modernization of terminology, as well as an acceptance of the notion of progress, without the reality always having changed.

Once again, a way to integrate into modernity without losing yourself completely.

Absolutely! But in regard to modernity, I would like to stress that in Bali, the role of capital is more important than that of labor. The wages are ridiculously low.

You may well be a college graduate and have to settle for a monthly salary of three million rupiah [about USD210], barely enough to support a family.

The two are still linked, right? Shouldn't you be able to build up capital with what you earn working?

Wage employment cannot be a basis for building capital in Bali. Business, good luck, even tricks, are much surer ways to accumulate money. This is where my skepticism about the future of Bali comes back: you see an underclass in Bali or underclasses, if you take ethnic factors into account. Grassroots workers, day laborers, have no rights. If they are Balinese, they remain protected by family and village networks. But how long will traditional relations of solidarity protect them from the bewilderment of new experiences such as migration, urban sprawl, and the mutation of forms of housing which pass from the collective to the individual?

The prevalence of capital over wages is also an official finding, in the sense that the creation of small businesses is encouraged by facilitating micro-loans for villagers. There is therefore a political will consistent with the aim of helping to get around the difficulties of building up capital.

Yes, the handicraft sector has benefited the most from microcredit, which sometimes compensates for the lack of funds for investment at the local level.

Look at the example of Kedonganan, next to Jimbaran, where the Village Credit Organization (LPD) has championed microcredit for residents, and even received international praise for its effectiveness. And Kedonganan was only a poor fishing village ...

Yes, but it was mostly used to create the beach restaurants in Jimbaran Bay, which have destroyed and polluted this beautiful place! Yes, it is indisputable, there has been a conversion: the fishermen have become restaurateurs; or rather, the fishing bosses have, because nepotism also played its part in the allocation of lots. People talk about nepotism at the political level, but it is no less at the village level. I prefer the case of Sanur, where community leaders, Brahmins, prioritized local villagers. Remember that the Brahmins must protect their *sisia*, their clientele, if they want in turn to enjoy the respect due to them. In short, it is very complicated, and the quality of the leaders at the village level is very important.

Who are the Balinese left behind in this development of the last 50 years?

All the current surplus population of the villages of the island. The first to move to the city were the rural Balinese elites, *brahmana* and *satria*. They sent their children there to study, then, urbanizing, they bought land when it was not too expensive. Today, settling in the city is getting more complicated and requires more resources and more specialized skills. But the villages in the interior, especially those in the north and east of the island, continue to dump their surplus of semi-educated youth on towns and tourist areas. It is out of the question for these young people to buy land, which has become unaffordable, nor therefore to integrate durably into the local collective structures of their urban environment, unlike their well-born predecessors of the 1970s and 1980s. So, there is a certain disintegration of the social fabric. Another problem is the labor market, in particular in the field of tourism. Many young people enter the labor market with basic skills, of course, but they are offered essentially unpaid positions. They are made interns (*magang*) whose temporary contracts are endlessly renewed without leading to being hired. Sometimes they are fed or accommodated, or their transport costs are defrayed. Their hope is to accumulate experience, certificates, and contacts, in the hope of getting a real job later. Yet all this does not prevent them from smiling. We are far from labor riots!

Are there any geographic areas that are being left behind in Bali?

I immediately think of the beggars in the eastern region of Buleleng, or of certain slopes of Mount Agung,[205] which are very poor. They were ravaged by the eruption of the Agung volcano in 1963, which diverted rivers and made farming impossible. All kinds of "social diseases" are found in these areas, helped by the perversity of some foreigners.

How would one draw the social stratification of Bali?

At the top, there are very rich Jakartans, often Chinese-Indonesians. They have goods, land, property, businesses. They live in Jakarta or Surabaya, but now get married here in Bali, often with great fanfare. The origin of their presence dates back to the period of Suharto. Their political role is invisible, as they operate through networks of influence. At the bottom is the transient proletariat from outside: the day laborers on the short week, so to speak, in a fluctuating domicile. In between, toward the top are some *Cokorda* or other princes, who have taken advantage of tourism, and a handful of new tourism entrepreneurs, in Kuta, Sanur, and Ubud, then the classic middle class, made up of notables, teachers of higher education, the liberal professions; further down the ladder are craftsmen, farmers, drivers, and the providers of services.

Here, too, as we have said previously, this middle class is divided in two, between the outsiders and the indigenous, the first being more powerful economically than the second.

Yes ... I think it is the capital outside the island that controls Bali except for certain sectors such as culture. Non-Balinese capital has indeed taken control of everything in Bali except its much-vaunted culture. By over-valuing this culture in official discourse, the rest is ignored, and Jakarta is quietly allowed to take over Bali. I am exaggerating, of course, but not that much. The Balinese are not blind. Moreover, it is this fear that Bali will be controlled by non-Balinese that is behind the fight against reclamation in the bay of Benoa. Note also that the technicians in Bali electricians, mechanics, computer experts, etc.

---

[205] Mount Agung: Bali's highest volcano, thought for over a hundred years to be extinct until its eruption in 1963-1964, with great loss of life.

are often Javanese.

Are the disadvantaged classes also divided in two, between the local and the non-Balinese?

Yes, and with a double identity discourse that intrudes between these two proletariats. On the one hand there's *Ajeg Bali*,[206] the Balinese identity discourse promoted by the *Bali Post*; and, on the other hand, the classic Islamist discourse. Both are entering Balinese politics. While support for either of these should not be overestimated, it is there nonetheless. That said, the outsider underclass is less homogeneous than one might think. The new hard-pressed are no longer poor Muslims migrants from Java and Lombok; the latest arrivals are migrants from NTT, the great East of Indonesia, and often Christians. This is visible here and at the national level: it's a phenomenon of globalization. Modern Balinese society, by mutating, has led to relative prosperity. However, one may wonder to what extent the ongoing ethno-cultural or religious crystallizations might herald new breaks ...

In this social stratification that you have just described, what about foreigners, in the sense of non-nationals? We know that foreigners have almost no rights in Indonesia, just the right to be tourists, and yet they have been there, for decades now; they represent an economic force. Do they have their place in Bali?

Unquestionably. When it comes to their personal behavior, their influence is not always for the best, as there is undeniably foreign predation in Bali. But, on a strictly economic level, the most creative people are the foreign residents! This is a phenomenon that dates back to Walter Spies and to Rudolph Bonnet in the 1930s. Ideas in crafts or neo-crafts, in textiles, in tourism, come from foreign residents. Beach fashion and design are still in foreign hands now even though designers from Jakarta have also joined in. Like it or not, foreigners are present in the social stratification of the island.

Bali has also made a name for itself in the international culinary world, with a number of foreign chefs.

Yes, and now it's the local chefs who are showing their creativity. It's an interesting change. I remember Javanese in the 1970s making the rounds in the villages of Bali with their *kaki lima*[207] carts selling *bakso*.[208] This was followed by vendors of *mie goreng*[209] and others selling *nasi goreng*.[210] The Balinese didn't eat these things, except in town. As for so-called Western food, you were told point blank that it did not conform to Asian tastes. It's much different today. Some Balinese

---

[206] *Ajeg Bali*: slogan meaning "Bali upright, firm, erect," with a provocative Balicentric agenda in favor of preserving aspects of Balinese culture.

[207] *Kaki lima*: pushcart vendor selling hot prepared dishes.

[208] *Bakso*: meatballs in soup.

[209] *Mie goreng*: fried noodles

[210] *Nasi goreng*: fried rice.

chefs have made a name for themselves in Bali, but also in the Gulf countries and elsewhere.

To come back to these foreign residents whose presence does not exist in the official view in Bali, their visibility is denied despite their presence here for 50 years now, that is to say half a century ...

Yes, and that tells us something interesting about people's state of mind. You often see Balinese or Indonesian women whose success is highlighted in the press. But they almost always forget to mention the foreign husband! There is another paradox. Foreigners demand that Balinese be proud of themselves and of their culture, not noticing that they themselves have seized power in parts of the economic and even cultural sectors.

This is one of the great problems of Indonesia in the broad sense, that the nationalism necessary to hold this great disparate country together, and the rejection of external influences that this implies, will become a handicap to its advancement in the long term.

Yes, including the inherent ambiguity in this situation. Because, when it comes to openness to the outside world, apart from Bali and certain Chinese-Indonesian circles, there is little cosmopolitanism in the positive sense of the term. There are too few people capable of a double reading of phenomena local reading and global reading. This would require going beyond the obsession with identity.

Finally, what is the middle class in Bali?

As everywhere, the middle class is supposed to be the bearer of democracy, necessarily because it is the backbone of the economy. But it comes up against the entrenched behaviors linked to castes, nepotic groups, religions, etc. In Java, this middle class is structured mainly, in its lower component, around mild Islamism.[211] Here in Bali, around Hinduism. Can it be a bearer of progress? That's another problem.

In the national political discourse, yes, the middle class brings progress.

Yes, but isn't that an expectation of foreign origin?

So, like neoliberal economics, would democracy also be an import?

It is not impossible, even if comprador capitalism,[212] after launching development at the time of Suharto, ended up generating mechanisms that are contradictory to it, with, ultimately, a bourgeoisie of "clean" entrepreneurs. The best example of this is President Jokowi, who strives to rid the country of the stranglehold of the oligarchy inherited from Suharto. But one wonders if, below this bourgeoisie

---

[211] See the article by Thamrin Amal Tomagola, "Basis Sosio-Kultural Kekerasan-Radikalisme Perkotaan" in *Spektrum Budaya*, Festschrift HUT ke-84 Toeti Heraty, Museum Toeti Heraty, Jakarta (2017), pp. 280-301.
[212] Comprador capitalism: capitalism benefiting foreign investors.

of entrepreneurs in power, there is perhaps a petty bourgeoisie whose demand for social justice will be expressed more and more in matters of religion, in the absence of a discourse of modern social justice.

8. Pollution, Over-Population, Over-Exploitation, Chaos

Before the chaos and pollution brought by modernization, Bali was beautiful. Jean Couteau indulges in a bit of nostalgia. He remembers the human being in nature and nature in human spaces, he remembers a space of harmony where surplus production was devoted to the divine. Indeed, I can only go farther and say that Bali was beauty itself, *All The Beauty Of The World*, to quote the title of a film by the French director Marc Esposito. As this beauty, this harmony, began to disappear, they became objects in themselves, were articulated in discourse, as in the famous *Tri Hita Karana*[213] principles, which are a recent invention. We review the most visible outrages the island has suffered in recent decades. Weren't the Balinese at all prepared for these changes? Jean recalls that Suharto introduced economic dynamics and that modernity has always been imposed from the outside. Locally, there has never been any urban planning or reflection on the problem of vehicles; there has never been any communalization of land; pollution was allowed to invade rivers and beaches. Reklamasi, the reclamation of Benoa Bay, against which many Balinese have mobilized, has been the burning environmental issue in recent years, but is the protest really environmental? Or is it rather about identity? We note across Indonesia the recent appearance of politicians who are committed to being accountable to their constituents. Unfortunately, the pyramid scheme of authority is often an obstacle to managerial effectiveness. Finally, there is a pitfall here in Bali that few people dare to mention: a syndrome of over-idealization of the past and traditional methods. And to face the challenges of modernity, this does not work.

Eric Buvelot. **The adverse impacts linked to development are endless in Bali, the chaos is frightening.**

Jean Couteau. I think you first have to start with the reverse. Forty or 50 years ago Bali was a space of absolute order. Everything was managed by natural standards. The architecture was made of natural elements, stone, bamboo, mud brick there was nothing imported, nothing industrial. Everything was linked to nature! The space itself was sculpted, mixing the presence of the human being in nature, for example the paddy fields, or the altars in the forest, and the presence of nature in human spaces, such as huge *waringin* [214] trees in the middle of the villages. It was truly a space of harmony. The structure of the village itself was based on ecological standards. There was the upper part of the village, with the pure waters and the temple of the community; and the lower part of the village,

---

[213] *Tri Hita Karana*: Balinese philosophy that defines the "three causes of well-being," that is, harmony of humans with each other, with the environment, and with God.
[214] *Waringin*: giant fig, sacred tree in Bali.

with the drainage water and the cemetery. All this was perfectly coherent, a society perfectly adapted to its space, with an ad hoc cosmology ...

Perfect order!

Yes. When the Balinese bought or sold food, they wrapped it in banana leaves. Plastic packaging was not yet imaginable. As for religion, it was one of surplus. All surplus production, such as flowers, fruits, rice, was consecrated to the divine, transmuted into offerings. The whole culture was an ode to this harmony between nature and man. It is no myth to talk about the harmony of Bali!

Hence the fascination of the first visitors.

It was beautiful. It was beautiful everywhere! There were no buildings along the roads. They were found only in villages, in areas where agriculture was not established. This whole universe was harmonious, except for the frequent outbreak of disease, with a very high infant mortality and a low life expectancy. But, otherwise, it was almost perfect. I knew this Bali. Perhaps this is the source of my frequent cynicism.

What about the famous principles of *Tri Hita Karana*?

The paradox is that the Balinese theorized about this harmony just when it was starting to disappear. These principles were formulated in the late 1960s by a wise old man I knew, Gusti Ketut Kaler, who produced some of the most interesting texts on Balinese customary law.[215] The forest once occupied a very large physical space in Bali. I have known people from here whose family memory includes the opening of this or that forest, especially in Tabanan, or in the mountainous regions, which were very sparsely populated. Today there are four times as many inhabitants in Bali as in the 19th century.

For example, the famous Muslims of the mountains of Kintamani or Bedugul, where do they come from?

From outside Bali, of course; they occupied virgin spaces, forests, etc., particularly when they were freed from political constraints, such as the Sasaks [216] of Karangasem, liberated by the Dutch. They ceased to be serfs and were allowed to settle in the mountainous areas. Then there were also Madurese. These places took on a particular aura because mountains and the forest were places of meditation, the domain of the guardian Barong,[217] or Banaspati Raja, considered the lord of the forest! Between the villages there were no-man's lands which were sometimes used as battlefields. In the area overlooking Kintamani on one side, or Tejakula on the other, there were forests which were all cut down starting in the 1980s, used only for handicrafts, for tourism and export.

---

[215] Michel Picard, in *Kebalian – La construction dialogique de l'identité balinaise, Association Archipel,* 2017, p. 190, says that the Tri Hita Karana was conceived by Mertha Sutedja.

[216] *Sasak*: original ethnic group of Lombok Island, to the east of Bali.

[217] *Barong, Banaspati Raja*: Balinese mythological creature resembling a lion.

But isn't there a sacred connection to trees in Bali?

Yes, they are considered living beings. They are called *eka pramana* in the local tradition, which means that they are supported by a single life principle.[218] Before cutting them down, one must make an offering, then also replant. Nature is rendered sacred. Traditionally, there is an everyday relationship with trees. For example, sculptors cut whole slats directly from the bark of large trees to make sacred masks. Barongs whose masks are carved from the same tree are considered brothers, and will visit each other in procession, from one village to another, with crowds and music in support. Here we are in the midst of the magic of Balinese culture, but also in the symbolic respect for nature.

Have any forests survived?

The one in West Bali, in the national park, but it is not in very good condition. Otherwise, on the slopes of Mount Batukaru and in a few remaining pockets ...

Do you have any other phenomena in mind that would symbolize a major difference between before and after?

The original Balinese black pigs have almost disappeared, replaced by a species imported from Europe, called *bule* (albino). It symbolizes the ongoing transformation of Bali, especially as *bule* pigs have huge balls. And they are given the same *bule* name as white foreigners!

By the 19th century, Balinese pigs were already sold for export, especially to Chinese merchants.

The dogs are different, too! The famous Kintamani dog is a European herding dog said to have originated from a mix in the early 20th century with Balinese street dogs.

Nonetheless, the breed is internationally recognized and its pedigree officially certified.

In terms of ecology, we must also note that the entire coral reef around Bali has almost disappeared. Until the 1980s, coral was taken to make slaked lime for building. The natural protection of the Balinese coast having thus disappeared, the abrasion of the coast is accelerating.

Yes, we immediately think of Candi Dasa where the coral reef has been replaced by horrible concrete blocks to contain the abrasion ...

Like in Sanur. The coastal landscapes have taken a nasty blow.

What about the mangroves?

---

[218] Animals are said to be inhabited by two life principles, *dwi pramana* they can move; humans by three, *tri pramana* they can speak.

They're relatively protected. But the beaches in Bali are indeed disappearing, due to the abrasion of the coastline. Think of the road network and its consequences for urbanization and land use. Not to mention the landscapes, ravaged by construction along almost all the roads.

Is it Indonesia on the move?

Yes, with the urbanization of coastal areas everything has changed visually. Bali is no longer recognizable.

What about the architecture with this rampant urbanization of developing Indonesia?

When the Balinese began to structure their religion and modern thinking,[219] they also structured their architecture in a systematic and no longer hereditary local way. And they did so at the same time as they were theorizing the principles of the *Tri Hita Karana*. These are the standards that are applied in the Renon district of Denpasar and in the hotels of Nusa Dua. But, if we look at the historical developments that followed, the famous classical Balinese architecture, organized around the sea-mountain axis and the local cardinal points, has almost disappeared! Again, at the same time as the Balinese were setting standards, the subject of those standards was starting to disappear.

Yes, when the need to create standards arises, it is already too late.

We have gone from a traditional system in which the architecture reproduces both the human body and the cosmos, to a decorative system that only needs a vague carved relief of Arjuna for a building to be described as "typically Balinese". In fact, the principles of Balinese architecture are gradually crumbling. The paradox is that as they are disappearing, people insist ever more vehemently that traditional norms are the reality.

You also need a lot of space for the traditional Balinese house, but today the land is expensive …

There's the problem. Formerly, it was indeed necessary to have enough land so that each son of the master of the place could have his own living space. Each new enclosure was built as a duplicate of the father's enclosure, with a temple to honor the ancestors, a building for the parents, another for the children, and another for the elderly, all in a courtyard around an open space. It was in symbiosis with nature, a place where art could be born! This relationship to art has also changed with the disappearance of the symbiotic aspect. This type of habitat is endangered Arta.

What else has been ravaged with development?

The rivers.

---

[219] They started doing so in the 1970s, as part of a general reflection about tourism and the preservation of Balinese architecture. The lead thinkers in the matter were Ida Bagus Tugur and the 'Javanese' architect Roby Sularto.

Yet it is said that the Balinese religion is the religion of water, *agama tirta*.

Yes, if the religion of Bali is indeed the religion of water, the Balinese person is a drop of water. The water descends from the heavens, like the ancestor, who is himself a drop of water (*titisan*). In addition, each village has multiple sacred water points, the *beji*, where temple palanquins and effigies are washed ahead of the gods' visit in temple festivals. And the main work of high priests is to prepare different types of holy water (*tirta*) for the great rites of life and death. All this is hardly due to chance, because water is nourishing, it purifies. The origin, purity corresponds to upstream. Impurity, the end, death, to downstream. It is said, moreover, that the "field of pain," Hell, is located in the depths of the sea. All this is obviously linked to the dynamics of irrigation and it is here that the grip of humanity is nested within that of nature. Why, under these ideal conditions, did the Balinese let plastic trash take hold of rivers and block irrigation networks, why did they put aside the old ecological balances of their tradition? Big question!

It seems that the Balinese do not know how to react to the developments that are occurring on their island. Why can't they predict them?

There's the speed of change, but I think a lot of that has to do with the nature of Suharto's military regime, which initiated this change. For even though he nominally planned development and set it in motion, the regime was in fact based on networks of private interests roughly speaking, the more or less neutral agents or survivors of the repression of 1965-1966. It was impossible to take measures that economically contravened the interest of those networks for example, putting in place a coherent policy for regional planning, with green zones, areas to be developed, etc.

Political discourse on the organization of society in Indonesia never lags behind in awareness of the problems, but in practice it still seems that there is often a lack of action.

There are certainly aspects inherited from Suharto's military regime, but there is also something more traditional: rather than defending a truth, if necessary, by appealing to the law, people prefer loyalty. It is according to loyalty that the rules are made or broken. In Balinese culture, as I said before, it is more important to be loyal than to be right. It works in traditional settings, as it does in the modern state.

It's the spirit of belonging, to family, friends, village, region, ethnicity, etc., with the nation coming last in a series of concentric circles which gradually recede in decreasing order of importance.

Along with belonging, there is also dependency. In 1965-66, if the strongman of your village, say, a clan cousin always ready to help you, told you to become a *tameng*, [220]

---

[220] *Tameng*: this word means "shield". These were the death squad members, operating from lists provided by the military.

and therefore to go hunting for communists in the evening, well, you had no choice! It was because of him that you got your piece of land ... So, no hesitation. You became, if not a killer yourself, at least a witness and accomplice of the killers.

Indonesia is a gigantic country populated by people who function at the village level, making it difficult to coordinate all these villagers into citizens of a nation. This is the structural challenge of Indonesian national identity and the basis of its fervent nationalist ideology.

Yes, the Majapahit empire, founded in Java, was already a kind of conglomerate of villages. You said a moment ago that the nation comes last. Yes and no. Because the ideology and the bureaucratic heart of the state work. The constant repetition of words, slogans, and principles such as *bangsa*,[221] NKRI,[222] Indonesia, Pancasila may sound irritating, but it reflects an unquestionable desire to create Indonesian "togetherness". And the key institutions, like the army, the judiciary, the police, are genuinely national, that is to say multi-ethnic and multi-religious. The Balinese have their temples in this national space, and the Christians their churches.

Is the organization of society, now democratic, even more difficult than it was in the authoritarian days of the *Orde Baru*?

No. Despite the fact that the political parties represent only the elites and tend to generate corruption, there is a certain democracy, that is, consultation mechanisms that work. This democracy, called *Reformasi*, has sometimes had perverse effects, particularly after the implementation of the 2004 Regional Autonomy Law, when newly settled populations in Bali found themselves obliged to have a residence permit, KIPEM;[223] this generated real discrimination against non-Balinese. Since Jokowi, these regional decrees have been repealed.[224] Overall, *Reformasi* moved corruption from the center to the peripheries. It was inevitable and arguably preferable, because there has been some improvement. The elites at the center can no longer do whatever they want. Local, national, and other loyalties are expressed openly, and politicians must heed this. In Bali, the *Reklamasi* issue illustrates this complex state of affairs well. Under hidden military pressure, the former governor Made Mangku Pastika[225] was long forced to pretend to support this project, even though, in fact, he constantly postponed any decision, throwing the ball back into the court of the Jakarta government. He was aware that the crux of the issue was not the economic benefits promised by those who supported the project, nor the environmental dimension emphasized by those who opposed it, but the ethno-religious balances that he had to maintain. Thus, we come back to the role of discourse, to the significance of the identity phenomenon among

---

[221] *Bangsa*: nation.

[222] NKRI, *Negara Kesatuan Republik Indonesia* or Unitary Nation of the Republic of Indonesia.

[223] KIPEM: identity card and temporary residence permit in Bali.

[224] In other regions, discrimination was against lukewarm Muslim women, who were obliged to wear the headscarf in government offices.

[225] Made Mangku Pastika: Governor of Bali from 2008 to 2013 and from 2013 to 2018.

certain elites, and to the idea of defending Bali to the death.[226] Strange return to the *puputan,* which initiated Balinese modernity, isn't it?

The *Reklamasi* issue is therefore not ecological but identity-based.

Basically, yes, even if people claim the opposite. Nonetheless, I think things are better managed since *Reformasi*. National and regional balances are better taken into account. And above all, there's a new generation, freer and more autonomous in their way of thinking, with a small elite that's very aware of major international issues, ecological in particular.

This improvement has come through education, openness to the world, the internet ...

Yes, by a whole set of mutations ... first by way of the *Orde Baru*. It was Suharto's regime that set the economic machine in motion. Its relative success paradoxically generated the sociological changes that led to his fall from power including mass education. Now, in the *Reformasi* era everything is more complex and better managed. The real difficulty remains in putting in place, in a coherent and non-traumatic manner, the infrastructure and institutions needed for modern socio-economic development, and in raising the standard of living at the same time. There are still huge challenges in education, urban infrastructure, wastewater and waste management. This in an environment in which all the traditional socio-economic and socio-political networks are in the process of transformation, sometimes even disintegration.

Are these developments manageable? That's the whole point ... I've always felt that decision-makers are behind on issues.

The answer is very simple. Modernity has been imposed from the outside. First through colonization and then, perhaps more fundamentally, through tourism. How have the Balinese reacted so far? By taking refuge in a pseudo-tradition that they are constantly reshaping. This is problematic because it prevents them from confronting change rationally. Change still tends to be perceived as an intrusion from the West. But you can't really blame them.

This feeling of distrust towards foreigners, so typical of decolonized developing countries, probably comes from Indonesian intellectuals, who are traditionally critical of the West ...

Yes, but it's also true that Westerners are often incorrigibly didactic: "You have to do it like this, don't do it like that!"

Indeed, their remarks often lack nuance, but rarely relevance... What about this umpteenth ban on plastic bags in Denpasar in convenience stores and supermarkets?

---

[226] Especially in regard to *Reklamasi*. A famous singer / philosopher Sarasdewi mentioned it in a text that was widely circulated in Bali.

Yes, plastic trash is a hazard for tourism. All of this requires action, especially as people talk about it in the newspapers, on social media networks. Ultimately, politicians are forced to take action even if there is no comprehensive preventive vision on ecological issues, precisely because of the idealization of the past.

It seems that the current governor, Wayan Koster, is determined to take on the problem of the landfill of Suwung.[227] Is that correct?

I am not sure ... Whether it's for reasons of nationalism or because it involves many interests at the grassroots level, it seems that the local Balinese government does not want to put a foreign company in charge of recycling trash. Also note that the production of electricity is very polluting here, because the power stations run on coal.

The issue of production by nuclear power plants comes up regularly but has never really advanced although the Indonesian nuclear agency has been operating a laboratory reactor for over thirty years in Java ...

Yes, but Indonesia has never even mentioned nuclear ambitions. And then, the country has so many natural resources that promote clean energy that it would be a shame if it took this path.

Good, but let's get back to the chaos of today! What else about the degradation of this fabulous island?

The destruction of landscapes! It is absolutely catastrophic! First, the construction along the roads, like the tourist shops near the rice fields of Tegallalang, the fish restaurants in Jimbaran Bay or the *tempat rekreasi*[228] in Batur or Bedugul.

There, you cite only examples of degradation linked to tourism. This is not always the case; I would even say that most of the destruction of beauty in Bali is more due to national development, to Indonesia's economic growth ...

I think the two are linked in Bali, since the development of the island depends on tourism. And then there is above all the question of the rule of law. Whenever green zones have been designated, they have never been respected. There has never been any real urban planning. Not to mention the problem of vehicles. There are 3.2 million vehicles registered in Bali (20% cars and 80% two-wheelers) for a population of 4,225,000 people.[229] This figure does not include vehicles registered elsewhere. The island is at saturation point! And how to get in and out of all those narrow streets in cars!

Looking at the uncontrolled urbanization of Bali, one has the feeling that what amounts to the common benefit is always the minimum

---

227 Suwung: Bali's largest landfill, where trash piles up untreated; located in south Bali between Kuta and Sanur.

228 *Tempat rekreasi*: recreation places.

229 Source: *Radar Bali* (2018).

acceptable. Narrow streets, no parking areas, no parks, gardens, or benches ...

Yes, there has never been a communalization of land, for shared use by citizens. There's no such thing. This raises the question of the concepts of law and *cadastre*: there is no tax on speculative capital gains in land. These taxes are used in many countries to finance social services, especially social housing; not here.

Let's get back to the pollution of rivers and shores in Bali. Why do we still see people throwing bags of garbage in rivers when awareness campaigns started 20 years ago?

People are not really aware. Historically, trash used to be all biodegradable ...

Yes, but Bali has been rubbing up against consumer society for almost 50 years, two generations. Isn't that enough time to understand that plastic packaging does not disappear by magic?

I come back again to the over-idealization of the past and of tradition, which is paramount in Bali. It does not encourage people to face the challenge of modernity, nor its realities. Even the reverse is true.

With Indonesia being the world's second largest plastic polluter of the oceans, there is an urgent need!

Yes, there is no real processing plant in Bali ...

There were attempts, but they did not register over time. I think of the Sanur, Kuta and Denpasar sewage and drainage system, a 130 km sewerage project funded and built by Japan in 2004-2008, which never really worked. The treatment stations have not been operational for a long time ...

It is impossible for a foreign company to do anything. Imagine a foreign investor in waste management, when local officials, down to district and village level, demand bribes not only for the slightest authorization, but also for collection. It's unmanageable. Traditionally, there are habits which signal a sensitivity to environmental problems, but they have never been successfully adapted to the challenges of contemporary society.

I think this should also be the responsibility of the central government. There has been indeed a sufficiently coherent national environmental discourse on these issues for a long time, since the Suharto years. On the other hand, there are people in this country who are competent enough to solve these problems and yet ...

It is very difficult to be effective in Indonesia. The mechanisms for delegating authority don't work. There are smart people in the driver's seat, but they often don't want to delegate, and often can't. Here, no one wants to speak to the saints, everyone wants to speak directly to God! No one wants to deal with assistants, everyone wants the minister, the boss! This blocks all operational functioning.

Why?

It's the notion of power, I think, its centrality …

Isn't there a problem related to education, a problem of the broadening of skills, which today is still the prerogative of too small a minority?

Often times, yes … And there is also this problem of overvaluing whoever is in a position of power. It is true that God is God, but if we want him to be effective, we must resort to his saints; that will give him more time to excel! This notion has been understood in developed countries; it's not yet the case here.

Yes, but maybe the saints here don't have enough skills and degrees. It's possible that knowledge has not yet become sufficiently generalized for one to be able to trust the subordinates.

Yes, for sure … especially since the mechanisms for appointing people to positions of responsibility are based more on criteria of loyalty, seniority, or pseudo-diplomas than on skills. But that may be changing.

With elections at the national, regional, departmental levels, etc., this does not favor the choice based on skills either, but rather popularity.

Still, there's the positive example of mayors in recent years. Leading politicians have appeared on the national political scene after having been good managers at the city level. This is the case of President Joko Widodo, mayor of Solo and then governor of Jakarta, and also of Ridwan Kamil in Bandung or Tri Rismaharini in Surabaya.

Yes, these elected politicians have incorporated the notion that they are accountable to their constituents …

They've also incorporated the idea of the public good.

Is there a figure that stands out from the crowd yet in Bali?

Ida Bagus Rai Dharmawijaya Mantra, who is the son of the former governor Ida Bagus Mantra, is a good manager. He is currently mayor of Denpasar. But doesn't that also have to do with his father's aura?

Speaking of good management, what can we say about the management of the urban space of Denpasar?

The infrastructure has never been put in place to be able to properly manage the urban space. There is no real ring road, for example …

Yes, or these roads are created after the fact, sometimes pushing back buildings …

There is no public transportation system. The Sarbagita bus system has been a total failure. There is no planning; it's as if the future does not exist!

On the one hand, there is a total neglect of planning for the common good and on the other, the almost certain possibility of organizing spaces for private real estate projects.

Today, urban planning projects increasingly consist of discovering a few hectares that are still free for private development projects, for private capital ...

The Benoa Bay reclamation project, the famous *Reklamasi*, is a perfect example. Can we say that the Balinese find themselves robbed of their land?

There is no study on the subject. But, yes, in a way, they are being robbed ... At the same time, there is a kind of idealized notion that the land should not be sold to foreigners. It is in fact enshrined in national law.

True, it is not sold, but it is nonetheless leased and often exploited by foreign interests.

What's emerging here are changes in the distribution of access to land that are associated with ethno-demographic and ethno-religious changes with big problems to come if these changes are mismanaged. The current governor, Wayan Koster, wants to "re-Balinize" Bali. People have to dress in Balinese clothes every Thursday at their workplace, for example ...

This is still popular with the Balinese!

Yes, but it can create tension among people outside the culture of the island.

PART THREE

DARMA

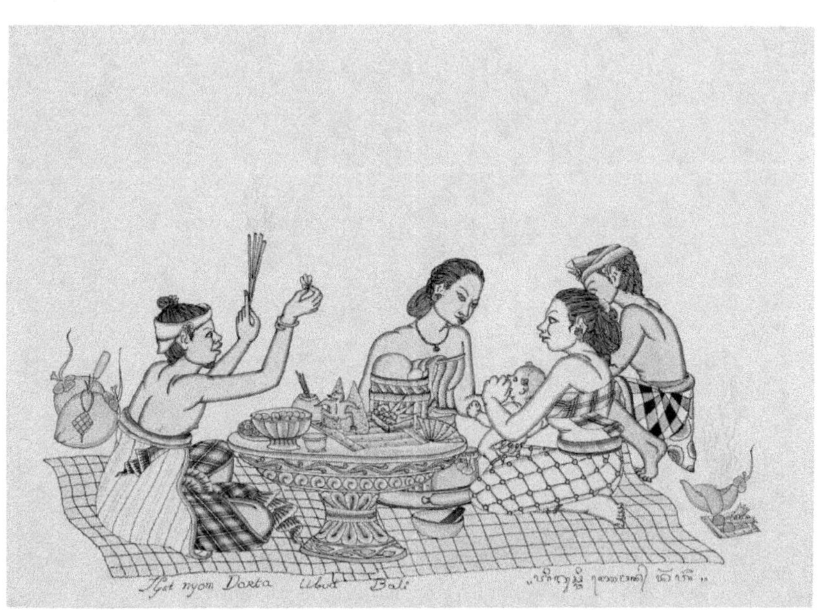

12 Days Ceremony by I Gusti Nyoman Darta, 24 x 34cm, paper.

9. Social Order, Society, Social Equilibrium, Women's Rights

In Bali there has been a transformation of the caste system. But what indeed is the caste system? Jean Couteau explains to us its origins and also that local criticism of this system is not based on the usual Western values, as one might erroneously suppose. We also learn that there have always been significant segments of the population who refused this system. And that there is another, older classification, between clan groups. When the colonial Dutch codified the caste system, many people strived to join the main lineages, with the origins of prestigious lines going back to Majapahit. In the 1950s, when it became necessary for the Balinese to prove that their religion met national criteria, they borrowed from their old Balinese or ancient Indianized past, and from there created the identity of their religion. The Balinese are also becoming Indianized in a modern way and thus find their place in international Hindu spaces. Locally, has a new social equilibrium been found? What about social cohesion following these transformations? Is caste giving way to class? Then we turn to women's rights and identity. Does the Balinese woman identify more as a Balinese than as a woman? And what about the "eternal wound" of her genitals that made her impure? Jean explains to us that the Indonesian government has always focused on women's economic emancipation. He also says that postmodernism is often used to justify the current identity discourse. The West demands recognition of individual rights, but here it is not the individual who carries the values. In the end, women are too often excluded from many social mechanisms, even if progress has been made because their full emancipation would induce a loss of control over them; we see this with questions related to inheritance rights, which Jean recounts in detail. Otherwise, are there modern and fully free Balinese? With regard to this, we briefly discuss issues related to LGBT people, recent developments in marriage, and the fate of the Bali Aga Balinese who have preserved older, different customs.

ERIC BUVELOT. Can you give us an idea of the Balinese social order from a historical perspective?

JEAN COUTEAU. Until the Dutch took over Bali over a hundred years ago, the historical development of Balinese society was still very slow. The weight of a modern economy was barely felt. By brutally bringing capitalism in 1849 to the north and in 1906-1908 to the south, the Dutch introduced a change in discourse together with practical changes. Indonesians who passed through Dutch schools espoused the notion of progress (*kemajuan*), which implied accepting, among other things, transformation of the caste system and, to some extent, the emancipation of women. This view lasted throughout the revolutionary period and early Independence, then during the presidency of Sukarno. But it should be understood that these educated circles, formed in Western thinking, constituted only a tiny minority.

Yes, what happened next?

After Suharto came to power, and especially with the spread of education, there was a reversal. It was no longer change and therefore the future that was valued, but tradition, the affirmation of Balinese cultural identity, and therefore the past. And this at the same time that irreversible changes were taking place in the deep structures of society. There were also mutations even faster than those which took place during the Dutch colonization, because they involved both land and the mind, and affected the entire population. The transformation of all socio-economic structures was accompanied by a sort of ideology of cultural immobilization.

Will this lead to conflict one day?

I couldn't really say. But one can still pose the question, at least on a strictly ideological level. When the Westerners arrived, they brought, along with the notion of progress, that of conflict. Marxism, with its notion of class struggle as an analytic measurement of social transformations, is a convincing illustration of this. Was it relevant for the analysis of existing social structures?

And especially in relation to the caste system ...

Yes. The caste system is criticized. But this criticism, since the military regime at least (1965-1998), rests on bases other than Western and Marxist criticism ...

So, the caste struggle is not the class struggle?

Absolutely not, it is the product of a look back at identity. Current Balinese modernism no longer refers to change in itself, to progress, but to the reinvention of a past cleansed of its backward residues. Modern Balinese no longer refer ideologically to the West, but to an imaginary non-Balinese past that they increasingly seek in India, in a mythical Hinduism of origins, that of the **Vedas**. Accordingly, at least for the majority of thinking elites, the caste system should reflect actual social reality, as in the original Vedic texts, and not the status inherited from one's ancestors, according to the *wangsa*.[230] If you work in religious affairs, you are Brahmin, *brahmana*. If you work in the upper administration, you are *satria*. If you are a merchant, you are *wesia*. They reread the past in a way that allows them to deny the *wangsa* inherited from their history.

Yes, they reread a past that does not really belong to them and, in doing so, do indeed abandon their Balinese past, the cult of ancestors ...

---

[230] *Wangsa:* Bali's own caste system.

I think there is also a desire for order in this choice. In Balinese tradition, the system was amorphous and flexible. There was no real conceptual border, no ideological barrier, because there was no structuring of thought, no desire to think of Balinese religion or society as a coherent system. All of that has changed. The mere fact of education has forced the Balinese to organize themselves, especially in relation to other Indonesians, to Christians, Muslims, and so forth. After they gained official recognition as "Hindu" by the central Indonesian authorities, they had to somehow become so, to rediscover and therefore, in some way, reinvent their past links with India.

There is therefore a clear responsibility of the Indonesian government in this phenomenon, which dates back to the 1950s, when it was necessary for the Balinese religion to be identified ...

Yes, although the government was hardly the first or the only actor. The whole of society moved in the same direction under the fact of modernity, since the Dutch period. As early as 1950, when the Balinese demanded that their religious traditions be recognized,[231] they were told: "You want your religion to be recognized, but what really is your religion?" At that point there was very strong pressure from modernist Muslims, from those who practice an open, albeit hesitant, reading of Islam. These Muslims were ready to let the state recognize the Balinese religion, as long as it was identifiable as a religion, that is, it had one God, a holy book, and prophets. It was therefore necessary to make the Balinese religion pass as a "religion of the book".

What happened?

A committee of Balinese opinion leaders took up the challenge, and eventually succeeded. How? They borrowed from their local written tradition, they also borrowed from India, and from these contributions they formed what can be called a religion. They formalized it with principles, such as the oneness of the divine and the presence of prophets, which made this religion acceptable to Islam and in conformity with the five principles of the nation, *Pancasila*. They then plastered the model of this religion on the Balinese tradition, "forcing" a little here and there to make it fit. And it is this syncretized Hinduism, formalized and made official in 1959 after a long struggle, which has since spread in Balinese society, thanks to schools and the bureaucracy. Michel Picard [232] has described the phenomenon in detail, including its tensions between supporters of the local Balinese substratum and those aligned with modern reformed Hinduism.

---

[231] The first negotiations began in 1950, as soon as Indonesia was finally liberated, when the minister of religious affairs came to Bali to inquire about the local religious situation. A year later, the main local religious organizations demanded official recognition of their religion. A petition from Balinese figures to President Sukarno followed, which led to the formation of the Indonesian Council of Hindu Affairs (Parisada Hindu Dharma) and full recognition of Hinduism in 1959.

[232] In *Kebalian – La construction dialogique de l'identité balinaise*, Association Archipel (2017). Michel Picard is a researcher at the CNRS and member of the Centre Asie du Sud-Est (CNRS-EHESS). He is also the author of, among others, *Bali – Tourisme culturel et culture touristique* (1992).

Did this upset Balinese religious practice?

Originally this changed little in terms of ritual. On the other hand, the explanation became theological. All this shifted little by little. Exchanges multiplied, education became widespread, new media appeared. Today there are multiple direct channels of transmission of the Indian Hindu corpus, and a free circulation previously impossible of treatises from the Javano-Balinese tradition. Thus, ancestor worship is less and less emphasized in intellectual life, even if in reality, in ritual practice, it continues to come first, albeit penetrated by more and more mantras or prayers from the Old Javanese/Kawi and/or Indian Sanskrit corpus.

Yes, the Balinese do not address the gods of India!

Not really ... That is, it depends on the context. The family temple is Balinese, it is still the sanctuary of ancestral spirits. But there is an incontestable slide of the gods and ancestors towards the God of heights more than simply mountainous. Yet, the evolution is complex: there are Balinese who perceive the references to India as real intrusions; and there are those who accept them with open arms. In the end there is a new wave of syncretism, after that of the first millennium, and that which followed the 1343 Majapahit invasion.

Have Balinese ever refused the caste system?

Yes, there have always been significant segments of Balinese society that refused the caste system, in the Bali Aga regions, those that remained aloof from post-Majapahit Javanization. But maybe we have to go back to the origins. What is the caste system in Bali?[233] This is called the *wangsa*, a Sanskrit word which gave the word "nation" in Indonesian, *bangsa*. Basically, the people were divided between the small group of *triwangsa* on one side, and the majority *sudra wangsa* on the other. This corresponded to the division between *satria* princes and *brahmana* high priests on the one hand, and the lower *jaba* people those on the outside of the court, corresponding to *sudra wangsa*, on the other. The function of the high priests was to justify the power of the princes, to produce legitimate ideology. But this caste system, which arose out of these two main groups, operated within principalities which were independent of each other and which often only imperfectly controlled their entire territory. Each principality had its hierarchy of castes (*wangsa*) and clans (*soroh*), themselves hierarchical, around which were organized most of the rites and, sometimes, local power, the *wangsa* being only a simple normative envelope. Complicating matters further, no one really advertised themselves as *wesia*, the third normative group of the *triwangsa*. When Bali was unified by the Dutch in 1908, problems arose.

For example?

---

[233] For an explanation of the system, see *Kebalian – La construction dialogique de l'identité balinaise*, Association Archipel, 2017, in particular, p. 40. See also *Bali in the Early Nineteenth Century: The Ethnographic Accounts of Pierre Dubois*, Brill, by Helen Creese, 2016, pp. 206-212.

The origins of a prince of Denpasar are not the same as those of a prince of Karangasem or Ubud. This was not a problem when everyone was in their kingdom or principality, but when, under the magical leadership of the Dutch, they found themselves united in the same Balinese space, all hierarchical primacies were called into question. This shook up a lot of things, and forced the Dutch to codify the system at the island level and no longer at the local level. And as belonging to the governing clans, to that of Cokorda in particular, depended on patrilineal descent and the rites associated with it, everyone then endeavored to join the main lineages, royal or otherwise. There were openings in the matter: there are lineages for which affiliation is quite well known, but in many other cases there is no authentic historical chronicle; these are more or less mythical lineages. What do people do then? Well, they do some research in the manuscripts, and, if need be, they go see the *balian* to "find" their ancestors ... perhaps imaginary. The richer one is, the more easily one finds them!

Is there a de facto hierarchy among all these lineages?

Normally, the origin of prestigious lineages goes back to the conquering warriors of Majapahit, who invaded Bali in 1343. The primary lineage is that of the Dalem[234] of Gelgel. Starting in the Gelgel period, the Dalem and members of their retinue, the Arya, spread across the island. In the course of time, land along with a few families of peasants, architects, priests, sometimes from Java, were attributed to a prince; and, within a few decades, a principality appeared in the middle of the forest. This is how we find sub-clans of Dalem origin in the region of Ubud, Peliatan and Sukawati. Other princely lineages, often titled "Gusti,"[235] appeared later, after Gusti Agung Maruti's revolt against the Dalem in the 17th century. The unity of Bali was then in tatters. The kingdom of Mengwi was born where Maruti had taken refuge, and later spread westward and even seized part of Java. Other kingdoms, in Karangasem and Buleleng, emerged around the same time. The Dalem dynasty of Gelgel also resettled, right next to Gelgel, in Klungkung.

Why do the kingdoms of West Bali seem to have less historical prestige?

These are sub-clans of Mengwi, Gusti who became Anak Agung, that is, rulers. It all sounds a bit complicated and today it just doesn't work anymore, except on the occasion of certain rites. It's important to point out that these rites are what cause the relative impoverishment of many princely families, with the exception of those who have been able to convert to tourism. Many princely families no longer have the means to maintain the rites corresponding to their status, losing some of their prestige. They can no longer support their former subjects (*panjak*) during the labor-intensive cremation rites.

---

[234] *Dalem*: member of the royal family, direct descendant of Arya Kepakisan, the first raja of Bali under the rule of Majapahit.

[235] *Gusti*: lord. One of the many clans of Bali. *Gusti Agung* was sometimes a title for kings.

Could you please elaborate on that?

These ceremonies entail a great deal of preparation of offerings and ritual paraphernalia by the labor of *panjak* followers, who must be fed for weeks on end. If a prince can no longer afford to feed "his people" during ritual preparations, there is inevitably a loosening of the bond between the two parties. Moreover, today these "little people" are often educated and have sources of income beyond the land provided by the *puri*. But it depends on the principalities. Ubud is a special case. Its princes arrived late on the political scene, at the end of the 19th century, but the memory of its founders is still alive and they still have the means to maintain their rank through ritual.

And the social cohesion that goes with it?

Yes! On the other hand, if there is a decline in the economic power of princely families, it's the Brahmins who benefit first. Why? Because, as the common people get richer, this translates into more elaborate religious festivals and more solicitations of the priesthood. So, in the end, more orders to the *brahmana* for offerings. These are phenomena of modernity internal to religion, but it is certain that this shakes up the traditional stratification of the *wangsa*, which is becoming less and less operative now.

So, can it be said that the caste system is becoming less prevalent?

Undeniably. If a Brahmin family is prosperous and it has the means to maintain its status, it may very well decide to strengthen its caste identity, by avoiding language transgressions, and by insisting on the maintenance of certain prohibitions, of marriage in particular, even by causing the breakup of the *banjar*. But most of the time, especially in the city, the opposite happens: loosening of the language, weakening of prohibitions, etc. So, I would say that there are evolutions a bit in all directions, with a slow slide toward openness.

You spoke of marriage a moment ago; is endogamy breaking down, have unions with non-Balinese developed? Is there a discourse that accompanies these phenomena?

Yes, the practice of marrying only within one's caste is slowly breaking down, often with tears. As for unions with non-Balinese, the rule is clear: the man takes the woman. No question. Whether a Balinese man marries a Muslim Indonesian woman or a Westerner, the wife, with the help of ritual, automatically becomes affiliated with her husband's network of temples. In the case of a Balinese woman marrying a non-Balinese, it is the reverse: the woman adopts the religion of her husband, except, of course, the postmodern fantasy of some white men who feel obliged to become Hindu.

The woman is therefore in all cases less valued.

There's little doubt of that, whatever the intellectual contortions of those who claim otherwise. If we refer to some classical Balinese texts, such as *Kakawin Nitisastra*[236] or the *Sarasamuscaya*,[237] it is said of the woman that she is endowed with an eternal wound: her sex. We can also read that she is eight times more capable of pleasure than men, which the latter obviously strive, in deeds, to deny. Modern Balinese ignore the misogynistic aspects of these texts.

Good, but back to interfaith marriage. It is not easy, it is even forbidden, according to the law of the Prophet, for a Muslim to marry a non-Muslim.

No problem. The Balinese who marries a Javanese woman will go through the motions of becoming Muslim. For him, having two religions doesn't cause any heartbreak …

But if he marries a Muslim Javanese woman, she has to become a Hindu, right?

Of course! Both! He will not see any contradiction! In the deepest Balinese tradition, religions are all the same. Pretending to become a Muslim is of no fundamental importance. The important thing is the *purusa*,[238] the position of the male.

This is not the case with Muslims, no question of pretending!

No, of course not. But strictness among Muslims is recent. Until a few decades ago, some Muslim Balinese villagers still did not object giving their daughters in marriage to their Balinese neighbors. This of course depended on their degree of Islamization, their relationship with the Balinese, and the origin of these populations. For example, in Loloan, West Bali, local Muslims, more tied to the archipelago's Islamic networks, were more strict. On the other hand, in other Muslim kampongs, in Tabanan, Mengwi, Denpasar, where Muslims have long been affiliated with local princely houses, this sort of exchange of women happens more often.

Today, complete sincerity is required from a candidate for conversion to Islam.

Yes, more and more, with official documents to back it up; but old habits persist. Sometimes there is a burlesque side to these religious issues, as happened with the Javanese wife of a Balinese friend of mine. She had stayed in Java for several months to take care of her dying mother. Upon her return to Bali, her Balinese husband naturally wanted to make love with her. But she refused. Not because she did not love him, but because she had been re-Islamized, and she felt that making love with him would be fornication, because he was not a Muslim. You

---

[236] *Kakawin Nitisastra*: a popular moral didactic poem in Java and Bali since the 18th century, based on an older Indian work.

[237] *Sarasamuscaya*: a sacred Hindu text originating in Java in the 9th century.

[238] *Purusa*: the masculine principle, which represents the spiritual.

can imagine the situation. I wanted to publish their story. I'm still waiting for my editor's approval.

If we come back to the differences between men and women, what prevails is ethnicity rather than gender, right? Does the Balinese woman identify more as Balinese than as a woman?

I think so. In any case, that is how she is viewed in most circles. This is also how she considers herself: it is indeed difficult to criticize the condition of Balinese women in front of more than one female Balinese intellectual. Why? Because developments are going in all directions, and changing from one environment to another. On the one hand, there are the sociological and legal developments linked to the emancipation of women through professional activities; on the other, the contradictory pressures of the ideological systems of the West versus the Indonesian state, one side advocating individual responsibility, the other, identity and the maintenance of a collective system of values.

Are you saying that change is slowed by religion?

Yes, I would say rather by religions and thus by the culture of the state. Because, here, it is not the individual who carries the values. At least, the values are not transmitted by the individual, but by communities, which are all religious by virtue of the Constitution. It is impossible to announce yourself as religiously marginal and see this marginality respected.

So, what's going on?

All in all, there is openness over the long term, but with multiple counter-current effects. Many Balinese are ready to accept the principles of equality between men and women; on the other hand, they don't want to hear about the individual responsibility advocated by the West with regard to sexuality, therefore of the use that one makes of one's body. This has an impact in particular on LGBT people, long tolerated, now officially condemned! And therefore totally marginalized.

They were present in popular performances, in movies, on television, whereas today they are expressly prohibited, following official directives.[239]

Yes, we used to laugh with them. But then they did not exist as such, as LGBT people.

We mostly laughed at them. Which was not necessarily the solution either. But today, they are invisible in the media by decree. Still, Bali still has its LGBT neighborhood ...

Now people label everything around one identity or the other ethnic, gender, sexual preferences, etc. In the past, LGBT people were accepted because they

---

[239] Since 2016, the Indonesian broadcast authority (Komisi Penyiaran Indonesia) has banned the appearance of gay people on television, including in fiction produced by the channels.

were not named. Since their difference is now identified and talked about, it is extremely difficult for them to find their place in the social system.

Why is there this cultural hiatus with the West?

Because Westerners demand recognition of the law, they want to impose their universalism, their well-delineated legal system. It works for them, but not here. Indeed, the setting of standards, the organization of thought, values, religion, etc., at first creates intolerance. Western tolerance rests on individual behavior, on the right to be different, on the recognition of difference, which is then the object of legal rulings. But traditional Indonesian tolerance is based on the fact that everything is blurry, the famous *saru-saru gremeng*. The difference is not viewed as such. However, moving from traditional tolerance to a modern one automatically creates tensions, simply because of the contact of cultures and the different way people deal with difference. People see the behavior of the West firsthand and cannot take them as role models. I'm thinking here of pedophilia in the north of the island and of those foreigners who, construing responsibility being an individual matter, take advantage of their economic superiority to permit themselves all kinds of sexual manipulation with local people. Little surprise therefore that Indonesian and Balinese modernity is taking a path other than that of sexual tolerance.

Pedophilia also exists locally ... the taste for very young girls exists everywhere in Asia. Here, it's prestigious to have a very young mistress. The expression of sexuality is not the preserve of Westerners alone.

Yes, it is not a solely Western matter. But here, it is traditional power which had complete sexual freedom; whereas with Westerners, it is political power and the power of the money that buys it. What is exercised as an individual choice by one side is inevitably seen by the other side as aggression, at least on the part of many modern Indonesians.

You spoke earlier about the "wound that never heals." Can we come back to this notion of the impurity of women and see how it has evolved historically?

Fundamentally, the notion of female impurity is related to blood, to the impurity of blood. During her period, a woman cannot go to the temple or prepare offerings. In the past, in some villages, she couldn't even sleep wherever she wanted in her own house. She was totally isolated. This is no longer the case today. There are women who hide their periods, and men who don't care ... Some Balinese will tell you: it is not the woman who is impure, but her blood, which is a way of saying: we are no longer in the patriarchy. This, it must be said, had its happy paradoxes. In pre-colonial times, if the wives of princes were expected to *masatia*,[240] that is, to throw themselves alive into the flames of their husband's cremation fire, those who had their period were exempt from this ultimate sacrifice. Impurity had its

---

[240] The last documented case of *satia* occurred in Tabanan, in 1903, when two women self-sacrificed at the cremation of the king.

advantages. Finally, I must add that the blood of men is impure, too. A wounded man is also banned from the temple.

How do you see the evolution of the status of Balinese women?

I think it's continuing to improve as their role in the economy increases, but it will be extremely slow. Decisions have been taken to give equal rights to women, especially with regard to inheritance. So, there are parents who might decide to share the *gono-gini*, that is, the goods acquired together, in an egalitarian way between boys and girls. More and more people are making donations to their daughters. But, in real social practice, in village society, which is very macho, it does not work, or it's rare. Often brothers disagree, arguing that they will be responsible for their parents, their cremations. Remember that the Balinese feel they owe their sons a debt on this issue. We must add two things, which explain the resilience of these traditional phenomena. First, the urbanized villager is still in some ways tied to his original temples in the village. This slows down change. Second, there is no unity of tradition: each village has its own ways, with differences that the villagers are proud of.

Haven't there been changes in recent years?

There is now a rewriting of customary law, for those aspects which are considered not to conform with modernity. But that doesn't mean that habits are changing. Or rather very slowly. This makes some of them more rigid. In fact, everything to do with women changes more slowly. And not just in Bali.

This could however create a new case law.

Yes, because according to the *adat* customary law, the woman is not entitled to anything. It is the *purusa*, the patriarchy, that prevails. Ancestors, property, everything passes into the male line. Women, for example, never have access to the management of the traditional village community, the *desa*.[241] Some modernists anxious to justify their tradition will say that what matters is the couple, as in the past in the West, with the notion of the hearth. But in reality, women are excluded from all the main decision-making mechanisms of the customary framework.

Is male inheritance still an important issue?

Yes, so much so that when a family does not have a male heir, it creates one through customary law by the adoption of a child or, better, the enthronement by marriage of a son-in-law in the status of *sentana*, in which he abandons his original clan and adopts that of his wife, with all the related ritual responsibilities. Many men refuse to become *sentana*. They perceive it as a humiliation. They are sometimes deemed to be mere fortune hunters.

Even among the lower castes?

---

[241] On the other hand, within the framework of the administrative village, the *desa dinas*, also called *kelurahan*, there are some village heads who are women.

Yes, of course. However, beware of the words "low caste". There have always been villages in Bali where the stratification imposed on them by the descendants of Majapahit was refused. There is a strong substratum of traditional village democracy. We often don't see it, fascinated as we often are by the splendor of the great principalities. People of such villages refused the caste system. If one day they saw a guy arrive on their territory, for example a prince on the run who had slept with one of the wives of a king, they might grant him asylum, but on the condition that he give up his prerogatives. He was accepted but lost his titles of nobility. But it was not lost in memory. You still meet common people who say, "Actually, I am descended from such and such a king, and I lost my caste title by settling here." I would say that in the sociological reality of most Balinese villages, the rule of law of the upper castes is refused. But this is not a new phenomenon.

In practice, inheritance through sons means that as long as families make daughters, they continue to have children ...

Yes.

In the time of the *Orde Baru*, the family planning slogan read: "Two children is enough," but here it has never had much effect – what matters is having sons. In fact, Governor Wayan Koster recently said that the Balinese can have up to four children today ...

That is for demographic reasons, to offset the number of *pendatang*.

So, social classes replacing castes, is there a concept, a political discourse, which would justify this change?

Almost no one writes about the caste system these days, but when it appears, it is only with reference to normative Hinduism, that of the **Vedas**. Generally, people avoid conflict by staying in the *saru-saru gremeng*, the vague, a kind of artistic vagueness about important things. For example, the term "twice born" (*dwijati*) formerly reserved for Brahmin priests may now be officially recognized for high priests without *brahmana* descent, but nobody makes much fuss about it. However, avoid talking to Brahmins about this.

And at the political level, what is the discourse?

Frankly, nobody talks about it in the political sphere either. It is not an issue. Of course, if one takes a sociological perspective, there are economic, and hence class advantages linked to caste status. The first Balinese to urbanize and thus become modern were people from the upper castes. Now it's the common people's turn to go to the city, but it was originally an opportunity for the upper castes. This means that in the heart of Denpasar, it is often high caste people who control much of the space natives of Ubud, Klungkung, Tabanan and elsewhere who, in the 1930s, came to settle in the city.

What was their motivation?

Usually, as members or sons of the elites, it was to study and work in the colonial administration. Some even went to study on other islands in Probolinggo, Malang, Makassar ...

Yes, the local elites collaborated with the occupier, like everywhere in the world.

Yes, but this is also where they forged links with other princely families in Java and elsewhere, alliances that would be at the origin of Indonesian nationalism. The Balinese also started to express themselves more and more in Malay,[242] and this is where another sociological foundation of Indonesian nationalism lies. It is important to point all this out. What the West has also changed here was the discourse, as I said earlier, with the grand ideas of the Enlightenment and Marxism with its theories of conflict and social class. By the way, it is no coincidence that after the banishment of Marxism in 1965-1966, the old social stratification was somewhat resumed, but the fabric was already shredding. Things are evolving now without any blockage, without the ideologies of conflict, contradiction, liberation. I sometimes wonder if this is not better!

It is difficult to imagine that Marxism ever had a voice in this island! What a shock!

It is true that, with Marxism, some Balinese espoused Western illusions. Yet, without analytical Marxism, something is missing now: an instrument to evaluate politics and analyze social structure. But regarding political Marxism, should we reintroduce it into Indonesia? No way! We saw the results in Cambodia!

Isn't it postmodernism that has replaced Marxism here?

Yes! Postmodernism has brought to light the illusions of modernism, i.e., the promises of communism, progress, etc. It has criticized universalism and the mono-linearity of evolution, denounced by Jacques Derrida[243] and others in their time. Yet, since according to this theory universalism does not exist, the deconstruction dear to postmodernists has been directed toward Western intrusion, in the name of criticism of the standardization of social, political, cultural, or sexual behavior. Fine! The paradox is that among these Indonesian critics of the *narasi besar*[244] or the grand narratives of the West, there are many Muslims! In this case, they forget that the *narasi besar* of Islam is not bad either! It is even more absolute because it does not often tolerate criticism!

Has the caste system always been frozen in its structure?

---

[242] Malay already existed as a lingua franca in traditional port areas.

[243] Jacques Derrida (1930-2004) created and developed the school of thought called deconstructionism.

[244] *Narasi besar*: literally "big story". Reference to the concept of "meta-narrative" by French philosopher Jean-François Lyotard (1924-1998), according to which there are systems for explaining history.

Yes and no. It's very complicated.[245] At the historical roots of it, there is a system of three upper castes of Indian origin, the *triwangsa*: *brahmana*, *satria* and *wesia*. Below are the *sudra wangsa*, the common people. There is another more indigenous classification, between *menak* and *jaba*. The *menak* are the *triwangsa* aristocrats, while the *jaba* constitute the populace, those outside the court; therefore, the *sudra*. Among the aristocrats, the king was the Dalem, "of the interior," associated with the deities. There are also the *soroh*. These are clan groups. And some of these groups are considered more indigenous than others. There are the Pasek, for example, who are not related to the Majapahit. They are of local origin.

It's a very common name in Bali.

Yes, this is one of the more widespread clan groups, like the Pande, the metal smiths. Between them, there are the Dewa, the Gusti, all kinds of more or less hierarchical sub-clans. Each clan has its temple of origin. Each family has its ancestral temple in the household itself, then another in the village for the local clan, in the region for the large clan group, then yet another at the foot of the mountain, to take souls to the mountain of the ancestral origins at the end of the cremation rituals. In every region or former political space, there is the *pura penataran* temple, which is often the temple of the local principality. There the clan hierarchy is often reproduced in the hierarchy of ancestral altars. And this same hierarchy rules over the rites.

Are all Balinese fully aware of these subtleties?

Yes, and increasingly more so ... They often even try to find their ancestors, having forgotten where they came from! They knew their origins from this or that temple a few kilometers from their home, but they no longer knew where they came from further afield. One often finds such people at the *balian* in search of their lineage, eager to reintegrate into a clan network ...

So, you confirm that today there is a general revival of interest in the past among the Balinese?

I think so, in the Balinese past, that of the clan chronicles. Except among certain intellectuals who claim that it does not make sense, who refuse or diminish the importance of ancestor worship. These are being re-Indianized in a new modern way, and they sometimes transform their ritual accordingly. Some of them become members of Indian sects, such as Sai Baba, based in Bali. They join Indian rites, join ashrams.

Where do these "reformers" express themselves?

They are quite powerful. There are tens of thousands of them. They make themselves

---

[245] There is no question here of exhausting the complexity of the subject or of comparing Balinese and Indian castes. Remember, however, that the colonial Dutch interfered with the castes. They have since lost all legal status.

heard, they have their own centers in Bali. Many also go to India to learn, directly to Sai Baba or some other spiritual center. This circulation of Balinese in international Hinduized spaces is a real phenomenon.

How is the individualization brought about by the West theorized? Is it rejected? What do people fear behind this individualization?

It is rejected only when it becomes uncomfortable. For example, when it induces a loss of control over women. If women are allowed to make choices that are based individually and no longer by society, they escape control. Groups of Balinese women are expected to clean around the temples and villages; their presence is required in the community, so they must not stand out as individuals and make their own choices. So, usually the shift toward sects and Neo-Hinduism is on the part of the couple, in an urban environment.

The age of marriage, both for men and for women, has been pushed back in the last 50 years or so. Isn't this a sign of the individualization of women?

Yes, I think so. Among the people who demand more autonomy, obviously many are women. For good reasons: if they work, they integrate more easily into modernity than men. They have better time management and are more reliable. Now we hear women talking about a lot of things, including sexual violence.

Modernity offers women a more rewarding position than the one they traditionally occupied.

Work gives ordinary women better marriage possibilities. But in Bali, as elsewhere in Indonesia, smart young women find it difficult to meet men not only at their level, but who accept them. In fact, many intellectual women are not married.

This phenomenon exists everywhere in the world, including in the West.

Yes, the man finds it difficult to accept the woman in a position of strength. But there is also the customary world, worse for women here in Bali than in Javanese Islam, even though the spread of Sharia law in Java is beginning to negatively influence the division of property between male and female heirs.[246]

Are there modern and free-thinking Balinese?

It depends on what you mean by those terms. If we mean resolutely individualized and indifferent to religion, there are no doubt very few. Even Balinese who live among foreigners in the south of the island remain steeped in tradition. The modernity of Bali, in its depths, is very recent, only thirty or forty years old;

---

[246] What can we say to old parents who gather their children to announce to them: "My children, we have decided to share our goods according to the law of the Prophet: one part for our sons, half a part for our daughters," thus rendering obsolete the egalitarian sharing of the Javanese tradition?

it came with the development of education on top of economic changes. It is a little older in the north of the island, where the Dutch formed the first local elites at the end of the 19th century. It was in this region that the first criticism of the caste system and perverse aspects of Balinese tradition emerged. There the Dutch let traditional structures evolve on their own, whereas in the south they propped them up to develop tourism, in the 1920s and '30s, leading to today's overvaluation of the tradition.

How do the Balinese justify their traditions?

It's complex. In terms of cultural referent, what was generally called the "Balinese religion" thirty years ago, and to which I refer most often, was communicated in the tradition of the Javanized villages of Bali. Here we have the *lontar* manuscripts, known only to a minority, and the shadow-puppet theatre, through which were disseminated the key aspects of the tradition. It was from these two channels that Javano-Indianized thought spread, in a symbolic and rather vague form. What is fascinating about Bali is this continuum of assimilation of concepts coming from India, over a long period.

Very long indeed!

Yes. And this happened both from the Javanese universe toward that of the remote Bali Aga village for more than five hundred years, and also, today, from the neo-Indianizing world toward that of the Javanese and of the Bali Aga. This phenomenon of syncretism is extraordinary by its historical duration.

Was there never a break? Is syncretism still working?

Yes. So far, there have never been any real ideological, theological, and social barriers formally separating groups in the name of their differences except in the modern case of the communists. That said, you have to be careful. It is possible that this case, far from being an aberration, is in fact, over the long historical period, the first of a series of historical breaks still to come, around identity, religion (or religions). Unless it is the opposite, that the traditional *gado-gado* continues, that Bali continues to have no real, hard ideological anchor point and that, once past the fashion for identity, syncretism returns in force, perhaps under the aegis, itself potentially syncretic, of the national Pancasila and its multiple interpretations. This is what I hope for.

The confrontation of Bali with the West was of a completely different nature in the north and the south of the island. On the one hand, there was the colonizer, while on the other, there was the tourist.

Yes, the way of integrating the West was different. In Singaraja it was the ruler, while in the south, in Ubud in particular, it was the ...

The vacationer!

No, the cosmopolitan and famous artist, moreover serving the palace! The palaces received visiting Westerners into the traditional system, such as Walter Spies and his cohorts. In Bali there has always been a well-established tradition of welcoming strangers into the eco-political system. When the Bugis,[247] for example, arrived on the coasts of Bali to escape the Dutch who had just seized Makassar at the end of the seventeenth century, they were hired as mercenaries by the princely houses. In Loloan, the mercenaries were refugees from Malaya. As for the Chinese, they brought various techniques and tools which were used by the Balinese, in particular firearms. Indeed, why did Ubud succeed in expanding its territory at the end of the 19th century? Because its warriors had guns. All these foreigners were originally confined to the spaces allotted to them. They all nonetheless eventually integrated.

What can we say about the Bali Aga?

Generally speaking, they are gathered in villages where ancient rites and beliefs have been preserved, thus escaping the Javanization of post-1343.

You say "Javanization". Is that on purpose? Don't you mean "Hinduization"?

In a sense, they were already Hindu, even though they have their own village pantheons. There had been inflows from ancient India via Java, dating back to the first millennium. When people study the Bali Aga today in Bali, there is always reference to Rsi Markandeya,[248] who, according to legend, was the first to Hinduize the island. The Bali Aga themselves, at least some intellectuals among them, are also reconstructing their history. They redefine themselves according to certain mythical characters. So, there, too, you have the real and the new Bali Aga, concerned with identity, as with other Balinese, but with a different discourse.

"Identity"! Can you expand?

Well, for example, there is the village of Tenganan, which continues today as it is idealized by my friend, the biologist and researcher Georges Breguet,[249] or as shown by the way Bali Aga people are being re-Hinduized: now, Hindu missionaries go to the Bali Aga to teach them the good word by *dharma wacana*.[250] They are expected to stop burying their dead and to burn them instead. Their temples are being reshaped so that they contain an altar of the One God. This is happening right now.

How are the Bali Aga different from other Balinese?

---

[247] *Bugis*: ethnic group from South Sulawesi.

[248] Rsi Markandeya: legendary Shivaite priest from southern India, who is said to have arrived in the Indonesian archipelago in the 8th century. He is said to be the founder of the mother temple of Besakih, at the foot of Mount Agung.

[249] Georges Breguet: Swiss genetic researcher with a degree in human biology and author of numerous studies on the anthropological origin of Bali Aga.

[250] *Dharma wacana*: religious preaching, usually in a traditional environment.

The Bali Aga never integrated the Javanese culture of the Balinese principalities that emerged from the conquest of the island in the 14th century. Starting with social structures. The Bali Aga do not have caste stratification, the *wangsa*. Their privileged class is that of the descendants of the founders, real or mythical, of the villages. It was also a time when populations were evolutionary. When these increased, families would move to vacant land a few kilometers away. The *barong* of these villages were often affiliated with each other. These were democratic village societies with the seniority of families as a factor determining privileges and responsibilities.

And with the arrival of the customs and traditions of Java, of Majapahit?

This is where the caste system comes in. It means that language distinguishes people from each other according to their caste. Social status is now present at all times.

What's happening to the Bali Aga in today's modernity?

As I just said, some complain of being attacked by Parisada Hindu Dharma,[251] which wants to make good Hindus out of them! It happens through school, too. And this is reflected in particular in the establishing of new altars in the temples of Bali Aga villages. For example, the *padmasana*, which did not previously exist among the Bali Aga.[252] Nowadays, we see it more and more! Except in villages which more or less consciously resist this process of Indianization.

Are there many Bali Aga, also called "Bali Mula," today?

They represent only 1% of the island's population. People know their mythical villages, like Tenganan or Trunyan, but there are also more importantly clans which are integrated into Javanese spaces and which in fact refute the caste system. The percentage of Balinese villages and clans that reject the caste system is much higher.

---

[251] Parisada Hindu Dharma: Indonesian Hindu Affairs Council founded in 1959.
[252] There was often a bamboo altar dedicated to Surya, the Sun, or Siwa, the embodiment of pantheistic Oneness.

10. Morality, Ethics, Customs, Tradition, Religion

> Has morality strengthened? Locally, people think of balance between conflicting rather than moral forces. Do people accommodate good and evil? Loyalty to the group is foremost; the notion of morality is relative, Jean Couteau reminds us. The intervention of invisible forces is stronger than individual responsibility. As elsewhere, there are normative codes and here the collective standard operates. Words that relate to morals are often of foreign origin, Jean continues. In terms of ethics, however, in Bali as elsewhere, one must also comply with the practices and customs, with propriety, I point out. Yes, but here the notion of karma pervades mentalities. As a result, one must be on the side of the Good; modern Hinduism has left its mark, even if the old Balinese tradition, different, remains over-idealized. We look into the issues of Balinese identity and Indonesian identity as well as the popularity of President Jokowi in Bali. Balinese tradition has a totalitarian aspect: each village can enact its own rules. The tradition exerts a terrible pressure from childhood; one does not escape the group; a Balinese is never alone. There are fines for non-compliance with community duties. We consider the mechanisms of *banjar*, villages, rites: how do they work? Then other questions appear: what are the obligations due to the community? Are there women priests? We also evoke the demographic pressure of outsiders on customs, and we finish on the recent prohibition of plastic bags in shops and the way it is integrated, or not, in the community psyche.

ERIC BUVELOT. What do we mean by "moral," by "propriety," from a Balinese point of view?

JEAN COUTEAU. From a Balinese perspective, it is not the truth that matters, it is loyalty to the group first. This means that even if someone does something stupid, the village will always take their side. This is a fundamental principle. If your village is in conflict with another village, let alone with people from outside Bali, you are forced to side with your village. Traditionally, if it occurs to you to hold a contrary opinion, you will find yourself exposed to community sanction with, at its maximum, the inability to gain access to the cremation grounds for you and your family. It means that the souls of your dead will not find their way toward sublime peace and will fail to end up in the ancestors' abode above the mountains. All this is important and forces us to relativize the notion of morality in the case of the Balinese. Loyalty comes first.

In this case, can individual responsibility exist?

Indeed, these are collective standards; but the notion of individual responsibility is another story. There is loyalty, certainly, but there is also the belief that people are subject to forces that are beyond their control. For example, if your daughter loses her virginity to the village Don Juan, it may not be her fault. You may well think that she was bewitched, victim of invisible forces. The guy had a ring that gave him magical powers she was unable to counter. Here we are witnessing the intervention of the *niskala*. So, what do you do in a such case? You go see a *balian*, who will then try to compensate for the power that has come into play here with his own manipulation of invisible powers. So, there are definitely forces which are stronger than individual responsibility.

But are there still codes of conduct?

Yes, there are normative codes, but not moral codes in the rigid sense of Western morality. These are codes that define the way of being together, the constraints of the group, the village, the *banjar*, the clan. Of course, I am exaggerating a little: it is obvious that Balinese society is modernizing and that the notion of individual responsibility is more and more present. There are some psychologists and psychiatrists in Bali, although very few become a super-*balian*, like the most famous of them.[253] There is therefore a tension between these two sets of norms, the traditional one and the modern one.

Yes, because individualization brings its share of new behaviors.

We see this in aspects of modernity, in economic behavior, in judgments relating to corruption, indeed in sexuality, gender. But, in the final instance, in cases of corruption, even in criminal cases,[254] what often matters more is the loyalty to the group. Priority is given to the interests of a narrow group, whether connected to the family or the village, rather than to the wider social circle of the nation.

Let's come back to this notion of forces which are beyond us. It also works in forced marriages, as we have already seen.

Absolutely, when a woman does not want to marry the suitor who is imposed on her or who imposes himself on her, she is sometimes said to be the victim of magic.[255] This is a matter to be dealt with through ritual. She is put under pressure by the *balian*'s help, and, after a few days, she is broken and finally gives in. It is the collective standard that takes over here.

How much of this is still valid today?

Difficult to say because, for the same individual, both sets of behavior are operative now. There are times when he reacts in a modern way, driven by an expectation of honesty and independence, then there are other times when he

---

[253] Luh Ketut Suryani, psychiatrist and influential figure in Balinese social and political life, also founder of the Suryani Institute for Mental Health Foundation.

[254] There are (non-)legal consequences to this loyalty. The press, although it sometimes reports lynchings, never announces the verdict or the names of the lynchers: the village is solidly united.

[255] This is most famously depicted in *Tresnané lebur ajur satonden kembang* by Jelantik Santha, 1981.

will react in a more traditional way. How important are modern behaviors? Hard to say. Sociologically, I would say that between 20% to 30% of the population has modern behaviors, mainly among urbanites. This does not mean that these people do not have times when they are subject to traditional beliefs. Such beliefs have been in the depths of their psyches since infancy; this is especially true for people over forty, whose mind has been shaped by a different Bali: Bali before the car, the cell phone, education …

An example?

A guy has a road accident. He hits a motorbike with his car and the rider dies. How is it interpreted? It wasn't the driver who killed the motorcyclist, it was the *niskala* forces at work. The one who died was destined to die because he had left the "field of pain," the Balinese purgatory of his previous incarnation, before having fully paid his debt. The same with the story of the guy who killed his father with a keris during a trance ceremony, two years ago. In cases like this, individual responsibility is not part of the interpretation. And events are concretely linked by karma across the incarnations.

Are there other aspects of morality?

One thing to note is that words relating to morality are mostly of foreign origin. *Adat, ethos, moral, karma, tatua,*[256] are of Arabic, European, and Indian origin.

Does that mean that locally, people haven't thought about these concepts, these notions?

Traditionally people see things in different terms: as a matter of balance between contradictory *niskala* invisible forces. If someone finds himself in a situation of imbalance, it is because destructive forces have taken control of his personality. These forces must therefore be countered. Hence the importance of offerings, and of locating the causes at the level of the *niskala* world; hence, too, the importance of the *balian* (shamans) to identify what is going wrong.

Do people then adapt to Evil as well as to Good? Is it a balance?

It's a kind of balance. I don't think we have to conceptualize all of this. This is one of the problems in the West, there is a tendency to put conceptual barriers where there are none. But, yes, it's a balancing act, which doesn't mean that people aren't aware of what's right and what's wrong. But Good as opposed to Evil, with a barrier between the two, is indeed a concept of recent origin here, introduced by the Western and Arab legal and religious systems.

Here are two cultures where Evil must be defeated!

There is also the notion of karma, although it is also ultimately of foreign origin.

---

[256] *Tatua*: religious philosophy.

It is the notion that there are always consequences to one's actions. But it is not karma in the Indian Hindu sense of the word. Here it often refers to what the Balinese call *karma cicih*, that is, the consequences of our actions during our life, and not afterwards. Furthermore, it is different from the kind of karma that subjects the soul to a *samsara*[257] cycle of reincarnation. Being reincarnated as a dog or a maggot does not seem to trouble the minds of the Balinese, since they believe that they reincarnate among their own descendants. Ancestor worship is clearly more important than formal Hinduism. In Balinese stories, one is at worst judged at the entrance of purgatory by Sang Suratma, the equivalent of Saint Peter; one is then tortured in the *tegal penyangsaran* (temporary hell/purgatory) for x years; and then one returns among his own. Where? In Bali.

Is that changing today?

Yes, more and more with the spreading of the new formal Hindu reading of religion. This implies the idea that one might not be reincarnated among his own people depending on the quality of his actions.

Are there political consequences of all this?

Yes, and here we come back to the notion of the lack of individual responsibility. If you obey the requests of your group, you also obey those of your master. This accounts to a large extent for the anti-communist massacres of 1965-66. At that time, a whole ideological apparatus was called in, sometimes of Indian origin: the massacres were but the consequence of the exercise of *darma*.[258] In the *Bhagavad Gita*,[259] you have to side with your *darma*, duty, even if it means you have to kill your cousins; this is the case with Arjuna. It's agonizing, but you do your duty and you kill.

In this case, aren't we witnessing a struggle between Good and Evil?

Yes and no. The *darma* is not only Good, it is also duty and religion. I am going to play the advocate of postmodernity: modernity here has built narrow binary classifications. Traditionally, the Balinese did not need intellectual consistency to justify their actions.

Yes, but in Bali as elsewhere, we must nonetheless comply with habits and customs, propriety, good manners, *adat* ...

Ah! *Adat* is something else! It is an Arabic word re-appropriated by the Dutch to mean "customary law." What did they do with this law? They recognized it in order to better formalize and restructure it according to their interests. In Java, the primary focus was on enabling planters to use village land. In Bali, the

---

[257] *Samsara*: the cycle of reincarnations in the formal Hindu tradition.

[258] *Darma* (also *dharma*): it is a question here of the duty corresponding to one's position.

[259] *Bhagavad Gita*: central part of the epic poem Mahabharata and one of the fundamental writings of Hinduism. The text was not known to the Balinese before Independence, but the story of Arjuna's dialogue with Krishna was already known through the *wayang* shadow-puppet theatre.

intrusion was less violent, but just as real. This involved modernizing or even banning certain "inhuman" customs, such as the sacrifice of widows and the abduction of women, or tidying up caste titles. Bali had to be "paradise".

And after Independence?

Yes, the Balinese continued to standardize *adat*, especially by producing a written version of it. The Majelis Adat Bali[260] determines what is acceptable with regard to modernity and what is not. It has been around since the *Orde Baru*. In fact the situation is very complicated. Because, despite all efforts, many elements of the old *adat* still endure, including the more backward ones. Another factor is that customs differ from village to village; the Balinese pride themselves on this and say that this is part of their cultural richness. But, at the same, Balinese customary law, now written down and renamed *adat*, tends to transmute into an instrument of modernity, aimed at ensuring the sustainability of cultural identity in a Bali increasingly jostled by tourism.[261]

In the ancient *lontar* texts, wasn't there any guide to peoples' behavior? A written text ...

There were many. People were told how to behave toward their father, toward power, and so forth. For example, there was the code of the *suputra*, the good son, who had to obey his four masters, the *catur guru*: his father, his biological master; his teacher, master of knowledge; his lord, master of power; and, finally, God, his sublime master. The code of the *catur guru* used to be constantly repeated in the shadow-puppet theatre, so it permeated mentalities. Remember that it was through the theatre that the norms concerning the village, the temples, traditional practices, etc. were transmitted, usually during the intervention of the clowns, who appeared after the central characters in the story.[262]

How does one get acquainted with these standards today if shadow theatre is becoming rarer?

It is the schools now that transmit the social standards. But it's not the same. The main principles are now religious: the *panca sradha* of the Hindu religion.[263] They were introduced in Bali from the beginning of the 20th century and take up the pattern of Indian reformism. A modern Hinduism, therefore, with one God who has little in common with tradition, and which is superimposed on

---

[260] Majelis Adat Bali: council on Balinese customary law.

[261] See *Bali: Cultural Tourism and Touristic Culture* by Michel Picard, Editions Didier Millet (1996).

[262] One speaks in the play of the behavior of the *suputra*, the good son, the one who respects the *catur guru*.

[263] *Panca sradha*: respectively: 1) belief in one God (principle of Brahman); 2) belief in the soul (*atman*); 3) belief in the principle of *karmapala* (every act carries consequences); 4) belief in the principle of *punarbhawa* (reincarnation); and 5) belief in *moksa* (final liberation).

the rites and prayers of the old traditional ways.[264] Formerly people practiced *sesontengan*,[265] that is, they addressed their prayers in Balinese, with no particular form, to the ancestors, to a *hyang* or spirit of any place, god of the river, of the tree, of the mountain, etc., or to an unspecified Ratu Gede, according to the needs of the moment. In the mountains, there was also the master of the sky, Ratu Tangkeb Langit. That was in remote villages. Meanwhile in the princely palaces and the *brahmana* houses, there were, of course, the gods of India, but they were discreet, except when they donned their habit of the older cults. In other words, in the Bali of old, the oneness of the divine was not a problem and the issue was never raised. Now, even if the local Balinese deities still endure, they are increasingly made into *manifestasi* of the supreme God,[266] and the original names are being erased. There is a long slide towards monotheism, increasingly colored by Indian Hindu reformism.

Apart from school, are there other means and institutions that play a role in this transformation?

Yes, there are sermons, which are increasingly popular as universities produce more religious graduates, and cell phones and social media become more popular. The first sermons appeared on TV in the 1990s, organized by the Department of Religious Affairs; then there were the sermons of the *pedanda* Made Gunung on Bali TV. Now, more and more sermons are organized on the occasion of important religious festivals and involve *sulinggih* high priests, some of whom have become talented orators, mixing humor and religious teaching.

So, it's a bit like the theatre.

Yes and no. Yes, in the sense that it is the return of the power of speech, as it used to be, when clowns intervened between episodes of the story to remind people of their ritual obligations. No, in the sense that the content is totally different. The content is no longer as it once was, the myth and its heroes; it is religious norms, definition after definition, interspersed with jokes.

So, there is a fundamental difference.

Essentially, yes. We are in the process of moving, with school, sermons, cell phones, and new media, from a religion based on the symbol, implicitly emanating from the narrative fact of the theatre, to a religion based on the principle, emanating from teaching. There is a shift from the relative to the absolute and, if one isn't careful, from tolerance to intolerance. This transition is that much faster and more dramatic as cell phones kill the old Balinese memory, anchored in the theatre. The

---

[264] *Panca Sembah*: the five (new) ways to pray thought to have been designed in the 1960s by I Gusti Ketut Kaler.

[265] *Sesontengan*: term for traditional invocations in the Balinese language, while the mantras are in Kawi, and now in Sanskrit.

[266] The prayers are focused on the one God, Sang Hyang Widi Wasa, often through one of his *istadewata* (manifestations), whose original expression is in Sanskrit, therefore Indian.

wayang shadow play has become rare and everyone has a cell phone. The mutation is accelerating, with the attendant risks.

What do you mean?

All this creates ruptures. Cell phones and social media are not only transforming the space and content of religion, but dramatizing it. It is not only Neo-Hindu reformism that benefits from YouTube, but also the reaction against this reformism. Certain Balinese see in the current rise of Neo-Hinduism as a threat against the traditional worship of the ancestors, which remains at the heart, if not of the interpretative system, at least of the ritual practice of the Balinese.

What then does this ancestor worship consist of?

In the Balinese tradition, life is a passage waiting for a return. The ancestral soul descends from the mountain heights, is embodied in one of its descendants, and must maintain an existence balanced by rites addressed to the gods, ancestors, and lower forces. Any imbalance and, in particular, any neglect of one's obligations towards the ancestors, results in misfortune. Visits to *balian* (shamans), in particular after a birth, death, or a calamity, maintain the link with the dead and make it possible to identify the problems and then restore, in ritual, the lost balances. Complex funerary rites cremation, dispersing the ashes into the sea, etc. allow the soul of the deceased to reach the "old country" above the mountains, awaiting a new incarnation.

So, there is no question of reincarnation according to one's karma, nor of gods from the Hindu tradition?

Very little. During trance, it is never the Indian Hindu gods who seize the individual. These are Balinese deities, with typical Balinese names. The Hindu gods, say the old texts,[267] did come from India, transferring "pieces of Mount Meru" (the Mahameru) from India to Java, then from Java to Bali, but they remain on their mountains. Unlike the local gods, they do not intervene in rites or trances.

What does that imply?

This means that historically the structured theories of formal Hinduism have, until very recently, hardly penetrated the local religious tradition. These theories are found only in narrow erudite circles, in particular of *brahmana*. Their motto was to not reveal the content of mantras and sacred manuscripts in their possession. *Aja wera*, do not reveal our knowledge, they said; and indeed the power of the *pedanda* priesthood is largely based on the esoteric aspect of their knowledge.

But don't the Balinese know the Indian gods?

---

[267] In the *Tantu Pegelaran* text for Java and the *Babad Pasek* chronicle for Bali, the mantras mention by name the gods of the different mountains, where the gods transferred from India and Java are said to reside.

Certainly, they do, these gods inhabit the theatre. They are the actors of the great myths. They are also the remote architects of the cosmos. But they are not the ones who determine the day-to-day. They are present, but over there, in the distance ...

And, coming back to our discussion, is it this system of ancestor worship that Neo-Hindus are transforming?

Yes, more or less consciously, because there are a lot of intermediate attitudes. But formally, ancestor worship, however dominant in Balinese ritual, is not one of the basic tenets of official Hinduism. And as long as someone emphasizes this difference between Balinese tradition on the one hand, with its ancestor worship, and official Hinduism on the other, there is a potential clash.

But nobody talks about it?

So far, very little, as the Balinese are not fond of formal rhetoric and don't care about contradictions. But, with the teaching of official Hinduism, which is now spreading in the villages, this may be changing, if we are to believe at least what happened recently with Nusa Penida and its ancestral gods.

Can you explain?

Wedakarna, known to be a great defender of Hinduism, recently declared that the ancestral gods of the temple Dalem Peed, in Nusa Dua, known for their magical powers, were in fact only saints (*makhluk suci*), and not real gods. No sooner had his statement made the rounds of social networks than a series of trances took place in that temple, with priests and worshippers swearing to fight to the death in defense of their gods. We can clearly see the toxic effect of the over-dramatization generated by social networks.

Did everyone join in?

No, far from that. But, presently, there is undoubtedly a high level of intellectual and religious activities that is widening the social space occupied by official Hinduism. Some people set out to discover Indian philosophy, or seek its traces in ancient Javanese texts. Others, often tired by the ritual demands of village life, or seduced by the notion of karma and the sophisticated cosmological pantheism found in Indian tradition, withdraw instead into *bhakti*, that is, their main gods are no longer the ancestors but rather the masters of the cosmos. This is what recruiters from sects from India such as Sai Baba, Hare Krisna, Brahma Kumaris or Ananda Marga, all of which have their Balinese chapter are waiting for. Hindu gurus of all sorts now abound, not to mention the New Age gurus on the prowl for Western followers, such as the famous Ratu Bagus, who practices shaking yoga in an ashram in Muncan.

On another subject, does the feeling of national belonging contradict that of ethnicity?

Absolutely not. We must dispel the illusions of Westerners that the Balinese are against Muslims, against national sentiment, against other Indonesians, etc. Westerners who think that the Balinese want independence are deeply misled. Being Balinese is not at all contradictory to being Indonesian. Many deeply Hindu Balinese are in fact hard-leaning nationalists. It is the "Pancasila-ist" state that protects against Islamism and which enables Hinduism be present in Sumatra, Borneo and elsewhere in Indonesia.

Is the popularity of President Joko Widodo in Bali proof of this?

Absolutely! In fact, the Balinese have been so good at asserting their rights that they recently managed to get the president to grant state university status to Universitas Hindu Indonesia. They know how to use national institutions and their "modernizing" spirit to demand and obtain reforms of the local tradition for example, on the subject of women's rights, or in certain constraints of custom which are considered backward. Criticism of tradition in the name of Pancasila which indeed protects their religion goes down much better in Bali than criticism in the name of Islam or the West. One example is the case of male-female twins born to common people, which traditionally results in the family being banished from the village.[268]

Such banishment has not been enforced for a long time!

To the contrary, there was a case in Buleleng recently. There are still many villagers who believe that male-female twins create impurity and therefore bring calamity to the village. More generally, these phenomena generate tensions. *Adat* is on the one hand idealized, in the name of identity, but it is also expected by others, such as Windia[269] to follow "universal" humanist standards in the name of modernity. All of this stirs things up and conflicts sometimes arise.

If *adat* is idealized, it is not without reason.

Yes, even though there are sometimes abuses, the spirit of *adat* is the organization of collaboration among villagers. And this is where the very spirit of Balinese-ness is revealed: the organization of associations of which all Balinese are members: clan (*soroh*), village (*desa*), neighborhood (*banjar*), this or that temple or dance group. It shows an extraordinary density of togetherness and sociability.

It is idealized, but doesn't it entail constraints?

Yes, of course: collective work, preparation of rites and festivals, what the Balinese call *ayahan*, ritual duty. With now, its modern and constraining aspects: it often

---

[268] Banishment: male-female twins are called *manak salah* in commoner families, and are considered ritually impure; elaborate purification rites entail temporary banishment of the family to the outskirts of the village. Among aristocrats, on the contrary, male-female twins are considered a blessing, associated with the 14th-century ruling couple of Bali, Masula-Masuli, who were male-female twins.

[269] Wayan P. Windia: law professor at Udayana University and intellectual figure who proposes an open reading of tradition.

happens that Balinese, who work at the city, have to pay someone to take their place in this unpaid *ayahan* work.

Isn't this a paradox, since it introduces a capitalist practice into the exercise of community tasks?

There is indeed a paradox. The more society modernizes, the more it transforms, and despite this, the more it is idealized as a traditional society unspoiled by modernity. This is what worries me. The burdens of capitalist society will be increasingly heavy, and the question already arises whether the Balinese will be able to produce the intellectual instruments that will allow them to manage its transformations and thus overcome this paradox.

Aren't some constraints imposed on the Balinese to respect the codes of their culture accentuated today? Are the various fines and penalties for those who refuse to comply with them on the rise?

Yes, I think so. But it depends on the village. Each village has its own rules. The Balinese say: "*Desa mawa cara.*" This means that each village has its own way. They also say: "*Desa kala patra,*" meaning that things change according to "place (*desa*)," "time (*kala*)" and "circumstances (*patra*)." Things are further complicated by the fact that the notion of what a village is covers different realities and varies from place to place. In some parts of the island, a customary village (*desa adat / desa pakraman*) has only one *banjar* as a community unit. In others, a customary village may have dozens of *banjar*, as in the customary village of Denpasar, which has, I believe, almost a hundred.[270]

So, again, there are general rules, but does each village do what it wants?

It's a bit like that, yes. With temple communities, *banjar*, villages (*desa pakraman*), clans and sub-clans, there is such a wealth of social organizations that there is no general set of rules. This is something Westerners have difficulty understanding.

So, there is a certain freedom to act differently, but within a general spirit of community?

Yes, but there is another paradox. Whereas in matters of belief, things are vague, in matters of social and ritual obligations, it is different: there is a very constricting aspect: compulsory attendance at meetings and activities, and precise definition of one's obligations towards the village and ritual for example, collective making of certain offerings; exact calculations about how many satay sticks one prepares and receives, and so forth.

Is the weight of *adat* in Bali heavier now, in the 21ˢᵗ century?

This is a complicated question. In the past, collective decisions were taken by

---

[270] Denpasar: in fact, there are 95 *banjar* in the capital of Bali. In practice; therefore, it is the *banjar* that is the heart of Balinese community and ritual organization.

consensus (*parerem*) at a general assembly (*paruman* or *sangkep*), which reflected a balance between local clans, but the decisions had the force of law. Everyone accepted. If too much tension arose between groups, they consulted, under very formal circumstances, the prince, the priest, or some other respected personage. The pageantry of this audience, the formalities, the prayers, everything gave the decision the seal of the sacred. There was no rejection of the judgment; or if so, it was open conflict.

What happened to this system?

It continues to operate to a certain extent. It is enough to see visitors from the surrounding villages present themselves in audience before Cokorda Putra, the prince of Ubud, to measure the impact of the traditional system, not on the law, but on the socio-religious life of the village.

Is it always that harmonious?

Things are changing. The administrative hold, the land conflicts resulting from the transformation of access rights to land, the fact that many *banjar* or village heads are now educated, not to mention the presence of foreigners and the introduction of the concept of human rights, all this is weakening traditional mechanisms. *Adat* is turned upside down. The customary is becoming modern.

Is it consequently threatened?

No! In the past, custom was taken for granted. But this is no longer the case; it has become a reference. But it is changing. Whereas before it was an oral tradition and unquestioned, it is now written down formalized and discussed, in relation to national and even international positions. Sometimes its sanctions are reinforced. It's interesting to observe Kuta, for example, in this regard. Most of the Balinese from Kuta are fastidious in their reading of their customs. They demand that the tourism sector respect their rights and, above all, that it makes maximum use of local skills.

I'm curious to know if Balinese try to evade their customs?

I know some who do not hesitate in private to directly mock Balinese customs. Quite a few refuse to become temple priests as required by their position in society. But it entails risks. If they fall ill, this may be interpreted as a vengeance from the ancestors for their refusal to accede to the temple priesthood. This is the whole problem! Balinese custom exerts terrible pressure, starting in childhood!

Can you have your secret garden when you are Balinese? Or is one like an open book all the time?

There's no escaping the group. Even with urbanization, even with tourism, if you go to Kuta or Denpasar, you always come across someone you know, who is part of a common network, be it kinship, school, village, or clan. A Balinese is never alone. I would even say that today, this visibility is multiplied by social networks.

There is no secret garden. If a Balinese takes a mistress, everyone knows it the next day. However, if he is a powerful man, no one will say anything. So, there are tremendous pressures to conform.

So, in this case, modernity does not destroy mutual surveillance, it even reinforces it.

Here I am going to reveal myself as a Westerner and even a bit Marxist: considering these enormous transformations, the problem is to know whether there will be a real breaking point. Or are we in a mechanism that has the capacity to adapt spontaneously? We don't know! It will ultimately depend on what happens outside of Bali.

Or perhaps it depends on the discourse that accompanies these phenomena, since, as you say, the theory that intellectualizes them does not conform to reality. If you are under an illusion, you can cope with all changes, as long as the discourse holds.

You are right, but I think it's necessary to repeat that we must avoid our Western categorizations, our absolutisms of judgment. Even if these interviews we are carrying out are to try to understand phenomena, to give definitions, I must admit that everything is still unclear.

What about the fines for failing to comply with customary duties? Are they more frequent now?

Yes, I think so. At the same time, these fines have become trivial. These transgressions of *adat* are often referred to as *dosa*, meaning "wrongdoing," but that is no longer how they are seen. It's become part of the economic system a compensation. Those who have moved to the city provide for a relative who has remained in the village to take on the work and responsibilities related to religious duties.

Capitalism at work, once again!

Absolutely. But this capitalism also takes account of local status. For example: when young people solicit donations make their *ogoh-ogoh*,[271] they post a list stating the names of donors and the amounts of the contributions. You must therefore give according to your rank, that is, if you are rich and powerful, you give more. It is not spoken: it is an implicit rule.

Is the role of the *banjar* more important today?

I see the *banjar* as what remains, what endures. And the temple communities, as well. These are the bastions of what it is to be Balinese. Banjar members meet in *paruman* every thirty-five days of the *pawukon* calendar. The *banjar* continues to manage community life and rituals very strictly. It is the "muscles"

---

[271] *Ogoh-ogoh*: large bamboo and papier-mâché monsters paraded on the eve of Nyepi, the Day of Silence.

of the *desa*, so to speak, and therefore of the village and its three core temples. But there are other temple communities, for the clan, the old principalities, the irrigation units. Each has its organization, its meetings, its obligations to contribute to this or that. The individual is at the crossroads of all these communities.

What are the obligations owed to the community, such as *gotong royong*,[272] the *poskamling*,[273] and others? Are they different today?

With the latest technology, this has evolved, especially for night surveillance of the neighborhood. There are now surveillance cameras, and even a suitable Android app that makes it easy. In principle, however, the *kelihan*[274] and the *sinoman*[275] tour the households of the place to remind designated members of the community of their duty of night patrol or vigil until the early hours of the morning on a small *bale*.[276]

I experienced this personally until the early 2000s.

There are also other traditions, those related to the temple, such as *makemit*, where a group of men have to keep watch in a temple all night long. Usually, when there is a ceremony in a village or family temple, everything is organized and decided in detail, under the aegis of a *kelihan* appointed by the community. A certain number of ritual items and food for the village must be paid for and provided for a certain number of days. These elements are very strictly accounted for by the *kelihan* and his assistants. This continues today, but this is also where there are changes.

I also wonder how sustainable all of this is in the neighborhoods of towns where the majority of people are *pendatang*. Will there be enough Balinese left in Monang Maning or Canggu to properly carry out the ritual ceremonies?

The Balinese are indeed under increasing economic pressure in these urbanized areas where the non-native population is significant. If the *banjar* decides to collect donations to pay for temple repairs or organize events, there is no assurance that the *pendatang* will agree to fund rites that are not theirs. Most often they are exempted from it against a nominal monthly contribution.

One gets the impression now that some areas of the urbanized south of the island are beyond the control of the Balinese, at least as far as religion is concerned.

---

[272] *Gotong royong*: typical Indonesian mutual aid and general interest community work.
[273] *Poskamling*: neighborhood watch post, generally active at night.
[274] *Kelihan* (or *klian*): group leader; literally "elder," from *kelih*.
[275] *Sinoman*: person responsible for communicating public announcements.
[276] *Bale*: pavilion for meeting and relaxing.

Yes, as Wahyu Nugroho, a young sociologist and admirer of Bourdieu[277] once told me, "When a Balinese has a Javanese neighbor, that's okay. When he's got three, it is still fine. But when he's got eight or ten, he moves to a new location, because he has lost his cultural capital." This is how identity ghettos are built. And it's not just in Bali.

I recently read an article in *Kompas*[278] which spoke of a supposed invasion of Bali by Westerners. The place cited as an example was Kerobokan, described by the journalist as a village, whereas it is rather a large suburb of Denpasar ...

Yes, that's right, the West brings about other types of behavior, and therefore all kinds of lifestyle changes.

He explained that in the morning, these Westerners walked around Kerobokan as if they owned the place! In short, xenophobic tirades are always popular!

It's true in a way. And yet, if you talk about xenophobia, we can also talk about xenophilia. The Balinese are hyper-tolerant towards Westerners.

Yes, but these Westerners will not automatically transform themselves into Balinese ... Moreover, the journalist further quotes an inhabitant of a Kerobokan *banjar* who recognizes that, since these foreigners are not Hindus, the local population does not expect them to come to the temple or participate in the custom.

I would say that Westerners are less and less curious about this. When I lived in Ubud, Western people of my generation were fascinated by ceremonies. A Balinese friend would tell us to come by a certain temple: there would be dances, etc., and we would go. Now the roads around temples are closed or clogged with cars and you don't know what's going on there. In the past, there were some modern aspects of course, but everything was Balinese, the music, the dance, in the whole space. We moved about on foot, there were offerings everywhere, no plastic, no cars. Today, it's over; the culture that is still exclusively "Balinese" is now only found in a limited number of physical spaces, such as around temples and within the family compound, and is limited to behaviors associated with *adat*. For the rest, it's the modern world and Indonesia.

Has the space dedicated to the community diminished?

Yes. Not so long ago, the *dalang* set up his shadow theatre on the road, there was no traffic! Now land is put up for sale, Javanese are setting up *pasar malam*,[279] foreigners are building villas.

---

[277] Pierre Bourdieu (1930-2002) is a French socio-anthropologist and philosopher whose works about social determinism have had a strong impact in late 20th-century social sciences.

[278] *Kompas*: major national Indonesian daily newspaper and television news channel, where Jean Couteau has had a regular column since 2012.

[279] *Pasar malam*: night markets.

To come back to the village. What is the definition of a *desa pakraman*, exactly?

Krama is the citizen. The *desa pakraman* is the village in the sense of community. It is a relatively recent term, whose official use dates from the law of regional autonomy introduced in the early 2000s. In the past, the term *desa adat* or "customary village" prevailed. As for the word *desa*, its original meaning is the "territory".

Why are there several types of villages?

It's a result of colonization. Thus, the *desa dinas* manages administrative affairs; its name comes from the Dutch word *dienst*, which means "service". It generally covers several *desa adat*.[280] It is the *desa adat* that the Balinese usually mean when they speak of *desa*, because it is a territorial and ritual unit. And this village normally has three communal temples: the *pura desa*, that of the territory, located upstream; *pura puseh*, that of the founding ancestors; and *pura dalem*, the temple of the dead on the downstream side. These three temples usually have the same communities of worshippers, sometimes with variations for the *pura dalem* for caste reasons.[281]

Is there an entity lower than this *desa pakraman*?

Yes, the *banjar!* Some villages have tens of thousands of inhabitants. At the neighborhood level, there is the *banjar*. The word initially means the "row" of houses. In the *banjar*, there is also a small temple, with a meeting pavilion. There is a *paruman*, a meeting, every thirty-five days. All the married men, never women! It is at the level of the banjar that the work related to ritual is decided.[282] Normally, everyone should come, at the risk of exposure to sanctions that is, fines (*dosa*). And sometimes only the *kelihan* are present.

How are decisions taken?

It varies a lot from region to region, depending on whether or not there is a princely house (*puri*) or Brahmin house (*gria*) that influences decisions. But there is a general principle. Discussions can be heated, but it is the voice of the majority that wins, without counting the prevailing voice is that with the most nods of assent. In the *desa*, this often reflects the dominant position of certain local clans, and even of certain families. The balance of power can change. This may result in

---

[280] *Desa adat*: Thus, there are 606 *desa dinas* and 1,384 *desa pakraman* (*desa adat*) in Bali, which means that one *desa pakraman*, defined by its three temples, has an average of 3,000 inhabitants. A *banjar* generally corresponds to 150-300 families. There is also a duality between the *banjar dinas*, the administrative community, and the *banjar adat*, the customary community. The customary community is socially the most important.

[281] Members of the upper castes often ask for their own cemetery and burning grounds.

[282] And also smaller divisions of the *banjar*, called *tempekan*, with about fifteen people assigned to them.

tensions, and sometimes splits.[283] But the decisions taken are always imperative.

Can you give some examples of what is being decided there?

How many satay to prepare for a ceremony, how to finance temple renovation work. How to subdivide the work to be done in common. It is often complicated, because of caste. In theory, since Independence, villagers all have the same duties and must pay the same contributions. But there are *brahmana*, for example, who do not want to be subject to the collective rules of the village temple. Why? It is normally out of the question for them to carry the corpse of a non-caste person, of a *sudra*, during a cremation. A *sudra* can carry the body of a *brahmana* or a *satria*, but the opposite is not allowed. Compelling the members of the upper castes can lead to splits. People can create a new *banjar* that brings together people from upper castes, as happened for example in Batuan. After the split, members of the upper castes therefore find themselves with their own cemetery, or corner of the cemetery. Sometimes the *triwangsa*[284] have become democratic. They pay their contributions like everyone else, but they are usually exempt from complying with certain obligations. So, there are all kinds of conflicting situations that are resolved through compromises especially since *sudra* often feel obligated by a moral debt. For example, the *brahmana* family X has provided them with their holy waters for generations. Or they were once given a piece of land by an old local aristocratic family. They may feel indebted to the Brahmin house or the palace for generations.

Does this represent some kind of eternal debt?

Admittedly, if today a *sudra* has gone to college and got a master's degree in whatever, that is indeed a game-changer.[285] In fact there are all kinds of scenarios, and this is where Balinese society is shaken. There are conflicts linked to the sale of land, to urbanization or to the establishment of minorities, including their cemeteries in communalized spaces. So, it is not surprising that the *paru/man desa*, the village meetings, are sometimes very lively.

Exactly what is the status of newly established villagers who are not Balinese?

There is the notion of *krama tamiu*, of outsider citizens, which has been developed relatively recently. But the Balinese are not very demanding in this area; they ask the newcomers to pay a monthly membership fee and that's it. Sometimes also a contribution for the repair of buildings for community structures.

---

[283] This most often occurs when some villages want to impose constraints on the local *triwangsa* (high caste) clans, who therefore create their own *banjar*. Politics also plays a role. See the magazine *Sarad* of 20 April 2010, p. 11.

[284] *Triwangsa*: members of the three upper castes (*brahmana, satria, wesia*).

[285] He could forget his grandfather's pledge to help cremate today's princes by bringing their bodies to the burning ground, a pledge made in exchange for the gift of land once made by their ancestor, the prince Cok Lingsir. Or he can go to court to transform his right of use on the same land, based on an oral gift, into a right of ownership. Education changes power relations.

This can easily become a source of conflict, as from *banjar* to *banjar* the conditions for these newcomers are not necessarily the same ...

Yes, each *banjar* is autonomous to make its own sovereign rules, and this can be misunderstood. But as soon as there is tension, the Balinese unite! However, tensions can also arise between Balinese clans, and a local family may be prohibited from using the local cemetery. Land can also be seized if it is considered to belong to the village. There are all kinds of retaliatory measures.

What else must one know about the villages today?

Perhaps it's that there are all kinds of temples and temple congregations in the villages at the level of the territorial village, rice fields, old principalities, clans. There are also the communities of the great temples of the island, the *kahyangan*. The intersections between these communities of devotees are extremely complex. And this is where Bali endures, with *banjar* and *desa adat* at the heart of the system. As long as this system persists, and adapts, Bali will remain Bali.

Doesn't this whole system lack coherence and unity?

It is true that there have been attempts to harmonize traditional customs since the Dutch times. Things that were considered not to conform to modern humanism, such as kidnapping a young woman to marry her by force, or the option to execute a person by throwing them into the sea, have become illegal. However, the implementation of reforms is not always obligatory or even possible. Transforming the status of women is more complicated than a simple question of inheritance. Who is in charge of the ancestral temple? It is the youngest of the sons, except for aristocrats, in which case it is the eldest. And he is under strain a rationale that conservatives point to for maintaining the permanence of male power. The Dutch first, then Suharto's *Orde Baru*, and now democracy have all tried to formalize Balinese custom in their own way and to modernize it.

Has it paid off?

Yes, there are trends emerging a tendency to monogamy, to the registration of marriages in the civil record, the appearance of personal choices as to religion and way of life. And the establishment of a national administrative system which is increasingly efficient and effective, and which is difficult to evade today. There are also more and more people who have completed their studies and are returning to the village educated. But the formal status of women is always dependent on *pradana*[286] being subjected to *purusa,* the masculine.

How does one become a *mangku*?[287]

They usually become so because of an intervention by the *niskala*, during a

---

[286] *Pradana*: the material.
[287] *Mangku* or *pamangku* = temple priest. Only born once (*ekajati*), unlike the twice-born (*dwijati*) high-priest (*sulinggih*).

ceremony. A *jero tapakan* or equivalent is called upon, that is, a man or a woman who is *melik*, who has the power to transmit the will of the forces of the invisible world. It is he or she who interprets for the village the signs of *niskala* formulated by the *jero tapakan* in trance.

Must they be exclusively *brahmana*?

No. Unlike the high priests, he or she is a temple priest, and they are of all origins. The mechanism of transmission of the position of *pamangku* by descent is not expressed as such, except in some villages. It nevertheless takes place, transmitted from father to son, from father to cousin, within the clan group, etc. It is not standardized. There are also female *pamangku*, called *mangku istri*, often the wife of a deceased *pamangku*, initiated with him at the same time.

If one is designated, can one escape this call of invisible forces?

If one refuses, there is a chance that whatever happens in their life, and especially their misfortunes, will be seen as caused by the *niskala* forces. No one escapes the *niskala*.

In Bali, is the number of priests increasing or decreasing?

I would say it remains stable. And that there are more women, especially among the interpreters of the forces of the invisible world (*niskala*). Yet, although this tradition continues, there is also the rise of new types of priest, including "new look" priests who sow their cult in the villages and Indianize the inhabitants with their sermons. There is a (beginning of) loss of ritual homogeneity.

If morality has not necessarily strengthened, has it at least changed?

Yes, there is a permeation of new and modern moral standards from the Western world through schools, NGOs, the media and, more generally, the global political correctness discourse. I am thinking here of the notions of honesty, sexual responsibility, respect for the environment. These are standards that have started permeating modern Indonesian society at large. Because these concepts are Western, they are not particularly liked but they are penetrating society little by little, either by denial of what these new norms attack, for example patriarchal violence, or by legal advances, most often step by step. So, there is a slow individualization of behavior and the slow replacement of a collective norm based on irrational religio-magic, by a collective legal norm based on individual responsibility. How long will it take to become widespread? Only God knows.

Does religion hold the same place as before?

In terms of behavior, much less. Why? Formerly, when Bali was still authentically agrarian, calendar time with its considerations of the pure and the impure, the auspicious and the unfavorable framed the totality of everyday life. People did not plant rice or engage in building a house, or creating a painting, on just any day or any time; such things were prescribed, and were undertaken with a ritual. Thus, there were times when making love was forbidden for calendrical reasons for example, during the last week of the *pawukon* calendar, corresponding to the myth of the incestuous son, Watugunung. It all went without saying. Today, not only is the role of the *balian* and other interpreters of temporality reduced, but the system of Balinese hours, the *dauh*, has disappeared. Many young Balinese have never heard of it. Time is no longer thought of the same way. Balinese time gives way to Gregorian time. It is now counted in units of productivity and in cash, and it is secularized. Today, the sphere of religion tightens around a few festivals and rites which are emphasized all the more as they more strongly affirm the power of the person (say, in marriage) or of the clan (cremation). At each holy day, people now send one another "Happy Galungan or Happy Saraswati" etc. greetings through their ubiquitous handphone. In the end, if religion has lost the measure of Balinese time, it takes hold of the conscience. While the "other" is revealed in religious and social difference, the Balinese difference is affirmed in parallel terms, but by seeking its codifying logic in an increasingly mythologized Indian origin.

In this regard, is the new and latest ban on plastic bags in mini-markets and supermarkets in the south of the island an illustration of this transformation of mentalities?

Indisputably. Because beyond identity there is, for a very small enlightened minority, trans-identity, that is to say modern universalism with, among other things, its ecological awareness. But at the same time, the extended autonomy of the individual based on this universalism is not fully accepted across the board. For the most part, contradictions persist. The more the Balinese become Westernized, the more they also assert themselves as different from Westerners. And to do this, they hang on the weight of certain traditions. This ensures the preservation of identity, but also blocks certain necessary evolutions.

11. Quality Of Education, Identity, Language, Migrants

In the past in Bali, people learned by mimicry. There was little explanation, everything was based on observation, transmission through a process of reproduction of one's guru's gestures. This changed with the first Malay-language schools instituted by the colonial Dutch, which brought in the notion of analytical knowledge. But the real period of literacy began in the 1970s with the Suharto regime. Indonesian language, Balinese language, ready-made formulas, relation to words Jean dissects how today's Balinese think of themselves through languages and expressions, then underlines that this corresponds to a desire for modernity. We then consider the extraordinary boom in the number of students in universities. While underlining the progress in the average level of education, we note that the PISA[288] ranking of education in Indonesia is regularly among the lowest in the world. Jean points out, however, that advances in education have benefited women, who are usually the most gifted students. Where are we today with the use of the Balinese language? Is this language, with its multilevel system due to caste hierarchy, adapted to modernity? What about the identity discourse concerning migrants from other islands? We try to find answers and detail the history of migratory phenomena in Bali, since now people define themselves here above all in relation to the "other".

Eric Buvelot. What is traditional Balinese education?

Jean Couteau. For techniques, it is mainly through mimicry, with a guru. In the past, and even now in certain artistic circles, children or adolescents were entrusted to the care of a master of the art or the trade, and it was the ability to imitate this guru that was at work. A bit like during the Middle Ages in Europe. In the old tradition, this mimicry was even considered a transfer of *taksu*,[289] magical power. The guru was not paid in cash. It was enough that the *sisia*[290] bring him some rice or some fruit or do him a favor.

Has this system endured?

Yes, through tourism and crafts. When formal education began to develop in the 1970s, there was very little money in circulation. In the handicraft-rich areas

---

[288] PISA: Program for International Student Assessment is a regular OECD (Organization for Economic Co-operation and Development) study of 15-year-old high school students in 70 countries.

[289] *Taksu*: supernatural power, inspiration, from Sanskrit *caksu*, the cosmic eye. This *taksu* is usually attached to certain temples. To this day, artists systematically tour the temples believed to be able to irradiate them with cosmic *taksu*.

[290] *Sisia* here has the meaning of pupil, disciple, apprentice.

of Ubud and Gianyar, one way in which children paid their school fees was to learn about crafts. They found a master, often a neighbor or a relative. If they did not pay him in rice, they left him at least part of the work they did, which the master sold for his own needs. It was a system based on a complex balance of services between clan networks and villagers. For the teaching of dance, the dance master or mistress transmitted their gestures either through mimicry by placing their *sisia* behind them, or, firmly grasping the limbs or body of the *sisia*, and directing their gestures. A painter, on the other hand, asked his pupil to go over his pencil sketch in Chinese ink. In all cases, there was a demonstration for mimetic purposes, never analysis.

Yes, but not everyone is necessarily an artist either! What happened with ordinary small trades, those related to the fields, to utilitarian crafts?

It was all about observation. Children learned by watching their elders. It was only in the 1970s, after literacy had risen from 15% to over 60%, that attitudes began to really change. However, there are still traces of the old system. The Balinese have always had, and still have, an extremely keen visual memory. The making of offerings helps one to remember details and sharpens memory. This largely explains their talent. But the shift from transmission through mimicry to analytical knowledge, through school, has certainly initiated a profound change.

This mimicry apart, how is culture, in the noble sense of the term, transmitted?

As in the arts, one must find a guru and become his *sisia* (disciple). To do this, it is best to be a *sisia* of a Brahmanic house, or a *parekan*[291] of a princely house. Typically, around the prince, formerly very cultivated, or around the Brahmin, or during an evening at a temple festival, all the masters and pupils of the place would gather in a group. Those of the inner circle read, sing, and translate a selected text. Those outside listen and learn, by hearing, repetition after repetition, each at their own pace. This is the *makakawin*.[292] Unfortunately, this teaching system is no longer as strong as it used to be, even if the *makakawin* still persists during major temple festivals, or through citizen-band radio.

Why this end of the transmission of traditional knowledge?

Because the elites, high caste or not, have abandoned their places in the villages. They started coming to Denpasar, or Singaraja, the former capital in the colonial period, even before World War II. They urbanized after Independence, at the same time as they took the reins of modern power. This interrupted the process of traditional knowledge transmission in the villages. Also, school competed with shadow theatre, and this totally changed the system of transmitting knowledge.

---

[291] *Parekan*: a subject close to the court.
[292] The *makakawin* sessions study literature in Old Javanese or Kawi (the *kakawin*). There are also *makidung* sessions that study literature in Middle Balinese.

It was still a closed system ...

Of course. The system remained very hierarchical, with the language levels to remind everyone of their place. The princely courts and great Brahmanic houses infused their environment with their culture, marked by the myths and cosmogony of Indianized Java. But the further away one moved, the more the indigenous substratum asserted itself. Despite this, the center, the palace, remained sacred. The common people competed for the princes' leftover food, "sacred" leftovers, they said. Yet, outside the court lived those who had no place either close to the palace or among the Brahmins. Social stratification was integrated into the value system. It also revealed the aristocracy's role as a provider of food.

Did the transition to modern education go smoothly?

At the beginning, some Balinese refused to go to school, which they saw as alien. When they sent their sons there, it was sometimes with a representative of the tradition, for example, a Brahmin, who would sit at the back of the class to make sure that all went well with these foreigners.[293]

How was it eventually accepted?

The first Malay-language schools were opened by the Dutch at the turn of the 20th century in Singaraja, at that time the capital, where the first local intellectuals came from. When the Dutch seized the south of Bali between 1906 and 1908, the Cokorda of Denpasar recounted this invasion in Malay. Malay was already a sociological and literary reality.

It is often said that Malay was the lingua franca of the Indonesian archipelago, so it was also a literary language?

Yes, the Dutch relied on Malay, which had a long-lasting historical presence, as a complement to their own language. In the end, it was of course Malay that won, officially taking the name "Indonesian" at the *Sumpah Pemuda*[294] congress of 1928 in Batavia. So, contrary to what some people say, Indonesian is definitely not an artificial language. Numerous texts written in Malay, including literary texts, have circulated throughout the archipelago for a thousand years, spread by peoples of the straits and coastal areas, but also from the 19th century by Chinese-Malays and Chinese-Indonesians. This is the origin of Bahasa Indonesia.[295] In the 1920s, the first journals to appear in Bali were written in Malay. It was also in Malay that the first Hindu conceptualization of the Balinese religion took shape, at the beginning of the 20th century, which from then on began to permeate local mentalities.[296]

---

[293] See *Tjokord Gde Agung Sukawati: Reminiscence of a Balinese Prince*, as dictated to Rosemary Hilbery, *South East Asian Studies*, University of Hawaii (1979).

[294] *Sumpah Pemuda*: the "Youth Oath" is the founding episode of the Indonesian independence movement. It represents the first declaration of values governing the future republic of Indonesia.

[295] Bahasa Indonesia: the Indonesian language

[296] On this subject, see the controversies between *Surya Kanta* and *Bali Adnyana, in Kebalian – La construction dialogique de l'identité balinaise* by Michel Picard, Association Archipel (2017).

Was Independence immediately followed by a great period of literacy?

Not really. Literacy is above all the accomplishment of the military regime of Suharto. When I arrived in Bali in the early seventies, schools were being built absolutely everywhere!

Are you saying that during the Sukarno period education was neglected?

The Sukarno years were a period of poverty for Indonesia. Sukarno certainly focused on education, but he didn't have the means to implement it,[297] and so there was not the surge of literacy that we saw later, under the *Orde Baru* in the 1970s. This surge also had economic causes. Development policy and openness to investment required the rapid training of a skilled workforce. And it happened in a very short period of time! In the 1980s, the few graduates of higher education almost automatically became university lecturers. At the same time, private universities opened everywhere. Department after department. From S1 (bachelor's degrees) to S2 (master's degrees), and soon from master's degrees to doctorates.

What did this change?

There was a shift from Balinese culture to national culture. The movement gained momentum in the 1980s with television. Everything was now formulated in Bahasa Indonesia, all the abstract vocabulary in particular. This was a linguistic reversal that seemed to pose no problem to anyone. It was also a sign of the acceptance of nation-building.

Hasn't the creation of local television channels allowed a return of the Balinese language?

Yes, but at first it was the other way around. When national television became mainstream in the 1980s, it created a strong Indonesian "togetherness," which the military regime used for its propaganda. This reinforced the shift from Balinese to Indonesian. Bali TV was not established until 2002, with few programs in Balinese. Too late therefore to compensate for the linguistic Indonesianization of society.

How do the Balinese relate to words?

Many educated Balinese today define their identity with words and expressions of an incantatory nature, corresponding to a need for modern identity affirmation. If you ask them what best describes Bali, some will answer: "*Tat twam asi*," which, they add, means "I am you." In fact, if you refer to the sentence of the original text, "*Tat twam asi*" means quite another thing: "You are the whole," the sublime reality. They thus reinvent the meaning of

---

[297] In Bali, an embryonic humanities faculty was set up in 1958, followed by a medical faculty in 1962.

a Sanskrit sentence to justify their humanist Balinese-ness! This is typical of their normative, performative reconstruction of identity by borrowing from India. But that's not all, they also invent all kinds of expressions to re-Balinize themselves in a modern fashion.

For example?

There is now *"Rahajeng semeng"* to say "Good morning" or *"Rahajeng rahina Galungan lan Kuningan"* during the festivals of Galungan and Kuningan,[298] as well as all possible variations for the other festivals all this is recent. Or the famous *"Om swastiastu"* that people now use to exchange formal greetings. More recent still is *"Mugi-mugi awor ing Acintya* (May he join the Invisible)," pronounced when someone has died. All these expressions are recent inventions just like, in a slightly different register, the daily *Trisandya* prayers, morning, noon, and evening.

When did this phenomenon appear?

It's been around 20 years or so. *Om swastiastu* appeared at the same time as *Salaam alaikum* was generalized for Muslims. Indonesians have started to put religion everywhere in all their social relationships.[299] In the past, during a first encounter, always tense, the Balinese inquired about their respective statutory positions, their caste.[300] When they already knew each other, a *kejitan*, a slight movement of the eyebrows, was enough of a greeting, something that is disappearing today. *Om swastiastu* did not exist. They didn't need it.

What else is recent and yet so iconic?

The concept of *Tri Hita Karana* which today's Balinese claim is the essence of Balinese-ness. This expression signifies the balance between three aspects of everyday life, the relationship of human beings with each other, with the environment, and with God. In fact, the *Tri Hita Karana* was invented in the 1960s. It was born from the idea that the village, the epitome of Balinese harmony, is the place of a balance based on the meeting of three components: the gods, with the *parhyangan* temples; the *palemahan* territory; and the *pawongan* community. From the awareness of this village balance, Gusti Ketut Kaler made a theory. Whatever those concerned might say, it is a phenomenon of modernity, of the restructuration of tradition in a modern concept.

All this corresponds to a desire for ordering ...

Yes, this is part of the need to rationalize Balinese culture. Balinese today wish to justify their social being, to build a homogeneous body of Balinese knowledge,

---

[298] *Galungan, Kuningan*: major Balinese religious festivals, corresponding to a long visit of the ancestors among their living descendants.

[299] President Abdurrahman Wahid (affectionately known as Gus Dur), whom many Indonesians consider an exemplar of tolerance, blatantly scoffed at this formalist Islam. But even he, the great cleric of traditional Islam, could do nothing against changing mentalities.

[300] The standard formula was *"Dija antuk linggih?"* (What is your position/ rank/level?)

and no longer to get by with something amorphous and animistic, as their culture was before. To do this, they substitute for the original local expression a similar or modernized expression, in Sanskrit or Old Javanese. People also speak of *kearifan lokal*, local wisdom, which is a modern expression. Greetings, prayers, slogans, principles: everything changes, transformed and replenished by an expression in the language of the origins, even if these origins are imaginary, and even if the use of the Balinese language is waning. Note that in the modern space, one uses English, to better mark that one is part of that space.

What else can we add from a linguistic point of view?

The reality is complex: the Balinese language is indeed fading from some spaces, but it is reestablishing itself in others. Generally, though, we are unquestionably witnessing a shrinking of the sociological spaces where it is practiced and also a loss of vocabulary. Almost all discussions about Balinese culture, including those held in princely palaces, take place in Indonesian, apart from long polite introductory remarks. This is the biggest revolution since the era of Majapahit, when Javanese arrived here with their language. And nobody talks about it as such. I find it quite extraordinary!

The Balinese are enriched by the Indonesian language, but also other languages that are spoken more and more on the island due to tourism.

This is indicative of the "cargo cult"[301] aspect of Balinese society. Everything that is perceived as positive is integrated. If we look back at the history of Bali, there is always someone who comes from a land beyond the seas to spread a new truth. This is the case with Hinduism, on several occasions. With Rsi Markandeya[302] first, in the mythic past, then Dang Hyang Nirarta[303] in the 16th century, who is said to have founded some of most of the important temples around the island.

These mythifications are a constant in island societies.

Yes, for example, in Java as in Bali, there was Begawan Byasa, who is credited with the origin of writing. In India, he is said to have written the *Mahabharata*.

There are also English words that are found integrated into everyday

---

[301] Cargo cult: Originally a Melanesian belief system based on the expectation of the arrival of ancestral spirits on ships full of food and other goods. Today, a description of how a community assimilates contributions from outside into its own culture.

[302] Rsi Markandeya: mythical founder of Bali already known in India. He is said to have crossed the Straits of Bali with his followers and founded the mother temple of Besakih, at the same time founding the Balinese religion.

[303] Dang Hyang Nirartha, also known as Dwijendra and "Pedanda Sakti Wawu Rauh," was a 16th-century wandering Shivaite priest. He is credited with introducing the lineage of the *brahmana* Siwa priesthood to Bali, as well as the *padmasana* altar to the holiest corner of most temples. The upper part of this altar, which symbolizes the world, is the open seat of the inconceivable Açintya, or Siwa the Supreme, lord of the pantheism of palace culture.

language. I am thinking for example of the English word "crowded" which has become *krodit* here and which is now used to designate congested roads in road safety bulletins.

This ability to absorb words, and beyond that to syncretize concepts, ideas, has always been extraordinary. We usually think that syncretism works for a few generations at most, but no! Here it is over two thousand years! When you look at the Balinese religious corpus, there are things that date back to the megalithic. Certain rites have survived, often around well-brandished *lingga*[304] in particular among the Bali Aga,[305] where we find traces of the initial stages of Indianization. And that's without mentioning mythical characters such as the king Mayadenawa, for example, whose defeat one is supposed to celebrate at Galungan. He is perceived as a villain because he attacked the temple rituals by trying to suppress the system of offerings. But some say, *mezzo voce*, that it was to get back to basics: he was a supporter of Buddhism, the first form of Indianization in Bali. Finally, there was cultural Javanization after the occupation of Bali by the warriors of Majapahit in 1343, which permeates Balinese literature to this day.

Nowadays, does everyone have access to university studies in Bali?

More and more. The numbers are fantastic! Almost a hundred thousand young people in private and public universities, according to the latest published data.

So, there is an extraordinary boom in the number of students, there is also an extraordinary success rate in exams,[306] but let's get to the criticism: when you look at the PISA ranking of education in Indonesia, it still ranks among the worst in the world. The exams are sometimes rigged, there are private universities that churn out degrees with success rates of 99.5%!

Yes, but things are improving. To me, the main problem, which I've noticed while teaching here, is that the majority of young people who come to college have a poor knowledge of abstract vocabulary, which signals the weakness of general culture that should have been acquired during secondary education. I once asked my master's students to write about "politics in art." I had brought pictures of Napoleon, Lenin, and Mao Tse Tung. They had never heard of Lenin or Mao!

To me, that's hardly surprising in a country that massacred all of its communist citizens in the 1960s!

Only one student had heard of them, but he was Korean! Indeed, there is a

---

[304] *Lingga*: phallus; associated with Shiva.

[305] *Bali Aga*: Balinese people who still retain traditions and customs that predate the Hinduism brought by Java.

[306] Jean Couteau explains: "When you give your students too many bad marks, the rector calls you in to tell you: 'Sir, we cannot make two-thirds of the class fail. There are forty students waiting to register for next year.'"

considerable problem of political knowledge here. But beyond that, in Indonesia in general, where do we see the most dynamic intelligent people here? Among activists, among artists.

Yes, but we must not forget the children of the elites who are sent to study abroad.

If they come back! Indonesia needs them. The whole problem with Indonesian education is that it is not selective enough. This deficit is especially true for what we call the humanities in the West, that is, all the teaching that corresponds to areas of questioning, such as literature, sociology, law. Teaching here does not so much produce questioning as instill norms. It tends to standardize thought. Yet, there is indeed a certain transfer of knowledge, even if this transfer rests too often on memorization.

Aren't you exaggerating a little?

Yes, of course. Things are changing fast, and for the better. In fact, we are now seeing the emergence of academics producing knowledge that poses itself as its own object, instead of being, as in the past, obscured by ideology and identity. Now, young writers studying Hinduism no longer hesitate to openly raise the issue of the Neo-Hindu, Indianizing drift of Balinese society.[307] More and more Balinese academics are also joining international university networks. Universitas Hindu Indonesia has even just created an English-language journal. This shows the impact of modern media, which is pulling Bali out of its intellectual isolation.

What is the role of teachers in these deficiencies?

There is sometimes a problem of competence, often caused by nepotism, especially in Singaraja. The best are graduates of foreign universities. But there are fewer candidates than you might think. Until recently, if you got a scholarship to study abroad, you would not rise in rank while you were away. When you got back, you would find that your colleagues had advanced to places of power, and were often jealous because their PhD was local. They could block your career advancement while you taught freshmen for five years before someone realized you were out of place. Another problem, and this is an ideological one, teachers are obliged to prove that they adhere to the principles of Pancasila to be appointed university lecturers. This has the advantage of reducing the number of extremists at university, but it also tells us something about how democracy works in Indonesia.

Recent polls have indeed shown that a growing number of students adhere to fundamentalist ideas of Islam. Similar measures have been taken in mosques. This is to protect the Republic of Indonesia and its pluralistic values.

Yes, given the developments in the country, for me that makes sense! Socio-

---

[307] See, for example, the work by I Gusti Agung Paramita, *Wajah Tuhan dan Sifat Pemuja* (The Face of God and Attitude of the Faithful), Sarwa Tatwa Pustaka, Denpasar (2020).

political balance is more important than formal democracy.

Despite these harsh observations that we have made, can we say that education has improved?

Yes, I think so, despite all the shortcomings. There is a historical leap, a qualitative leap in knowledge which is considerable. The Indonesians are catching up.

As a tourist island, Bali offers many courses on tourism. Can we say that the training is of good quality?

Yes, even high quality. The first school, the BPLP,[308] was created in 1978 with funds from the World Bank, initially with foreign or local teachers trained abroad like Gede Ardika, who later became Minister of Tourism. The training is excellent.

So, education has improved, that's undeniable, and that of women in particular. Do women have the same access to education?

Yes, for the last 20 years. In fact, the most gifted students are often women. One of them told me that women have a better sense of time, because they have to manage the preparation of offerings in advance, and with precision.

Was there a period of mixed education in Bali, that is, shared between the school of the Republic of Indonesia and the traditional transmission of knowledge?

Yes, I mentioned it when we talked about learning crafts, which for many was a very interesting intermediate phase. Young people went to school in the morning, and in the afternoon to their guru to learn a craft. It was a way of entering modernity while keeping one foot in tradition.

How do the Balinese take care of their children at home? Has it evolved?

Urbanization has changed things for many of them, but I would say that traditionally there aren't really any constraints in the family. In the countryside, children have great freedom of movement. They move from house to house, they are in contact with nature, they are very comfortable with their bodies. Too comfortable, sometimes. But school has put things in order, so to speak. Otherwise, the transmission of the norms of social behavior is done as much by the village associations, the system of the temples, the organizations of young people, as by the family or relatives. Yet the father is certainly a very important character, although not in the rigid way of the Western-style paterfamilias. There is more tactile contact with children than in Western cultures.[309] Then, of course, regarding daughters, there is a sudden break in all intimacy with them when they are "taken," to use the term, by their husbands, since when they marry, they switch

---

[308] BPLP: Balai Pendidikan dan Latihan Pariwisata Bali (Bali Tourism Education and Training Center).

[309] See *Balinese Character: A Photographic Analysis* by Gregory Bateson and Margaret Mead, New York Academy of Sciences (1942).

allegiance to their husband's ancestors. On the other hand, the *sentana*, or male heir, enjoys a favorable position. He escapes parental pressure because it is he who will be responsible for their final passage, post mortem, to their ancestral abode above the mountains.

Does the male heir therefore have a privileged position in the family? Is he therefore the preferred son? The most pampered?

Yes, indeed. But in return he has to take care of his parents. He is the eldest for the aristocrats, the youngest for the common people. The big difference is between girls and boys.

Let's talk about the role of girls at home. Does the fact that they are required to do household chores continue to this day with modernity?

Yes, I'm sure. They live by duplicating themselves. They make their offerings, then go to work or college. Yet, there are also more and more women living independently in city *kos* unthinkable 25 years ago. They refuse to find themselves in the kitchen preparing tea for the men of the house. Some associations promote women's autonomy, sometimes directly on campus.

Let us return to the Balinese language. What about the current use of this language?

Since I began living here in Denpasar, I speak more and more Indonesian and less and less Balinese. There is a narrowing of the sociological spaces in which Balinese is used. If, while shopping, you speak in Balinese to a Javanese saleswoman, she will not understand, or will pretend not to understand. Balinese language is not valued by non-Balinese, unlike what we see in Java in Jogjakarta for example, where the students are all picking up the local language. Here in Bali, *pendatang* don't get into Balinese. At the same time, the Balinese themselves find this quite normal. There is inevitably a depletion of vocabulary in the practice of this language, with all the abstract words increasingly coming from Indonesian.

Is this true even in the religious sphere, and in particular in the villages?

Yes, but the shift is different. Temple priests and *balian* tend more and more to substitute formulas in Sanskrit or Old Javanese for exhortations and prayers they used to utter in Balinese (*sesontengan*). In addition, fashionable preachers, who for twenty years have been spreading the Neo-Hindu good word, often mix Balinese and Indonesian, the first for jokes, the second for abstract explanatory aspects. They even add, here and there, Sanskrit expressions, the very obscurity of which guarantees both their status and their knowledge.

What are people doing to save the language?

Schoolchildren often complain that Balinese is too difficult. In fact, quite often the teachers haven't been properly trained, although Balinese teaching departments have now been set up in some universities. Yet there is a rebirth of poetry and short stories in Balinese. A short-lived renaissance, no doubt, as local newspapers, threatened by the internet, have reduced their columns in Balinese. At the same time, there is a certain literary production. So, I cannot say where we are going. Will the Balinese language be reduced to a small niche in a largely Indonesian-language environment? Or are we going to witness a historic revival? We have seen others! Ukrainian recently, Hebrew 70 years ago. But I'm quite skeptical.

There are a lot of international schools in Bali! Especially for foreign communities that have established themselves there ...

A lot. Also because of tourism. There is a demand for knowledge of foreign languages, which is met by all kinds of more or less bilingual courses and schools, including at secondary level. English is undoubtedly more and more current. There is also an Alliance Française and a French high school. Russian, Korean, and, of course, Mandarin are all taught. So, it's not surprising that there is a shrinking of Balinese cultural space. Also bear in mind that in addition to foreign languages, instruction is in Indonesian. As for the books on Hinduism, they are in Indonesian but translated from English. And don't think that all Balinese texts are readable. As soon as one leaves short stories or modern poetry, one is dealing with a mix of Balinese and Kawi (Old Javanese). Reading older Balinese texts is a bit like reading *Beowulf* in the original pre-Norman version. English is easy in comparison.

Since Balinese is a multi-level language, that complicates things, right? How does one cope with caste differences and in what language level does one write?

For literature, it's complicated: those who hold the tradition want to maintain High Balinese, and there are those who wish for the advent of a popular variety of Balinese. In the spoken language, a balance of sorts is established between the variants of the language. Usually, people speak Balinese only when they know each other and have identified their caste affiliation. So, this only happens in closed sociological spaces.

Why? Isn't it the same all over Bali?

Not exactly. In urban Bali, the caste composition is as mixed as the population, because the people of the towns come from all over the island. But originally, this system existed in a form specific to each socio-political space and hierarchy, to each area. People immediately knew how to talk to whom, based on location and name. Today, outside these defined spaces and in the presence of other Balinese whose rank they do not necessarily know, Balinese tend to use Indonesian. Personally, I use Indonesian more and more with the Balinese, because when you are uncomfortable, well, you switch to Indonesian. Example: you meet someone and talk to them in High Balinese, but they, thinking that you are from a lower caste, answer you in Low Balinese. It's like they're somehow stepping on you. On the other hand, if you address them from the start in Middle Balinese or Low Balinese, they may be the one who will be upset or embarrassed! Result: everyone switches to Indonesian, mixed up with keywords to denote that one is Balinese: *tiang* (I), *inggih* (yes), *ten* (no), etc. It's a matter of etiquette.

When the authorities communicate on the need to teach and speak Balinese, what level of language are they speaking? The low, the middle, the High Balinese?

They speak Indonesian! But today there are *penyuluh*, that is, people whose mission is to popularize the language and spread what is considered correct Balinese to people in the villages. They broadcast a form of Middle Balinese.

In the end, can one adapt this language to the constraints of modernity?

I'm skeptical. But that will depend on political will. There are ambiguities in the local government, with the emphasis sometimes on unity, sometimes on pluralism, depending on the readings of Pancasila and the understanding of the national motto: *Bhinneka tunggal ika*.[310] There is also national policy and regional policy, each with its own ways!

From an academic point of view, there is an obligation to put this language in the Latin alphabet. What constraints does this imply?

Some would like to use the original Balinese alphabet, but this is more a demand for identity than anything else. The Latin alphabet is here to stay. The Balinese alphabet can be used to decorate the names of the streets, but not much more. Very few people can read the lontar manuscripts. More important to note: the Balinese vocabulary contains a Kawi corpus of Sanskrit origin which is slowly infiltrating Indonesian. There is also a Balino-Indonesian vocabulary which is not yet formally recognized by the *Kamus Besar Bahasa Indonesia*[311] but which does exist especially all the words that relate to Balinese culture.

So, because of their constant decrease in percentage of the total population living in Bali, can it be said that the Balinese are now developing a mentality of being under siege?

Sometimes. I remember, for example, a poem by Wianta on this subject, which we give as an opening epigraph to this book. He talks of Bali as a small, surrounded island. At the same time, we shouldn't see things only from a Western angle, that is, to overemphasize existing contradictions.

Yes, but when Governor Wayan Koster says that the national policy of two children per family is not enough and he asks the Balinese to make four, it is indeed an observation that goes in that sense!

Yes, his predecessor Made Mangku Pastika had a more national perspective;

---

[310] *Bhinneka tunggal ika*: Unity in Diversity.
[311] *Kamus Besar Bahasa Indonesia*: Indonesian language dictionary.

Wayan Koster was elected more on the basis of identity. But is there a siege mentality? Yes and no. Even if you hear people here and there in favor of more autonomy, the Balinese are definitely part of the Indonesian national project.

Yes, the separatist reflex only appears when there are extremely disruptive events, such as the Islamist attacks of the 2000s ...

In fact, I don't think so. After the 2002 bombing, during an activist meeting, there was, I was told, only one voice, whose name I will not mention here, that demanded retaliatory measures against Muslims. Personally, I don't hear hate speech against non-Balinese. Nothing at all like the kind of talk you hear in Europe. However, I've heard that in the universities it is starting a bit ...

I remember when Abdurrahman Wahid[312] was chosen over Megawati Sukarnoputri[313] by the electoral council in the 1999 presidential election, the Balinese were not happy. A riot and acts of vandalism ensued ...

It was a political protest by supporters of the nationalist party. In the Balinese tradition, you have to be loyal, whether you want to be or not. These same mechanisms are at work in the issue of *Reklamasi*[314] at Benoa Bay. Indeed, in some circles there is the idea, and not without reason, that Bali no longer belongs to the Balinese. Balinese politicians sometimes speak in private about the problems of ethno-demographic balance. But they say this more often from a national rather than an ethnocentric perspective. On paper, the land reclamation project of the Bay of Benoa should lead to jobs, which will mean even more *pendatang* in south Bali. *Reklamasi* is therefore part of a dynamics of demographic changes already underway on the island.

With this clarification, we are beyond the claim of identity in principle, but in a practical calculation with regard to the indigenous and non-native populations.

The *Reklamasi* project is generating identity. For example, Sugi Lanus, a young analyst of classical texts, has said that the bay of Benoa was indeed a sacred space as such. And this was approved by Parisada. Yet although there are many places of worship in this bay, individually sacred, no one before Lanus had yet thought of designating the whole, the entire bay, as a sacred place. It was a dramatic change, which could only reinforce the rising identity discourse. What was an issue of ecology became a religious issue. And, in the end, there was politicization of religion.

The environmental dimension of the issue, which has nevertheless been highlighted, is therefore irrelevant?

---

[312] Abdurrahman Wahid (1940-2009) was the fourth President of the Republic of Indonesia (1999-2001).

[313] Megawati Sukarnoputri is one of the daughters of Sukarno, the proclaimer and first president of the Republic of Indonesia. She was president of Indonesia from 2001 to 2004.

[314] *Reklamasi*: a vast land reclamation project in the bay of Benoa in southern Bali, which has met with determined protest from the Balinese coastal population of the south.

Not totally. There are indeed green associations concerned, with Gendo,[315] the lawyer and pro-Bali activist at their head. But the religious aspect has become the most prominent, the one that Balinese are most sensitive to, even if in reality the most important is the socio-economic aspect. If *Reklamasi* is carried out, it would confirm the loss of Balinese control over the economy of their island with, in the not-so-distant future, a probable reversal of the ethno-demographic balance in the island. All the elements of a true crystallization are therefore present. But it is hidden.

How?

No one wants to call a spade a spade. This is the problem with current Indonesia, the fruit of the "success" of the military regime: the social has been replaced by the religious, which inevitably turns into a very dangerous face-off, while the problem lies elsewhere. But no one wants to say it and take the appropriate measures. This allows the obsession with identity to rise. And nothing is being done to counter this phenomenon.

Since when have migrant groups come to Bali from other islands in the archipelago?

I would say that it was the Dutch who initiated the modern form of migration. Previously, there were indeed migrants who were granted informal resident status in unoccupied spaces of the island, for example in Loloan, in a marshy area that would seem unwelcoming. Or in spaces where these migrants had a specific social function. The Muslim *parekan* of Karangasem thus were granted their own *banjar* to assume their function as mercenaries of the prince. He trusted them more than Balinese! But at that time, there weren't really any migratory phenomena, except perhaps that of the Bugis.[316] Next to Banyuwangi in East Java, there is a small bay where once hundreds of Bugis anchored their junks. In the 18th century, it was from this center that they radiated to the coasts of Bali. There were the *wong sunantara*, sea raiders who occasionally came to plunder the coasts and thus forced the inhabitants of northern Bali to settle in the hills. Among the other historical settlements of non-Balinese, we can also mention, more recently, after their liberation by the Dutch from all feudal allegiances, the establishment of certain Sasaks [317] from Karangasem in the once uninhabited mountainous areas of the center of the island. Finally, there are Madurese from East Java, who mostly settle in non-rice-growing areas.

Another migratory phenomenon is that of the Republic of Indonesia with its *Transmigrasi* program ...

Yes, nationally, an organized phenomenon that consisted of moving populations, including Balinese, to underpopulated areas of the archipelago that needed to be

---

[315] Gendo Suardana: activist and lawyer, leader in the fight against land reclamation in Benoa.
[316] Bugis: ethnic group of South Sulawesi.
[317] Sasak: ethnic group of Lombok.

developed. This is why there are now Balinese villages in Lampung, in the south of Sumatra, and in Sulawesi.

What about the migration to Bali?

It is economic in nature. To understand it, you have to go back in history a bit. I remember in the 1980s, when tourism in Bali was still emerging, there was a lot of construction work going on. The Balinese each still had their own piece of land. So, there was no itinerant proletariat like in Java, no absolute poverty. Therefore, Balinese labor was expensive. For this reason, when investors opened their construction sites in Nusa Dua, instead of hiring Balinese, their contractors went to look for workers in Java. Tens of thousands of people thus came to settle in Bali in an environment that was neither that of *Transmigrasi* nor that of individual initiative. The phenomenon continues to this day.

What about the migrations organized by the Dutch in Bali?

In the 1920s, they brought in Javanese laborers to build the Benoa jetty. And others to teach in Malay-language schools, thus constituting the first modern urban networks in the south of the island, which later served as a support for Indonesian nationalist discourse in Bali. It was demographically insignificant.

Finally, how can one build the Republic of Indonesia without destroying local traditions? We see that President Joko Widodo is pushing for ever greater interconnectivity of the country's provinces by developing infrastructure while encouraging Indonesians to wear their traditional costumes every Thursday. Isn't there a paradox here?

It is an Indonesian contradiction, born under the military regime. The various levels of government focus on local identities and traditions with the hope that they will simply sublimate into national identity. Are Indonesians better equipped than others to overcome this paradox? I don't know... I hope so. There is a long Indonesian tradition of emphasizing the similarities rather than the differences. So, we must remain optimistic. But, the emphasis on religion in and beyond the educational system does not help matters.

What to do?

The problem is, if you over-universalize the teaching of religions, as Europeans have done, it can lead to the end of faith. Obviously *ulemas* and priests don't want this. So, you let the religious rise in strength. How then do you channel the unity of the country? The medium that has worked in Indonesia so far is nationalism although this nationalism is rather bizarre, since it involves religion and there is no enemy! It is generally professed as a humanism.

Sandiaga Uno, Prabowo Subianto's running mate for the 2019 presidential election, proposed during his campaign to make Bali a halal tourist destination, an idea that comes up regularly ... What do you make of it?

Public outcry in Bali, like every time someone comes up with this idea. But now that he has become minister of tourism, following the covid crisis, his idea is simply to focus on VIP tourism.

How do all these issues around Bali affect the mentality of the Balinese today?

There is an identity trap. There is this admiration of foreigners who continue to present an idyllic image of Bali, an image taken over by the Balinese themselves! The Balinese now use the outside world to assert their universalism. Tourism is organized around this idea, and it penetrates mentalities. But there are economic and socio-cultural burdens that are increasingly difficult to bear, which accentuate the demand for identity. This is why, in the immediate future, the only real upheaval to fear is the interruption of tourism! This interruption is now happening with the pandemic. What do the Balinese dream of? The return of the old days of tourism. And no radical politics.

12. Relation to the Outside World, to the Other, Bali's Role, Identity Formation

In former times, the Balinese did not focus on ethnic otherness, but on statutory otherness. In their relationship to each other and to the outside world, the symbol of "elsewhere" was Java. In terms In former times, the Balinese did not focus on ethnic otherness, but on statutory otherness. In their relationship to each other and to the outside world, the symbol of "elsewhere" was Java. In terms of religion, legend tells of a transfer of the gods and mountains from the Himalayas to Java, and from Java to Bali. As for ethnic links between the two islands, this, too, is mythologized: the Hindus of Java are said to have fled in large numbers to Bali to avoid Islam. Jean Couteau tries here to sort out conventional ideas which do not necessarily reflect reality. Indeed, as we often recall in this book, Islam has always represented a form of modernity in Bali. In the relations of Bali to the outside world, Jean also recalls the Balinese invasions of Lombok and Sumbawa. Yes, it's hard to imagine Balinese kingdoms as belligerent powers, or the island as one of the world's slave trade centers. What is the "other" called here? *Jaba, Londo, Bule.* We take a look at these terms that are more or less racist depending on the context. Jean explains the current identity by past repression of the left and the manipulation of religion. While orthodox Islam is gaining ground today, Jean recalls that it was Christians who were the most theologically aggressive before. What is Bali's current position in the Republic of Indonesia? What is its local image? Can we now say that Balinese society thinks of itself as a whole?

ERIC BUVELOT. How do people envision the relationship with the "other" in Bali?

JEAN COUTEAU. The Balinese do not emphasize ethnic or even racial otherness. First, the foreigner is not "other," since he too can become an ancestor, and this applies to everyone. There are ancestral shrines addressed to Chinese ancestors, to ancestors from Mecca (Muslims), and even in a few instances to European ancestors, such as castoffs. Yet, within their own community, the Balinese emphasize otherness in status, materialized by the caste system. That said, just because ethno-religious otherness is understated doesn't mean that it does not exist. The notion of the "exterior" has always existed. *Jawa*, meaning Java, is closely related to *jaba* in Balinese, which means *"outside"*. I remember in my early years in Bali I was often asked when I was going to return to *Jawa*, the outside world being the world of Java. The concept of *jaba* people is to be understood as those "outside" the aristocratic castes. Meanwhile, the island of Java has always existed in the Balinese imagination in a complex way. Bali is both connected to and separate from Java.

Can you give a concrete example of that?

Yes, there is the story of Ida Bagus Angkeran, where Java is connected by land with Bali, Bali being the tail of a dragon whose head and body are in Java. The hero cuts off the dragon's tail, separating one from the other and creating Bali. Another example, linked this time to the contributions of the outside world, is the introduction of Hinduism: in Balinese and Javanese mythologies, it is said that there was a transfer of the gods and mountains from the Himalayas to Java, which gave rise to Semeru (Mount Meru), Bromo, and other mountains of Java. But in the *Babad Pasek* chronicle, we read of the transfer of pieces of Semeru from Java to Bali, giving rise to Mount Agung. Between Java and Bali, there is therefore a link which is also a separation.

And in regard to the two peoples? What is the historical perception?

The ethnic bond is also mythologized. Most Balinese elites claim to be of Javanese origin. In their ancestral temples, there is often a *menjangan seluang*, a carved wooden deer head which marks them as descendants of the Arya[318] warriors of Majapahit who seized Bali in 1343, an occupation that I would describe as similar to that of the conquest of England by the Franco-Normans in the 11th century. There was a replacement of the elites. It is a point of pride to participate in this link with the empire of Majapahit, which, in the narrative of modern Indonesia and associated mythology, is presented as the empire that unified the entire archipelago.[319] But alongside the history of the unity of Bali and Java, there is also that of a break between the two islands, with the flight to Bali of a number of Brahmins, Dang Hyang Nirartha[320] in particular, who are said to have left Java in the 16th century, when Java was becoming Islamized, and these Brahmins refused Islam.

This is a story you often hear in Bali even today.

Yes, it is a legend that gave rise to a myth that Hindus from Java fled in large numbers to Bali to escape from Islam. This only affected a few hundred people at best, individually. There has never been a mass migration from Java to escape Islam.

What is the position of Bali in the history of the Indonesian archipelago?

There have been other connections, contacts, and conflicts with the outside world than those with Java. In the 16th and 17th centuries, the Balinese invaded Lombok and Sumbawa, to the east, and Blambangan to the west, a part of East Java that was Islamized relatively late, in the 18th century. There was even an

---

[318] Arya: group of clans descended from the warriors of Majapahit. Foundation of the Balinese aristocracy.

[319] There are also stories of resistance against Majapahit occupation, in particular that of Kebo Iwo, a giant whom the Javanese could only defeat by deceit.

[320] Dang Hyang Nirartha, also known as "Pedanda Sakti Wawu Rauh," was a 16th-century wandering Shivaite priest. He is the founder of the *brahmana* Shaiva priesthood in Bali.

expedition mounted by the kingdom of Mengwi towards the site of Majapahit in Java. Today to make a leap into contemporary history some people talk of the re-Hinduization of Indonesia! It may sound at odds with how Westerners view Indonesia right now, but the Republic of Indonesia offers the legal possibility for Hinduism to spill over into the entire territory of the archipelago. Indeed, ever since the Balinese became prosperous from tourism, they have been opening temples everywhere. The Mandara Giri temple located at the foot of the Semeru volcano in Senduro, East Java, receives tens of thousands of Balinese visitors each year. Islam may be growing in Bali, but Balinese Hinduism is spreading throughout the Indonesian archipelago. It is on this reality that the idea of a possible re-Hinduization is grafted.

Majapahit's Empire Strikes Back?

There's a myth supporting this idea, the myth of Sabdo Palon,[321] popular in villages in both Bali and Java. In Java it appeals to reluctant Muslims who reject the hardening of Islam and claim that the Majapahit days of grandeur will be back. Some Balinese are aware of the power of this idea and advocate it, even if it's a story originally imported from Java. It expresses a longing for a national space that would be Hindu rather than Muslim.

What motivated Balinese conquests of neighboring islands?

In Java, this corresponded to the collapse of Majapahit. Muslim merchants seized the maritime economy and succeeded in transforming it into political power by establishing themselves, with religion in mind, on the north Java coast, in Demak. It should also be noted that Sunda[322] was still Hindu until the arrival of the Portuguese in the early 16th century. These Portuguese newcomers broke the power of the maritime sultanates. There was therefore a weakening of both the Javanese powers and all the maritime sultanates. The Balinese took advantage of this weakening to project themselves beyond their island.

But to launch these conquests, they had to move armies in ships! Did the Balinese kingdoms have this power?

The islands of Lombok and Sumbawa are not very remote from Bali. Also, religious identities were not very pronounced at the time; it did not separate people. There were also a lot of Bugis[323] mercenaries, a Muslim sea-faring people, in these Balinese armies.

This tradition of warlike conquests is not the first thing that comes to mind when one thinks about Bali. Even if we know that these conquests existed …

---

[321] Sabdo Palon was an advisor to King Brawijaya V, the last Buddhist monarch of the Majapahit Empire in Java.
[322] Sunda: kingdom in western Java.
[323] Bugis: ethnic group from South Sulawesi.

And yet, the Balinese are known to have been very effective henchmen for the Dutch colonizers. Excellent warriors like Untung Suropati, a former slave and soldier of the East India Company at the end of the 17th century. Arrested for falling in love with a Dutch woman, he turned against his masters and led a famous rebellion. He even established a kingdom in Java, in the regions of Pasuruan, Malang and Probolinggo, which took the Dutch a long time to undo. Today he is considered a national hero. The Balinese who controlled these parts of East Java until the early 18th century eventually became Islamized. Between Islam and Hinduism, in fact, many capillaries have established themselves over time. The notion of *kafir* did not work in this context. Religion did not create ruptures. I think the Muslim classification of the Balinese as "others" came much later. This is a colonial Dutch import. Even when Amangkurat II[324] displaced populations en masse, replacing Hindus from Blambangan with locals from Central Java, in a form of ethnic cleansing of the time, there was no identity tension. People were simply bending to the power of the moment.

Unlike our contemporary times!

It's complicated. In fact, I would say that even now, in the depths of Balinese society, as in Javanese society, ordinary village people of modest education, the *wong cilik*, do not care about ethno-religious identity. Many Balinese have become Muslim after marrying a Javanese woman; this does not prevent them from celebrating Galungan and Kuningan[325] in Balinese fashion. And with their more or less Muslim wives, from celebrating Lebaran (Eid el-Kebir) in Java. In short, many Balinese and Javanese do not emphasize religious distancing! The same for women who change their religion to follow their husbands. It's not a problem. However, the more educated people are, the more this religious indifference crumbles, except for the minute cosmopolitan minority.

Can this become problematic?

It wasn't a problem in former times. Keep in mind that until fairly recently, until the mid-20th century, members of a western Balinese village, Banyubiru, could convert to Islam while maintaining the *banjar* system and, in part, ancestor worship.[326] So, why were they converting? Because Islam meant trade with Java and represented progress, wealth, the outside world, medicine! In Balinese villages, Islam was also represented by the *dukun*,[327] with their mantras taken from the Quranic text, and Muslim butchers. Ultimately, Islam had the power of positive otherness, it was

---

[324] Amangkurat II was the monarch of Mataram (in what is now Central Java) between 1677 and 1703. He worked extensively with the Dutch East India Company (VOC) to maintain his throne.
[325] *Galungan, Kuningan*: major Balinese religious festivals, corresponding to a long visit of the ancestors among their living descendants.
[326] "Bali et l'islam, Coexistence et perspectives contemporaines" by Jean Couteau, *Archipel* No. 60 (2000).
[327] *Dukun:* shaman.

the "cargo cult"[328] before the arrival of Europeans.

It's hard to get Westerners to admit it today, but Islam represented modernity.

It should be emphasized that in Indonesia generally, and, until recently, these notions of ethnic and religious belonging had been very vague for a long time. But modernity on the move is probably changing this, as we see in our discussions.

By being accommodating, you create a space of freedom, you open the field of possibilities ... This is also Indonesia.

To come back to otherness, we can also mention the notion of *segara rupek* between Bali and Java, that is, the idea that the sea is rough between the two islands. Proof of separation, therefore of otherness.

Since when did Bali reveal itself as Hindu? I don't mean from a legal point of view or conforming to the principles of Pancasila, but from a historical point of view ...

Westerners were the first to point out Bali as marked by India. This dates from the time of Raffles,[329] at the beginning of the 19th century, when Brahmins presented the British with texts which bore similarities to what the latter knew about India. The word Hindu was not stated as such. But one thing led to another and it was indeed Westerners who declared Bali "Hindu".

Not completely without reason, anyway.

Certainly, but above all operating on the sole criteria of the presence of Brahmins who, sociologically, had a rather thin power base. In any case, it helped to relate Bali's identity to that of India. This continued in the same century with the Sanskritists and their analyses of the texts of various *lontar*. Bali was soon imagined as a place in which the Hinduism was more perfect than in India. But the Balinese themselves did not know they were Hindus.

And after?

Well, as you said, after that there was Independence, Sukarno, and the need to adapt the Balinese religion to the principles of Pancasila, and in particular to the notion of one supreme deity. The Balinese themselves took part in the struggle for Indonesian independence. It gave them rights and provided them with networks. The sons of kings, sons of Brahmins and others had been sent to Java at the turn of the century for their studies. They forged strong links there with the Javanese

---

[328] Cargo cult: originally a Melanesian belief system based on the expectation of the arrival of ancestral spirits on ships full of food and other goods. Today, a description of how a community assimilates contributions from outside into its own culture.

[329] Thomas Stamford Bingley Raffles (1781-1826) was a British statesman and naturalist famous for founding the city of Singapore. He was also lieutenant-governor of the Dutch East Indies during the British interregnum from 1811 to 1816.

elites, the families of the sultans of Yogyakarta, Solo and elsewhere. This is how the Balinese reconnected to the myth of Majapahit, and wanted to give it a new reality. These elites immediately thought of themselves as Indonesian. The assertion of Indonesianity followed at the Sumpah Pemuda[330] in 1928.

In this positioning, there is indeed a relationship to the "other," the Dutch, the colonizer. This union is to confront another otherness.

The arrival of the Dutch is, of course, another otherness. It is often viewed in an ambiguous, if not positive, way, except perhaps in the Tabanan area, the main site of national resistance against the Dutch. It is mainly through the education provided at school that the image of the Dutch is negative. The several *puputan* that took place mythologized Bali as one of the great places of national resistance. But the Dutch also brought modernity *kemajuan* or progress and in the 1920s and '30s, they created the image of paradisiacal Bali on which today's tourism is based. Thus, Bali acquired its current importance largely because of the colonial Dutch. With several returns of the favor: the Balinese grant figures such as Walter Spies and Rudolf Bonnet a bigger role than they actually had. They made myths of them. The princes of Ubud contributed to this mythical construction: they benefited from it. Their reputation was enhanced for their patronage of foreign artists fascinated by Bali who were in fact, from their traditional point of view, their courtiers, their servants, as Tjokorde Agung Sukawati[331] put it. This gave them enormous prestige. Rather ambiguous, no? In the book I co-authored on Walter Spies,[332] I wanted to bring these myths back to reality.

As local potentates, didn't the princes primarily serve the interests of the Dutch crown?

Of course, but there has definitely been an image shift with the arrival of culture; here I mean Balinese culture plus Culture with a capital C, to sublimate the whole. In this particular sense, the culture of Bali is a Western creation, adopted by the Balinese themselves. In all of this, of course, we can read an overvaluation of the foreigner, despite a very real Indonesian nationalism. To sum it up, I would say that the Balinese, especially older ones, find it hard to hate the Dutch. You don't hear pejorative terms used for them.

In Java, there is *Londo*.[333]

Yes, in Java resentment towards the Dutch is stronger. I remember once, when I was walking the streets of Surabaya, I would hear people heckle me with *Kontol*

---

[330] Sumpah Pemuda: The "Youth Oath" is the founding episode of the Indonesian independence movement. It represents the first declaration of values governing the founding of the future republic of Indonesia.

[331] Tjokorde Agung Sukawati (1910-1978) was a prince of Ubud.

[332] Walter Spies Collectors Suite: *Walter Spies: The Art of Life and Walter Spies: A Life in Art*, by John Stowell and Jean Couteau (2011/2012).

[333] *Londo*: from "Belanda," Holland.

kuda[334] as I walked by. But that was a long time ago. In Bali, such things never occurred. On the contrary. Until recently, most Balinese used the word *tamiu*, a High Balinese term meaning "guest," or more simply *Jawa Perancis* (Javanese from France).

Yes, but the word *bule* is now used everywhere to refer to whites.

I saw it spread in the 1980s, that word, *bule*.

This is a real racist term!

Yes, it came from Jakarta. It was literally racist in the beginning, because the term means "albino".

Yes, it is both a genetic defect, a kind of disease, but also a disease that affects the skin and its color! And in Balinese culture for that matter, it was even considered a curse. It couldn't be more racist!

OK, but now it has somehow stopped being racist. Today, this term is used as well to refer to foreigners of all sorts: Japanese, Koreans, even Africans!

I remain very skeptical on this subject. It's like in Europe or the United States in the 1960s or '70s, when people still said "Negro" without bad intent. It had passed into everyday language to the extent that people no longer saw its racist charge. But it persisted nonetheless ...

Again, this is the problem with categorizations.

Categories don't forgive everything. Can we say that there is racism in Bali?

These categorizations are becoming more and more apparent, in the various media for example. And from there, it begins to create realities: ethno-religious affiliation is more and more accentuated. There is one point we must emphasize, however: until the first Islamist attack in 2002, Balinese focused their sense of belonging locally, on the village and the clan. At least among the common people. Since then, identity has broadened both spatially and sociologically; it has become Hindu-Balinese, which means that local identities are undermined and have faded in favor of a Balinese Hindu identity at the national level.

Nowadays, who is the "other" of Indonesian nationality? Is that anyone from outside Bali, like *jaba* before?

Today it is the impoverished Muslim. Rich Muslims do not mention their religion here, they are on vacation, they go to beautiful hotels. It is only recently that we have really seen an accentuation of religious identity to which, it must be stressed, many are opposed. Remember that Balinese espoused the values of the Republic of Indonesia all the more easily because Sukarno was half Balinese. It was he who granted the Balinese official recognition of their religion. In the

---

[334] *Kontol kuda*: horse cock.

Sukarno days in Java and Bali, people did not think of themselves in terms of ethnicity and even less of religion. Their main concern was to get out of poverty, rather than gain recognition for their particularities. Indonesian humanism still worked very well ...

How has it evolved then?

There was the rise of communism and the events of 1965-1966. How did one counter this doctrine? By putting the emphasis on religion and tradition. From that time onward, the teaching of religion has consisted of restructuring religion, in fact transforming a popular practice considered deviant and thus potentially open to communism. In the case of Bali, Hindu dogmas were thus imported for some, locally "manufactured" for others.[335] We see now the result on the ground. Little by little, people talked less about ancestor worship, they played down the role of animism, and, in the process, Bali became increasingly monotheistic: Sang Hyang Widi and its *manifestasi* is now highlighted in official prayers, ensuring the pantheistic link between popular polytheism and rigorous monotheism! This transformation took place through national education, and was the result of an increasingly literal reading of religious texts by more and more people. Thus, what was originally a political instrument against the left and its dreams of social justice has over time become a fixation on religious identity!

Should this also be seen as an expression of nationalism, the left being at its core internationalist?

Yes! This is another aspect, but more recent. Although initially politically driven against the left, the religious domain, once it had become popular in the 1980s, turned into a favorite weapon against the intrusion of non-Balinese capital. We have already talked about this in connection with Bali's economic alienation and demographic changes on its soil. All this has dramatically accentuated the feeling of identity of the Balinese.

Regarding this identity, didn't you say that the Balinese easily assimilate outsiders?

Yes, the Balinese easily assimilate individuals. Not so much groups of outsiders. There has always been separation. In former times, Muslim and Chinese Indonesians had their own status, their own space, with rights granted to them by kings. They were traders on the coast, and mercenaries near the center of the kingdoms.

What about now?

There is separation between ethno-religious groups. The only spaces of real mixed social intercourse are at the level of national institutions such as the judiciary, the army and police, or among members of the cosmopolitan elite in the South. And among artists, to a certain extent.

---

[335] From the Brahmanic tradition and the Kawi literature introduced by post-1343 Javanization.

What about education?

Schoolchildren and university students mix, usually with no problem. The real problem is at another level. While I was going through an official publication from Udayana University, I discovered to my dismay that all the higher staff of the university, from the dean up, are ethnic Balinese. Among the 35 of them, not a single Muslim, not a single Christian, even though minorities make up 15% to 20% of the population. Thus, we have an institution, and there are certainly others of the same ilk at the regional level, in which people regularly sing the national anthem, regularly claim that the Balinese are tolerant, but who "naturally" practice a strict ethno-nepotism that blocks the access of non-Balinese to power. An institution that should be an instrument of enlightenment is becoming an instrument of blindness. It is all the more worrying as the discrimination is pervasive, and people aren't even aware of it.

About this "other" of Indonesian nationality, do the Balinese make a difference today between the Javanese, the Sumatran, the Timorese?

These days, yes. There is a differentiated perception. In the past, the "other" Indonesians were Javanese. They integrated easily because they did not yet bring a Muslim discourse. In the 1980s, this was still the case. There weren't many of them and it wasn't a problem. It was later that they began to create homogeneous Muslim spaces. It was also at this time that ethno-religious separations started to appear separations accentuated by an orthodox Islam, formerly invisible or discreet.

Are there new phenomena of discrimination?

With the establishment of Indonesian *pendatang* and foreign residents, there are more and more places that are increasingly ethnically homogeneous, and thus separate. In the past, land was controlled by villages, whereas today it is individual property. But there is also discrimination linked to tourism. There are Western clubs which are de facto closed to the Balinese. Beaches are occasionally forbidden to them.

Not especially the Balinese, I would say... These are private places where the selection is made by money and perhaps also by what brings their clientele together. There have indeed been attempts by certain hotels to privatize portions of the beaches, but this is illegal and difficult to achieve in practice. I do not believe these rumors of a local brand of apartheid, that we hear from time to time.

Yes, but there is an indisputable exclusivity among certain foreign populations in Bali. Discrimination operates through economic and cultural filtering. Some establishments offer services or products aimed exclusively at the tastes of a well-defined clientele ...

So, Bali does not reflect a neocolonialist attitude, contrary to what these recurring rumors implicitly suggest?

It's more complex. The exclusivity is now accentuated by our smartphones, all over the world. Foreigners in Bali no longer need to assimilate, as you and I did in the past. There is implicit discrimination.

There are also more discreet forms of discrimination. With the sprouting of *warung muslim*[336] all over Bali, we have seen the emergence of Hindu *warung*. But in fact cuisine in Bali was never subject to particular religious constraints, even with regard to beef.

Food can create separation: the sexual fluidity that once existed between Hindus and Muslims is disappearing among the educated population. This is the most worrying aspect of these recent phenomena of discrimination.

With the lynchings, perhaps?

These come in waves and are based on rumors that suddenly take hold of populations. But there are a lot fewer than in the past. The last decade has been very prosperous, which no doubt explains this decline. It would also seem that they are now more directed towards the latest waves of migrants, people from NTT. No one really takes offense at the lynchings and discriminatory measures against non-Balinese, except perhaps a handful of intellectuals. And the lynchings have not crystallized in structured racism of the kind one finds in the West. There is no hate speech behind these acts. The next day, those who participated in the lynching, will buy *bakso*[337] from a peddler hardly different from the one they roughed up the day before.

The differentiation between groups is also reinforced by eating behaviors and ad hoc clothing, which did not exist in the past.

Of course! In the old days, you could joke with Muslims about pork, nobody cared, everyone laughed! Today, we are seeing disturbing changes. The separation is made and affirmed in the way of dressing, in the new rigor of eating halal among Muslims and of eating *sukla*[338] among certain Balinese.

How does Christianity fare today in Bali? Don't Christians come mainly from the eastern part of the Indonesian archipelago, from NTT ...

In the past, Christians, headed by Dutch missionaries, were the most aggressive in spreading their good word. Today, there are Balinese who convert to Christianity, and others to Islam, for that matter. Some because of the pressures that Balinese tradition places on them, others to marry someone from a different faith.

What is Bali's current position in the Republic of Indonesia?

In moderately Islamized national circles, Bali is Indonesia's international showcase. There is real pride in Bali. For some Javanese, Bali is even what Java

---

[336] *Warung muslim*: modest roadside cafe-restaurant, in this case, halal.
[337] *Bakso*: rice balls with meat, often sold by Javanese.
[338] *Sukla*: a Balinese term meaning "fit for (Balinese Hindu) ritual use."

should have remained.

What about Bali's economic weight at the national level?

This is where the Balinese complain; some believe they are being robbed of their revenues. But it gives them a certain prestige.

Of course. Not only are the Balinese beautiful, rich in a unique culture, but they also generate a lot of money!

Yes, but some Indonesians also complain about the cliché that everyone overseas knows Bali, but no one knows Indonesia. Foreigners are all thought to believe that Bali is an independent country.

Is there separatism?

I think not. Some in the West will say that Indonesia is a Muslim construct. No, really! There was indeed a call for a referendum in Bali in 1998, when a national politician declared that a Hindu could not be president.[339] But he was quickly put back in his place, he apologized, and it was not followed up; or rather the politician involved was accused of not being a nationalist, because he was disrespectful of Pancasila. Indonesia is first and foremost a multicultural construct with religion as one of its basic principles. Is it solid? Brittle? I do not know. However, I tend to think it's solid, because of Indonesia's inherent cultural flexibility.

Can we say that Indonesia is indeed a Javanese construction?

Yes, in a way, but again, things are vague and that's all the better! But can we really say that Indonesia is Javanese when Bahasa Indonesia is the language of a very Islamized minority, the Malays of the Straits of Malacca? Not to mention that the great Javanese literature, very little Islamized, is not taught in schools.

What is Bali's role in the Indonesian archipelago?

It's a key role: without Bali, Indonesia can't claim to be a multicultural country! This island is the symbol of Indonesian pluralism. This is what allows Indonesians to say: we are not a Muslim country.

There are also more than twenty million Christians in Indonesia. But they do not have the same symbolic value since Muslim countries with a Christian minority are quite common, aren't they?

Yes, Bali holds a key position and has a strong symbolic value.

And conversely, how does Bali relate to Islam?

There are demographic changes in the urban areas of the south of the island where the presence of Muslims is estimated at 25-30% of the population, and undoubtedly even a majority of non-Balinese in certain areas of south Badung.

---

[339] The politician was A.M. Saefuffin.

This of course changes the perception of Islam among the Balinese. Traditionally the Balino-Muslims, who originate from the Muslim villages of the island, speak Balinese among themselves and are very well integrated. They often say, "We are Balinese, but Muslims." In the past, they were called *"nyama slam /* our Muslim brothers," and Balinese kings participated in the construction of their mosques.[340] Balino-Muslims participated in some Balinese rites with their own rites and music. They intermarried with Hindu Balinese. We find traces of this Muslim presence all over the island, often around *puri.*[341] However, they are now very much in the minority among all Muslims living in Bali. One must also mention that the first Muslims who settled in Bali were raised by their descendants to the status of Balinese-style ancestors. They became "the ancestors from Mecca," complete with their temples and pork-free offerings. In short, their descendants were Balinized an instance in which Islam was swallowed by Bali. But this was centuries ago.

What happens between Javanese kampong and Balinese kampong?

Things sometimes get tense, especially when it comes to new immigrants from Java. Why? Because the traditions are different. Not so much the food traditions like pork, which the Balinese adore and the Muslim ban but above all the management of death. Imagine a Muslim funeral procession passing in front of a temple: the purity of the territory, and that of the temple, can be considered defiled. It will need a purification ceremony. But who will have to pay for it? Muslims? But, for some of them, paying for a ceremony for gods who are not God is forbidden, *sirik.* So, there are tensions.

It hasn't always been like that, has it?

Muslims not only have their traditional cemeteries all over the island, but some tombs have become sacred places for the Balinese, with guardians who are Balinese as well, as in Seseh, not far from Canggu.

So, it's a lot more complicated than one might think. What about Chinese-Indonesians in Bali? In former times didn't they completely integrate into the villages, speak Balinese and sometimes become Hindu?

Yes. Absolutely. The earlier Chinese had their Balinese altar, and some Balinese have an altar for their distant Chinese ancestors. But the recently arrived Chinese, who moved to Bali from Java, are much less close to the Balinese, except in the Ubud region, where they are the main buyers of Balinese paintings. They are probably better viewed in Ubud than anywhere else in Indonesia.

We also find a trend of separation by Westerners residing on the island

---

[340] See *Menyama Braya: Studi Perubahan Masyarakat Bali* by Wayan Damayana, UKSW (2011).

[341] *Puri:* palace, residence of the nobility. The dependents of the *puri* live near the palace, in *banjar pekandelan* (literally, *banjar* of the loyal).

today. Those of the past were still fascinated by the local culture and mingled easily with the Balinese, while those of today live in their villas, in neighborhoods they created, where they have their own restaurants, shops, etc.

Yes, that's true. There is also the language factor. In the old days, to live here, you had to learn Indonesian, if not Balinese. Today, English is enough to live in some spaces.

In this panoply of differences, where does the biggest obstacle lie for the Balinese?

In the evolution of Islam. One of the candidates for one of the four senatorial seats attributed to Bali has recently run in the name of Islam, albeit as a moderate. There are also Balinese universities with a significant number of students coming from other islands. Up to 40% of students at Udayana University are from outside Bali. (There is no fixed quota, but at the students' selection levels, steps are taken to guarantee a national mix.) Some female students wear the full veil. These communities live in urban spaces where they de facto self-marginalize. Yet, relations remain very good. There is no hate speech.

In previous centuries, Bali not being a unified whole, the relationship to the outside world was probably not uniform either?

Yes, Bali was made up of kingdoms that were at war with each other. And wars were frequent. This left traces in the toponymy, in many place names. For example, in Denpasar, the *banjar* Tainsiat means *taen siat,* i.e., "there was war". *Jagapati*, in Badung, means "Watch out for death." *Anggapati*, "death". Identities then were crystallized around kings and princes.

So, at that time, the other was first and foremost other Balinese.

Yes, due to different allegiances, networks of different clan temples. But the networks crossed, and there were large common religious ceremonies, especially at Besakih and in the large territorial temples, the *kahyangan jagat.*

Except that some major events on the religious calendar were not celebrated at the same time during the time of the kingdoms.

Yes, that's true. For example, Nyepi.[342] There were all kinds of Nyepi, depending on the village.

Yes, yet based today on the lunar calendar. Another thing that I would like to mention is the fact that until the 19th century, Bali was one of the most important centers of the slave trade outside the Atlantic world. After Zanzibar, however, located on the other side of the Indian Ocean.

In the 18th century, ships came to Bali from Île de France and Île Bourbon in the

---

[342] *Nyepi*: the Day of Silence, which marks the new year of the Saka lunar calendar in Bali.

Indian Ocean to buy slaves. There were then only a few thousand people on these French lands and the genetic heritage of the populations that inhabit them today undoubtedly includes Balinese blood.

Yes, we must not forget to mention the fact that these slaves sold by Balinese merchants were Balinese.

Yes, until the 18th century, Balinese slaves made up between 20% and 30% of Betawi, the population of Batavia, now Jakarta. Panji Sakti, king of Buleleng at the end of the 17th century, was known to be a major supplier of slaves.

When you know Bali today, so proud of its identity and unity, it's hard to imagine it as an agglomerate of kingdoms waging war against each other and selling their respective populations as slaves.

In fact, the island was neither politically nor economically united. The only way to cross the many deep river ravines was by bamboo footbridges. It was the Dutch who unified the island by building a network of roads and bridges.

Each kingdom had to be autonomous, self-sufficient.

Yes, the many valleys and gorges, gouged out by seismic activity and erosion, were difficult to cross; this created separations and to a large extent defined the political and economic units. Also, the island was not fully populated then, many forest areas remained, which created buffer zones and physically separated the Balinese who claimed descent from Majapahit from others. That is, between the Javanized aristocrats of the low plains and the villagers of the interior, the *Bali Aga*.[343]

Can we say that Balinese society today thinks of itself as a whole?

Yes. Bali thinks of itself as a whole in relation to the other, but in relation to Bali, definitely not!

---

[343] *Bali Aga*: Balinese people who still retain traditions and customs that predate the Hinduism brought by Java.

PART FOUR

MOKSA

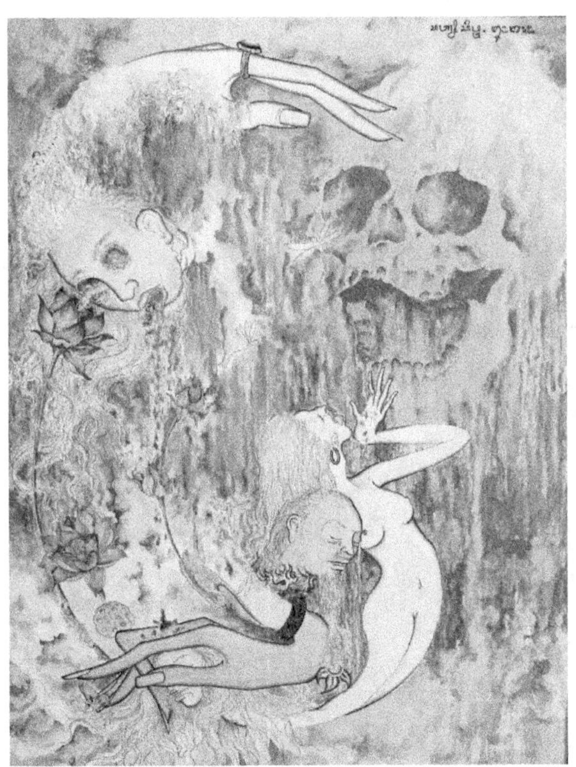

Spirits of The Forest by Satya Cipta, 29,7 cm x 42cm,
24ct gold, mixed media on arches paper

13. Evolution and Role of Religion, Religious Pressure, Commercialization

The Balinese religion is fundamentally a village religion, a cult of ancestors coupled with a cult of nature. Moreover, the importance of nature is found in traditional architecture, and it is directly part of the human organization of space, explains Jean Couteau in this interview. As for Hinduism, it came to Bali not from India but from Java, the "old country". In former times, God didn't have to be justified, it was taken for granted. Today, the obsession with identity takes precedence. Now, Westerners expect the Balinese to produce a Hindu paradise, thus catching them in a "narcissistic trap." Jean also reflects on the influence of tourism on the Balinese religion. When did the Balinese start to think of themselves as Hindus? Are there increased pressures on religious duty today? We then discuss new types of priesthood; the Balinese who go to India to seek holy water; the introduction of prayer which interrupts television programs... All this contributes to changes in religious experience. Is there a commodification of ritual today? Jean reminds us again that the Balinese have no need for intellectual coherence to justify all these sometimes contradictory phenomena.

Eric Buvelot. **What is the Balinese religion today?**

Jean Couteau. These days, if you ask Balinese what their religion is, most of them will say they are Hindu. Some go so far as to follow Indian rites, such as *agni hotra*, others refer to the Hindu trinity, the Trimurti; but in reality, if we go to the foundations of their beliefs, the village dimension, we find that they are in fact not very Hindu. In the villages, people primarily address their ancestors. When there are temple festivals, the attending gods are ancestral deities, accompanied by all kinds of *ancangan*,[344] not the Hindu gods. These may reside on the mountains, as the old treatises say, but they do not come down "visiting" like the temple gods. Except Durga,[345] in the magical rite of the Barong. They therefore command things from the heights without really interfering in the ritual. This says a lot about syncretism: the Balinese religion is a cult of ancestors embellished with a cult of nature on which is superimposed an Indianized cosmological reading and which the Balinese are in the process of re-Indianizing in modernity.

Justified, nonetheless, by history.

Yes, you are right to say so. This phenomenon of superposition has indeed existed

---

[344] *Ancangan*: companion of the gods.
[345] *Durga*: the goddess Durga, also known as "Shakti" or "Devi," is the protective mother of the universe.

for more than a thousand years, but in a different way according to the social spaces. Indian traditions, let's say the Hindu gods, penetrated from the "top," via palaces and networks of Brahmins and associated meditators; they then spread through the theatre, the *wayang*[346] in particular. This "Hinduism" arrived not from India, but from Java in different waves during the twists and turns of history, the strongest of these being the Javanese invasion by the Majapahit empire. There is hardly any genetic Indian trace in the Balinese population. Remember, too, that before Hinduism, from the sixth century there was a Buddhist presence in Bali. Some may say that it is almost the same thing and that the difference is in the way one reads the cosmic mechanics. Of course, but it also shows the complexity of things. Especially since these external influences vary from place to place. Thus, death rituals are less Indianized in isolated regions of Bali: cremation is not practiced there; besides, the cremation rite of *ngaben* is more Balinese than Hindu. Its object is certainly to separate the bodily elements from the spiritual elements, in the Hindu manner except that these bodily elements will end up in the sea, passing first, most often, by the river, while the soul will ultimately be taken back, in rite after rite, to the mountain of its origins where it will "become water" (*dadi yeh*), as people say, awaiting its return as "drops" (*titisan*), the reincarnated ancestor. It is all very Balinese.[347] As for liberation from the chain of incarnations, this is mainly a dream of old scholars, mostly Brahmins, and contemporary devotees obsessed with re-Indianization. All the clan groups on the island also have temples at the foot of the mountains, mainly in Besakih. This is where, at the end of the death rites, the deceased are sent back to the heights above the mountains in the "land of deified souls". So, we are very much in Bali.

The notion of reincarnation is still of Indian origin.

Yes, but here it is Balinized, translated by the symbol of the droplet, or *titisan*. We can see the amalgamation of the cult of nature, here water, and the cult of ancestors, because ancestors have become water. Between the cult of nature that of the mountain, of water and the notion of reincarnation, well, it all blends together, each into the other. This syncretic fusion is a reality that can still be found throughout Southeast Asia: there is, fundamentally, the cult of ancestors, and, imbedded in it, the Indian discourse of the transmigration of souls and of unification with the great Whole: *moksa, nirwana, pelepasan*, according to traditions.

So, Westerners are mistaken when they say that Bali is Hindu?

For some reason, or rather because of the ongoing re-Indianization, they take official religious discourse for social reality. They want to see Hindu or Buddhist meditators everywhere. It is as if Japanese visitors mistook all French people for Cistercian monks and went to stay on the banks of the Loire in search of French

---

[346] *Wayang*: shadow-puppet theatre; traditional performance from Java and Bali.

[347] There is also, very frequently, the rite of the exhumation of the dead (*ngagah*) that was once found throughout the Archipelago and beyond, as far as Madagascar. See "The Pre-Hindu Substrate of Ancestor Worship: Rite of the Dead in Bali", Jean Couteau, *Archipel* No. 97, 2019, pp. 151-172.

wisdom! Popular religion in Bali is very different from the advertised religious norm, which is recent.

Can you expand on the importance of nature in Balinese religion and culture?

It's fundamental. For example, in architecture: all constructions are physically oriented along two natural axes of symbolic purity: the upstream / downstream axis (*kaja / kelod*) and the axis of the rising and setting of the sun (*kangin / kauh*). The temple of the household is located *kaja kangin*, that is, upstream, toward the mountain and the rising sun; while the outlet of wastewater and impurities is *kelod kauh* downstream, toward the sea and the setting sun. In the villages, the temple of the dead is located on the downstream side, toward setting sun. Nature, and with it, sacredness, is thus directly embedded in the human organization of space. Large trees are sacred. They have their own spirit: people wrap them with a sash of cloth; some even have an altar for their holy "resident" (*duwe*).

This is the animist basis of the Balinese religion.

It is indeed extraordinary. There are plenty of examples. Banyan leaves are used to make effigies of the dead for the post-cremation *nyekah* mortuary ceremony, before sending the soul to the mountain heights. To make the Barong, the wood of the mask is ceremonially cut from the *kepuh* tree. In the Calonarang dance, the goddess Durga, the avenger, descends to incarnate through a tree before sowing terror. We must also mention the *majegau* tree, a symbol of Shiva, whose wood is used to make certain altars. In fact, all the elements of nature are sacred in one way or another. [348]

Do people really believe in all these things? And in the effectiveness of the rites linked to them?

The Balinese do not question this or that element of their beliefs, even if the animist aspects are obvious. They have been submerged in it since infancy. However, in ritual matters, they take more account of economic factors. They might choose a simple version of a rite, rather than a complex one, but without questioning the rite itself. So, things are changing: for example, in regard to cremation, people have gone from burning wood to using a gas burner and, now, to cremation in crematoriums, ritually complete of course. And they justify this mutation by ad hoc quotations from sacred texts.

The economy therefore forces the Balinese to question centuries-old rites!

Yes. Some rites are simplified. On the other hand, for those who can afford it, sumptuous rites are still there, as a way of revitalizing your prestige. The aristocrats, *triwangsa*, want to maintain their status intact, the nouveau riche *sudra*, to assert

---

[348] There are treatises on wood, their quality, and their positioning in the compass rose of the universe.

themselves as their equals. All this shakes up not only the social structure, but also religion and all the ideological apparatus which supports it.

So, what is the position of the state?

Regarding social structure, it has always naturally leaned toward democratization despite the reluctance of the *triwangsa*. There, everyone agrees. But where it has been, and remains, complicated is in the realm of religion, because it was necessary to make the religion of Bali compatible with the other religions of Indonesia.

Is there thus a desire for Islamization?

No. The state is undoubtedly under the influence of Islam, but Indonesia is not an Islamic state, far from it. However, as early as Independence, there was much to be done to make the Balinese religion acceptable from the monotheistic perspective demanded by Pancasila. Apart from the pantheistic speculations of a few Brahmins, the notion of God as the One barely existed in Bali, or rather did not have to exist, for the majority of Balinese. People didn't have to state it, as they do now. God was and still is for many people the *Ratu Gede*, the deity of the particular place, or the *sesuhunan*, the one to be implored, who does not need a name with a special meaning.

Is it because God goes without saying?

Above all, God does not have to be justified, nor even defined. People speak of the god of the *kepuh*[349] tree *(betara punyan kepuh)*, or east of the river *(betara dangin tukad)*. It is not known whether it is personified or abstract. It depends on the people. According to the classic manuscript *Gong Besi*,[350] it is said that God, or the divine, descends and that he has a different name depending on where he sits. God does not need, or rather did not need in the past, to be named in a specific way. This way of relating to religion was obviously not to please Muslims or staunch Christians, not to mention certain Balinese sensitive to mockery.[351] Since the recognition of their religion in 1958 and their formal acceptance of monotheism, modern Balinese, supported by the state, therefore tell you that the god of the *kepuh* tree is a *manifestasi* of Sang Hyang Widi, the one God, which is a way of refusing animism. This does not simplify the situation on the ground. There is a continuum, from those who firmly believe in the presence of a *betara*[352] in the tree, to those who are convinced that they are making an act of monotheism by equating all local gods and all Indian gods to *manifestasi* of the One. Good for them.

Why all these nuances? Is it because Bali is an island with a culture that was little exposed to elsewhere and to others?

---

[349] *Kepuh*: *Sterculia foetida*, Java olive tree.

[350] *Tutur Gong Besi* is a current book which lists the values of the Balinese religion and which is based on a *lontar* written in Old Javanese.

[351] Putu Setia, in *Menggugat Bali* (*Accusing Bali*), 1986, and *Bali Menggugat* (Bali Accuses), 2014.

[352] *Betara*: god, divinity.

I think so. We come back to what Michel Picard said, it is indeed largely in the relation to the "other" that the Balinese have finally, and recently, been obliged to define their system of convictions, or rather their system of explanatory references of the world, by using a terminology that is not their own. The Indian contributions of a thousand years ago constituted only a half-system which penetrated by capillary action over the long term, without overturning tradition, irrigating it here and there with Indian cosmology according to the needs, especially political, of the moment. It was able to generate "twice born" high priests, producers of holy water, and spread great stories, but did not destroy ancestor worship.

When did the shock come for this cult?

With the arrival of the West and of modernity. For example, the word *agama*, which now means "religion," is of Indian origin. The Balinese did not need such a word. It is only with the arrival of otherness, in particular the political otherness of the colonizing West, that, because they had to define themselves, they came to define their beliefs in the Western sense of religion as a coherent system. As Michel Picard explains, the colonizing Dutch attributed to the Balinese a religion or *agama* called "Hindu" and made this classification make sense. In other words, they set in motion the conceptual machine, which was taken over by the Balinese. Consequently, not only do the Balinese now call themselves "Hindu," or more exactly "Hindu-Dharma," but they are determined to become so.

Has that always been the only name?

Balinese religion has long been labeled *siwa-buda*, because of its Majapahit origins, or as *gama tirta*, the religion of water, because of the role of holy water, irrigation water, and descent in Balinese life. These were several names among many, since none were supposed to be definitive. There used to be no real need for standardization or conceptualization. Now it is exactly the other way around. There has been a reversal of attitudes in a few decades. It has gone from a certain indifference to concepts of religion to a need for an explanatory definition of the world. Ultimately, it ends up a situation of over-valuing the religious domain, which is increasingly imported and defined ever more strictly around a neo-Shivaite orthodoxy built around old classical Indian texts and disseminated through the regional state apparatus, through Parisada,[353] and school and university education.

Wouldn't there be two sorts of relations to the outside world that explain this evolution of religion? A first, which represents the period of colonization when the Dutch define the Balinese as "Hindus," and a second, that of modern Bali where the Balinese must play their role of Hindu tourist curiosity?

You are forgetting another aspect. Besides the role of the Balinese as a tourist object,

---

[353] For the history of Parisada, see *Kebalian – La construction dialogique de l'identité balinaise* by Michel Picard, Association Archipel, 2017, pp. 177-209.

they have a national role in the Republic of Indonesia. They accept Indonesia because it reserves for them a space in which their religion is recognized, even in the minority. Everywhere in the Indonesian archipelago where there are Balinese communities, there are temples and a symbol of the return of Hinduism, in Java and elsewhere. The Balinese even built a very large Hindu-Balinese temple on the slopes of Semeru, the ancient magical mountain of Java, and regained the Tenggerese of East Java to their religion.[354] This is an acting out of the myth of the return of the Hindu-Javanese empire of Majapahit, a myth that works all the better as it is also claimed by part of the national elites.

Can we talk a bit more about the influence of tourism on religion in Bali? It is well known that Balinese take great pride in being a tourist destination based on their culture and traditions. Have there been changes or modifications made to their religion based on this assumed image of cultural tourism?

It comes back to politics. Before 1965-1966 and the massacres of communists, many Balinese had adopted the grand ideas of what can be called "modernism," including grand social ideas like communism, which was not that of Marx or Lenin but which represented a hope for justice carried by certain Westernized elites in the country. After the massacres, the new military power in charge turned things around by emphasizing religion and traditions, that is, anything but social issues. People were therefore forced to define themselves in relation to their faith. But there was tourism, which was to provide for the Balinese. It was therefore necessary to adjust the erotic image of Bali, dear to Westerners, with the idea of a Hindu society of perfect harmony, dear to the Balinese. As tourists, Westerners expect the Balinese to produce a Hindu paradise. This has undeniably contributed to a shaping of Bali, leading to the crystallization of identity that we are witnessing today.

Aren't you a little harsh on tourism?

I don't think so. Tourism has undoubtedly contributed largely to this mythification of tradition, and by extension, of culture, then, finally, of the Balinese religion elements which were not formerly differentiated from each other. Western tourists are also partly responsible for the political concern of some Balinese, especially with regard to Islam, since tourists and semi-residents tend to ask the Balinese around them about their relation to Islam.

Mightn't the Balinese have fallen into a trap of narcissism?

Absolutely, here is a perfect formula. And they can't get out of it. In the past, this narcissism was the opposite of what it has become today, because it was only defined in relation to itself: there was really only Bali and a vague idea of an outside world. Now, reeling from otherness, some Balinese believe that Bali

---

[354] Tenggerese: population which occupies the flanks of Bromo and which escaped the Islamization of the island of Java.

represents the ideal future of the world. Made aware of the world's ecological problems, they no longer hesitate to suggest that the world adopt the principles of *Tri Hita Karana*, or the Day of Silence with "Nyepi for the World" and so forth.

Yes, the amazing slogan "BALI FOR THE WORLD" of some years ago!

There is a kind of shift in cultural themes which reflects a profound change in Balinese society. Bali is coming out of its shell. I have already mentioned the temples that the Balinese are opening all over Indonesia. Now, not only are they nationalizing, but they are also internationalizing. They are taking the plunge abroad, as people go on pilgrimage to India, and even to the great religious festival Kumbh Mela which is held at the confluence of the Ganges and the Yamuna. They go to seek the truth in India, or find stones, construed as divine gifts (*pica*) and sources of magical powers. In art, statues inspired by Indian iconography are now becoming more common.[355]

Based on all these configurations, do you have any idea how tourism could have changed the relationship to faith here? I think of this simple illustration of the phenomenon: when the Balinese go to the temple today, they are very likely to be photographed from all angles by tourists. Are they constantly being portrayed, in a sort of "society of Balinese spectacle," as I have written in an article, daring to maliciously adapt Guy Debord here?[356]

It is certain that from the 1970s, when Westerners arrived en masse in the Far East with their own obsession with identity, they wanted to adopt other identities. Here, in Bali, they wanted to become Balinese. This resulted in a number of transformations, and a lot of misunderstandings: Ubud, from a simple village, became a New Age mecca. This led to manipulations of the Balinese religion. Mick Jagger had a Balinese wedding here. David Bowie wished his ashes to be scattered in Bali. This still occurs, but it also means that one has recourse to a local priest in reality a simple reciter of mantras who operates certain purification mechanisms borrowed from Balinese rites and who, at the same time, internationalizes them, to the delight of lovers of universalist paradise from the confused West!

Like in India in the 1970s ...

Yes, but I think they are more naive here. Westerners go to India to learn the truth, whereas here, they come to dispense it. The truth has always been on the side of the Westerners here. They can fabricate their own Hinduism here.

Here is an assertion which can be debated! I believe Westerners have also come here to admire. The notion of image is fundamental in this magical and idealized relationship between one world and another.

---

[355] The most famous, and least noticed, is that of Saraswati, the goddess of knowledge. But one might find Ganesha, Siwa Natar Raja, etc.

[356] Guy Debord (1931-1994) is a French intellectual who founded the Situationist International. He wrote *The Society of the Spectacle* in 1967, a book considered the seminal text of Situationism.

Almost a pious image!

Idealized, certainly, because there is also the issue of commodification that comes into play. The whole system of tourism produces images which ensure the persistence of the myth. It's only marketing, but it helps make reality!

Speaking of marketing, what have the Balinese produced as texts about their own religion, historically?

A number of traditional para-philosophical texts, but they have never been structured into a coherent and homogeneous corpus. So, there is no single holy book, [357] but there are explanatory and exploratory attempts, stories and interpretations that border on magic and philosophy. For example, the multiple treatises on the *catur sanak* (four siblings) which are the four elements that accompany the birth of a child: the amniotic fluid, the placenta, the fat, and the blood, construed as the four energies that will protect a child all its life. This is a tradition that exists, in one variant or another, throughout the Indonesian archipelago and is therefore much older than Indian influences. But these nevertheless appear in magico-philosophical speculations concerning the dialectic between the human microcosm (*buana alit*) and the macrocosm (*buana agung*), symbolized by the "four siblings". The rites relating to these little siblings frame the person throughout his life. The four siblings are symbolized by the placenta, which is buried in the family compound and throughout life given offerings on appropriate days. There is also the altar of *taksu*,[358] that is, the altar of everyone's cosmic double. In Bali, it is said that the body is inhabited by forces, divine and chthonic,[359] which each have their equivalent in the cosmos, an Indianized term. There is similar speculation about many other aspects of Balinese culture, such as the architecture of houses and temples which are also cosmological models. One should also mention the speculations around letters of Balinese script, including magical letters, the *modre aksara*, used to achieve *Ongkara*, non-duality.[360] Did these speculations spread with Indo-Javanese influences at the turn of the first millennium only to find themselves fully structured and codified now, in the great ordering that modernity imposes on Bali? It's possible. But there are also many treatises which offer modern readings of the system of offerings, discussing for example the links between colors and cardinal points, between micro and macro. All this often on a mix between the magical and the philosophical, between Bali, India and Java.

Let's go back to the influences of tourism on the Balinese religion.

Many Balinese tend to see themselves as foreigners want to see them. This

---

[357] Except perhaps the *Sarasamuscaya*, but Indianized Balinese prefer to mention the *Vedas*, the *Bhagavad Gita*, the Indian purana, etc.

[358] *Taksu* is a Balinese concept that brings together notions of charisma, spiritual strength, and inspiration necessary to attract the attention of humans and gods alike.

[359] *Chthonian*: relating to the underworld.

[360] *Ongkara*: a composite letter, the equivalent of Om / Aum, well known among Buddhists.

establishes a somewhat ambiguous complicity, because it is at odds with the Indonesian national space. As I mentioned earlier, some foreigners are waiting for Bali to declare itself Islamophobic, to secede, and so forth. There is a kind of misunderstanding of the deep Indonesian national culture of which the Balinese are obviously a part.

Do the Balinese like to please that much? Are they afraid of disappointing their admirers?

It is difficult to criticize the Balinese. They continually assert their cultural egos, even the most ignorant! Often, I meet young Balinese, and not so young, who know their culture probably less well than I do, but I have to be quiet on certain sensitive subjects, such as identity, Hinduism, the ideal Bali ... It's sometimes very difficult to express an opinion! Especially since I am not politically correct, although I don't want to shock.

This is the whole problem of the relationship to the other when the other also gets involved.

Historically, the relationship to the other was first the relationship to Java. The Balinese say they were Hinduized by a holy man from Java, Rsi Markandeya.[361] Installed with his disciples on the flanks of Mount Raung in East Java, he had constantly in his view, on the other side of the strait, the majesty of Mount Agung, which moreover was not called "Agung" but "Tolangkir" or the "Man of the Mountain," whom he ended up subjugating, thus introducing religious Indian-ness to Bali. When? Some say in the 8th century. It doesn't matter. It is above all a question of reinforcing the idea that Balinese identity comes not only from Bali, but also from beyond the sea. One finds the same phenomenon of migration from Java in the 16th century, the century of Balinese grandeur, during the reign of Waturenggong,[362] about 200 years after the Javanese occupation of Bali in 1343. According to some, there were no castes then in Bali.[363] In Java, meanwhile, it was also the period of the erasure of the great Hindu-Buddhist tradition, causing the migration to Bali of a number of spiritual figures, the most important being Dang Hyang Nirartha, also called "the newly arrived Ancestor (*Betara wawu rau*)." This Brahmin Shivaite priest is said to have been in contact with Javanese Sufis, and therefore monotheists, in Java. In Bali, he created temples all over the island and also imposed a modification in these temples, adding an altar, the *padmasana*, which brings together all the gods of each temple. This altar, whose name means the "lotus seat," is located in the most auspicious position: in the corner where the line of the upstream intersects with that of the rising sun. It

---

[361] Rsi Markandeya: legendary Shivaite priest believed to be the originator of Besakih temple.
[362] Waturenggong: Balinese king of the mid-16th century associated with the idea of a golden age of the kingdom of Gelgel through its political, cultural and religious expansion.
[363] This is hotly debated. There was a clan aristocracy and a priesthood long before, but it is indisputable that this period saw the arrival from Java of Brahmin priests (*pedanda Siwa* and *pedanda Buda*) who then formed the core of the Balinese caste nomenclature.

is the seat of the Supreme God, alternately Surya, the Sun, or the Inconceivable (Acintya). It symbolizes a first version of Balinese pantheism, before the current one of Sang Hyang Widi qualified as monotheistic. Rare in the past, *padmasana* altars are now found all over Bali, a sign of the increasingly monotheistic spirit of our time. Here, too, the "other" is a generator of change.

At the time of these reforms, did the Balinese begin to think of themselves as Hindus?

No, this is recent. The word Hindu didn't even exist ... Furthermore, when Indonesia proclaimed independence in 1945, the Balinese didn't really need to show a strong ethnic or religious identity. They didn't think they were different from others. As in most islands and parts of Indonesia, to assert your religion was less important than to assert your nationalism. Sukarno himself being half-Balinese, they didn't have to assert their difference, especially since it was not particularly marked. That came later. After the first council of Hinduism was formed in 1959[364] and the religion was officially recognized in 1962.

So, today, what is the role of Parisada Hindu Dharma, the council that manages the Hindu religion, in this shaping of thought?

Founded by scholars, it was structured for a long time by former soldiers, especially during the era of military rule. This Council of Hindu Affairs has in fact created a distinction between those who claim to be in the Balinese tradition, especially Brahmins, and those who promote a normative reforming Hinduism based on the reading of the Indian Vedas.

Are these two trends still opposed today?

Yes, Parisada has created institutions for the dissemination of formal Hinduism, such as the Hindu Dharma Negeri Institute (now Universitas Hindu Negeri), which produces theology and explanatory texts that link the Balinese village and literate tradition to Indian tradition, but with an emphasis on the corrective aspect of the latter.[365] However, this modernist Parisada is far from unanimous. In fact, there is a real mishmash. Many Brahmins refused the main reform of Parisada Hindu Dharma, which consisted in opening the high priesthood of the "twice born" (*dwijati*) to non-Brahmins, with the possibility of officiating during the grandest rites.

So, it was about democratization?

Yes, each Brahmin house has its own privileges, its own mantras. It produces its own holy waters, has its own *sisia* clientele among certain clans, etc. When

---

[364] From the earliest days of effective independence, Balinese elites worried about the recognition of their religious tradition. It was originally a Balinese Hindu section (Bagian Hindu Bali) established within the Ministry of Religious Affairs of the Republic of Indonesia (Kagri).

[365] We note the names of Ida Bagus Agastia and Gede Sura for the religious aspects, and Wayan Windia for the legal aspects.

new high priests appeared who not only took over rites formerly associated with the *brahmana* caste, but also began to produce holy waters for their own clan clientele,[366] a break was inevitable especially since there was often a loss of clientele for the Brahmins and therefore economic consequences. A competing Parisada therefore appeared in 2001, the Parisada Campuan, with more local references, oriented towards the ancient Javanized tradition in the Kawi language, and academic support from another higher education institution, Universitas Hindu Indonesia.

Is there a conflict?

No, more like simple tensions on the ground, especially when a family group leaves the clientele of a Brahmin to join that of a new kind of priest. It is therefore better to speak of a cohabitation that's a bit uncomfortable, especially when the two groups officiate together at very large ceremonies, held at the level of the island or the district (*kabupaten*).

Who wins of the two camps?

Hard to say. The traditional Brahmins are undoubtedly in the majority. Their association held a general assembly at the end of 2019 bringing together no less than 500 *pedanda Siwa* and *pedanda Buda* priests. They have a new name, Dharma Ghosana, and they remain dominant in rural areas where people fear that any betrayal of the Brahmanic house of their ancestors will bring vengeance from the *niskala*. But there are many places without a Brahmanic tradition. And there, the new kind of high priests *empu, rsi, begawan,* etc. are multiplying.

And in modern spaces?

There the supporters of the new "democratic" priesthood clearly prevail, that is, the non-Brahmin high priests, joined by modernist Brahmin dissidents. All the more so as this demand for modernity and democracy also carries a claim for a pan-Hindu religious identity that is more assertive than among the traditionalists, because it is through this democratic reading that the Balinese increasingly call themselves members of an international Hindu community. Today there are thousands of Balinese who go to India to seek holy waters. This did not exist before!

Ultimately, they wish to align with Hinduism just as other believers align with their religion. They want to belong, they want certainties! They want a transnational religion; they want to go beyond their borders!

Yes. That said, even if they affirm their tolerance in the name of the principles of their religion and their tradition, their current obsession with identity results in a decrease of this tolerance towards the "other". Today, the other is increasingly the Muslim, whereas previously it was the member of another clan, let alone the

---

[366] The *empu* high priests serve the Pande and Pasek clans, the *rsi* and *begawan* high priests the *satria* clans, the *dukuh* high priests some mountain populations (the Bali Aga).

jaba / sudra for members of the upper castes. Social classification mattered more than religion.

Speaking of the common people, what about discrimination in the villages?

In traditional villages, clans were confined to their own areas, the *banjar* being more or less homogeneous. Moreover, the clans were not located just anywhere, anyhow, in relation to the princely house, if there was one. Brahmins and *satria* often had their own space. The same goes for the *sudra*, who had, according to their role, their particular *banjar* near the princely house. This was where those in whom the prince had complete confidence resided.[367] In terms of this reality, there was a kind of discrimination based on traditional status. At Independence, this discrimination was problematic. Some people declared that there could be no more castes. To the Brahmins, who were traditionally exempt from communal ritual labor (*ayahan*), they would say: "It's over, to work, like everyone else!" Some Brahmins accepted. But in many cases this created splits, in *banjars*, even villages. New *banjars* were immediately set up, thus maintaining clan and caste homogeneity. Yet, this created tensions, all the more so as other tensions arose from land reform. All these ruptures fed the pressures at the origin of the massacres of 1965-1966 and continue to leave their mark on the political life of the villages. Modernity has a cost.

All this sustained by what were then new ideas and concepts, made popular by the presence of the Dutch, the struggle for independence, and the whole mix of ideologies popular in the 20ᵗʰ century.

Absolutely! Modernity and the notion of progress also reached the villages. This brought about new types of solidarity and ideas: the nation, taking control of history, social justice, communism, etc. It went in all directions. Among the high castes, the reactions varied. For example, Ubud largely escaped splits. When there is a cremation of an important nobleman, people still come, they participate. Many still remember how they got their land, their privileges from their prince.

In the survival of these traditions in Ubud, and considering the splendor that they have recovered, is the perpetuation of custom due to fidelity to the prince, or is there in addition this notion of Balinese society as theatre? Ubud today is also iconic of Balinese-ness in relation to the tourism business.

You are right. There is the famous theory of Clifford Geertz [368] who speaks of Bali as a "theatre state" in which princes confront each other, less by war than

---

[367] The *banjars* called *pekandelan* are the *banjars* of the loyal (*andel*).
[368] Clifford Geertz (1926-2006) was an American anthropologist often described as postmodern, known for, among other things, his work on Java and Bali, in particular *Negara: The Theatre State in Nineteenth-Century Bali* (1980).

by pageantry. Even though it is a Weberian intellectual construct,[369] there is some truth to this statement. Ubud is indeed the prime example of this "theatre state".[370] Its princes have retained prestige in the eyes of Westerners because of the spectacle generously offered by their traditions.

Placed in a tourist market perspective, the princely house of Ubud has in a way always been very strong in communication and marketing.

I say of them that they are *satria sejati* to justify what they have achieved. The *satria sejati* is the proud knight who meditates, like Arjuna, but who remembers his social duties. In the past they generated clinics and schools, granted land. Nowadays, they make it known, if not to maintain their power, at least their influence.

Devoting oneself to social duties is generally a habit of the elites in Indonesia.

It's embedded in the *wayang* shadow theatre. The warrior goes to the mountain to meditate, then he returns to fight the ugly ogre. Fighting the ogre is social duties and the mountain is the quest for unification with the great Whole, the dream of sages, and only sages. Thus, the old tradition continues today in another guise.

Harley-Davidson owner clubs in Bali, and elsewhere in Indonesia, often do mountain rallies and social action by bringing money or material goods to underprivileged villages. Are we to conclude that local bikers are also modern-day *satria sejati*?

That's very interesting; it's probably unconscious ...

Maybe not ... If you consider yourself to be part of the elite, that you are so rich that you can afford a motorcycle that costs the price of three Japanese cars, you might consider yourself a 21st century Arjuna, and, instead of fighting the ogre, you distribute to the poor.

This is undoubtedly conscious in some members of the *satria* caste. And maybe in others too, you are right ...

We've talked about this from a community perspective in a previous discussion, but are there increased pressures today on the way to behave regarding religion?

Yes, there are. Initially, these pressures manifested themselves in an informal, but structural way, as the result of the military nature of the New Order regime. Originally, men and women still wore whatever colors they liked in their traditional dress, and with a certain elegance, too... and they did their temple

---

[369] "Ideal type," referring to a concept by Max Weber (1864-1920), a German economist and sociologist considered one of the fathers of sociology.

[370] See Graeme MacRae, "Negara Ubud: The Theatre state in Twenty-first-century Bali," December 2005, *History and Anthropology* 16 (4).

prayers in family groups in their own time, and their own way. Then, they started to wear what you could call regimental outfits for ceremonies, and to say temple prayers when ordered, the *panca sembah*, all together. Reformism was born in the city and has taken hold of the villages. Now, as a result, temple priests today use fewer Balinese and more Indian mantras. There's also the convention of the *Trisandya* prayer which, like the call of the muezzin broadcast on national television, cuts Balinese television programs at sunrise, sunset, and at noon. We are now approaching the completion of this transformation. Balinese who pray to the deities of the river, that is, to the animistic aspect of Balinese religion, are becoming a minority. The memory of old Bali is now a matter of nostalgia, not daily reality.

Don't they realize it?

They do, but to only to a certain extent. This is probably why the current governor, Wayan Koster, asks the Balinese to wear traditional dress every Thursday. This is supposed to allow a reintroduction of local culture into modern life. These phenomena are identity drifts which accompany the loss of memory. And finally, this is similar to the drift that seized Islam thirty years ago: piety turned into orthodoxy!

Would one dare to say that one is an atheist in Bali today?

Impossible – it is even punishable by Indonesian law. In the past, there was no barrier between being religious or not being religious. Remember, the notion of truth didn't matter. This is no longer the case: the truth matters! So, I'm worried about the political fallout.

Is all this the result of the work of Parisada Hindu Dharma Indonesia?

I think so; but it has been an ongoing process. I remember an Indian named Pandit Shastri who settled in Bali after Independence and who contributed to the spread of these new daily worship habits, with the help of Governor Ida Bagus Mantra.[371] It continues. More and more Balinese are receiving scholarships to study in New Delhi or Benares and soak up the new truth.

Is there a commercialization or commodification of religious or ritual exercise?

Balinese religion has become less physically accessible. When there are temple festivals, today there are road detours away from the temple. Cars, tourists, non-Balinese don't approach as easily as they once did. At the same time, there have been instances of fabricated ceremonies to satisfy tourist demand, for example in Taman Ayun, Mengwi. I do not know if this is still practiced: it created strong opposition.

---

[371] Ida Bagus Mantra (1928-1995) was governor of Bali from 1978 to 1988, with advanced degrees from universities in India.

I imagine that Parisada Hindu Dharma Indonesia would not see these fabricated ceremonies very favorably. It pushes the religious sphere inwardly to distance it from its dimension of spectacle for tourists.

Yes, that's what Michel Picard talks about, the conceptual separation of religion and art created by tourism and modernity. And then there is also the cultural policy, which means that the most iconic aspects of the Balinese tradition have been extracted from the ritual corpus. In particular, some of the welcoming dances for the deities have been slightly modified, shortened, feminized, if necessary, to be presented to tourists as art. Everything the new Balinese generations think of as culture comes from there! The gestures are the same, but the inner energy, the *taksu*, is different. I remind you here that *taksu* is the cosmic eye! So, there is a desacralization, that is undeniable. But with a little residue of tradition, too, because when these dances are performed in front of tourists, a small offering is made. This remainder confirms that Bali is not changing. Like those objects that remain on the edges of a whirlpool and are the last to be washed away.

Are we really witnessing a mutation of Balinese religious reality, where an ancestral cult would turn into normative Hinduism?

In some ways, Hinduism is gaining the upper hand, in a syncretic variant in which local memory is becoming minor. However, this is still an ongoing process, accompanying the transformation of socio-economic life and the emergence of modern intellectuals. And the road is long. Because if there is one thing that so far does not change much, it is the role of mediums, whether they are *balian* or *jero tapakan*. Because while the high priests address their prayers to the gods of Indian origin located on their mountains, or now in the distant cosmos, the *balian* give voice to the ancestors and the lower forces, while the *jero tapakan* serve as intermediaries to these same ancestors "visiting" the shrines dedicated to them. Ancestral gods, dark forces, and wandering souls still constitute the core of the Balinese cult. At least in the village sphere.

Yes, but you also say that this ancestor cult is disappearing in favor of normative Hinduism. What is the balance between the two?

There is no need for a final answer. This is syncretism in action. In the modern, urban social space, what people are talking about is increasingly Hinduism. In the traditional social space, in the village, it is still ancestors. With foreigners, the Balinese present themselves as Hindus and display the explanatory cosmological diagrams expected by lovers of the Orient. It's tricky. Some foreigners may live 20 years in Bali without realizing that there is anything else in Bali besides this good and proper Hinduism, be it Vishnuite or Vedanta or better yet, Tantric.

14. Relation with Islam, Islamic Attacks, Relation with Christians, to History and Time

In this interview, we return again to subjects related to religion, or to the religious interpretation of phenomena of modernity. What about the otherness between the Balinese religion and Islam, the difference between inside and outside the island? After all, in some Balinese temples there was once a space for Muslim prayer. The Balinese tradition did not put the blame for the Islamic attacks on the "other," but today how do things stand? In the history of the Republic of Indonesia, Suharto was the first to accelerate religion and tradition, for the purpose of national unity, but also, yes, for tolerance. Still, it is difficult to achieve formal equality between religions, Jean Couteau tells us, believing that Indonesia now must face one of its biggest historical challenges: rivalry of religions which it has itself established. From the relationship with Islam, we move to that with Christianity, detailing the evolution of Bali's relationship with these believers of another faith. How do the Balinese relate to history? We end this discussion on the notion of Balinese time and the strange Balinese Oedipus myth of the *pawukon* calendar, as well as the creation or transformation of certain religious festivals in modernity.

ERIC BUVELOT. **Traditionally, what about the notion of otherness in Bali, especially between the Balinese religion and Islam?**

JEAN COUTEAU. Otherness was never stated as such. It was introduced by the Dutch, the product of a very Western obsession. This is perhaps why it is all the more talked about, including by myself. In the past, people didn't think about it. It did exist potentially, for example in the orthodox reading of Islam, but that was not often found in Indonesian Islam, especially among Javanese. As for Bali itself, once the "others" settled in Bali, they were thought of as part of the Balinese conceptual space, then integrated into the ritual and social space. There are still *betara mekkah* or ancestors of Mecca associated with certain Balinese temples. This was a normal reflex: Muslims were present, so what to do with them? Well, when they died, they were made ancestors! Thus, they found themselves integrated into the Balinese system. At least that is what prevailed in the early days of Islam in Bali. So, there is no allegation of otherness in regard to religion. Then, when Muslims became more numerous, people found a compromise. For example, in the princely house of Bangli, there is a temple in which there is a *langgar*, a Muslim prayer space. It was built in the past for a Muslim family. Another situation, in regard to the dead: the very recent cult of *Wali Pitu*,[372] saints

---

[372] *Wali Pitu*: the Seven Sages, in reference to the *Wali Songo* (Nine Sages) of the Javanese tradition who are considered to be the first propagators of Islam in Java.

of Balinese Islam, who, it was decided, were the first to spread Islam in Bali.[373] The keepers of their graves are often Balinese. So, again, even when there is difference, it is not construed as otherness. Even when it potentially exists, ordinary Balinese don't want to see it.

Yet the Quran has a strong notion of otherness, there are Muslims and infidels …

That's not how the Balinese saw it. It is clear that they understood that the Quran is a strong text. So, what did they do with it? They took the *ayat*[374] that appealed to them and transformed them into Balinese mantras. You see *balian* going to Banyuwangi in East Java to seek magic formulas from old Muslim elders. Muslim women became Balinese Hindu by marriage a taboo of classical Islam! We have already mentioned that the princely elites had more confidence in their Muslim mercenaries than in their own Balinese cousins or even their brothers. Many of the Balinese princely houses were protected by Sasa or Bugis, all Muslims. We also find historical traces of integrative contact in the literature, with popular stories of Muslim heroes. As for everyday life, what attracted me to Bali for a long time was that there was hardly any racial otherness. But is that about to change? Modernity produces otherness …

So, what has changed?

The whole cultural environment. The Balinese religion is being redefined into formal Hinduism. From a polymorphic field and social bond as it was originally, it is becoming gradually less social and more structured and intellectualized, through the dissemination of a conceptual corpus partly imported from modern India, sometimes via branches of the BJP.[375] There were once vague cosmogonic theories, but these were based on treatises written in an Old Javanese/Kawi patois, were not disseminated as truth, and, above all, were the exclusive prerogative of scholars, Brahmins in particular. All in all, the peasant religion had few characteristics of Hinduism, only a pantheon of gods who remained on their mountains and who hardly interfered in non-Brahmanic rites, except to call the world to order during conflicts, earthquakes, and other signs that "the world is old". Now, not only are people importing texts from India in large numbers, but they are exhuming old treatises from the Brahmanic tradition to assert ever more clearly the "indisputable" Hinduism of Bali.

Does this create a different relationship with the "other"?

The transformation of Balinese tradition into full-fledged Hinduism undoubtedly changes the relationship with others, even if, from a strictly Hindu point of view, the notion of infidel is irrelevant. For the Balinese, the problem of Islam is not

---

[373] In fact, it is a recent invention, based on old graves. For a description of the phenomenon, see the review *Le Banian*, No. 21, 2016.

[374] *Ayat*: verse.

[375] BJP: The Hindu-centric Bharatiya Janata Party is one of India's two main political parties.

so much Islam itself, which is very diverse, as that its modern reading and the number of its practitioners can produce "disorder." Contrast and otherness are more likely to be found in sociological issues and politics than in religion. This is where the classic Hindu discourse "turns things inside out." One refers to one's political allies and foes as the gods and villains of the Mahabharata and, from there, fabricates an "other" that did not exist ...

This disorder, is that what happened with the Islamist attacks in Bali?

Yes and no. We will come back to this. The first reference to carriers of cosmic disorder, and therefore to troublemakers in the Hindu version, dates from 1965: at that time, the communists were sometimes compared to the Korawa[376] from the Mahabharata, whom their Pandawa cousins had to kill in the name of duty, of *darma*[377] as taught by Krishna.[378] The moral dilemma of Arjuna faced with this duty to kill or not to kill is a central theme of the *Bhagavad Gita*, the famous poem, once unknown in Bali except in shadow theatre. During the 2002 terrorist attacks in Bali, this mythical interpretation was revived, this time with Islam as the generator of cosmic disorder. However, for many Balinese, it is not Islam that is to be singled out as the cause of the disarray. Rather, it is a general deviation in behavior, generating impurity, and basically of Western origin. Sexual liberty, homosexuality all that disturbs harmony.

... all that creates disorder!

Yes, it creates disorder – not that sexual disorders are not found in Balinese society, but they are framed in customary law, rite, and especially power. All this came to the surface after the bomb. According to one version that has circulated,[379] the gods of Bali's temples gathered in Kuta's temple of death (*pura dalem*) and decided to seize the spirits of young Javanese to incite them to commit their misdeeds, the spilled blood then being an offering to Jero Gede Mecaling, a dangerous demon. If the demon is responsible, then Islam is not. However, there is also a more modern interpretation which blames Islam.

What has that changed?

It was after the 2002 attacks that the assertion of Balinese-ness emerged from elite circles to become a truly pan-Balinese phenomenon. Ordinary people began to declare themselves Hindus rather than just villagers of this or that clan. The tradition of Balinese tolerance started receding even more. Today, with demographic changes underway, this tendency is starting to strengthen and could become difficult to control and Westerners sometimes meddle with their concepts and theories of conflict, seeing difference where it does not necessarily exist.

---

[376] The Korawa are a legendary family from the epic Mahabharata, enemies of the heroic Pandawa brothers.
[377] *Darma* (Balinese): dharma, the cosmic law that underlies correct behavior and social order.
[378] Krishna: central deity of Hinduism; Krishna is the 8th incarnation of Vishnu.
[379] See the article by Jean Couteau in *La Gazette de Bali*, No. 89, October 2012.

Today, with the power of the internet to circulate information, it is not just Westerners who project their concepts; everyone is doing it, including Islam.

Yes, this is the spirit of the times. Indeed, we are in a time where identities are asserting themselves and rubbing against each other. I hope Indonesians have realized that national cohesion is threatened if nothing is done about it, especially in education. We must counter this. In my opinion, cohesion is certainly not threatened in the next five years. But in the next fifteen years, who knows?

So, to sum up, is there a difference in perception between old Balinese tradition and Neo-Hinduism about otherness?

Yes, text fabricates "truth." Traditional Balinese religion knows no dictatorship of the text. Now, with modernity, and therefore the influence of what Indonesians call the "religions of heaven," and therefore of the Word, there is the advent of a Balinese otherness based on text. Hindu texts are now read as being the Word.

In your opinion, is there excessive religiousness inherent in Indonesia?

No, the problem is that religion is weighted with identity.

There was much less religion before the advent of democracy, during Suharto's *Orde Baru.*

Yes, but differences were minimized during that time, for political reasons, and also because society was less modern. However, since the military regime, the sociological developments associated with the economy, in particular the displacement of populations, were so obvious that they would have weighed on national unity anyway. Dictatorships must last a very long time pass a certain course, economic and especially educational, as in South Korea for example before they accumulate enough physical, social, and cultural capital to finally lead to a modern and developed society. But thirty-two years of Suharto was not enough. He wasn't Lee Kuan Yew [380] either.

At the same time, we have already mentioned the fact that after the anti-communist massacres, the *Orde Baru* stimulated religion and tradition, without falling into the trap of Muslim extremism, which was muzzled, which democracy is now struggling to do ...

Yes, but remember the function of Pancasila. Its strength in society is certainly based on steady ideological hype, but it has produced a reality, both in terms of national unity and tolerance. And above all, Pancasila puts religions on a formal footing of equality. It works.

---

[380] Lee Kuan Yew (1923-2015) was a Singaporean lawyer and politician, prime minister of the city-state from 1959 to 1990. Known for his acumen and realism, he is the father of today's Singapore.

It worked under a strong regime, but it is less obvious in democratic times like today.

I understand your reservations. The problem is that equality between religions has turned into rivalry, including in Bali. There is now a de facto separation, which did not exist in the past, between the Balinese and outside populations. They do not know each other. The Indonesian political illusion is probably to think that the separation between religious groups, irrigated with tolerance by Pancasila and the state apparatus, will never translate into rivalry and intolerance. Whatever happens to the economy and demographics, Pancasila will remain *sakti*, strong enough to maintain national unity. That is what people say.

Where the shoe pinches, with the new migrant populations from neighboring islands, is that their faith often prohibits them from compromising with other beliefs ...

Yes, we have already talked about it. But I insist: this is a new phenomenon. It is the way faith is constructed that is changing. Twenty years ago, Haji Habib Adnan[381] boasted to me that he "prayed in the temples with his Balinese brothers". This tolerance still continues, even though traditional signs of tolerance like this are waning.

How do local religious institutions and intellectuals position themselves on this issue?

In public, they refer to Pancasila and the history of traditional tolerance, which is said to be inherent in the Balinese mentality. In private, people are more skeptical. Ultimately, it is the national state that guarantees religious neutrality.

Religions all have the right to speak ... and they don't hesitate to use it!

We must beware of preconceived ideas. From the Western point of view, it would only be Islam speaking, but in reality, other religions are also present. There are Mormons cycling in Indonesia today! The Bethel Christian Center has its own television channel. Their sermons are full of English quotes, and it is tolerated! The Balinese build temples wherever they are. From a Muslim majority perspective, it is irritating, to say the least.

Still, it's not all that free. Muslim traditions other than Sunni are persecuted, and there are strict mechanisms before building a religious edifice. The petitioning community must reach a certain number of members and the neighbors must sign a document of agreement. So, there are many possibilities to hinder the establishment of new places of worship.

The state fears that socio-religious changes, even local ones, threaten the political stability of the nation. Formal equality exists, except for a few minor details, in

---

[381] Haji Habib Adnan: former president of the Indonesian Ulema Council (MUI), Balinese branch.

large national institutions such as the army, justice, police, and higher education. On the other hand, there is a real problem with secondary education, where the national authorities are under the strong influence of the Muslim Brotherhood and the local Balinese authorities under the influence of Parisada's Neo-Hinduism.

Near Yogyakarta, a village refused to accept a new resident because he was a Christian. Is it out of fear that one day they will have to accommodate the building of a church?

It must be said that in Bali, too, there are villages where non-Balinese are prevented from settling or buying land. For example, they raise the rent of a *kos* to prevent Javanese from finding accommodation. But this is a matter of local operation. Discrimination is local. The village decides.

In this case, is it out of religious rivalry?

No, it's usually a matter of the demographics of the place. There is nothing religious about this phenomenon. At the same time, this is why there is a risk. If there is no ideological structuring of the prejudice, well, it comes and goes, and there is no coherent discourse that opposes these prejudices. The result is that when crystallization occurs, if it is accentuated, there is no way to counter it. The crowd can get out of hand. Anything is possible.

The principles of Pancasila seem not to be sufficient today and, at the same time, they remain sacrosanct, impossible to adjust them, to bring the slightest reform.

This is extremely delicate, but it is essential to prevent religions from competing with each other, as it tends to happen now. Since 1967, all Indonesians have studied religion in school. Their religion only. This generates competition and, inevitably, intolerance, despite Pancasila.

Does this mean one should be pessimistic?

No, because there are also many Indonesians, including many Balinese, who are trying to find resources in this tolerant Indonesianity which is the main medium of Pancasila. I am thinking here of construing Islam through the Javanese or, more broadly, the Indonesian tradition. Others, of secular tradition, such as the poet Radar Panca Dahana, appeal to Indonesian maritimism, that is, to the pre-Islamic and pre-Hindu substrate of the Archipelago. After all, Indonesia has not experienced ethnic trauma for 4,000 years. Apart from a Mongol incursion, the Dutch were the first real foreigners to dominate them. Without even invading them. An accident of history.

Are there other reasons for wanting to reconsider the founding principles of the country?

There is the rise of a stricter Islam. Without the accompaniment of a critical exegesis, the literal text becomes canonical. This can be precarious. Despite all the good things I think about the Indonesian Muslim organization Nahdlatul Ulama,[382] whose Balinese branch was founded in the 1920s, its members have begun to be increasingly literalist. The change is spurred, paradoxically, by education. In Bali these days, there are several kinds of Islam, each with its different tradition. For example, in Loloan, near Negara, Muslims are for the most part historically linked to the maritime migration of Malays from Malaya, as it was then, which places them in the most orthodox networks of the Archipelago. There was even a man from Loloan who was a preacher in Mecca a hundred years ago. Most other Balinese Muslims thrived in the shadow of princely courts, and their Islam was traditionally watered down to varying degrees. As in Pegayaman, north of Singaraja, where the rites are marked by the influence of traditional Java.

In the 1960s, Indonesia had a population of around 75 million, today it is 250 million. More than half are concentrated in Java. In this population of Java, there were the *abangan*, who refer to the Javanese tradition, and the *santri*, who refer above all to Islam. What is the impact of this demographic explosion?

Indeed, when Clifford Geertz[383] wrote his famous book *The Religion of Java*, he explained that the *abangan* refer to a tradition that predates Islam which is conveyed by *wayang* shadow theatre: an unstructured tradition that saw no major differences between Islam and Hinduism, and where stories from India were drawn into shadow theatre. Symbolism reigned, and the Quranic text was the prerogative of old ulemas, guarantors of balances. In shadow theatre, instead of focusing on the content of the *kalimat*[384] *syahadat*, the profession of faith, a magical weapon was drawn from the sound of this phrase, the *kalimosodo*, which the hero had only to utter to resolve conflicts and defeat the villains. In this kind of entanglement between Islam and Hinduism, the latter was culturally successful even if, in terms of nominative identity, this tradition was classified as Muslim. The spread of elementary education has changed everything: it fuels literalism. The situation has thus evolved from a Javanese Islam to an Islamized Java. The study of religion has gone from reading the innocent *kitab kuning*[385] of the old village *ulemas* to the imperious rhetoric of the masters of the Indian Tarbiyah, the Palestinian Hizbut Tahrir,[386] and Saudi Wahhabism. In doing so, it went from a culture of the symbol, fundamentally oral, to a culture of the creed, fundamentally written and foreign. People no longer speak about the **Quran** *the Book* being the "sublime untouchable" of its hidden meaning, in the Sufi manner,

---

[382] Nahdlatul Ulama: one of the two largest Muslim organizations in Indonesia, along with Muhammadiyah. Respectively founded in 1926 and 1912.

[383] Clifford Geertz (1926-2006) was an American anthropologist known, among other things, for his work on Java and Bali.

[384] *Kalimat*: sentence, formula.

[385] *Kitab kuning*: literally the "yellow book;" the set of Islamic texts used in the educational seminars of Quranic schools in Indonesia.

[386] The Gerakan Tarbiyah, a puritan educational movement, and the Hizbut Tahrir Indonesia, which has been banned in Indonesia, are two Muslim associations that advocate a literal reading of the *Quran*.

but they discuss its applicability. And this is done no longer only in Quranic schools, but in university classrooms and on the street. The great illusion is to think that literacy brings about Enlightenment. In Europe, it took us 300 years to go from Gutenberg to the Enlightenment.

So how does that translate?

For many people with minimum education, the sacred text is the word of God. At the time of the transition from oral to written, the physical text certainly had a sacred value. But no one opened the book except the ulema, who did what he wanted with it: it was the guarantor of his power. While now even the hadiths[387] taken from the Arab tradition bear the hallmark of the sacred, including when they relate to the hygienic habits of nomads in the year 2 of the Muslim calendar. This is the fundamentalism that we see now around the world. It's the sudden arrival of literacy, reading. Because the first reading, before being critical, is always literal. Balinese Hinduism is following the same path. There have been Christians obsessed with the Holy Land, Jews with Jerusalem, Arabs with jihad. Now it's the turn of Hindus with Kali Yuga.[388] Wouldn't it have been better to keep Jerusalem a heavenly goal instead of today's earthly one, and wouldn't it have been better, in Asia, to keep listening to the silent voice of meditators?

That said, in Indonesia, the *santri* who refer to the text and who belong to either Muhammadiyah[389] or Nahdlatul Ulama, aren't radicals.

No, they're not; I exaggerate. Of course, it is true that the oral tradition persists in spite of everything, even if it crumbles as the absolutism of the written word takes hold of mosques, institutions, and mentalities. The problem is that those who come up with another reading, as the former president Abdurrahman Wahid[390] did in his day, are intellectuals. They offer a symbolized reading of their tradition but it is not understood. It's too intellectual for ordinary people, whereas the raw text is easier to understand. Bali also sends Muslim participants to Quran memorization contests every year.

And here, how did the media react to the 2002 Islamist attacks?

The *Bali Post* played a positive role in highlighting that the first person to visit the scene of the attack and offer help was a local Muslim figure, Haji Bambang.[391] Remember, there were many Muslims among the victims. There were no anti-Muslim diatribes in the press, although there were a few stones thrown at

---

[387] *Hadith*: oral communication from the Prophet of Islam and, by extension, a collection of all the traditions relating to his actions and words.

[388] Kali Yuga, or "era of Kali" or "iron age," is the fourth and current age of Hindu cosmogony.

[389] Muhammadiyah: the other of Indonesia's two largest Muslim organizations, along with Nahdlatul Ulama.

[390] Abdurrahman Wahid (1940-2009) was the 4th President of the Republic of Indonesia (1999-2001), known for his daring liberal leanings.

[391] Haji Bambang (Haji Agus Bambang Priyanto): a Muslim community leader from Kuta who was among the first volunteers to help evacuate the dead and wounded after the 2002 bombing.

Muslim schools here and there because, indeed, that was the time when there began to be strong signs of Muslim otherness in Bali, such as women wearing the Muslim headscarf. That is, people whose religious difference was asserted as such. Nothing dramatic, however.

So, you're saying it didn't change anything?

I'm not saying that. It accelerated tensions. It was from the time of the bomb onward that one saw the crystallization of a discourse that classified the people of Bali according to their origins. The classification itself, based on a regional law passed under the 1999 Autonomy Law, appeared before the bomb. It differentiated Balinese originally from the village, *krama desa*, from Balinese born in a place other than their place of residence, *krama tamiu*, and the non-Balinese populations, *tamiu*. But the system hardened considerably after the bombing, especially when *pecalang* were given control of domestic passports created for the occasion. There were all kinds of abuse. Fortunately, Jokowi put an end to it when his first government abolished a number of regional laws.

And the man in the street, what did he think of the Islamist attacks?

The older ones saw the terrorist attacks as a sign of disorder in the world. Others, younger, started to talk about migrants as "Javanese guys," *jelma jawa*, rather than "Javanese brothers," *nyama jawa*.[392] And there are those, often better educated, who for the first time spoke about the dangers of Islam. Despite this, let's not exaggerate. The Javanese who arrive in Bali are generally very well received. This idea of difference should not be overstated.

Have the Islamist attacks changed something forever?

Maybe ... There are now many Balinese intellectuals who would like their island to be protected by a special regional status, *Daerah Istimewa Bali*. But they don't do anything to get it. In fact, it is extremely complicated in terms of the law, it is said, because Bali obtained its status as a province from a decision concerning all of the Lesser Sunda Islands. It's a Dutch legacy: Bali was part of a group of islands in the eastern archipelago, along with Lombok, Sumbawa and others. What would be the advantage of formal autonomy? Protected by its status, Bali could escape possible Islamization if Islam were to prevail in Jakarta in the future.

Indonesia is not there yet!

Yes, you're right. And despite my fears about changes in identity, I would say that Indonesia and its ideological apparatus, as well as the mentality of the people, bear a certain universalism. Everything possible should be done to preserve this. For that, one should not be too absolutist! People are wrong to say that human rights have disappeared under Jokowi just because not all of

---

[392] See I Wayan Damayana, "Menyama Braya," *Studi Perubahan Masyarakat Bali*, Universitas Kristen Satya Wacana, 2011.

the cases inherited from the military regime have been resolved.[393] We must understand that Indonesian democracy is based on balances that are difficult to inscribe over the long term: ethno-religious and political balance, and internal balance in the armed forces. Both are fragile. In this context, it is important to support Indonesian ideals, which are fundamentally very close to Western ideals and are not without impact on reality.

Can you clarify the similarities?

The great principles of the Enlightenment are all in Pancasila. They are articulated with typical Indonesian vocabulary and references. Why not?

Yes, but the first principle that requires belief in one God is still radically the opposite of the Enlightenment!

It took a long time for the Enlightenment to extinguish God! And Enlightenment itself turned into Darkness more than once. We have to put it all in a historical perspective, we can't require everyone to be an atheist.[394] Moreover, without reference to a neutral, interfaith God in some way, Indonesia would not exist. Belief in God was part of the political compromise on which it was built.[395]

About this compromise, what about NTT Christians flocking to Bali today? How are they and their religion perceived - a religion that was that of the former colonizer and which nowadays is declaimed in denominations that are sometimes a little eccentric? I think of those big meetings that are held in Bali where a preacher healed the sick thanks to the powers of Jesus which he mediated. The blind could see, the crippled could walk, etc.

Yes, this is the problem with Bethel, Pentecostal, and those kinds of churches, which have their own excesses, to which NTT people sometimes fall prey. That said, these eastern-island people are willing to do hard work. They can be found in all the jobs and trades at the bottom of the ladder: guards, construction workers; they are part of the new outsider underclass. They are mainly found in Denpasar and in the south of Bali. They are also the new henchmen, because they drink and are often the source of brawls.

Are they therefore less well regarded than the Muslim citizens who come from the west?

---

[393] In particular, the investigation into the anti-Communist massacres of 1965-1966, and the case of Munir Said Thalib (1965-2004), a human rights and anti-corruption activist, murdered in 2004 by the Indonesian secret service.

[394] It depends on the interpretation of Pancasila, says Jean Couteau. Thus, the late Toety Heraty, one of the great figures of Indonesian intellectual life, said that doing humanistic work and she mentioned Gorbachev "is the equivalent of formal faith in one God," in a personal discussion (November 2019).

[395] When independence was proclaimed in 1945, Muslim parties accepted that Islam should not be a state religion on the express condition that God was mentioned in the principles of the state. Hence Pancasila.

No doubt, but there is no real crystallization about them, especially as many are Catholics, less aggressive religiously than the Evangelicals. However, some people openly make racist remarks about them: they are black and sometimes have frizzy hair.

Many Balinese are themselves migrants to the outer islands. So, they should understand this phenomenon of the Indonesian economic migrant ...

Many Balinese are indeed migrants, or have family members who are. In particular through the *Transmigrasi* [396] program toward outer islands. So, they know the problem. But they react and manage as Balinese. They emigrated as a group to Sulawesi and South Sumatra in the 1960s and '70s and reconstituted their village-style Bali, the Bali of Covarrubias,[397] with *balian*, priests, and ceremonies. Quite astonishing. Others have settled in urban areas, in Java or elsewhere, and have a few temples there as well. Still others are isolated. These disappear, are diluted in the mass. To change religion for a Balinese, or to have two, is not a problem, as I've said.

While NTT Christians represent the latest wave of economic migrants in Bali, at the other end of the social scale are the rather wealthy Chinese-Indonesians. They have their churches, too ...

Yes, churches that are often mono-ethnic. Among Protestants, all it takes is a pastor to make a church. Certain churches become an exclusively Chinese refuge, often strongly Calvinist.

And mosques?

There are indeed more and more in Bali. In a way, this is normal, because the curve follows demographic trends. Some mosques are affiliated with government institutions. Most of them are controlled by Nahdlatul Ulama, the large organization of very moderate Indonesian Islam. So, there are very few radical sermons. The *ustad*, often of Sufi tradition, speak of brotherhood, never of exclusive truth. This is not to say that there is not a tightening of identity, even a crystallization of Muslim identity in certain circles. At university, for example, many lecturers recently hired from outside Bali keep separate from the Balinese environment. Outside of work, they live in a Muslim bubble, more so than ordinary Muslims.

Are there other problems?

You and I see the source of differences in the ideologies of religions. But, for ordinary people, tensions arise on another level, at the level of cultural signs. For

---

[396] *Transmigrasi*: displacement of populations organized by the government in underpopulated areas of the Archipelago that needed to be developed.

[397] Miguel Covarrubias (1904-1957) was a Mexican painter and cartoonist, but also a self-taught ethnologist and art historian who investigated Bali in the 1930s and wrote the classic *Island of Bali* (1937).

example, in my neighborhood here in Denpasar, there were about 40 Javanese employees working in a peanut factory. The factory owner, who had made his pilgrimage to Mecca, had made available a prayer room for his staff. One day, a child of one of the employees drowned in the river below. Immediately after the tragedy, the child's corpse was brought by the employees to rest into the prayer room. This posed a serious neighborhood problem. The prayer room was not a place dedicated to death in the Balinese space: to the Balinese, the whole neighborhood had thus become impure. There had to be a great purification ceremony (*rsi gana*). So, the Balinese went to the Muslims at the peanut factory and told them to take responsibility for the ceremony. But for the Muslims, there was no question of doing this ceremony, because it would be addressed to a god who is not God, since it is not theirs. On the one hand, there was the impurity of the village according to Balinese belief; on the other, there was the rigor of the Quranic text. Fortunately, the factory owner was a moderate and after discussion it was decided to simply close the prayer room.

How would it be today?

For young Muslims recently settled in Bali – who had gone through Quranic schools in Java and would consider that Hindus are infidels, unlike in the past – this kind of amicable solution would be more difficult to find. For the others, the problem does not arise. They know and adapt to Balinese traditions.

Could this type of conflict escalate in Bali today?

If a conflict takes an ethnic form in Bali, considering the mechanisms of solidarity that exist within Balinese society, it could turn out badly. But I don't think it would erupt around religion as such first. And the Balinese are wary of anything that would affect tourism. The danger is not now. It is rather in the evolution of people's mindset in the long run.

Observing the construction of mosques and churches in Bali, I noticed that mosques were increasingly lavish and spectacular while churches often incorporated elements of Balinese architecture.

We can see here the evolution in the mechanisms of tolerance and acceptance. Catholics in particular saw fit to adapt to local traditions and chose to build churches derived from Balinese architecture, and they also adapted the music. For some time, these adaptations were positively received by the Balinese. It meant that the Catholics could adapt to local conditions. But identity discourse got involved, with the concept of cultural appropriation. What had been proof of tolerance became a sign of domination. So, a famous Catholic school in Denpasar, which is now called Santo Yoseph, was originally called *Swastiastu*, a term which has meanwhile become a greeting among Balinese. The Balinese now claim full control over their symbols, even if such symbols, like saying *swastiastu* are modern inventions.

Let us return to the subject of Chinese-Indonesians, who, as we have seen, are often Christians, but also Confucians since President Abdurrahman Wahid authorized this belief. What can be said about them in matters of worship?

I would say they are a bit like the Balinese, in that fine points of theology weren't of great importance to them, which is what enabled them to convert to Christianity in the first place. The majority of Chinese-Indonesians are Christians, mainly Protestants, although some are Buddhists.

Their culture was banned by the military regime: Chinese names, ideograms, Chinese religions had to disappear. They were forced to embrace one of the five recognized religions then, and many chose to become Christian. It is often said that instead of converting to Islam, they preferred Christianity.

Yes, for some. But the Christianization of the Chinese had started before the military regime, in most cases. There is also a significant proportion of Chinese who are Muslim, although not in Bali. And here we are not talking about the Chinese we do not "see" as such. Now and then you may see a Balinese who will tell you that his father is Chinese. Many have been mixed for generations. Most were, however, forced to take Indonesian names.

Has the Balinese perception of Chinese-Indonesians changed today with this rise in the importance of identity?

I think the Balinese are less open toward Chinese-Indonesians today than they used to be. Many Chinese-Balinese who were established in Balinese mountains for a long time and who had the plantations there have now moved to the coast and joined with newly rich Chinese coming from the big cities of Java, who come here with a financial weight which allows them everything, especially in land, a sensitive subject here. So, their assimilation is not as great as it was.

Where do Balinese and non-Balinese Indonesians encounter each other and create a way of being together?

That's a good question. In their personal life, people tend to live in separate communities. Muslim officials have their mosque, Christians, their church. Students have their own associations, here Muslim, there Christian or Hindu. No one really knows the other's culture and religion. So, where do they meet? In the modern space, that of modern work, of school, the media, the city, in the modern arts and literature. In short, Indonesia. Indonesia is the identity that embraces differences and gives them meaning: different, but united. Indonesia allows for the expression of multiple identities. Attending an event in Indonesia that begins with the national anthem, preceded by an official prayer said by a member of the local religious majority, is a very impressive experience of smiling nationalism for a European today. Yes, nationalism can be smiling!

Let's talk a little about history. How do the Balinese shape it?

Most traditional Balinese don't really have a clue what history is. There is a linear dating in the Saka[398] calendar, but few indisputable facts. The past is mostly told in the form of clan chronicles (*babad*), telling the story of founding ancestors, without paying attention to dating.

And that's all?

No, of course not. Because ordinary modern Balinese need historical linearity. Using a mixture of Dutch historiography, authentic inscriptions (*prasasti*) and apologetic texts of dubious origin, they usually construct a vague history out of the characters they believe to have marked the phases of premodern Indianization a series of events and mythical ancestors that define the core of local historical consciousness. There was Rsi Markandeya[399] with the arrival of Hinduism in the 7th or 8th century; Mpu Kuturan,[400] who defined the system of three village temples in the 11th century; the Javanese invasion of Majapahit in 1343 with the contribution of *siwa-buda* teaching; Dang Hyang Nirartha and Dang Hyang Astapaka in the 16th century, who are said to be at the origin of the current Brahmanic clans and priesthoods, respectively Shivaite (*pedanda Siwa*) and para-Buddhist (*pedanda Buda*). In this rough timeline, we see an evolution taking shape, focused on the role of more or less legendary characters, and without much supporting evidence. And then, all of a sudden, we're in the colonial period and the resistance, sublimated in the fight to the death of the *puputan*, then on to Sukarno, another locally mythologized character. And then the anti-communist massacres of 1965-1966. But people forget them, except sometimes in the privacy of the home.

Yes, here we are again in the presence of the famous local "artistic blur". It must be said that between the current issues and the imprecise traces of the past, it is necessary to give some order, even if it means reinventing.

I would also say that many Balinese themselves are vaguely aware that this is all vague! They try to put things in order, but in a premodern way! The Lumières of the Enlightenment are not yet present, even if we can see lights in the distance. Luckily, there are still the lights of their tradition. The problem is to pass from one set of lights to the other.

So, what relationship do they have to history then?

Outside the universities, I know very few Balinese who think of history as an evolutionary and chronologically serial phenomenon in relation to the development of the production of goods, to the development of ideas, or of the human condition, over the long term and in a global space.

---

[398] Saka calendar: a lunar calendar of Indian origin, beginning in the year 78 CE.

[399] Rsi Markandeya: legendary Shivaite priest from southern India, said to be the founder of the Besakih temple complex and also the importer of the irrigation system.

[400] Mpu Kuturan: priest who came to Bali at the beginning of the 11th century from East Java, when there were close dynastic links between these two regions. It was during this period that the Hindu Trimurti of Brahma, Vishnu and Shiva would have been introduced in Bali.

Is it because history here is a perpetual restart?

Maybe … In any case, for the majority of Balinese, the question of the insertion of Bali in the Indonesian space is never raised. Neither historically nor economically. Nobody talks about the fact that the Dutch created an integrated economic space, for example. Except for a few intellectuals, nobody talks, like Denys Lombard,[401] about inter-island circuits as the real foundation over the long term of Indonesian nation-building. Yet, the Balinese call themselves nationalists and are proud of being Balinese. They do not see any contradiction between their two levels of identity. But this is where there is potentially a real problem, even if it is some way in the future, because too many young people, simply because of the education they receive, now see themselves through the prism of religion. They relate to developments which are as much those of India and Hinduism as those of Indonesia and Pancasila.

Yes, from an obscure belief in ancestors mixed with Hinduism, many Balinese have now joined the great global family of Hindus.

Exactly, they are creating a new reference space for themselves. Some say they have 5,000 years of history with Hinduism! So, we have 5,000 years of history on the side of religion, and 75 on the side of the Indonesian Republic. That is not necessarily a problem; Pancasila is accommodating. Of course! But it may become a cause for concern because, outside Bali a growing number of Muslims now ignore Javanese Islam, while becoming passionate about the battles of Badr and Yarmouk.[402] Meanwhile, the site of the great battle of Kurukshetra[403] in India is emerging as a favorite destination for Balinese pilgrims.

Why is this happening? Quite frankly, Indonesians as a whole seem to have little awareness of history. Neither theirs nor that of the world!

Economic causalities, demands for justice, the distribution of wealth, the management of conflicts, all this rhetoric of real history was removed from intellectual discourse after the events of 1965-1966. So, these issues come back in a new way that emphasizes the ideological aspects of nation and religion, except for a tiny elite of postmodern university lecturers. Either way, history is ignored altogether!

Are there also cultural reasons for this disappearance of history?

Obviously, but it also depends on the educational level of the people you are talking to. Changing mentalities takes time. Not so long ago, when you spoke to an ordinary farmer, he was incapable of thinking about time. When an old man dies, it is not uncommon to hear that he was over 100 years old. In the

---

[401] Denys Lombard (1938-1998) was a French historian specializing in East and Southeast Asia.
[402] The two battles that define the origin of Islam, the first one of the Prophet against the pagans of Mecca (624 AD), the second one against the Byzantines (636 AD).
[403] Kurukshetra: site of the famous battle between the Korawa and the Pandawa in the Mahabharata, located in Haryana, now a state in northern India.

past, there was no birth register, and age was calculated in relation to events. So-and-so was born before the Japanese arrived, after the Agung eruption, during the events of the G30S,[404] etc. There was no need-to-know time precisely. This was hardly conducive to the emergence of an articulate and inquisitive historical consciousness.

But there, paradoxically, history reappears, at least as a landmark of time. Before history, did the Balinese need benchmarks to calculate time?

Yes. The time they know best is the *pawukon*, the 210-day calendar. Why? It is from this calendar that most of the rites of the person and the clan are organized. An ordinary Balinese woman in any village will know when the *otonan*[405] of her children fall, when to make what type of offerings for a certain event on this calendar, and in how many days ... There, the Balinese know time. But it is a cyclical time, which does not accumulate years. Its sole function is to create order.

What's special about this 210-day calendar?

It's Oedipus, Balinese version,[406] articulated on a duration which is that of the rice-growing cycle. This is the key to the Balinese tradition; it is what defines the essence of the rites. But this calendar does not calculate the time in a chronology; it gives each moment a positive value and a negative value from the intersections of hours, months, days, etc., which exist within it. It's very complicated. There are ten types of weeks that each correspond to a hero in the history of Watugunung.[407] There are thus weeks of 1, 2, 3, 4, 5, 6, 7, 8, 9, and 10 days, which occur simultaneously and cyclically. The main ones are those of 5 and 3 days, which intersect in an identical manner every 15 days of the Gregorian calendar. When the days Kajeng and Kliwon intersect, a ceremony is done. There are also important 5-day and 7-day week intersections, every 35 days. It is at these multiple crossings that the main rites take place. The Balinese are very aware of these subtleties. And when it gets more complicated, they go to the priest.

Why Oedipus?

Indeed, the *pawukon* calendar is Oedipus, but Oedipus *à la balinaise*. In the Oedipus of the Greeks, when the Oedipus discovers that he has slept with his mother, he rips his eyes out and then walks across Greece, cursing the gods. In the Balinese Oedipus, Watugunung sleeps with his mother, rapes any women

---

[404] G30S: Acronym of *Gerakan 30 September*, or "30 September Movement," denoting the alleged Communist coup attempt of 30 September 30, 1965, which allowed General Suharto to seize power with the support of the American and British secret services.

[405] *Otonan*: a person's birthday according to the Balinese *pawukon* calendar.

[406] Watugunung is the son of Dang Hyang Kulagiri, king of Jalasanggara, and Dewi Sinta, with whom he had sex, as recounted by the lontar of the same name.

[407] See *Times, Rites and Festivals in Bali* by Georges Breguet, Jean Couteau and I Gusti Nyoman Darta, BABBOOKS, 2013.

he meets, and infuriates the gods. When his mother realizes that she slept with her own son, she decides to appeal to the gods. The gods attack Watugunung, but when Wisnu[408] is about to kill him, Siwa says, "No, make him master of the calendar!"

So, the calendar is organized on the phenomenon of incest prohibition?

Absolutely; it's reflected in the *pawukon* calendar. The last week is dedicated to Watugunung, the incestuous hero, while the first week of the new cycle is that of his mother. They are separated by the end of the calendar cycle. And what is the last day? The day of the goddess Saraswati,[409] the deity of knowledge. This knowledge is therefore at once that of time, of social organization, of ritual, and of sexuality. It is consciousness. One does not sleep with one's mother; it is not done. This is how man comes out of the darkness of animal life. This is a very important myth. It is not surprising that it is at the origin of most of the rites. It has nothing to do with India, except for the name of a few gods pasted onto the story.

Fantastic! But the Balinese have multiple calendars, don't they?

Yes, there is the luni-solar Saka calendar. The Balinese observe the full moon (*purnama*) and the dark of the moon (*tilem*) with offerings, and particular months have ritual significance. The Saka calendar is quantitative. Dated to the year 78 CE, it corresponds to a linear organization of time, a chronology, of which the New Year, *Nyepi*, falls just after the dark of the moon of the ninth month.

Wait! Are you talking about the New Year and the ninth luni-solar month? It doesn't make sense!

Yes, the New Year begins with the tenth month. It's odd, but there it is. In Bali, the New Year really begins with the tenth month in the Javano-Balinese calculation! This means that syncretism is not only contemporary, that it has always existed, fixing its quirks here and there in the calendar and in ritual. And it continues, as I will explain to you now, even if it means surprising you. *Nyepi*, as we know it, a day of strict silence preceded the day before by a fantastic parade of monsters, the *ogoh-ogoh* – well, this Nyepi is a very recent phenomenon.

Yes, we have already mentioned the fact that previously there existed several types of *Nyepi*! There is also history, right? Which goes back a long way. I know for example that the era of this calendar, the Saka era, is of Indian origin and is still used in India.[410]

Yes, no doubt about it. What I mean here is that *Nyepi* has totally transformed. In the past, let's say until the end of the 1970s, what mattered were the processions

---

[408] Wisnu, Balinese for Vishnu, is the second god of the Hindu trinity, along with Brahma and Siwa (Shiva).

[409] Saraswati is the goddess of knowledge, eloquence, wisdom, and the arts.

[410] The Saka era is said to date from the reign of Kanishka I, an Iranian-Scythian king of the 1st century CE.

to the sea to purify the effigies and sacred objects, which took place a few days before *Nyepi*. But above all, the day before, there was a great purification ritual at noon at the central crossroads of each village. Three priests officiated, one for each level of the world heavenly, human and chthonian. To finish up, they purified the world of demons with offerings and mantras. The next day was the day of silence, actually not very quiet. People could go for a walk, visit friends, ride a bicycle. It was fun.

That's no longer the case now. There is still the ritual, but impossible to go out. And no light at night. The *pecalang* are on patrol. And in recent years, no TV, radio, internet. Why all these changes?

The 1970s and '80s were key years. Why? Because universities had begun to produce intellectuals in numbers.[411] The *Bali Post* seethed with comments on religion (to strengthen!) and tourism (to develop!).[412] What could be better than to reinforce these opinions with some well-struck formula from an obscure treatise in Old Javanese? This gives an aura of the sacred. The chosen formula was perfect: on the day of silence, you must "kill all fire, kill all work, kill any going out, and kill all pleasure."[413] Such was the declaration about *Nyepi*, notably in a vocabulary of combat. So, on the day of *Nyepi*, no electricity, no work, no riding around, and no making love. Excellent! This formula immediately flourished in the *Bali Post*, the schools, and especially among the heads of department of the regional administration. People had to take silence seriously. The texts required it. It was only one step for the "conscience" of one's religious obligation to be transformed into official directives. The line was soon crossed. Before long, the compulsory silence of *Nyepi* day became a reality.

Fascinating to see how the text imposes its law because it is text. We thus see religion becoming frozen …

Yes, but that's not all because it was when foreigners were living it up Kuta, often with a marijuana cigarette in their lips. It was also when sweat merchants imported workers by thousands for the construction sites of Nusa Dua. And they were not alone. Following them like shadows were the beautiful, and the less beautiful, young widows or too-soon deflowered, who filled the brothels in tents on the building sites of the tourist paradise to come. Not to mention those from the seaside of Kedonganan. Meanwhile, in Denpasar, things were also changing: the city's Muslim kampongs saw the arrival of itinerant soup and noodle merchants in ever greater numbers. And the mosques of the city came out with ever more stringent injunctions to respect the pillars of Islam and to be wary of the scent of pork. Bali was taking in ever more Javanese, some of them beggars, others, graduates. All this changed people's mentalities.

---

[411] Udayana University was founded in 1962, but only a few courses were taught until 1975.

[412] Usadhi Wiratnaya, whom Jean Couteau describes as his mentor, was the favorite editorialist of the newspaper.

[413] The saying in Balinese: "*Amati api, amati karya, amati lelungan, amati lalanguan.*"

It's the identity crystallization you have told us about?

Yes, but here we see it around religion. On the one hand there were academics and senior officials, often from Java, imbued with Quranic verses; on the other hand, were foreigners propped up with artificial paradises in their heads and ever less formal faith. And then the Balinese, not the intellectuals, but ordinary Balinese discovered what they had so far refused recognize: otherness. The incredulity of the one who doubts and the contempt of the one who believes.

So, according to you, crystallization happened that way. Don't you exaggerate a little bit?

Barely. A sneer here, a call to prayer there, when the Balinese rediscovered "their" *Nyepi*, it awoke many things in them. It strengthened the idea, from one year to the next, that the silence had to be enforced throughout *Nyepi*, that is, for 24 hours, from sunrise to sunrise. In ten or fifteen years, what was only a vague and easy-going convention became an increasingly hard injunction. Now, beware those who transgress! The *pecalang* are watching. But that's not all…

That's not all? Yes, you haven't yet talked about the *ogoh-ogoh*!

Indeed, and that's where the bizarre is more bizarre again. Because at the same time as the Day of Nyepi became more serious, the evening before became wild the *ngrupuk* parade. In the past, nothing really happened, or almost nothing, after the village crossroads purification ceremony at mid-day. Just a few mantras and offerings, to see off the last demons, the *buta*, and to start the year in the total purity of Nyepi.

You're going to tell me that there were no *ogoh-ogoh* …

Exactly. The thousands of monsters on parade, everywhere throughout the island, coming out of each *banjar*, from every neighborhood; and all sorts witches on motorbikes, viruses, singers with guitars, each one more extraordinary than the next. Do you think this is traditional? No. It's a fact of modernity. The demons have always existed, the famous *buta* of shadow theatre and traditional painting. But they are now recycled in giant form as *ogoh-ogoh*, on the eve of *Nyepi*.

It's crazy. So, everything changed dimension. From a simple tradition of quiet, *Nyepi* became the day of silence. And the day before, which was about the invisible *buta*, became the extraordinary parade of *ogoh-ogoh*. What happened?

It started in a banal way, at the beginning of the 1980s, in Denpasar. At the time, the same intellectuals who had investigated the new truth of their religion in old texts in Kawi, or in recently translated holy books of India, these same intellectuals were engaged in debates on tourism, culture, and tradition. Everything but politics, of course, since 1965–1966 was not far in the past. But as *Nyepi* became serious, the demons exorcised the day before had to become more serious as well. Why not, instead of small symbolic figurines of cooked rice as before, make giant demonic characters to be let free in the streets? Tourists require exoticism and with this sort of entertainment, they would more easily accept the confinement of *Nyepi*. The idea was soon in the air. It's difficult to know who made the initial attempt: a group of young people, no doubt. But it was when the *Bali Post* got involved, with its star chronicler Gusti Ngurah Oka Suparta, that *ogoh-ogoh* appeared everywhere within two or three years. Thus, a relatively minor holy day, *Nyepi*, has in a few years become one of the strongest symbols of the Balinese tradition. And it was made the one national Hindu holiday.

You are here saying that one has, consciously and unconsciously, created tradition ...

Yes, and it's not the only case. Siwa Ratri, the "Night of Shiva," is even more patent. It is the holy day during the darkest night of the year, which usually falls in January.

I have never heard of this holiday.

It's not surprising, because it's relatively recent. In the past, no one meditated during that night, apart from a few Brahmin lovers of the old Kawi literature. Now, Balinese high school students are supposed to meditate all night addressing their thoughts to Shiva, or at least reading the referent Shivaite text:[414] the story of Lubdhaka the hunter in which the hero, threatened by a tiger, takes refuge on the branches of a *bila* tree overhanging a pond. To keep himself awake and thus from falling, he picks the leaves and drops them one by one into the pond, where there is a *lingga*, the symbol of Shiva, hidden underwater. Because he has unwittingly performed a Shivaite ritual, he achieves *moksa*.

Why Shiva?

Because Shiva is the supreme God, from a Shivaite perspective. It's a more classic name than Sang Hyang Widi. But there is another reason. The Night of Shiva was largely reinvented by Ida Bagus Agastia, a fine connoisseur of Kawi, an academic, and a Brahmin as well. So, an influential and respected man. He already knew the *Siwaratri Kalpa*, the text of the story I just recounted.[415] He started discussing it at the university with colleagues, then in a few articles. Finally, in 1986, with a few peers from Dwijendra University, they spent their first Night of Shiva reading and discussing the text and the meaning of the divine as they thought it should be, Balinese style.

Very interesting. Siwa Ratri is therefore a historical resurgence, reinterpreted in the light of modernity.

---

[414] This is *Siwaratri Kalpa*, a Kawi text of a tale of Indian origin, which would have been introduced around the 15th century, just before the maritime sultanates seized power in the Indian Ocean, and Bali, as a result, becomes isolated, in an increasingly Islamized political space.
[415] Meditation during Siwa Ratri had been institutionalized at the Parisada general assembly held in Campuhan in 1961, but the practice had not followed for more than 20 years (information from Michel Picard).

Yes, if you will, but it is even more complicated, because until the 1980s, before intellectuals rose in number as a result of education, classical texts were taboo. Only Brahmins or *sisia* who had gone through an initiation had access to them. Now a Brahmin was publicly promoting and interpreting in a manifestly deistic and open manner a classic Kawi text, until then more or less reserved for Brahmins. This was new. In a Balinese religious practice still clearly focused on ancestor worship, here was a Brahmin insisting on a local version of God, which he made accessible to everyone, instead of wanting to keep it for only Brahmans and initiates.

So, it was piety, the religious, that was in mutation?

Yes, access to university gives its graduates a new legitimacy, which allows them to break free from the shackles and taboos of the *puri* and *gria* (princely and Brahmanic houses) tradition. This inevitably results in new interpretations of classical texts and treatises, such as the *Sarasamuscaya*,[416] scrubbed of misogynist excesses. Besides these resurgences of past texts, there was the introduction of Indian Hindu texts translated from English, and, increasingly, sermons by graduates from India, all of which shakes things to the depths. Not only the religious understanding of ordinary Balinese, but of the Balinese as a whole.

So, is there really Indianization?

Yes and no. Yes, in the sense that one can effectively say that the cosmicized reading, directly Indian or taken from tradition, is taking over all religious interpretation. No, in the sense that ancestor worship continues to permeate ritual. There is a gap. There could be a tearing, but all in all there is a sort of adaptation of ritual to the new faith. The ancestors are inserted, supported by an Indian citation, in a conception of the divine which, although One, the "Brahman" of the new language, remains fundamentally pantheistic.

This is the famous Indonesian spirit of consensus ...

Yes; one avoids anathemas. New gurus are not taken seriously. But, in the end, people negotiate, they fabricate syncretisms of all kinds. More and more Indian, of course, as a new iconography reminds us, while remaining very Balinese. It's been like that forever. Thus, the 210-day *pawukon* cyclical calendar is unmistakably indigenous, but it has a little Indian twist: the names of the protagonists are often Indian. Moreover, even if the Saka calendar comes from India, who would dare to say that the purification rites that precede the Saka New Year are anything but Balinese?

Are all the ceremonies changing?

No! The cycle of festivals of Galungan Kuningan continues to be a long visitation of ancestral deities. The same goes for temple festivals. The prayers change a bit, with a touch of Kawi or Sanskrit, but the rite does not really change. And as

---

[416] *Sarasamuscaya*: a sacred Hindu text originating in Java, written in the 9th century.

for formal Hinduism, the interpretation is manipulated so that ancestor worship appears to conform to the Hindu ideal.

We have talked about the calendar, but how does the individual view their personal time?

First, in relation to the ancestors. There are times when Balinese think of themselves as having been present in the past. They sometimes say "I" when relating what a grandfather said or did. One doesn't study a family history; one acts it out through certain rites during temple festivals. The ancestor "descends" directly often through trance. He is present and dictates his wishes. But it is usually through the mask dancers that the family story is played out, based on *babad*, legendary chronicles. It is not the dates in the Saka year that matter in these chronicles. It is the fact that they deal with ancestors, and enable people to trace their origins. Because tracing one's origins informs about status. And therefore gives it a place in Balinese society.

How do they experience the phases of life?

They are standardized, in the old Javanized tradition anyway. There are four phases, each with an expected type of behavior. The first two are unsurprising: the *brahmacari* is the period of formation, and the *grhasta* that of founding a family. It is the last two that are decisive: *wanaprasta*, retirement in the forest on the verge of old age, that is, withdrawal from the active world; and the *bhiksuka*, the moment when withdrawal is total and wisdom attained. This categorization of phases of life has always been taught in the shadow theatre, in which old sages are said to isolate themselves in the forest to meditate in and on the expectation of death. This is certainly not the current situation. But when you're old, that's when you become a high priest. Many contemporary Balinese intellectuals have understood it well: instead of words, it is now holy water that they distribute as the truth. They thus finally wear the tiara of an aura that had often escaped them.

So, to sum up. The Balinese have a cyclical time, the *pawukon*. They have a linear time, the Saka. But they also have Gregorian time, don't they?

Yes, there are more and more Balinese whose mental space is organized around Western time, that is, essentially economic time. It is not without implications. Calendar taboos, especially *pawukon*, are increasingly neglected. The *dauh*, the traditional Balinese hours, have almost disappeared. And who respects calendar prohibitions in the area of sexuality? So, it's no surprise that old people say things are going wrong because people aren't behaving as they should. All of this explains a certain pervasive pessimism, such as saying that "the world [Bali] is already old," a phrase one often hears among older people.

How do the Balinese construct the modern chronological time of their Indonesian history?

In the educational system, this modern, national time is not so much event time, it is a superposition, or stacking, of modern identity time and mythical time. That is, culture and origins. Thus, there is Borobudur,[417] the origin, and Java. There is also Sriwijaya,[418] the beginning of the history and space of the Archipelago. All this remains vague but represents the will to build the Indonesian national space. After that, there is obviously Majapahit,[419] which is much the same as the reference to Sriwijaya, this time for Java. This story is built on strong landmarks, but there is no explication regarding the evolution from one strong historical moment to the next. Little is said about trade, its role and complexities, for example. It is only said that the Dutch plundered the Archipelago. It's also a story that is over-populated with personalities. There is Gajah Mada,[420] whose portrait all Indonesians know even though it was never depicted in his lifetime. There is Diponogoro[421] in Java, Imam Bonjol[422] in Sumatra. Then there is Sukarno, who combines Java and Bali, and therefore Islam and Hinduism, with a touch of 20th century ideology of progress. All these heroes refer to a kind of symbolic struggle between the Indianized aspects and the Islamized aspects of the whole country. All in all, history here remains essentially national and Javanese. The inhabitants of NTT do not know that the warriors of Bima[423] went to their shores until the 19th century to capture women. They say "we" when talking about Borobudur! Little is said of the major historical, technical, cultural, and economic mechanisms, whether local or *a fortiori* global.

That's the whole drama of Indonesia, especially the events of 1965-1966 ...

Yes, the anti-communist massacres were, besides everything else, an intellectual catastrophe. But is this the only factor? We must not forget that the cultural constraints, the referents in the matter, did not predispose Indonesians to think of history. On the other hand, once again, postmodernism has digested this, as a great rolling mill of classical knowledge!

And that suits everyone.

---

[417] Borobudur Temple is an imposing Buddhist edifice built in the center of the island of Java in the 8th and 9th centuries.

418 Sriwijaya is the name of a Buddhist city-state in South Sumatra that stood on the site of present-day Palembang. Its development began in the 7th century and lasted until the 14th century, when it came under the influence of the Javanese kingdom of Majapahit.

[419] Majapahit: kingdom located in the eastern part of Java. Founded in 1292, it reached its peak in the 14th and 15th centuries.

[420] Gajah Mada (died 1364) was military leader and prime minister of the kingdom of Majapahit.

[421] Diponegoro (1785-1855) was a Javanese prince who made war on Dutch colonial rule.

[422] Tuanku Imam Bonjol (1772-1864) was one of the leaders of the Padri Muslim movement in Sumatra which advocated a return to strict Islam.

[423] Bima: town located in the east of the island of Sumbawa.

15. Relation with the West, Hedonism, Atheism, and Individualism

In this penultimate interview, we discuss Bali's relationship to the Western world. And especially to some of its values. To what extent have Balinese adopted the myth of the world's paradise? How do they relate to Western universalism? Jean Couteau says some Balinese politicians today appear to think of Bali as the center of Indonesia, if not the world. Why and how did they adopt postmodernism? Why this overvaluation of Majapahit? Jean explains that the Islamist attacks in Bali were also seen as a sign of the disorder created by Westerners. How do the Balinese understand Western thought? What do they think about hedonism? Atheism? Individualism? And although the Western way of life is criticized by some intellectual circles, it is now widely practiced in the south of the island, which constitutes an intermediate zone, like a zone of experimentation, as we conclude in this chapter while recalling that the village is the last sacred territory.

ERIC BUVELOT. How do Balinese see themselves?

JEAN COUTEAU. They tend to see themselves through Westerners' eyes. There are historical reasons for this: the "discovery" of Bali in the 1920s; its image of paradise. That sometimes had rather bizarre consequences: the Balinese have adopted universalism and at times think of themselves as the light of the world. A bit like the French, crossed with ethnocentrism, but bluntly asserted. According to some local politicians, Bali is indeed the navel of Indonesia, if not the world, and, to at least one of them, Ubud is actually the navel of Bali. Where do they read the signs of it? In the fact that Sukarno, the founder of Indonesia, was half Balinese; also in the fact that Bali is the heir of Majapahit. And above all, in the fact that we admire them.

Are there any other recent signs that support this tendency to view Bali as the center of the world?

There are many. For example, *Nyepi*, the Day of Silence, is now proposed to the whole world as a moment of "cleansing" and ecological rest, for the greater good of humanity! They even have a slogan for it: "Bali for the world". Not to mention the invitation to the world to adopt the principles of *Tri Hita Karana*. I have an interesting anecdote on this. Ten years ago, I was a member of the small team, with Taufik Rahzen[424] and the philosopher Bambang Sugiharto, which conceptualized the 2013 World Cultural Forum for the government of Susilo

---

[424] Taufik Rahzen is an Indonesian intellectual, journalist, and publisher. He was also one of the advisors to the President of the Republic of Indonesia Susilo Bambang Yudhoyono.

Bambang Yudhoyono.[425] Our basic idea was to identify "indigenous ideologies" around the world similar to *Tri Hita Karana*, to reveal potential cultural kinship on an international scale and thus to spur cultural communication and enhance ecological awareness between and beyond nations. Sadly, the bureaucrats of the day mistook this project as a means to promote Indonesia's national principles, Pancasila, around the world! Our aim was to fight against all hegemonies. So, we failed to curb ethnocentrism. Nationalism won!

Very interesting!

Still in the same vein, Mertha Sutedja a retired army officer involved in the setting up of the Golkar[426] in Bali in the post-1965 years as well as a founder of today's ISI art institute toured the universities of the United States in the hope that the *Kakawin Sutasoma*,[427] from which the Indonesian national motto *Bhinneka Tunggal Ika* is derived, would be recognized as part of world heritage. He also came to see me at my house, wearing a tie, to ask me, without batting an eyelid, how to obtain the Nobel Peace Prize! But isn't it normal, after all, that the Balinese want to promote the harmony of their society? They, too, want to influence the world. But it also illustrates Balinese ethnocentrism. What is no less interesting is that this Balinese ethnocentrism is centrifugal, directed towards the outside, whereas the traditional ethnocentrism, formulated by the Brahmins, is centripetal. Remember that the directions of the compass rose and the corresponding gods are summed up in a center attributed to Siwa and symbolically associated with the Agung volcano. Here we find the ancient myth of Tolangkir,[428] Lord of the Mountain. It's just a step from one kind of ancient navel-gazing to another.

Is there a relation with the more formal development of Hinduism on the island?

No, the formal development of Hinduism, or the re-Indianization the island is going through, is a recent phenomenon. Modernity forces the Balinese to situate themselves in relation to the outside world. For centuries, they organized themselves only in relation to the village, the clan, and the mountain, and suddenly they are told in school that they are Hindus. They accept, read the holy books proposed to them, go on pilgrimage to the banks of the Ganges, visit Kurukshetra[429] where, it's said, the famous battle in the Mahabharata took place. It is still a reading of the world through a Balinese prism, but this prism is now fully Hindu. And they

---

[425] Susilo Bambang Yudhoyono: President of the Republic of Indonesia 2004-2009 and 2009-2014.

[426] Golkar: Golongan Karya, President Suharto's party and political instrument. Originally, a movement created by the military to counter the influence of political parties.

[427] *Kakawin Sutasoma* is a 14ᵗʰ-century Javanese poem which depicts the life of Lord Sutasoma, a manifestation of the Buddha. It is also the text behind the Indonesian national motto *Bhinneka Tunggal Ika*, Unity in Diversity.

[428] Tolangkir: old, mythical name of Mount Agung.

[429] Kurukshetra: site of the famous battle between the Korawa and the Pandawa, located in Haryana, now a state in northern India.

naturally find that they are not the only Hindus on this Earth.

This is no doubt due to the extra attention they have received from tourists for several generations now.

No doubt. They may be expressing a lack of self-confidence by over-affirming their identity. But they place themselves more in relation to the world. Bali is the world.

This is not wrong, since the whole world comes to Bali ...

Yes, if the world comes to them, it is because there is a recognition of their qualities. I am thinking of the famous Balinese smile, which we would like to see in other places around the world. Apart from the ecological balance, which is very damaged, we must recognize that there is a way of organizing social life in Bali that gives the appearance of harmony.

Elements that are sorely lacking in Western societies.

Although we are starting to see early signs of social disintegration in Bali which I am tracking here harmony remains a key principle, and it creates its own reality, against all odds: the art of being together. The Balinese announce it in their symbolism, in their controlled arts and dances, and, of course, in their famous *Tri Hita Karana*.

But foreigners do not necessarily have a positive impact.

Indeed, the fear of disorder and impurity is very strong in Bali, and there is a real misunderstanding with the West. What the Balinese do not understand is not only that these foreigners indulge in disorders and therefore generate impurity, but that they often prefer to be in disorder, in the name of freedom.

In Western societies, people have reached a stage where they demand disorder, where disorder must become order in turn, where it is the norm, a dynamic notion that is completely impossible to accept in Bali.

They find it difficult to understand that, instead of a stable behavioral system of norms with a narrow scope, one can have a very wide range of norms, plural in essence and regulated by law and therefore individual responsibility.

For the Balinese, when there is disorder, it must be remedied, right?

Order is restored through purifying rites: when the bombs exploded in Kuta in 2002, some Balinese saw in it a demand for blood, and thus for offerings, from Betara Nusa, the invisible master of the island of Nusa Penida located off the south coast of Bali. He was avenging himself for all the imbalances in Kuta, and Bali in general, caused by alcohol, sex, and greed. But his revenge created an even greater disorder, which had to be countered with a huge ceremony, a giant "clean-up".[430]

What else don't they understand about the West?

Women! That women have autonomy, sexual autonomy in particular. This is the principal disorder. Remember that in the Balinese language, to marry a woman is to "take" her. Thus, there is a very ambiguous behavior towards Western women. They are at once instruments of emancipation and scorned. A relationship with a Western woman is doomed to fail, at least according to short stories published over the years in the local press. The Balinese man desires her, but also disdains her, a common phenomenon in intercultural sexual relations.

By her predominantly financial power, which encroaches on that of men, the Western woman takes on the evil attributes of a witch ...

Yes, although she is not the only one. In some Balinese stories, all women, as they get older, are literally seen as monsters (*raksasi*) or witches! I don't see why the Western woman would escape it. After all, they sometimes have big eyes and long noses like the *raksasi*! At least to Balinese eyes.

Apart from a joke that may earn you the ire of our feminist readers, what do you think about all this?

The relationship with the West has evolved. In the past, although the West was seen as domineering, it was also understood as a vector of progress, especially by intellectuals. Mixed into the notion of progress there was also criticism of the caste system, a certain desire for equality, and even fantasies of revolution, which some have paid dearly for. Ideas about the emancipation of women have taken the same path ...

These ideas did not come out of thin air. These intellectuals were trained in the schools of the colonizers ...

Absolutely. They espoused Western categories, including, among others, with Sukarno, the notion of revolution or overthrow of social order, and not just the colonial order.[431] The dynamic then was in the ideas. It was only with Suharto that another reversal took place: ideas were no longer enough, it needed reality, but without selling one's soul to the devil. The emphasis was now on the economy, on development, repressing the revolutionary dream of equality and replacing it with the affirmation of tradition which has resulted, thanks to the drift of basic education, in the primacy of religious identity.

---

[430] The *Pamarisudha Karipurbhaya* rituals, that is to say a cleansing (*pamarisudha*) of danger (*karipurbhaya*), including a great exorcism (*tawur agung*), the cleansing of the location, a request for forgiveness for past faults (*guru piduka*) addressed to the spiritual forces of the world (*labuh gentuh*) and animal sacrifices including cows, goats, etc.

[431] It is no accident that communism and the events of 1965-1966 are often read in the light of the traditional notion of cosmic disorder.

What about time?

The Balinese today go by "watch" time, whereas in the old days they looked at the sky. In the 1980s, when Club Med brought in dance troupes for tourists, appointments were made according to Balinese hours, the *dauh*. No one wore a watch, except one that didn't work, as a sign of the person's modernity. Now everyone lives on their cell phone, at least in modern environments. Knowledge of traditional time is fading. Only the Day of Silence, *Nyepi*, is an exception, because it can be given a modern, ecological iconic connotation.

As we said, the Balinese already had two calendars of their own. They can therefore adopt a third: the Gregorian, down to its milliseconds …

[Laughs] Yes, indeed. But back to economics. Traditionally, the role of money has been overlooked. The economy was largely self-sufficient until the 19th century, and in the official culture, that of Brahmanic houses and courtyards, the possession of wealth was undervalued. For example, in the *Kakawin Nitisastra*,[432] it is said you can take wealth only as far as the cemetery, not beyond. In this regard, the changes are enormous, because more and more Balinese have a modern economic functioning.

How do Balinese intellectuals understand Western thought?

Some of the early modern Balinese intellectuals were Marxists, therefore champions of economic and social determinations. Now, especially since the fall of the *Orde Baru*, the most modern thinkers are postmodern. Both Marxism and postmodernism allow rejection of the hegemony of the West. The paradox is that in doing so they reinforce this hegemony: it's hard to find a social or political science thesis that doesn't mention Michel Foucault,[433] Jean Baudrillard,[434] Pierre Bourdieu[435] or Jacques Derrida.[436] It is not surprising that, unlike the Indians for example, no local intellectual has produced new conceptualizations that are operative outside Bali. What they produce are performative conceptualizations like *Tri Hita Karana*, *Nyepi*, "Bali for the World," etc., linked to this local version of a Neo-Hinduism that claims to be globalized.

Is hedonism an imported notion? Did it exist from a traditional point of view? Only for the princes, perhaps?

That's the whole problem! Desire as a raison d'être is something that has been

---

[432] *Kakawin Nitisastra*: popular didactic moral guide in Java and Bali since the 18th century, based on an older Indian work.
[433] Michel Foucault (1926-1984), a French philosopher known for his critiques of social institutions and for his work on the history of sexuality.
[434] Jean Baudrillard (1929-2007), a French philosopher theoretician of contemporary society.
[435] Pierre Bourdieu (1930-2002), a French socio-anthropologist and philosopher with significant impact in the human and social sciences of the 20th century.
[436] Jacques Derrida (1930-2004) created and developed the school of thought around deconstructionism.

fabricated largely by the West. There were Sade and Freud. And even in Western societies, sexual desire unrelated to procreation or power remains a relatively recent phenomenon. In Bali, there is Tantrism, a version of which probably existed in the past. But I dare not speak of hedonism.

Yes, but hedonism is not just about sex ...

Certainly, and here we come back to the system of equilibrium of Indian origin, also very significant in Balinese society. In Balinese Hinduism there is always this affirmation of the four principles of life, known from old treatises, which must be kept in balance. There is *kama*, which governs desire. There is *arta*, the principle of wealth. Then there is the notion of Good, of wisdom, *darma*. And, finally, *moksa*, disappearance. You have to keep all of this in balance, and that balance changes from one phase of existence to another. If there was an overvaluation of *kama*, of desire, there would be disorder, which is unacceptable. But its presence in everyday life is never denied. Especially in the villages, where primary, pre-Hindu sexuality remains the order of the day. In the most primitive temples, in the most sacred corner, one can see a *biu lalung*, meaning "naked banana". This is the crude phallic symbolism, probably older than the *lingga*, the Indian phallus.

Devoting oneself to pleasure, indulging in one's desires, is therefore a disorder ...

In excess, yes, it really is a disorder. This is Cupak,[437] who eats too much! In traditional theatre, it is people who are portrayed as negative.

It is therefore not surprising that the Balinese sometimes have a negative perception of tourists who come here for lounging about ...

Yes, there is a perception of the Westerner as "other" in behavior. As if anything at all could be expected from them.

To the point of believing and thinking that all Westerners are like that!

Yes, I know Balinese who do not understand why I don't try to cheat on my wife and have adventures. They really don't understand! You also know well that when you are invited somewhere and you are white, you are first offered alcohol. There are all these prejudices about Westerners! But it goes further. Basically, what many Balinese do not understand is that Westerners have autonomy of the person, that they themselves define their life choices, from the way of dressing to the way of thinking. None of this needs to be defined by the consensus of the community. For the Westerner, personal behavior is governed by the law; for the Balinese by the public social norm. In the West, there are a thousand ways of being. In Balinese society, only three or four, defined by caste, and more generally, by status.

---

[437] Cupak and Grantang are two characters from popular theatre. They are brothers with opposite personalities. Cupak is greedy and a thief, while Grantang is modest and honest.

What problems does this pose?

Westerners make things "dirty," create impurity with their behavior. It is therefore quite astonishing that this hasn't led to real anti-Western racism. But as we have already said, all these reflections do not form a structured racism. As always and in all areas, we remain in the "artistic vagueness" ...

Besides hedonism, is the atheism of the West seen as a major obstacle?

Yes and no. We have already spoken about it. Because religion, the structured belief in faith, is something relatively recent in Indonesia.

Yes, but you often say that for the Balinese, all religions are the same. So, what about the absence of belief?

This is not an issue in Bali. Belief does not have to be structured in faith for the Balinese. This is the artistic vagueness I was talking about. The divine does not have to be explained or affirmed: it is behind the river, lives in the tree, etc. What matters is the quality of actions, not what you believe or don't believe. In the Indonesian national state, however, it is different. Pancasila, taught in school, spread in the media, compels Indonesians to organize their religious thought, to declare their faith. Shaped and annealed, this faith becomes reality. But some Balinese, anxious to guard their Balinese-ness, to counter Indianization, then evoke the notion of emptiness to speak of God: *embang*, an indigenous Balinese word, not Sanskrit. So, there is Sang Hyang Widi, learned at school. Now, there is also Sang Hyang Embang, the sublime Void, both God and his opposite. In short, all this to say that there is no need to assert oneself as a deist or an atheist. It is left in limbo.

Are Westerners really said to have no god, no religion, therefore no faith?

Yes, and that's not a problem. Here, there is an affinity with the traditional Balinese attitude. That is, it doesn't matter. For the modern Westerner, it is not faith that matters, but actions, in a kind of individualized morality. Outwardly, it's just like the older generation Balinese. Because everything is changing. Teaching religion in school changes everything. The ancestors are eluded, religion is announced, proclaimed, transformed into ideology. With all the associated risks!

There is the taboo dimension of atheism, nationally, legally. If you call yourself an atheist, you are suspected of being a communist!

Yes, but it's political. Except in regard to the state, the Balinese don't care. What bothered them about communism was that "its supporters spoke too loudly." The notion of disorder! Having said that, the Balinese accept religious changes without flinching. This shows how unimportant one's professed religion is. It would be another story if they were told to forget the duties due to ancestors. Because the unvarying core of the religious in Bali is indeed the cult of the ancestors. It is not being Hindu, Christian, or otherwise.

Yes, but then again, and for Indonesians in general, they still fail to make that conceptualizing effort necessary for the end of God, for the death of God from a Nietzschean perspective!

This was the case with Europeans until the 18th century, and even into the 19th century. But, yes, indeed. I still think that they are right to do as they do, to remain in the vague.

I think they are less and less in the vague today. In any case at the national level. Twenty-five years ago, it was not uncommon to meet an Indonesian who casually asserted that he was "Islam KTP," that is, that his religion was written on his identity card but that he gave it little importance; today no one dares to say such a thing.

You are right, the vague is disappearing. The "Islam KTP" disappeared because of education. This resulted in literalism and sometimes radicalization of Islam in the Archipelago. Now, many Balinese are asserting themselves as Hindus. Will they become radical? Not yet, but there are some political signs. But there are multiple currents in the general artistic vagueness. Many refuse the re-Indianization of their religion. So, let's be careful. We must avoid categorizations, absolute barriers ...

Could you be more precise?

The big difference is that there are also more and more possible types of behavior, including in the religious domain. Many Balinese, for example, have now a passion for *malukat*, purification by ritual bath. This has always existed, of course, but the new trend is to find the temple with the best purifying waters. People go there in a group, for example with colleagues from the university, and, in a few years, from one mountain temple to another, they replenish their soul in divine strength and fresh mountain air sometimes without really knowing which god has irrigated them with his power. Some people will tell you, proud of the modern denomination, that it is Sang Hyang Widi or Brahman. Others that it is the gods of the *awang-awang* heavenly heights.[438] And who knows, as it happened to me, maybe a teacher of the Hindu religion will tell you, like Father Meslin in the 18th century, that this is all bullshit. There are no gods. It's the cosmos.

We have seen that there is a fashion for international sects. But is there an emergence of local sects?

There is a lot of sectarian aberration around self-inspired gurus, often *balian tetakson*, inspired shamans. In one case that I know personally, the shaman produces his own holy water, or rather, he controls a "visited" temple where he ritually asks for holy water through the intercession of his wife in trance. He says that the holy water produced by the priests of the temples of his village is the product of the gods of

---

[438] The magazine *Taksu* published an entire issue in 2017 on this topic, with youths dressing in white and going about looking for unknown *betara* they claim themselves ready to serve (*nyungsung*).

black magic, therefore of Rangda.[439] He alone produces pure holy water, that of Sang Hyang Embang (the sublime Void) or of Brahman, the creative principle. And when he utters mantras, they are *sesontengan* in Balinese, not Sanskrit or Kawi. So you see what is happening: this *balian*, who has hundreds of followers sometimes lining up for "consultation," is distancing himself from his original tradition: he refuses the gods of the Balinese temples; he also refuses Indian Hinduism. On the other hand, without being really aware of it, he promulgates his own monotheism, anchored in the Balinese tradition, but with one God (Brahman) of Indian origin. There are thousands of such gurus, of various inspirations often born if not from inspired ignorance or badly assimilated knowledge from tensions which arise between beliefs, faith, and reason; pantheistic past and the demand for modern monotheism; caste tradition and democratic requirement.

So, there are all kinds of sects!

Yes and no; actually, it's more complicated than that. What we are witnessing here is a modern version of the old tradition of learning, not so much from a text, but by affiliation with a master, a guru. The case of the Brahmins is well known. They have their *sisia* clientele. Some are co-opted by the guru, who gives them access to literature and other aspects of his knowledge. But there are other clienteles, other gurus. The key thing here is less the transfer of raw knowledge, especially written knowledge, than the circulation of holy water from demiurge maker and giver of holy water to recipients. There is transmission of spiritual power rather than knowledge. One is dependent on the other.

Are there other gurus besides Brahmins?

Yes, anyone can assert themselves as an intercessor and a guru of sorts. The important thing is to have an ad hoc altar, a seat of the divine force summoned by this intercessor, thanks to which he will eventually produce his holy water. These *balian* intercessors operate either alone or, as in the above case of my friend, through their own medium, in this case his wife. This system of transmission of knowledge by a guru in Balinese, *aguron-guron* has many forms, and the mysticism / knowledge relationship varies greatly. In many cases, one becomes attached to a guru if one is in search of mystical-magical power for reasons of black or white magic. The knowledge is often that of the *catur sanak*,[440] the four spiritual siblings. In other cases, the guru gives access to more or less esoteric texts, more or less imbued with cosmological speculation, and of more or less Kawi or Indian origin. There are therefore, according to the combination of these elements, multiple types of guru, each with his or her own clientele, his or her own mantras and written references, not to mention their holy waters and influence, local or pan-Balinese. Many are simple healers, others intellectuals, some serious, others

---

[439] Rangda is the demonic queen of the *leak*, supernatural creatures that take the form of, for example, a flying head from which bowels hang.

[440] *Catur sanak* (the four siblings; also *kanda empat*) are the amniotic fluid, the placenta, the fat and the blood, the four elements that accompany the birth of any child and will protect it throughout its life.

rough-hewn. A few produce publications, for example the magazine *Sabda*, ten years ago. Others, open ashrams. I know of one who, married to a Javanese and therefore administratively Muslim, went to Mecca and came back with water from Zamzam[441] and the belief that the Kaaba is none other than a Shivaite *lingga*. Good luck to him! All in all, in the great maelstrom of change, and even if structured sects appear, even if we see the emergence of fundamental criticisms of certain traditions,[442] everything remains fluid, without any marked identity fixation except around the guru, rather than in the text.

Aren't there political risks in this development of sects?

Yes, of course. Sects have always existed, but their content remained esoteric and one found them in very narrow sociological circles, most often Brahmanic. Now sects have not only become a modern urban phenomenon, but the speculations behind them are spreading to the villages via the sermons of fashionable preachers. Indeed, in their criticism of ancestor worship, which several sects want to replace with a more "orthodox" Hinduism, some preachers speak of this worship as "primitive" because it is based largely on trance and contact with the forces of *niskala*, the invisible world.

Are there real tensions?

There are indeed. In the tradition, differences merged into a generalized syncretic atmosphere. It is slowly changing today. Trance and other aspects of ancestor worship are openly criticized by supporters of *sampradaya*, or sects of Indian origin so much so that very recently Parisada had to step in and ban sects of non-Balinese tradition. To what extent this ban will be effective, no one knows. But one can nevertheless think that the evolution towards a greater rationality, and therefore a weakening of the cult of the ancestors which the reformists want to transform into Hindu saints seems inevitable.

Is it a generalized phenomenon?

No, because people's ways of thinking and behavior differ, depending on education, living environment, etc. During ceremonies, more and more Balinese are simply focusing on what they see or are doing. They no longer participate in the full psychological sense of the term. "You see," one of them told me some time ago, "we do all these post-mortem ceremonies, we prepare all these effigies and these offerings, so that our ancestors will return, say the elders, to the abode of the origins above the mountain." "And you, do you believe it?" I asked him. "Do you really believe that the soul journeys as they say?" "No," he said, "but I have to take part, I'm doing this for my family." For these Balinese, the paraphernalia of the rite is simply symbolism. They are among those who ask that the rite be simplified to focus on the essential: the prayer addressed to God, for the deceased. That is the reason for the building of more

---

[441] Zamzam is a well-located in Mecca, Saudi Arabia. Of miraculous origin, according to Islam.
[442] In particular contact with the souls of the dead via the *balian*.

and more crematoriums across the island in recent years. That said, what for some is a request for orthodoxy, for a religion purified of ritual, for others is a slide towards agnosticism, seldom affirmed as such.

Enough about religion, let's go back to the Balinese perception of Westerners. Are they ultimately anti-Western?

No. Absolutely not. Apart from the average tourist, whom they tolerate, there are two typical Western models in the local imagination: those bringing disorder, who come here to party; and those who are interested in Balinese culture, who are revered. I belong to the second group, as a sage or *begawan* of the Ayung River,[443] which has its ups and downs. [Laughs]

Has this close relationship with Westerners for 100 years given the Balinese a new vision of the world?

I think so, but this is where breaks appear, because there are new categories of Balinese. For the most part, it is less and less the village, less and less the clan and caste that shapes behavior; more and more it is the community of believers and the business community, therefore sometimes unbelievers, too. Things have changed from ritual to prayer and now, for a tiny minority, they might evolve from prayer toward doubt.

So, the Balinese have gone from a local cult to a global religion ...

Yes, a lot of them have. Social behavior follows this new order of things, with *bhakti*, contemplative prayer, at the top. Can we say that metaphysics is taking hold of Bali? In a way ... moderate and sponsored by Universitas Hindu Indonesia for traditionalists, and more intense for Universitas Hindu Negeri (UHN) and its Neo-Hindu modernists.[444]

Are there any intermediate postures?

Of course, of all kinds; but in modern and urban educated spaces, it is clearly Indian metaphysics that prevails, in a modernist Neo-Hindu version promoted by the UHN (Universitas Hindu Negeri) that dominates: people talk about *sangkya*, *sanatadharma*, Hindu *samaj*, 19th-century Indian reformism. Besides philosophy, it is the whole of spirituality that is called into question. We see it in the criticism, by some, of the cult of ancestors, of the *balian*, of trance and more generally of the Balinese *niskala*. We also see it, on the other hand, in the promotion of Indian rites such as *agni hotra*. All of these signs, not yet mainstream, are deep

---

[443] Sage of the Ayung River: in reference to Jean Couteau's place of residence.

[444] Jean Couteau specifies: the Universitas Hindu Indonesia (UNHI) is a private university founded by the former governor Ida Bagus Mantra in 1993 based on the Hindu Dharma Institute, founded in 1963. Its Indian tendencies are mitigated by a certain reverting to Balinity and studies of Balinese religious literature. It is the preferred university of the *triwangsa*. More focused on progressive Indian contributions, the Universitas Hindu Negeri (UHN) is a public university created in 2020 from the public Institut Hindu Dharma Negri (IHDN), founded in 2004, but with roots back to 1953. It is undoubtedly the main agent of the changes underway.

indications of the change in the way people think about themselves since Westerners called them "Hindus".

Is that where the break is that you were talking about?

Yes. This is a real break, all the more so as it is reinforced by very rapid socio-economic changes: urbanization; the fact that land has become a commodity; entrepreneurship. These things are reaching down to the depths of society. The phenomenon of the gurus mentioned above is another obvious sign. Not to mention the long Sanskrit names that have become fashionable for the younger generation to hide their origins: no more "Gobler" and "Koncreng". Now it's "Asmarajaya" and "Dwi Yustiawati." The hierarchy of caste is gradually fading in the face of the hierarchy of diplomas and of money.

What is happening with the person?

Has the famous notion of the individual arrived? I answer "yes". Today I personally know many Indonesians, including Balinese, who react as individual persons, who are no different from you and me, who have the same cultural references, and are autonomous. However, they are only a tiny minority, many of whom are in fact artists or academics. So, yes, the individual has appeared here.

But Western individualism remains criticized, right?

Yes, because of its hedonistic aspects. But what many Balinese ignore, and this is the problem, is that individualism, at least on a normative level, is associated with the notion of responsibility, which is based on law. Whereas here, when individualism arises, it often lacks this compensatory aspect and becomes more delusional than Western individualism total narcissism! It appears particularly in politics. This can be seen in the corrupt and shameless manipulation by some of loyalty to the original group. It is extremely difficult to control by the law because this individualism is a reflection of power; it only works for the rich and powerful. The other autonomous individuals produced by modernity do not yet have access to the law. The so-called civil society remains marginal. This is one of the great discoveries of the West, the fact that the leader must also comply with the law ...

So, the individual is just starting to appear but still effaces himself in front of the group ...

Absolutely, the individual becomes autonomous when he leaves his original group, but is no longer so when he returns to it. He therefore functions in a different way depending on the space where he is. In the daily social life of the village, as free and independent of mind as a Balinese may be, he will have to obey language conventions imposed by his caste, obey expectations in regard to age, gender, ritual, his peers at work, and so forth. He will be himself, independent, only in the confidences that he makes to curious foreigners, like me, or during certain discussions with educated peers. The fact is that standards are cracking everywhere today, but they are nonetheless collective standards, which are often over-asserted as a reaction.

How do you see this development in the future?

The whole issue, and I know we have a slightly different opinion on the subject, is whether it's going to break or transmute into something that will stay relatively harmonious. That's a big question. At the same time, we must also admit that there is a certain schizophrenia in Balinese society. On the one hand there is Kuta, and to a lesser extent Denpasar, which represent disorder, individualism, capitalism, questioning of identity, Neo-Hinduism and on the other hand, there are traditional villages anchored in the cult of ancestors and the *niskala*.

Don't Kuta, Sanur, Canggu and Denpasar rather represent a gray area, an intermediate sector, an airlock between two worlds?

No, it's another world already. Kuta can be even more disorderly than some Western societies; it is Babel ...

I still find the south of the island to be an intermediate zone, a mixed zone. This is a place for the Balinese to experiment. Some find themselves there for economic reasons and it will change their lives because of the encounters and discoveries they make there. Anything can happen in Kuta!

Yes, any fate can be turned upside down in Kuta. For sure ... This is also where the relationship to Islam really comes to life for Balinese going there for a job, because they are more confronted with it than in the village. This is where religions come into contact with each other in a modern, that is, identity-based way.

Consequently, all this induces for the person, but also for the Balinese community as a whole a new relation to the world which occurs on its own territory.

Yes, the world has invited itself to Bali. This breaks the traditional balances. It is the fruit of capitalism.

But the West has long ceased to be the sole master of capitalism. In Bali, there are a significant number of tourists and residents from other Asian countries.

Yes, many Japanese, Chinese, South Koreans ... But they operate from modern economic mechanisms which are of Western origin and which produce the same standardization in behavior! The real issue for Bali is whether or not the waves of identity politics we are witnessing now will fade away. This requires maintaining demographic balances between communities.

To conclude on the topics discussed today, what are the limits of personal autonomy in Balinese society?

The limit is undoubtedly the village. One must not interfere in its affairs. All Balinese bow to its decisions. You see an illustration of this with road traffic: as soon as there is a ceremony, car traffic must defer to it; traffic can be simply blocked. Village territory is a priority because it is the foundation of solidarity. It is sacred. It is still in this space that the Balinese continue to define what is possible and what is not. And do not think that urbanization marks an immediate rupture. It doesn't. The village remains a reference. People have their ancestors, they pay their contributions to the *banjar*, they go to the big temple festivals. People become urban, but they also remain villagers.

As a result, the villages or traditional neighborhoods in the south of the island have all the more challenges to meet with modernity as they are located in an area that's in full transition.

It's undeniable. So far, the villages are the winners. If, for example, you own a piece of land and the *desa pakraman*[445] opposes its sale, you will ultimately have to comply with its decision. Most often it's the village that has the last word.

Something tells me, however, that capitalism has all the assets it needs to win out of this type of conflict when it does occur. Against hard cash...

Indeed. This is the corruption I was talking about a moment ago. But the village remains first. And even a *camat*[446] (district head) can be fired if he harms locally powerful village interests.

In the end, does traditional Bali still have a future?

It's hard to say. But I was lucky enough to see the last moments when the system still had the appearance of consistency – in the 1970s until the mid-1980s. Very little urbanization; an intellectual formation still based on symbolism; the beginning of the opening with tourism "bringing something" more than "taking something;" the land not yet being a commodity and then, everywhere, without this being affirmed, homogeneity in architecture, in spaces, beauty in dance, collective gestures, balance in behavior, no cars ...

---

[445] *Desa pakraman*: literally "territory of the citizen," and formerly *desa adat* or "territory of custom".
[446] *Camat*: district manager (administrative subdivision of a *kabupaten*).

16. Self-Understanding, Change, Interpretation, Mental Formation

How do Balinese think of themselves? Does this question have any meaning? Jean Couteau reminds us here that the Balinese person must above all "keep things in order." While Bali still produces paradise for the global tourist market today, the impact of capitalism on social structures is enormous, as we have seen throughout these talks. For example, the notion of reincarnation is changing, rites are being commodified, and cultural tourism is nothing more than a faded dream. And the anthropologists who come to Bali say, with the consent of the Balinese, that Bali does not change, while everything is turned upside down! Jean, for his part, argues that local intellectuals find genuine social reflection difficult, resulting in a constantly erroneous analysis of the real sociological situation. On the other hand, the Neo-Hinduism that is taking hold of Bali, plays an explanatory role. At a time of increasingly lavish religious ceremonies, thanks to the money from tourism and Indonesia's economic development, Jean believes that the island has nothing to gain by taking refuge in this hyper-religiosity. How do institutions manage these changes? For Jean, it is above all necessary to fight the ethno-religious otherness which is gaining ground today in Indonesia. And before giving a quick inventory of the changes of the last 50 years as a conclusion to this series of interviews, he asserts that Bali must be understood as a society that will determine the way Indonesia copes with religious pluralism.

ERIC BUVELOT. Does the concept of self-understanding make sense in Bali?

JEAN COUTEAU. This subject is particularly difficult because the notion of the individual as an autonomous person does not exist in the Balinese tradition, in the sense that people exist, think about themselves, and react first in relation to the group. Added to this is ideology. The Balinese are told that they are the opposite of Westerners, who are supposedly hyper-individualists. I am essentializing here. In reality, as I have said, the autonomous person has already appeared.

Are the Balinese schizophrenic?

Yes and no ... that is, the Balinese person is located in a different temporal space than we are. I'm talking about the typical Balinese who still represents 80% of the population. Why? Because he was born now, but he belongs to the past: he came down from the mountain to reincarnate. In everyday life, when he has a problem, he tries to enter into a relationship with the ancestral souls who float above the mountain. To him, the events that occur in his life are caused by manifestations that come from the *niskala*. Moreover, when he thinks of himself in relation to the past you will tell me that this is a form of personalization it is not a question of objective history but of clan history, within kingdoms of Bali or Java, in which their ancestors, and therefore himself, are actors. This story is not precisely set out. It is mythical, and it is told in mask dances where the characters are key ancestors. Furthermore, as I have already mentioned, the Balinese say "I" when they speak of themselves in the present tense, but also when they speak of their ancestors, as if they are replaying the past. They are thus located in a sort of trans-historic space. I don't know how to define this absolute egocentricity in which the autonomous person, in the Western sense, does not exist.

Well, the person does not exist in the Western sense, but what should this Balinese person do? What do we expect from him or her?

The Balinese person must keep things in order around them. This results in ritual obligations, in particular towards the ancestors, but also towards the lower forces and the gods, that is, the three main levels of the world, through a variety of ritual ceremonies.[447] A Balinese must maintain the balance between these three levels. The person is therefore essentially situated in relation to this. When something is wrong, one must restore the balance through ceremonies, exorcisms, purifications and in difficult circumstances by consulting the *balian*, who is a link with the invisible forces of the *niskala*.

What about strictly personal issues?

They are not read as being the primary responsibility of oneself. They are linked to an imbalance of the aforementioned forces. As I explained before, someone has a car accident today because they left a debt unpaid in the ancestral purgatory or during a previous incarnation ...

This effectively removes the notion of responsibility in real life! And probably makes the notion of law impossible, too ...

Yes, of course. It provides a loophole. But this is also the case in other societies. However, this does not mean that society is not secularizing and that law, and psychology, is not on the way with the implicit notion of personal autonomy. We are witnessing sociological and mental shifts towards modernity which are all the more difficult to grasp as they are most often confused and often denied.

Under such conditions, how, or rather why, does Balinese society continue to function?

Essentially because they have found a narrative that still brings together all of its contradictory components. This narrative produces "paradise" for the global tourist market. Because of this, Bali has managed to maintain both certain structures and

---

[447] There are five main types of ceremonies: those addressed to the chthonic forces (*buta yadnya*); to the gods and ancestors (*dewa yadnya*); to the human world (*manusa yadnya*); to the dead (*pitra yadnya*); and to priests (*rsi yadnya*).

appearances of the tradition, plus a discourse of maintaining the balances of this paradise. On this pedestal, we do not see the breaks, we only see cracks ...

And in the future?

People have already seen the impact of communism, of the notion of progress imposed by the West. It resulted in massacres. Now we are observing the impact of capitalism on social structures but also on belief and the construction of the person. As people urbanize, their relationship with the gods changes. In a typical situation in the village, the gods are brought down to the temples in visits to their "children"; people then "put themselves at their service,"[448] through dance, theatre, offerings. One also occasionally consults the ancestors through a *balian*. But when you live in town and have a little education, what happens? For the newly urban, after a while, well, it just doesn't make sense anymore; you can be spiritually inspired and yet no longer know which gods to serve or which is descending. In the city, the rural divinities are no longer in their natural space! One doesn't understand them anymore.[449] Even if you put a small altar for them in your newly built house, the bond is not the same because you are suddenly alone. The god of the river, the god of the tree, the altar of the ancestor you no longer really know who they are or where they are; you are a little lost. Around these questions, and generally in semi-urban space, trances, revelations occur, groups are formed and new sects appear. The relationship with the divine changes; India intervenes. The person becomes more autonomous.

This is where Hinduism comes in. If you can no longer bring down the ancestors, you can now raise the prayers to heaven...

Absolutely! This is a reversal. From the spiritual which descends on visits as ancestors, we have passed to a spiritual which ascends toward God through the *bhakti* prayers. And this is where the construction and focus around the one God and "his manifestations" is taking root in the psyche of the Balinese. This is a very important phenomenon, especially as other aspects of India's impact are spreading. In particular the notion of reincarnation, which is in full transformation, in certain circles anyway. Instead of reincarnating among one's own, say the modernists, one now reincarnates according to one's karma. There is no concern for consistency; the two perceptions of karma coexist and these contradictions are maintained without bothering anyone – a sign that a new syncretism is forming.

I imagine that, on self-perception, there is no requirement for consistency yet either.

Yes, especially since we are also beginning to see people in urban spaces who function in a Western way, for example young women who, marginalized in the

---

[448] The term for participating in ritual is *ngayah*, to serve.
[449] In issue No. 261, 2017 of the magazine *Taksu*, devoted to the peculiarities of Balinese-ness, the writer speaks of the *"betara di awang-awang,"* the "gods in the clouds" in the metaphorical sense: young people would seek to serve gods (*nyungsung ida betara*) that are unknown to them.

tradition, ask questions about feminism and therefore empower themselves. These people are trained in the city, in a modern school; they are in contact with foreign ideologies. But developments remain hesitant and contradictory. You can see it in art. Thus, certain artists of the so-called "traditional" style, in Kutuh, Ubud, in particular, take refuge in thematic hyper-tradition, as if modernity did not exist. They portray the Bali of the past, with offerings and ceremonies, without cars or foreigners, in a sort of contemporary neo-realism where traditional forces subdue modernity. In contrast, there are the modernists who abstractly visualize official Neo-Hindu cosmological concepts. And then there are the contemporaries, a small minority, who think about the world and its impact on Bali, with the theme of ecology and the revolt of women. Three styles and three ways.

So, you are saying that the majority of Balinese painters produce works based on Neo-Hindu abstraction, except for a few, based in Ubud, whose traditional creations offer a denial of reality that rejects modernity?

Yes … These village artists say the tradition continues in its purity, while academically trained artists advocate Neo-Hinduism. This is the spirit of the times, which can be found among most educated Balinese. It is no coincidence that there are more and more references to the *yuga* system, the Indian eras, in written texts. Thus, we would currently be at the end of Dvapara Yuga[450] and entering Kali Yuga,[451] that is, just before the end of the world. I remember a Balinese, 20 years ago, who said he was Kalkî, the last incarnation of Vishnu, the one who announces the end of the world. This is unknown to the Balinese tradition, where old people sometimes say that "the world is old" (*gumi uba wayah*). We thus see the emergence of prophets and gurus of all kinds, a sign of the cracks in Balinese society. Some of these gurus, moreover, operate in other cracks, those of Western societies: they become New Age gurus for buyers of an Orient reinvented for them.

Are these to be seen as attempts to gain control over what is going on?

This is the big question. I think all of this is still part of an unconscious effort of ordering, of confused rationalization of the transformations underway. But this is also what is problematic, because it does not respond to the primary challenge to the village culture, which resists. There is a mismatch.

Apart from artists, are there other attempts to rationalize the upheavals that have occurred over the past 50 years? Are there intellectuals who try to conceptualize all these changes in books or articles?

There is the Hindu university,[452] which is the main agent of Indianization in Bali. It imports Neo-Hindu text from India and sends trainers to the villages

---

[450] Dvapara Yuga is the 3rd age in the cosmogony of formal Indian Hinduism; it is marked by greed and fraud.
[451] Kali Yuga, or "the Age of Kali" or "Iron Age" is the 4th and current age of Hindu cosmogony.
[452] Universitas Hindu Indonesia, Unhi.

who promote this Hinduism.[453] Are there real questioners, from a non-religious perspective? Not that I know of.

Does this make Neo-Hinduism the best ally of modernity in contemporary Bali?

Yes, this is the brand of new modernity, with its explanatory logic, but also its negative aspects. Bali is living in illusion. When tourism suddenly took hold of Bali in the 1970s, several phenomena emerged concurrently: a fixation on the original Balinese culture as a symbol of an unchanging identity, announced by the policy of cultural tourism; a practical objectifying of this culture, which allowed the Balinese to produce not only false ritual dances, but also false trances and even false processions; a shift from Balinese religious tradition to Indian religious tradition; and a negation of any change, in the name of that immutability of the identity mentioned above. There was thus a secularization of social acts at the same time as an identity fixation in religion. You can see the rupture!

Are the Balinese well aware of all this?

No! They have not drawn any significant intellectual consequences from it. They feel like they've got it under control! Particularly because this is the primary function of cultural tourism. One accepts the change involved by imagining that it is going to produce continuity, when in fact it produces a break. We forget the damage of objectification.

Tourism perpetuates, but it transforms ...

It has indirect effects which are terrible. Of course, it doesn't break everything, as has happened elsewhere, in Hawaii for example. The changes it causes maintain the myth of what Bali produces in the eyes of the world: the myth of a unique culture preserved by cultural tourism. In fact, it destroys while overvaluing what it destroys. There is a hiatus, a schizophrenia impossible to maintain over the long term. Everyone says change isn't happening when it's everywhere! Even some anthropologists who come here state that Bali is not changing, because they do not dare, in the name of objectivity, overvalue the historical era during which they arrived, when Bali was still a homogeneous space: a dream place. Everything in Bali is transforming tradition into a tourist object by claiming that it is preserved! This leads not to the sustainability of culture, but to the iconization of its key aspects.

What are the psychological effects?

Indeed, it rattles the Balinese. Some admit that they are annoyed that their traditions are reduced to objects, knowing full well that they make a living from it. I would like to add something here that might sound harsh because this is

---

[453] This is *dharma wacana*, sermons, the equivalent of *siar islamiah* in Indonesian Islam. Both aim, with the blessing of the state, to teach their respective truth to ordinary people.

true of Bali, but also of Indonesia at large. Few people dare to go beyond the perception common to their ethnic or religious group to proclaim their truth, that is, to describe reality as they perceive it individually: it would be rude. As we said, autonomy of the person is limited. Even educated people find it difficult to produce social reflection. That is, to distance themselves from the thing they want to observe, from the religious, from identity. And even if they have produced it, they have a hard time saying it point blank. So, they import Western theories, such as postmodernism, useful since it criticizes universalism and justifies the return to identity. This is of course illusory. But that at least allows one to continue to think that Bali creates a perennial culture, "light of the world," which in the end is only an intellectual, local, and inverted variant, because proposed by the Balinese, of the notion of "Balinese paradise" of the 1930s! And this has the function of obscuring the domination of contemporary capitalism, as the "Bali paradise" of the 1930s obscured colonial domination.

That's a very interesting theory! But back to psychology …

Coming back to what was said above, outside of Neo-Hindu circles, we are beginning to see Balinese who think and operate on an increasingly modern level. There are young artists who base their work on ecological concepts, women writers and artists who embrace themes of sexuality. So, the phenomena of dissociation produced by capitalism also favor the emergence of autonomous personalities in certain cultural spaces. These people make modern art, modern theatre! But they remain very marginal with regard to society in general. When you are Western and cultured in Bali, you tend to circulate mostly around these artists and give them an importance that they do not actually have! It's a common illusion here!

From the point of view of psychology, how does one grasp the notion of disorder when it takes hold of Balinese society?

You probably know the psychiatrist Luh Ketut Suryani,[454] who is known for dealing with the phenomena of the *niskala* in her work, that is, the presence of the intangible in the personality of her patients. She admits this to be a reality, as she believes that Western psychology is ethnocentric. Which is of course true, in a way!

This psychiatrist takes a very strong identity position …

That's the whole point. She's very ethnocentric herself. She tends to respond to psychological disorders in a way that involves identity with a theory of *niskala*. In her view, she is the only one who has the treatments and explanations, all Balinese, in particular therapies for collective "possession," on the border between science and *balian* shamanism. That said, it allows her patients to continue to be part of the group, to remain Balinese, while if they are treated on the basis of individual pathologies, they find themselves excluded and without hope.

---

[454] Luh Ketut Suryani, psychiatrist and influential figure in Balinese social and political life, also founder of the Suryani Institute for Mental Health Foundation.

Does the accumulation of wealth help overcome psychological problems caused by change?

The first objective of those who have succeeded in enriching themselves or in gaining power is to introduce themselves into the elite of the traditional system by building an even more beautiful residence and holding even more lavish ceremonies. In my opinion, there is no challenge as such. New wealth does not generate an immediate break. During temple festivals, the new rich, high officials, and super-graduates are seated with the Cokorda, the Brahmins and other elites. Indeed, although the nouveau riche might question the validity of the caste / *wangsa* system, they do not question the notion of Balinese status itself. The important thing is to be counted among the elect, the happy few, separated from the common people by a huge gap.

Do these changes also engender militant behavior? As we could see with the issue of *Reklamasi* in the bay of Benoa ...

This is a phenomenon that has not yet crystallized except among certain populations of the coast. *Reklamasi* projected such ecological and demographic transformations that the Balinese could not help but react. Bali is not Dubai. But there was nothing socially entrenched about the activism. Apart from a few militants, it was mostly local and ethnic in nature: it aimed to block control of non-Balinese capital, as we discussed.

For me, the mobilization against this project is something very new, the reactions to *Reklamasi* suggest a new psychology!

Without a doubt. But we saw a similar phenomenon before, in 1998, when Balinese *en masse* called for a referendum on leaving the Republic. An indelicate politician in Jakarta had claimed that a Hindu could not become president of Indonesia. He was referring to Megawati,[455] who had prayed in a Balinese temple although she is a Muslim. People thought, why be Indonesian if a Balinese cannot become president? This crisis was one of the first signs of the transformation of an identity oriented around the village into an island identity, then a Hindu one. But awareness of the self, as in being fully autonomous from ancestors, in the pursuit of pleasure, a career, or even the accumulation of wealth, all of this remains foreign to most Balinese.

Even among artists?

Here, artists want social recognition, or they want to formulate a religious neo-conviction. The notion of art as making what you want, or questioning, is rare here, as I've said.

Is the sense of fault that is inherent in all religions important here?

---

[455] Megawati Soekarnoputri, a daughter of Sukarno, Indonesia's first president, and herself president from 2001 to 2004.

It's *karma pala*, "the fruit of one's deeds," that's considered important here. It can occur after life; that's the classical Hindu notion of karma. Or is can happen during present life, *cicih* karma. Either way, it's a mechanism, more than guilt.

Speaking of mechanics, then by extension of the great cycles you mentioned earlier, like the *yuga*, would the Balinese be tempted to rationalize what is happening today based on these great cyclical periods?

Notions of upheaval, disorder or even the end of the world are not treated as social phenomena but as cosmic phenomena. To remedy this, the Balinese perform ceremonies. They do not redistribute wealth or power like the West tries to do, but ritual. This is why the temple festivals that take place at Besakih[456] are becoming bigger, as well as at other major temples of the island, corresponding to the mountains, to the cardinal points, or to a sojourn of founding figures of the religion.[457] It is in these places that the Balinese keep the system, symbolically, in order. It must be understood that what the Balinese person asks is to be in an orderly system. Whether from the traditional point of view, with the ancestral system, with the invisible forces of the *niskala*, with the offerings or from the point of view of current Hinduism, or even with the person. If there is disorder, you have to manage it. With ritual.

Is the island in a cycle that leads to upheaval, destruction?

This is what is to be feared, because when people talk about chaos, it is because they notice disruptions, social dysfunctions, which they refuse to address as such but which they attribute to cosmological disorders.

It's a way of rationalizing as well.

Yes ... But if this is not accompanied by real socio-political measures, it can generate even more disorder, given today's accelerating economic, demographic, and other changes. We come back to the old problematic of Indonesia as a whole: how to create instruments other than symbolic and religious to manage all these transformations. Because between the philosophy dating from the 7th century proposed by some Muslims and the destructive cycle of Kali Yuga of some Hindus, we are in the same mental mechanisms, the same refusal to see contemporary social reality. This is why Bali needs modern Balinese intellectuals, with a real ability to see things objectively. And they exist, of course, although in a very small minority. Bali has nothing to gain from taking refuge in either neo-traditional or Neo-Hindu hyper-Balineseness! Bali needs enlightened and pragmatic Balinese. It is not just a question of morals, of corrupt elites, because a moralistic view will lead to political extremism. You need people who understand complexity and act on it.

---

[456] Besakih: the largest temple in Bali, at the foot of the Agung volcano.

[457] Mantras directed to the divine always address the gods of the various mountains; and one does not make any big ceremony without visiting the island's main temples to beseech their residing gods for holy waters.

How do institutions manage change?

Certain institutions have undeniably been put in place. For example, when it was a question of reducing the birth rate, the family planning program of the *Orde Baru* was quite effective. The military regime indeed had set up development organizations that operated from the top down. But with democratization, they have disappeared in favor of new models which come from a grassroots system; but it doesn't really work.

These community organizations have not all disappeared yet. We still sometimes see, here and there, a sign that mentions that citizens are subject to family planning: two children per family ...

Yes, it's a paradox, because family planning no longer has the support of Governor Wayan Koster, who encourages large families so that the Balinese remain masters of their island! Coming back to the agents of change, we must also mention the graduate students who are dispatched to the villages to apply programs in the field of their studies. There is also the Lembaga Perkreditan Desa[458] which promotes microcredit, as well as numerous cooperatives. All these things are good. But in my opinion, there is currently a problem of managing new urban spaces which have village status but city problems. Like Ubud, which does not have a specific statute that allows it to levy real taxes and organize its own roads, for example, without going through the *bupati*.[459]

However, there is a mayor in Ubud, right?

A village head, but without power. The main budget flows go through Gianyar,[460] the capital of the regency. And Ubud's needs are no longer those of a simple village. The space in this in-between position in Bali, half-urban, half-village, is very large.

Do Balinese who have gone to live elsewhere better understand the current issues?

Without a doubt. Because on the outside, they find themselves in a minority position. For a long time, that was not a problem. But the fact is that many Balinese, despite their history, no longer see the "other" as the similar but as the dissimilar. It's something we see not just in Bali, but all over Indonesia. Is this one of the unintended and awkward consequences of the current teaching of Pancasila, which overemphasizes the religious? Perhaps one should leave spiritual discourse to the religious sphere, and prevent it from taking over social and political discourse!

If we leave everything to religion, there can be no construction of a social discourse adapted to the times.

---

[458] Lembaga Perkreditan Desa (LPD): village credit organization.

[459] *Bupati*: person responsible for *kabupaten*, elected by the citizens; formerly "regent".

[460] Gianyar: the provincial subdivision, or *kabupaten*, on which Ubud depends.

People who speak objectively of social discourse are extremely rare. Even if social issues shake traditional structures, it is never formulated as it should be! Intellectuals who have the means to see things objectively are absorbed into the system, for fear of being ostracized.

Is there a Balinese miracle?

I mainly think that there is an Indonesian miracle. And that's exactly what both enchants and appalls us: the absence of an ideology other than generally religious. In spite of crystallization here and there, as I explain here, we are still in this famous artistic vagueness in which most people say there are no differences from one ethno-religious group to another. Perhaps that is history. Indonesians have not experienced repeated barbarian invasions like Europeans. The Archipelago has preserved its peoples, and this is reflected in their smiles.

Is there a Javanese imperialism?

No! One can speak of course about the permeation of Indonesian culture by Javanese culture. That's undeniable. We see this in particular in the emphasis on some form of ethics, of behavioral control. This hinders decision-making. But to speak of Javanese imperialism is not to understand that the sea does not separate, it unites. And that Java permeates more than it dominates.

In the end, do the Balinese think they are a chosen people?

Yes and no! They think they are a chosen people because they have been chosen by the whole world as the inhabitants of a paradise on Earth. But beware: to be the elect, it was necessary for Europeans to tell them so.

And the list of those who said it is long, including you today!

Yes! That's the whole drama!

Finally, and by way of conclusion to our discussions, can you make a quick inventory of the changes in Bali?

To sum up, there is a kind of shift from tradition to modernity, which is accompanied by a continuation of elements of tradition in this modernity. However, it is sometimes contradictory. The first thing to highlight is that Bali is no longer an agrarian society. People constantly assert that it is a traditional agrarian society, when in fact it no longer is. Bali is a capitalist service society. Most behaviors, decisions, whether ritual or economic or otherwise, operate from the norms of capitalism. The land, the rites, even the offerings, everything today has a modern economic form, adapted to local constraints. The problem is, the Balinese do not want to recognize this reality and act on it. Many of them either have a premodern mentality or advertise themselves as such. As a result, the more capitalism dominates Bali, the more they deny its effects and close their eyes to the consequences. For example, when it comes to identity, it was long thought that Bali was definitely inscribed in Indonesian space. Sukarno was half-Balinese, and the Balinese participated in nation-building with their elite. But since the fall of Suharto's military regime, we can see that other forces are emerging. They risk leading to an increasingly marked crystallization of identity, as elsewhere in other parts of Indonesia. Balinese identity has become more and more ethno-religious and refocused on a new kind of Hinduism, that is to say re-Indianized. This is where there is a challenge. Because, just as we went from an Indonesian Islam to an international Islam, so in Bali we go from a local belief system to international Hinduism with all the possibility for conflict that that implies. Bali is also in the process of moving from a religion with a meaningful ritual present in all everyday gestures, to a more abstract and harsher religion. In doing so, there is a passage from vague symbol to dogma, from theatre to text, from signs to truth, from vague to definite, from relative to absolute. I find that utterly dramatic. These developments worry me. The solution would be to become aware of these changes and to act at the level of education.

Beyond Bali, I wonder if the shift to modernity that has been described here might not correspond to a general trend that many Westerners have not yet realized, obsessed as they are with their own model of modernity in which everything ends and dissolves in economic and behavioral individualism. In Bali, the passage in 50 years from an agrarian, homogeneous, largely illiterate society endowed with fluid and non-theological beliefs to a modern, heterogeneous and literate society does not inevitably translate into the emergence of the full autonomy of the person, the rationality of behavior, and the adoption of an identity and religious relativism, but at least as often, into its opposite, especially since the traditional modes of social cohesion are weakening due to urbanization, education, and the transformation of land into a commodity. While some Balinese, privileged and trained in today's globalized world, espouse universal codes and appreciate the new autonomy offered to them, many nevertheless suffer in contact with the "other" (Muslim, Christian, etc.), huge changes in their living environment (damaged), the way of working (not agrarian), and religion (the impact of structured religions, changes in the transmission of knowledge, school, the teaching of a truth, the new media). Many therefore react, not by universalism, but by a collectivism of a new kind, far from the villages of yesteryear: that of religious affiliation. Therefore, after having as illiterates espoused the nationalist and socialist illusions of the fathers of the nation, which led to massacres, here they are inventing, with faith, a Hindu past which never existed. In doing so, alas, they fabricate for themselves an otherness which does not need to exist.

It took 300 years for the literacy generated by Gutenberg's machine to produce what is known as the Enlightenment, and then almost 300 years more for those enlightened to generate anything other than darkness. So, it took a long time for the translation of the Bible to translate into its questioning. What will happen to the holy books of the day in Indonesia, considering all the excesses associated with them? Because the transition from a Javanese Islam to an Islamized Java on the one hand, and from a Balinized Hinduism to a Hindu Bali on the other hand promises surprises of all kinds, perhaps to the regret of the gods of the mountain.

Thank you, Jean, for these 20 hours of interview that you have been kind enough to grant me over several months.

260

Selected Bibliography

Aditjondro, George. Bali, Jakarta's Colony, Social and Ecological Impact of Jakarta-based Conglomerates in Bali's Tourism Industry. Perth: Asia Research Centre Working Paper, Murdoch University, 1995.

Artaud, Antonin. *Le théâtre et son double*. Paris: Gallimard, 1938.

Basset, Catherine and Picard, Michel, and Couteau, Jean. *Bali, l'ordre cosmique et la quotidienneté – Autrement hors série.* Paris: No. 66, Éditions Autrement, 1993.

Bateson, Gregory. *Steps to an Ecology of Mind*. Chicago: University of Chicago Press, 1972.

Bateson, Gregory and Mead, Margaret. *Balinese Character: A Photographic Analysis*. New York: New York Academy of Sciences, 1942.

Baum, Vicki. *Tale of Bali*. [*Liebe und Tod auf Bali*] Querido,1937. English translation by Basil Creighton, Oxford University Press, 1973.

Belo, Jane. *Bali: Temple Festival*. Seattle. University of Washington Press, 1953

Cabasset Christine, Couteau Jean et Picard Michel. "La poldérisation de la baie de Benoa à Bali, vers un nouveau puputan?" *Archipel,* No. 93, 2017, pp. 151-197.

Cerf, Muriel. *Le Diable Vert*. Paris: Mercure de France, 1975.

Couteau, Jean. "Bali et l'islam, Rencontre historique," *Archipel,* No. 58, 1999, pp. 159-188.

Couteau, Jean. "Bali et l'islam, Coexistence et perspectives contemporaines," *Archipel,* No. 60, 2000, pp. 45-64.

Couteau, Jean. *Bali Today, Modernity*. Jakarta: Kepustakaan Populer Gramedia, 2005.

Couteau, Jean. *Bali Today, Love and Social life*. Jakarta: Kepustakaan Populer Gramedia, 2008.

Couteau, Jean. "La bombe de Bali, une autre manière de penser l'événement," *La Gazette de Bali*, No. 89, October 2012.

Couteau, Jean. "Les sept saints de l'islam balinais," *Le Banian,* No. 21, Paris, 2016, pp. 219-226.

Couteau, Jean. "Tolérance et Religion: Bali," *Le Banian*, No. 21, 2016, pp. 32-47.

Couteau, Jean. *Myth, Magic and Mystery in Bali*, Jakarta: Phoenix Communications, 2017.

Couteau, Jean. "Le Substrat pré-hindou du culte des ancêtres: rite des morts à Bali," *Archipel,* No. 97, 2019.

Couteau, Jean. *Now Bali* magazine, monthly articles from 2008.

Covarrubias Miguel. *Island of Bali*, New York: Alfred A. Knopf, 1937.

Creese, Helen. "Curious Modernities: Early Twentieth-Century Balinese Textual Explorations," *The Journal of Asian Studies,* Vol. 66, No. 3, August 2007.

Creese, Helen. *Bali in the Early Nineteenth Century: The Ethnographic Accounts of Pierre Dubois*, Leiden: Brill, 2016.

Damayana, I Wayan. Menyama Braya : Studi Perubahan Masyarakat Bali. Salatiga: Fakultas Teologi Universitas Kristen Satya Wacana, 2011.

Darling, Diana. *The Painted Alphabet*. Singapore: Editions Didier Millet, 2019 [New York: Houghton Mifflin, 1992].

Darma Putra, I Nyoman. *A Literary Mirror:Balinese Reflections on Modernity and Identity in the Twentieth Century*. Leiden: Brill, 2004.

Darma Putra, I Nyoman. *Wanita Bali Tempo Doeloe: Perspektif Masa Kini.* Denpasar: Pustaka Larasan, 2007.

Darta, I Gusti Nyoman and Couteau, Jean and Breguet, Georges. *Time, Rites and Festivals in Bali*, Jakarta: Babbooks, 2013.

Debord, Guy. La société du spectacle. Paris: Buchet-Chastel, 1967. [The Society of the Spectacle. English translation by Donald Nicholson-Smith. Zone Books edition, 1994].

Djelantik, A.A.M. The Birthmark: Memoirs of a Balinese Prince. Singapore: Periplus Editions, 1997.

Fassola, Jacques. *Bali, Jardin des Immortels*. Paris: Éditions du Chêne, 1983.

Foucault, Michel. *Folie et Déraison: Histoire de la folie à l'âge classique*. Paris: 1961. (*Madness and Civilization: A History of Insanity in the Age of Reason.* Trans. by Jonathan Murphy and Jean Khalfa. Routledge, 2006.

Geertz, Clifford. "Form and Variation in Balinese Village Structure." *American Anthropologist,* Vol. 61, Issue 6, 1959.

Geertz, Clifford. *Negara: The Theatre State in Nineteenth Century Bali*. Princeton: Princeton University Press, 1980.

Geertz, Clifford. Person, Time and Conduct in Bali. Cultural Report Series No. 14, Yale University: *Southeast Asia Studies,*1966.

Goris, Roelof. "Holidays and Holy Days." *Bali: Studies in Life, Thought and Ritual*. The Hague and Bandung: Van Hoeve, 1960.

Hanna, Willard A. *Bali Chronicles: Fascinating People and Events in Balinese History*. Hong Kong: Periplus Editions, 2004 [Originally *Bali Profile: People, Events, Circumstances (1001-1976)*. New York: American Universities Field Staff, 1976].

Jacobs, Julius. *Eenigen tijd onder de Baliërs; eene reisbeschrijving met aantekeningen betreffende hygiëne, land- en volkenkunde van de eilanden Bali en Lombok (Some time among the Balinese; a travel description with annotations concerning hygiene, land and ethnology from the islands of Bali and Lombok)* Batavia: 1883.

Lampedusa, Giuseppe Tomasi di. *Il Gattopardo*. Milan: Feltrinelli, 1958. [English translation by Archibald Colquhoun, The Leopard, originally published in 1960 by Collins (in the UK) and Pantheon Books (in the US).]

Lansing, Stephen J. *Priests and Programmers: technologies of powers in the engineered landscape of Bali*. Princeton, N.J.: Princeton University Press, 1991.

Lindsey, Timothy. *The Romance of K'tut Tantri and Indonesia*. Kuala Lumpur; New York: Oxford University Press, 1997.

MacRae, Graeme S. *Economy, Ritual and History in a Balinese Tourist Town*, PhD Dissertation, University of Auckland, 1997.

MacRae, Graeme. "Negara Ubud: The Theatre state in Twenty-first-century Bali." *History and Anthropology* 16 (4), December 2005.

Mathews, Anna. *The Night of Purnama*. London: Jonathan Cape, 1963.

McPhee, Colin. *A House in Bali*. New York: Day, 1946.

Palguna, IBM Dharma, Shastra Wangsa (*Kamus Istilah Wangsa Bali Pustaka, Pusaka Manusia*). *Sadampaty Aksara*. Denpasar: Bali Wisdom, 2018.

Paramita, I Gusti Agung. *Wajah Tuhan dan Sifat Pemuja* (*The Face of God and Attitude of the Faithful*). Denpasar: Sarwa Tatwa Pustaka, 2020.

Picard, Michel: *Bali – Tourisme culturel et culture Touristique*. Paris: L'Harmattan, 1993. [English translation by Diana Darling. *Bali: Cultural Tourism and Touristic Culture*. Singapore: Archipelago Press, 1996.]

Picard, Michel. *Kebalian – La construction dialogique de l'identité balinaise*. Paris: Association Archipel, 2017.

Robinson, Geoffrey. *The Dark Side of Paradise: Political Violence in Bali*. Ithaca: Cornell University Press, 1995.

Santha, IGG Djelantik. *Tresnané Ajur Lebur Setonden Kembang*, Denpasar: 1981.

Schulte Nordholt, Henk. *The Spell of Power: a history of Balinese politics 1650-1940*. Leiden: KITLV Press, 1996.

Schulte Nordholt, Henk. *Bali, an Open Fortress, Regional Autonomy, Electoral Democracy and Entrenched Identities*. Singapore: National University of Singapore, 2007.

Stowell, John and Couteau, Jean. *Walter Spies: The Art of Life and Walter Spies: A Life in Art, Walter Spies Collectors Suite*. Jakarta: Afterhours Books, 2012.

Sukawati, Tjokorda Gde Agung Sukawati. *Tjokorda Gde Agung Sukawati*: Reminiscence of a Balinese Prince, as dictated to Rosemary Hilbery, South East Asian Studies, University of Hawaii,1979.

Supatra, Kanduk. "Nyungsung Batara di Awang Awang." *Taksu*. Edisi 261, 2017.

Suryawan, I Ngurah Suryawan. Saru Gremeng. *Bali: Sepilihan Esai Kritik Kebudayaan*. Denpasar: Pustaka Larasan, 2020.

Tantri, K'tut. *Revolt in Paradise*. London: William Heinemann, 1960.

Tomagola, Thamrin Amal. "Basis Sosio-Kultural Kekerasan-Radikalisme Perkotaan" in *Spektrum Budaya, Festschrift HUT ke-84 Toeti Heraty*. Jakarta: Museum Toeti Heraty, 2017.

Vickers, Adrian. *Bali: A Paradise Created*. Roweville, Vic.:Penguin, 1989. [Revised version, Vermont: Tuttle, 2013].

Wiana, Ketut and Santri, Raka. *Kasta dalam Hindu: Kesalapahaman Berabad-abad (Caste in Hinduism: Centuries of Misunderstanding)*. Denpasar: Yayasan Dharma Naradha, 1993.

Wijaya, Made. *Architecture of Bali: a source book of traditional and modern forms*. Singapore: Archipelago Press & Wijaya Words. 2002.

Wijaya, Made. *The Best of Stranger in Paradise, 1996-2008*. Denpasar: Wijaya Words, 2008.

Wiryatnaya, Usadi and Couteau, Jean (ed.). *Bali di persimpangan jalan*. Denpasar: Nusa Data Indobudaya Editions, 1995.

FILMS

Goona Goona or *The Kriss* (1932) by Andre Roosevelt and Armand Denis.

Virgins of Bali (1932) by Deane H. Dickason.

Legong: Dance of the Virgins (1935) by Gaston Glass and Henry de la Falaise.

Road to Bali (1952) by Hal Walker.

Gods of Bali (1952) by Sidney Carroll.

Incontro d'amore (Bali) (1970) by Ugo Liberatore and Paolo Heusch.

The Ring of Fire, an Indonesian Odyssey (1972) by Lorne Blaire and Lawrence Blaire.

Emmanuelle 2: L'antivierge (1975) by Francis Giacobetti.

The Eleven Powers: the Festival of Eka Dasa Rudra (1979) by Larry Gartenstein.

Lempad of Bali (1980) by John Darling and Lorne Blaire.

Mystics in Bali (1981) by H. Tjut Djalil.

Bali Triptych (1987) by John Darling.

Baraka (1992) by Ron Fricke.

Done Bali (1993) by Kerry Negara.

Endless Summer II (1994) by Robert Weaver and Patrick O'Connell.

Les 1001 danseurs du Kecak Dance (2004) by Douchan Gersi.

Toute La Beauté du Monde (2006) by Marc Esposito.

The Fall (2006) by Tarsem Singh.

Cowboys in Paradise (2009) by Amit Virmani.

A Loving Friend (2009) by Kerry Negara.
Eat Pray Love (2010) by Ryan Murphy.
Alex Cross (2012) by James Patterson.
The Healing of Bali (2013) by John Darling.
Bitter Honey (2014) by Robert Lemelson.
Bali: Heaven and Hell (2014) by Phil Jarratt.

Chronological Landmarks

Bali

Area: 5,780 km². Population: 4,362 million (2019). Density: 750 inhabitants/km²

Chronology

7th-8th century AD. Buddhist presence.

9th century. First Hinduized kingdom.

10th-11th century. Reign of Airlangga in Java; dynastic union of Bali and East Java under the reign of Udayana.

14th century. Having regained full independence, Bali is attacked and invaded in 1343 by warriors from the Javanese maritime empire of Majapahit. There follows a replacement of the elites, a bit like post-Franco-Norman England. Kawi (Old Javanese) becomes the language of culture. Only certain villages in remote areas, known as "Bali Aga," remain safe from this Javanization. The capital of the new dynasty is Gelgel where the *Dalem* (king) resides. Gelgel quickly frees itself from the suzerainty of Java.

16th century. Java is inexorably Islamized in the wake of maritime trade developed by Majapahit. This Islamization is refused by some priests who retreat to Bali. In particular Dang Hyang Nirartha, who will be at the origin of the six lines of *pedanda Siwa* (high priests), and Dang Hyang Astapaka, at the origin of the line of *pedanda Buda*.

First contacts with the Portuguese.

1597. A Dutch flotilla stops in Bali to replenish its water supply and is then received at the court of Gelgel.

1619. Foundation of Batavia (now Jakarta) by the Dutch East India Company. The Dutch then extend their hold over the archipelago by defeating the maritime sultanates, in particular that of Macassar in 1669; then, they gradually take control of Java, which will be completed in 1755 by the Treaty of Giyanti.

≈ 1650. Vizier (*patih*) Gusti Agung Maruti seizes power in Gelgel. The island of Bali loses its political unity, although the royal line, restored at the turn of the century, establishes its capital just outside Gelgel in Klungkung. A powerful kingdom will appear in Mengwi, which will control Blambangan in East Java until the 18th century. Other kingdoms will appear in Buleleng, Karangasem, Bangli and Denpasar.

Balinese slave trade by the Dutch until the end of the 18th century, towards Batavia and even Reunion.

Beginning of the 19th century. After the dissolution of the Dutch East India Company (1799) and the French and English interludes (1810-1816) on Java, first English studies of Bali.

1820-1839. Multiplication of contacts with Bali by whalers and European merchants; Java War / Revolt of the Javanese Prince Diponegoro against colonial rule (1825-1830). The Dutch open a trading post in Kuta and seek to transform trade agreements into recognition of suzerainty.

1846-1849. Dutch military expeditions against the kingdom of Buleleng. Dutch occupation of Buleleng in the north of the island and Jembrana in the west. The Dutch are held in check at Kusamba in Klungkung after the death of General Michiels.

1850-1890. Constant pressure from the Dutch on the Balinese kings to formalize their suzerainty agreements. Ambitions of Klungkung eager to restore its royal primacy. Appearance of Tjokorde Gde Sukawati, warlord in Ubud.

1891. Destruction of Negara and Mengwi.

1894. Karangasem comes under Dutch control.

1900. At the instigation of Tjokorde Gde, the kingdom of Gianyar comes under Dutch protection.

1906. *Puputan* (fight to the death) in Badung (Denpasar).

1908. *Puputan* in Klungkung. Bangli submits. Bali now fully under Dutch rule.

1909. First promotion of tourism.

1912. Gregor Krause publishes his first photos of Balinese bathing, creating the image of Bali paradise.

1925. Musician and painter Walter Spies arrives in Bali. Without intending to, he will make Bali one of the hotspots of the cosmopolitan intelligentsia of the interwar years. Supported by this audience, Bali experiences a cultural renewal in the fields of painting, music, and dance.

1920-1940. Indonesian nationalism is growing; the use of the Indonesian language spreads with the opening of schools in the villages. A Hindu reformist movement emerges in certain educated circles.

1942-1945. Japanese occupation and Dutch withdrawal; death of Walter Spies and internment of European residents.

17 August 1945. Proclamation of Indonesian independence, two days after the Japanese surrender.

March 1946-December 1949. Return of the Dutch; creation of the state of Eastern Indonesia (Negara Indonesia Timur); crushing of the Balinese resistance in Margarana. Recognition of independence at the end of 1949. Abolition of the puppet state and union with the Indonesian Republic. Human cost of the fight in Bali: 2,000 dead.

1950-1965. Evolution of an initially democratic regime into a "guided democracy" under the aegis of President Sukarno, born to a Balinese mother; attempt to establish Indonesian socialism; economic crisis; tensions among Muslim parties, the army, and the Indonesian Communist Party. In Bali, tensions between the Nationalist Party and the Communist Party.

1963. Eruption of Mount Agung at the time of the great ceremony of Eka Dasa Rudra; destruction of crops; great misery.

1965. Aborted coup attempt in Jakarta of 30 September 1965. Suharto ousts Sukarno and undertakes the repression of the Communist Party and the left. Approximately 80,000 dead in Bali.

1967. Suharto officially becomes president and opens the country to foreign investment. Hippies begin to come to Kuta.

1971. The tourism master plan provides for the concentration of tourism development in the Nusa Dua region. As a result, priority is given to large foreign investments, both Jakartan and foreign, rather than to local tourism dynamics. Formally, a policy of "cultural tourism" rather than "tourist culture;" but, in reality, a focus on tradition, recycled to produce "authenticity" with a triple objective: to avoid social protest, to produce cultural pride, and to provide shows for tourist consumption.

7 December 1975. Indonesian invasion of East Timor, until then a Portuguese colony, in the grip of a civil war following the Carnation Revolution of April 1974.

1994. First movement of protest against tourism development during the construction of the Bali Nirwana Resort, a hotel complex built overlooking the most famous temple in Bali, Pura Tanah Lot.

1997-1998. Asian financial crisis with serious consequences on the Indonesian economy, causing social discontent that will contribute to the fall of Suharto.

21 May 1998. Following huge student protests, accompanied by anti-Chinese riots and losing military support, Suharto is forced to resign. BJ Habibie, the vice-president, becomes president pending the organization of elections. Many Chinese-Indonesians settle in Bali, which is considered safer than Jakarta.

14 October 1998. LH Saifuddin, Minister of Food and Horticulture, who has presidential ambitions, having learned that Megawati Sukarnoputri had prayed in a temple, publicly asks: "Are the Indonesian people ready to accept a Hindu president?" Very quickly, some Balinese activists demand that a referendum on independence be held if indeed a Hindu cannot become president. Large protests take place. Saifuddin is condemned by the entire political class and Bali calms down. One lesson, however: the Balinese refuse the political Islamization of the country, a condition of its unity.

30 August 1999. Referendum in Timor Leste. Independence wins the day.

1999. First democratic elections since 1955. Abdurrahman Wahid (alias "Gus Dur") is elected president by both legislative chambers, despite Megawati's party having won the election. Demonstrations in Bali turn violent, with the destruction of several government buildings. Decentralization legislation: the transfer of authority to local governments will allow them to attempt to control migratory movements through the creation of an internal passport called "KIPEM," which will be banned in 2018.

23 July 2001. Megawati is elected president after the impeachment of Gus Dur, considered too liberal by the army and facing violent interfaith conflicts in eastern Indonesia.

12 October 2002. Islamist car bomb attack in Kuta: 202 dead and more than 200 injured.

2004-2014. Susilo Bambang Yudhoyono (SBY) is president, in first presidential election by direct ballot; economic growth.

1 October 2005. New round of suicide and car bombings. Bombs explode at two sites, Jimbaran Beach and Kuta, 30 km away, killing 20 and injuring more than 100.

2012. *Reklamasi,* the Dubai-like project of land reclamation in the bay of Benoa in the south of the island meets hostility from the population. Investors want to transform the bay into a luxury resort complex. Over the long term, not only would the project destroy the environment, but it would threaten demographic balances. The project causes tensions even at the top levels of the state.

2014-2019. Joko Widodo president of Indonesia; sustained growth. The so-called *Reformasi* era since 1998 has brought democracy, but some protest silence on investigations into human rights violations during the military regime (1965-1998); a latent separatist conflict in Papua; crumbling of tradition and slow rise of Islamism in Java. Exponential growth in tourism in Bali, from 5,000 arrivals by air in 1968 to 6.3 million in 2019. Economic progress; emergence of a Balinese middle class. Demographic change. Non-Hindus constitute more than 15% of the local population, compared to barely 1% in 1930.

2019. Joko Widodo is re-elected president for five years.

2020. The COVID-19 pandemic imposes a total halt to tourism activities in Bali causing an unprecedented economic crisis.

Acknowledgments from Jean Couteau

It is impossible for me to express my thanks to all those who have contributed, phase after phase, to my knowledge of Balinese culture. The artists I visited house to house in the 1980s, around Ubud and Batuan; the villagers I questioned here and there when, from 1990 to 1994, I produced daily articles in the *Bali Post* on Balinese culture and society; fellow teachers at the Denpasar School of Art; the artists I wrote about in the mainstream Balinese and Indonesian press; Balinese intellectuals and others whom I have met and appreciated during conferences, discussions; and also politicians who have seen and read in me a quest for encounter and knowledge driven more by the truth of the heart than by the whims of the mind.

Since Bali is one of the high places of ancestor worship, I would like to first thank those who will hear me only through the waves of my voice rising to the dead, residing, it is said, on the heights of the world: my teacher and mentor, Usadi Wiratnaya, philosopher, good man, and outstanding columnist for the *Bali Post*; Made Wianta, an artist who wished, in his performance *Art and Peace* at the end of the millennium, to attach Bali to the peaceful memory of the world; Wayan Sadha, companion of my *Bali Post* writings, incomparable illustrator and witness to everyday life; Luh Kertiasih, disappeared in the exercise of her loyalty.

I also owe thanks to those whose support and friendship have enabled me, year after year, to obtain the rights to work and residence in Bali: Prof. Made Bandem and Prof. Wayan Dibia, both masters of Balinese dance; Prof. Wayan Rai, master of Balinese music; and Mangku Pastika, destroyer of terrorists and yet friend and governor.

I cannot forget also the friends of the heart who have never ceased to support me: Intan Wianta; Cynthia Nuarta and her husband and Nyoman Nuarta, master sculptor, creator of *Garuda Wisnu Kencana*; Anak Agung Rai and Gung Biang, owners of the ARMA Museum; Cokorda Putra, prince of Ubud and friend, and his brother Cok Ace, vice-governor; Gung Lingsir from Puri Kauhan Ubud and his family, who knew how to welcome me at the difficult beginnings of my wanderings; Putu Fajar Arcana, friend, great reporter of *Kompas* and editor of my columns in this same great newspaper; Alistair and Edward Speirs, editors of my columns in *Now! Bali* magazine.

What to say if not thank you also to Gusti Nyoman Darta, master illustrator; Ketut Budiana, maestro of the fantastic; Dewa Putu Kantor; Wayan Sundra; Wayan Westa for his clarification on the details of ritual and philosophy; Susan Ruddy for her occasional editing. To all my friends: Putu Suasta, Taufik Rahzen, Pino Confessa; Made Kaek, Yudha Bantono, Ema, Gusde Santrian, Kun Adnyna, Nawa Tunggal, Gustra, my editors the much-missed Rafli and Brahmantyo, and all my friends in Bali, painters, writers and others.

Thanks to my French and Swiss friends: Michel Picard, without whom the final text in French would have kept many mistakes; my friend Georges Breguet; Henri Chambert-Loir, for his support over the years; Claude and Marie-France Cherki, Thierry Vincent, and Georges Beurnier. Special thanks to Diana Darling, for her fine translation and the light changes to the text she suggested.

Thank you also to relatives and keepers of the secrets: Jais Darga, the faithful; Warih Wisatsana, melancholy poet and unparalleled contradictor. My wife Inez (Nazrina Zuryani), gentle and patient with me as well as with her students; and my children Florent, Charles (Nyo), Joseph, and Jasmine.

Finally, thank you, Eric, always so calm, because without you, these ramblings would never have taken written form.

Acknowledgments from Eric Buvelot

Sukma Dewi Hamid, Thierry Vincent, Georges Beurnier, Claude Cherki, Michel Picard, Diana Darling, Serge Davis, and Aimery Joëssel.

For the front cover image: *Ceremony of Happiness*, Made Wianta, 52x42cm, Chinese ink on golden paper, 1984. Collection Of Nicolaus F Kuswanto (Galeri Zen1), bought and collected from Made Wianta in 2018.